A History of Irish Economic Thought

T0313243

For a country that can boast a distinguished tradition of political economy from Sir William Petty through Swift, Berkeley, Hutcheson, Burke and Cantillon through to that of Longfield, Cairnes, Bastable, Edgeworth, Geary and Gorman, it is surprising that no systematic study of Irish political economy has been undertaken.

In this book the contributors redress this glaring omission in the history of political economy, for the first time providing an overview of developments in Irish political economy from the seventeenth to the twentieth century. Logistically this is achieved through the provision of individual contributions from a group of recognised experts, both Irish and international, who address the contribution of major historical figures in Irish political economy along the analysis of major thematic issues, schools of thought and major policy debates within the Irish context over this extended period.

This volume goes beyond a discussion of Irish economists in relation to Ireland-specific economic issues to recognise the contribution of Irish economists to economic thought more generally. It is a comprehensive overview that will be of interest to researchers and students of economic thought and Irish history alike.

Thomas Boylan is Professor of Economics at the University of Galway, Ireland.
Renee Prendergast is Reader in Economics at Queens University, Belfast, UK.
John D. Turner is Professor of Finance at Queens University, Belfast, UK.

Routledge history of economic thought

Edited by Mark Blaug
Co-Director Erasmus Center for History in
Management and Economics, Erasmus University,
the Netherlands

A History of Irish Economic Thought

Edited by Thomas Boylan,
Renee Prendergast and
John D. Turner

Routledge
Taylor & Francis Group

LONDON AND NEW YORK

First published 2011
by Routledge
2 Park Square, Milton Park, Abingdon, Oxfordshire OX14 4RN

Simultaneously published in the USA and Canada
by Routledge
711 Third Avenue, New York, NY 10017

First issued in paperback 2014
Routledge is an imprint of the Taylor and Francis Group, an informa business

© 2011 selection and editorial matter; Tom Boylan, Renee Prendergast
and John D. Turner, individual chapters; the contributors

Typeset in Times by Wearset Ltd, Boldon, Tyne and Wear

British Library Cataloguing in Publication Data
A catalogue record for this book is available from the British Library

Library of Congress Cataloging in Publication Data
A catalog record for this book has been requested

ISBN 978-0-415-42340-3 (hbk)
ISBN 978-1-138-80707-5 (pbk)
ISBN 978-0-203-84632-2 (ebk)

Contents

Illustrations

Figures

Tables

Contributors

Alberto Baccini is a full Professor of Economics at the Facoltà di Giurisprudenza Dipartimento di Economia Politica, University of Siena, Italy. He is an expert of Francis Ysidro Edgeworth's work, and has published several articles for leading international journals on Edgeworth, the history of probability theory and John Maynard Keynes. Recently he has been working on the application of network analysis techniques to the study of economic and statistical thought.

Roger E. Backhouse is Professor of the History and Philosophy of Economics at the Department of Economics, University of Birmingham, Edgbaston, Birmingham, UK. Publications include *The Penguin History of Economics/ The Ordinary Business of Life* (2002), *The Cambridge Companion to Keynes* (2006, co-edited with Bradley W. Bateman), and *No Wealth but Life: Welfare Economics and the Welfare State in Britain, 1880–1950* (forthcoming, co-edited with Tamotsu Nishizawa). He is currently working, with Philippe Fontaine, on the history of the social sciences since the Second World War. He teaches the history of economics at Birmingham, Erasmus University Rotterdam and the University of Oporto.

Frank Barry is Professor of International Business and Development at the School of Business, Trinity College Dublin, Ireland. He holds a Ph.D. in Economics from Queen's University, Ontario, and has previously held positions at the Universities of California, Stockholm and New South Wales, and with the Harvard Institute for International Development. He is a specialist in the areas of international trade, foreign direct investment and economic development. Amongst his publications are an edited volume on *Understanding Ireland's Economic Growth* (Macmillan Press, 1999) and a co-authored book on *Multinational Firms in the World Economy* (Princeton University Press, 2004).

Daniel Blackshields is a Lecturer in Economics at the Department of Economics, College of Business and Law, University College, Cork, Ireland. He has been a member of the Department of Economics since 1997. Currently he is a participant in the Irish Integrative Learning Project. His research interests include Linking Research and Teaching, Sherlock Holmes' Problem-solving Pedagogies for Economics, Austrian Economics and the Economics of the Entertainment Industry and the History of Economic Thought.

Tom Boylan is Personal Professor of Economics at the Department of Economics, National University of Ireland, Galway, Ireland. His principal areas of research include growth and development, history of economic thought, post-Keynesian economics, and the philosophy of economics. He has published in a wide array of international journals and has co-authored a number of works which include *Political Economy and Colonial Ireland* (Routledge, 1992, with T. Foley) and *Beyond Rhetoric and Realism: Towards a Reformulation of Economic Methodology* (Routledge, 1995, with P.F. O'Gorman), and co-edited a number of major projects, including both the four-volume anthology, *Irish Political Economy* (Routledge, 2003, with T. Foley), and the six-volume collection, *John Elliot Cairnes: the Complete Works* (Routledge, 2004, with T. Foley). His most recent works include *Popper and Economic Methodology: Contemporary Challenges* (Routledge, 2008, co-edited with P.F. O'Gorman) and *Economics, Rational Choice and Normative Philosophy* (Routledge, 2009, co-edited with R. Gekker).

Anthony Brewer is Emeritus Professor of the History of Economics at the School of Economics, Finance and Management, The University of Bristol, UK. He has worked on various aspects of economic theory, but has in recent years focused mainly on the history of economic thought in the eighteenth and nineteenth centuries. He is the author of *Richard Cantillon: Pioneer of Economic Theory* and of other books and articles in the field, and is currently Vice-President of the European Society for the History of Economic Thought.

Graham Brownlow is a Lecturer in Economics at the Queen's University Management School, Queen's University Belfast, Northern Ireland. His research, which has been published recently in a variety of outlets including the *Cambridge Journal of Economics* and the *Economic History Review*, is focused on institutional and evolutionary economics and economic history. He is a member of QUB's Economic & Financial Institutions Research Group (EFIRG).

John Considine is a Lecturer in Economics at the Department of Economics, College of Business and Law, University College, Cork, Ireland. He has written about the economic thought of Edmund Burke and James M. Buchanan in the *Journal of History of Economic Thought* and in the *European Journal of History of Economic Thought*. He has also published in the *Journal of Economic Education* explaining how the TV show *The Simpsons* follows the satirical tradition of Jonathan Swift. John acted as research assistant to Terence Gorman during the summer of 1990.

Tadhg Foley is a Professor of English at the Department of English, National University of Ireland, Galway, Ireland. He was educated at NUI, Galway and the University of Oxford. With Tom Boylan he is the author of *Political Economy and Colonial Ireland: The Propagation and Ideological Function of Economic Discourse in the Nineteenth Century* (Routledge, 1992). He is also the joint editor, with Professor Boylan, of both the four-volume anthology, *Irish Political Economy* (Routledge, 2003) and *John Elliot Cairnes: The Complete Works* in six volumes (Routledge, 2004).

Charles Hickson is a former Senior Lecturer at the Queen's University Management School, Queen's University Belfast, Northern Ireland. He received his BA in economics from the University of Michigan in 1976 and his Ph.D. in economics from UCLA in 1986. He taught economics at both UCLA and The University of Washington. His research interests are in the area of economic and financial history, particularly from an evolutionary perspective.

Patrick Honohan is Governor of the Central Bank of Ireland, Central Bank and Financial Services Authority of Ireland, Dublin, Ireland. He was previously Professor of International Financial Economics and Development at Trinity College Dublin and a Senior Advisor in the World Bank working on issues of financial policy reform. During the 1980s he was Economic Advisor to the Taoiseach and spent several years at the Economic and Social Research Institute, Dublin, and at the Central Bank of Ireland. A graduate of UCD and of the London School of Economics, from which he received his Ph.D. in 1978, Dr Honohan has published widely on issues ranging from exchange rate regimes and purchasing-power parity, to migration, cost-benefit analysis and statistical methodology.

Edward McPhail is an Associate Professor of Economics at the Department of Economics, Dickinson College, Carlisle, Pennsylvania, USA. His research interests in the history of economic thought include path dependency and socialism, the role of endogenous preferences and human sociality, and the golden rule and the greatest happiness principle. With Andrew Farrant he is the author of 'Hayek, Samuelson, and the Logic of the Mixed Economy?' (*Journal of Economic Behavior and Organization* 2009). He is the author of 'Socialism After Hayek and Human Sociality' (*Review of Austrian Economics* 2008) and 'Does the Road to Serfdom Lead to the Servile State?' (*European Journal of Political Economy* 2005).

John Maloney is a Professor of Economics at the University of Exeter Business School, Exeter, UK. He was previously at the University of Plymouth. He teaches macroeconomics, international finance and the history of political economy. His research interests are in macroeconomics and the history of economic thought. He is currently researching the macroeconomic policies of the 1970s and a range of topics on voting behaviour.

Laurence Moss, until his untimely death in 2009, was Professor of Law and Economics at the Division of Economics, Babson College, Massachusetts, USA. He earned a BA and MA at Queens College, an MA and Ph.D. at Columbia University, and a Jurist Doctor (law) at Suffolk University. He was the author of several books and many articles on the history of economic thought, with *Mountifort Longfield: Ireland's First Professor of Political Economy* being one of his best-known works.

Peter Neary is Professor of Economics at the Department of Economics, Oxford University, Manor Road, Oxford, UK. He is also a Professorial Fellow of

Merton College. Educated at University College Dublin and Oxford, he was Professor of Political Economy at University College Dublin from 1980 to 2006. He is the author of *Measuring the Restrictiveness of International Trade Policy* (with Jim Anderson, MIT Press, 2005) and of various scholarly articles, mainly on international economics. He is a Research Fellow of the Centre for Economic Policy Research in London, a Fellow of the Econometric Society and the British Academy, a Member of Academia Europaea and the Royal Irish Academy, and a past President of the European Economic Association.

Renee Prendergast is a Reader in Economics at the Queen's University Management School, Queen's University Belfast, Northern Ireland. Her research interests are in development and the history of economic thought. Recent publications in these areas have been published in *Cambridge Journal of Economics, History of Political Economy and the European Journal of History of Economic Thought.* She is joint editor, with Antoin Murphy, of *Contributions to the History of Economic Thought: Essays in Honour of R.D.C. Black.*

Salim Rashid is Professor of Economics at the Department of Economics, University of Illinois at Urbana-Champaign, Illinois, USA. His primary interests are in economic development and economic methodology. He has published in the areas of mathematical economics, history of economics and economic development. He is the author of *The Myth of Adam Smith* and takes special interest in Anglican clergymen-economists. The role of Christianity in the economic development of Europe and the impact of religion on economic development in general are two of his principal areas of study.

John E. Spencer is Emeritus Professor at the Queen's University Management School, Queen's University Belfast, Northern Ireland. He was formerly a Lecturer in Economics at the LSE and Professor of Economics at the University of Ulster and the Queen's University of Belfast. Former Henry Fellow at Yale University, he is the author of many articles in Economics and Statistics journals. His publications include work on statistics, on financial intermediaries and on computable general equilibrium. He is co-editor of a book on the economies of both parts of Ireland and one on Northern Ireland and was the first President of the Irish Economic Association.

John D. Turner is Professor of Financial Economics at Queen's University Management School, Queen's University Belfast, Northern Ireland. Previously he had been a lecturer at Queen's University and a visiting scholar at the Bank of England. His main research interest is in the evolution of law, property rights, and financial institutions. His work in this area has been published in the *Journal of Economic History*, the *Economic History Review*, the *European Review of Economic History*, and *Explorations in Economic History*. He has recently completed a major ESRC-sponsored project examining the evolution of the British equity market in the nineteenth century.

Acknowledgements

Thanks to Philip Lane and the other editors of the *Economic and Social Review* for permission to reprint Honohan, Patrick and Neary, J. Peter (2003) 'W.M. Gorman (1923–2003)', *Economic and Social Review* 34: 195–209.

Introduction

Tom Boylan, Renee Prendergast and John D. Turner

The present work is the first substantial attempt to survey the history of Irish economic thought from the late seventeenth to the twentieth centuries. It builds on the foundations provided by R.D.C. Black's *Economic Thought and the Irish Question* as well as more recent contributions by Boylan and Foley (1992), Brewer (1992), Daly (1997), Johnston (1970), Murphy (1983, 1986) and Moss (1976). The approach taken is both thematic and focused on the contributions of individual economists, with the work organised into four chronological parts. The first of these, entitled 'Ireland and the birth of political economy', relates to the Irish contribution to pre-Smithian classical political economy. The second covers the rise and fall of laissez-faire in the century following the publication of the *Wealth of Nations*. The third part is devoted to the contributions of four individual economists who made pioneering contributions to modern economics in the late nineteenth and twentieth centuries. The final part surveys the development and contribution of political economy in the context of twentieth-century Ireland.

In attempting to delineate the scope of a work on Irish economic thought, two main approaches were considered neither of which is entirely satisfactory. One is to focus on the work of Irish political economists designating as Irish those who were born in Ireland and/or those who worked mainly in Ireland. The other is to focus on the work of those whose writings in political economy were concerned primarily with Irish issues. While there is something to be said for both approaches, the view taken here is that an exclusive focus on Irish issues would fail to take adequate account of important contributions to the more abstract parts of the subject. Consequently, our survey of Irish economic thought is based on the consideration of the work of significant Irish political economists and this is supplemented by an issues-based approach.

In determining who should be regarded as 'Irish' for this work, we have opted for an inclusive approach. We regard as Irish those political economists who were born in and educated in Ireland regardless of where they subsequently lived. We also include settlers such as William Petty, an Englishman who first came to Ireland as Physician General to Cromwell's army in 1652 and became interested in 'political anatomy' in the course of surveying the country in preparation for the confiscation of Irish lands. Richard Cantillon and Arthur O'Connor were Irish born and bred but spent much of their lives in France. Johnathan Swift and George Berkeley, both of Anglo-Irish stock, were born in Ireland and educated in Trinity College Dublin, but they were at home in England as well as Ireland. Francis Hutcheson, on the other hand, was the grandson of Scottish immigrants. A dissenter, he received his university education at Glasgow to which he eventually returned as Professor of Moral Philosophy. Francis Edgeworth and Terence Gorman were both educated at Trinity College, but spent most of their careers in British universities.

Whilst decisions about the designation of individual contributors as Irish or not-Irish provides a means of identifying the potential subject matter of a work on the history of Irish economic thought, it runs the risk of neglecting the contribution of British political economists such as John Stuart Mill who were deeply engaged with Irish matters particularly issues relating to land tenure. The same applies to the more peripheral contributions to Irish issues of Ricardo, Malthus, Senior and McCulloch.

Just as it was natural for British economists to consider Irish matters especially during the two centuries in which Ireland formed part of the United Kingdom, there was no necessity for those born in Ireland to focus on purely Irish matters especially if they made their careers elsewhere. Edmund Burke was not primarily a political economist and his work features only peripherally in this volume[1] but he provides a good example of someone whose contributions bore traces of his Irish upbringing but whose writings on political economy related to Britain and France and Britain's relationships with Ireland, America and India. As far as the abstract contributions of Cantillon, Edgeworth and Gorman are concerned, there is no discernable connection with the birthplace of their creators. The same also holds for some of the contributions of the likes of Berkeley and Geary, whose main body of work was primarily motivated by concerns about Irish conditions. The view taken here is that this makes the work in question no less Irish. Rather, it shows that Irishmen and, at times, groups of Irish men have made important contributions to the wider development of the discipline.

A focus on the work of significant theoreticians is by no means the whole story. As Oliver MacDonagh (1962) pointed out with reference to nineteenth-century Ireland in his review of R.D.C. Black's *Economic Thought and the Irish Question* (1960), there were issues on which 'the theoretical economists limped behind – and often a considerable distance behind the native agrarian philanthropists and agitators in the development of economic thought'. What MacDonagh has in mind is the work of men such as William Conner and Frank Lawlor whose contributions were examined in some detail by Black. While important historically, the contribution of these authors is not primarily economic and is only briefly discussed in the present work. According to Cliffe Leslie, the historical political economist, 'political economy is not a body ... of universal and immutable truths, but an assemblage of speculations and doctrines which are the result of a particular history' (Cliffe Leslie 1870). If Leslie's relativist hypothesis is correct, a study of Irish political economy would be expected to uncover some specifically Irish characteristics either in terms of problems addressed, institutional assumptions made or approaches adopted. The work presented here demonstrates that there is some truth in Leslie's proposition. At various points in the development of Ireland's political economy, the questions which preoccupied its practitioners were the product of the particular conjuncture which included Ireland's complex and varied relationship with Great Britain and British political economy.

Economic backwardness and development

The question of how to overcome the country's relative backwardness was a consistent issue for Irish political economy from the late seventeenth century to the late twentieth century. However, except in the early eighteenth century, concern with this issue does not appear to have generated a recognisable political economy of development. In different time periods, the discussion focused on different issues or groups of issues whose relative importance varied over time. The contributions of what Rashid (1988) calls the Irish School of Development Economics (1720–1750) appear to have had a limited impact on actual development or even development policy, not because of any weakness in the proposals themselves, but because the distribution of rights over resources did not provide the necessary initial conditions. On the other hand, in his discussion of the Irish development experience in the second half of the twentieth century, Frank Barry in his chapter shows that policy and experiment often led theory rather than the other way around. For example, Ireland's experiments in incentivising foreign direct investment were not theoretically based. Likewise the somewhat controversial theory of expansionary fiscal contraction was a product of the growth experiences of Ireland and Denmark in the wake of fiscal contractions in the 1980s.

Despite the fact that there is no recognisably Irish school of development economics persisting over time, two related themes which arose early deserve our attention both because of their persistence and their wider significance. The first of these relates to the importance of an inclusive approach to development. Petty, Hutcheson and Berkeley all took the view that the cultivation of higher living standards and aspirations amongst the poor could help to break the vicious cycle of underdevelopment. This theme was re-iterated at the close of the eighteenth century by O'Connor (1998: 74); and, in the early nineteenth century, Ricardo, Malthus and McCulloch all saw the creation of a taste for objects other than food amongst the mass of the population as a necessary aspect of development (Black 1960: 137).

The second theme which also emerged with Petty relates to the social basis of development. In Book V of *Wealth of Nations* (*WN*: V.II.ii.2), Adam Smith (1976a) pointed out that the security of property requires the existence of civil government. Civil government, in turn, requires the consent of the ruled. The link between consent and the security of property rights and the importance of both for development had been recognised earlier by William Petty who in

The Political Anatomy of Ireland wrote: 'Why should men endeavour to get estates, where the legislative power is not agreed upon; and where tricks and words destroy natural right and property?' (Petty 1899: 146).

In the century that followed, property rights were stabilised but as Arthur O'Connor argued in his *State of Ireland*, the existing monopoly of property was a major obstacle to Ireland's economic development. O'Connor argued that the laws which monopolised property also monopolised power and the direction which these laws gave to the descent of property influenced the nature of government. Entail and other restrictions which prevented the natural tendency of land to break into smaller portions were detrimental to productivity because small owner-occupied holdings were generally more productive than large holdings. A small proprietor would make more durable improvements because he had 'the whole benefit of his improvement secured to him and his family' (O'Connor 1998: 70–1).

O'Connor's proposals for revolution and reform came to nothing but, in the long run, they were to prove prescient. In the nineteenth century, most of the classical economists acknowledged that Irish agriculture was inefficient and backward and thought that the solution lay in supplanting the cottier system which had by then developed by capitalist farming, on the English model (Black 1960: 18). This, in turn, would have required the removal of a great part of the rural population from the land, something which could not happen given that the industry which might absorb this surplus population did not exist. Part of the explanation for this, canvassed by no less an authority than Ricardo, was the insecurity of property rights in Ireland. This, according to Senior, was 'the great evil of Ireland … arising from the detestation by the mass of the people, of her existing institutions, and their attempts to substitute for them an insurrectionary law of their own' (Senior 1868: 50).

The insecurity of property rights encompassed a number of different dimensions. It may have discouraged the flow of foreign capital into Ireland as Ricardo had intimated. From the point of view of tenant farmers, insecurity of tenure and issues relating to tenant compensation acted as a brake on investment. Arguments for fixity of tenure and peasant proprietorship were put forward by members of the Young Ireland group including Thomas Davis and Gavan Duffy (Black 1960). Although such reforms might have been easier to achieve than the proposals of the classical economists, they were not viewed favourably either by established political economists or those who controlled wealth and power. Recognition of the wider possibilities for reform came only after the extraordinary upheaval of the Great Famine. Continental influences as well the contributions of Cairnes, Mill and others led to recognition that forms of tenure such as peasant proprietorship had much to offer in terms of efficiency and incentives.

What all of this appears to show is that development paths which are feasible in one situation or country may not be in another and that economic development has social dimensions and rests on a degree of social consensus. This is not merely a question of stability of property rights. As Frank Barry shows in his paper on Irish development in the second half of the twentieth century, the achievement of consensus around particular policies is no easy matter. Barry refers to the social partnership of the late 1980s as providing political cover for fiscal consolidation. This undoubtedly captures an element of what social partnership was about but policy is likely to be socially sustainable only if it generates sufficiently widespread benefits. This, of course, does not mean that reforms will always be implemented when they are potentially beneficial.

Ireland and the birth of political economy

This part chronicles the Irish contribution to political economy in the late seventeenth to the end of the eighteenth centuries. The four papers constituting this part deal with some of the pioneering contributions to modern political economy. Apart from Cantillon, the key figures were English and Scots colonists and their descendants. As Anthony Brewer suggests in the opening chapter, Petty's engagement with the colonial project through his conduct of the Down survey was a major turning point in his life and in his intellectual focus. It may also have provided him with the base data on which he developed his estimates of Irish national income. Petty's contribution to political economy is foundational for two main reasons. First, he tried to place political economy on a sound empirical footing, expressing himself in terms of *number, weight or measure.* Second, whereas most economic writing before Petty focused on international trade and money, Petty conceived the economic system as a whole and insofar as he examined international trade and money did so in the context of the wider system. Despite his declared antipathy to purely intellectual arguments, Petty appears to have had a natural tendency to theorise and, as Brewer puts it, spun off ideas in profusion although many of these remained underdeveloped.

Cantillon was born in Ireland but became part of the Irish Catholic diaspora in France. Emerging as a banker in Paris, he profited greatly from the John Law's Mississippi Scheme and later from the South Sea Company in London. The *Essay* on which Cantillon's fame rests was first published in 1755, twenty-five years after it was written and over twenty years after his probable death. Described by Jevons as 'the cradle of political economy', the *Essay* is a work of pure theory that analyses the economy as an integrated system. As Brewer notes, Cantillon brushes ethics and politics aside and focuses on material wealth as his subject matter. He provides a clear exposition of the role of prices in linking production and consumption, an endogenous theory of population growth and a sophisticated version of the quantity theory of money. Despite being a work of pure theory, the *Essay* is clearly the work of an acute observer who is thoroughly familiar with the workings of the economic system. This suggests, as Brewer notes, that the contrast between the approaches of Cantillon and Petty would seem less striking if we had access to Cantillon's lost statistical supplement.

Chapter 2 deals with Swift and Berkeley's approaches to economic development. In doing so, it shows that the two authors have an expansive concept of human well-being and that they have a sophisticated view of the human actor which they liken to the modern capability approach of Amartya Sen, (1999).

Both authors sought to develop real world, practical policies which were relevant to the pressing economic problems of the time. Despite their common approach to human development, there were a number of important differences between the authors. This is especially the case with regard to the issues related to money and banking where Berkeley's practical and theoretical understanding as displayed in *The Querist* was much superior to Swift's.

Rashid and McPhail's emphasis on human development in Berkeley and Swift ties in neatly with the debates on the nature of the human economic actor which took place in the first half of the eighteenth century which are discussed by Prendergast in Chapter 3. Jonathan Swift had a marginal role in this debate, but Francis Hutcheson and George Berkeley were amongst the leading opponents of Bernard Mandeville who, in a clear challenge to Christian ethics, had argued in his *Fable of the Bees* that private vices were not only consistent with the public good but were in fact necessary to promote economic prosperity. The strong version of Mandeville's thesis depended on a very stringent definition of vice and the juxtaposition of two quite different moral standards. Of the three Irish writers, only Swift can be regarded as having comprehensively rejected the utilitarian point of view. Berkeley was a theological utilitarian in that he believed that the happiness of mankind in this world and in the next was the proper end of human action. However, because of the fallibility of human agents, he considered that the happiness of mankind was best pursued by following general moral rules that were arrived at through experience. Hutcheson's position is a bit more complicated. In his view, objects or actions were pursued not because of advantage or interest but because they were approved by the moral sense. Nonetheless, when it came to choosing between different available actions, utilitarian considerations came into play and that action was judged best which produced the greatest happiness for the greatest number. Hutcheson was also very clear that while benevolence might be a motive for action in matters relating to family and friends, in relation to mankind in general it would be insufficient to secure universal diligence.

Hutcheson's view that benevolence which could motivate action in relation to family and friends was inadequate when it came to wider economic relationships was to be reflected in the work of his student, Adam Smith. In his *Theory of Moral Sentiments*, Smith (1976b) focused on moral questions but he accepted that self-interest was the prime motivating factor in the *Wealth of Nations*. In his *State of Ireland*, Arthur O'Connor adopted the framework of the *Wealth of Nations* including its emphasis on self-interest and used it to analyse the economic condition of the country at the end of the eighteenth century. As Blackshields and Considine show in the final chapter in this part, O'Connor went beyond Adam Smith in his application of *homo economicus* to the governance of a country and his exploration of the implications of that governance for economic performance. No one before O'Connor seems to have engaged in this decidedly modern enterprise. The chapter also demonstrates that Connor's radical legacy was taken forward by his nephew, Fergus O'Connor of Chartist fame and by his illegitimate son, William Conner. As noted above, the latter analysed the implications of the land tenure system and made important proposals for reform before the need for these was recognised by more established political economists.

The classical era: the rise and fall of laissez-faire

Like Hutcheson and Berkeley before him, Richard Whately, Archbishop of Dublin, saw the pursuit of wealth and good as compatible objectives. As Laurence Moss shows in the opening chapter of Part II, Whately and the occupants of the chair of political economy he founded at Trinity College were proponents of a species of natural theology according to which political economy showed the beneficent nature of the status quo from which all classes of society could benefit. At least in the 'wrong' hands, the dominant Ricardian approach to political economy could be used to highlight the distributional conflict between landlords, capitalists and workers. By focusing on exchange instead of production and on market values instead of labour values, Montifort Longfield and other members of the 'Trinity School' could show that there was a general tendency for the three classes to prosper together. Whatever their purposes, the Whately professors were no mere ideologues. Longfield offered a deeply original account of how supply and demand interacted to establish market prices which in important respects anticipated the marginal approach which became dominant after 1870. Longfield's work was taken forward by Butt who focused his attention on the development of Longfield's insights with respect to the marginal productivity theory of distribution. Partly because their work was ignored by the likes of Mill and Cairnes and partly because the intervention of the Great Irish Famine meant that the later occupants of the Whately chair had very different preoccupations, these pioneering analytical contributions of the Trinity school were not carried forward.

While the industrial revolution proceeded apace in early nineteenth-century England, in Ireland the majority of the people remained dependent on agriculture the productivity of which was, therefore, a key economic issue. Broadly speaking, before the Great Famine, the classical economists focused their attention on the consolidation of holdings and the provision of appropriate incentives to encourage investment including in some cases compensation for tenants. The issue of free trade in land also received attention towards the mid-century. While some of its advocates believed that, by itself, free trade in land would be sufficient to ensure that land would eventually be held by those in a position to use it most effectively, other advocates argued that measures facilitating transfer of ownership should be combined with provision for tenant compensation (Black 1960: 33). In his chapter on the classical economists and reform legislation of landed property, Charles Hickson examines the classical economists' analysis of the strict settlement system which prevented free trade in land. Hickson argues that the settlement system had some social advantages which were overlooked by the classical economists. Hickson also carries out a detailed examination of the analysis of the landlord–tenant relationship provided by McCulloch and

Senior whose focus was primarily on efficiency issues, and contrasts it with the work of John Stuart Mill and John Elliot Cairnes who he regards as being interested in redistribution as well as efficiency. The influence of Mill and Cairnes on subsequent legislation is examined and its shortcomings are identified. While much of the writing of the period correctly identified the incentive issues associated with different forms of land tenure, Hickson argues that various proposals for reform were deficient in failing to take into account the transaction costs associated with the compensation of tenants.

Although writers such as McCulloch provided a detailed analysis of the incentives for investment provided by different contractual relations between landlords and tenants, they tended to accept the absolute nature of property rights in land. The first orthodox economist to challenge the absolute nature of property rights was John Elliot Cairnes. As Boylan and Foley demonstrate, Cairnes' argument against the absolute nature of property rights had a number of different facets. First, he contrasted the absolutist view of the landlord's property rights with the view that that the landlord had no claim to the value added to the land by others. Second, and more radically, he argued that the landlord's right should be subordinate to the public welfare. In general, Cairnes argued that laissez-faire could not be justified where the pursuit of individual interest was not consistent with the good of the whole.

Cairnes' doctrine of the limited nature of landed property became widely accepted and with it came acceptance that the contract between owners and cultivators of land could be interfered with by law. The acceptance of the limited applicability of the doctrine of laissez-faire had wider implications in that it undermined the notion that political economy was a body of natural laws or immutable truths and paved the way for the development of historical economics.

In his chapter on the Irish historical economists, T.E. Cliffe Leslie and John Kells Ingram, Roger Backhouse shows that Cliffe Leslie was the leading figure in the historicist school which represented the strongest challenge to English classical political economy in the 1870s. Both Ingram, a follower of Comte, and Leslie emphasised the importance of broad historical influences for the nature of economic activity in any given period. Given the importance of particular history, deductive methods which abstracted from particularity could not provide the basis for scientific analysis. Moreover, the evolutionary nature of economic life meant the future could not be known and the knowledge assumptions implicit in deductive approaches to analysis were likely to be seriously misleading. Backhouse notes that Leslie and Ingram are commonly regarded as leaders of the *English* Historical School. This is not just a matter of Imperial prejudice but reflects the fact that both authors were integrated into British economics and did not form part of a separate Irish economics community. Although there had been intimations of an historicist position in political writings of Edmund Burke in the late eighteenth century, Cliffe Leslie's historical economics seems to have owed more to the historical jurisprudence of Henry Maine than it did to his fellow countryman.

John Elliot Cairnes is often regarded as the last of the classical economists. However, Boylan and Maloney's chapter shows that Charles Francis Bastable who occupied the Whately Chair of Political Economy in Trinity College for a full half century combined a commitment to the classical tradition with a commitment to the broader evolutionary perspective derived from his acquaintance with the work of the German Historical School as well as the work of his compatriots Leslie and Ingram. Bastable's main contributions to economics were in the field of international trade where he is regarded as one of leading theorists of his generation. Most of Bastable's contributions were refinements or extensions of international trade theory as it had been left by J.S. Mill. Broadly speaking, Bastable was a strong proponent of free trade and developed a particularly stringent test for the applicability of the infant industry argument. Perhaps not surprisingly, the Fiscal Inquiry Committee set up to consider the case for increased protection in the new Irish State found reasons to take no action. Bastable's other major contribution to economics was in the field of public finance.

In the final chapter of Part II, John Turner examines Irish contributions to nineteenth-century monetary and banking debates. Turner shows that the suspension of convertibility into gold at the end of the eighteenth century was accompanied by the depreciation of the Irish currency. A Parliamentary Committee of inquiry was set up in 1804 to identify the causes and seek remedies. Anti-bullionists attributed the depreciation to the adverse balance of payments whereas pro-bullionists argued that the cause was lax monetary policy attributable to the suspension of convertibility. The latter position was that articulated in the Committee's final report which, however, acknowledged that the expansion of credit could be justified as a source of emergency war time finance. Although the report was largely ignored by Parliament, it had a significant impact on the pro-bullionist Bullion Report of 1810.

In a pamphlet which he published in 1804, Henry Parnell suggested that parliamentary oversight over the Bank of Ireland restrained the issue of paper as it had done in the case of the Bank of England. Just over twenty years later, Parnell's views had changed dramatically and, instead of parliamentary oversight, he argued that the Bank of England should be subject to the discipline of competition. Parnell's later work is widely regarded as the first major contribution to the free banking school of monetary theory. In the event, the free banking school lost the policy debate in the 1840s and, as a result, its influence waned.

Into the twentieth century – Irish contributions to economic theory

Part III of the present work examines the contribution of three of Ireland's greatest theorists: Francis Ysidoro Edgeworth, Roy Geary and Terence Gorman. Edgeworth and Gorman were born in Ireland and educated in Trinity College Dublin but did their main economic work in British universities. Both were amongst the leading theorists of their generation and made major lasting contributions to economic analysis. Roy Geary studied mathematics at University College, Dublin and in the Sorbonne in Paris. He was one of the leading statisticians of the twentieth century and although his economic contributions were a minor part of his overall work, they were of major significance in their own right.

Edgeworth's many contributions to the foundations of economic analysis are familiar to students of modern microeconomics. However, because they have been absorbed into the common stock of knowledge, the original source of these contributions has mostly been forgotten. Furthermore, as noted by Baccini, the process of absorption may have involved distortion of Edgeworth's original vision. Thus, in discussing Edgeworth's two equilibrium concepts, Baccini notes that Edgeworth's central interest was the indeterminateness of contracts and not the conditions for their perfect determination. Baccini's chapter is not simply interested in Edgeworth the economist. Rather his purpose is to uncover the unity in a pattern of research which switched abruptly from ethics, to economics, to probability theory and finally to statistics. Baccini shows that underlying what is often seen as Edgeworth's crass utilitarianism was a search for a common foundation for the social sciences. Edgeworth's conception of man as a pleasure machine depended on the possibility of roughly measuring utility and, for him, the calculus of probability was based on the possibility of roughly measuring probability. For Edgeworth, both measurement processes were grounded in the Spenserian view that the human nervous system incorporates a priori knowledge within its structure.

Roy Geary is best known for his contributions to mathematical statistics especially his work on the sampling theory of ratios and normality testing but, as John Spencer shows, these theoretical contributions which were produced while he worked as an official statistician or as director of the Economic Research Institute were primarily the result of thinking about practical problems. In addition to his theoretical work, Geary also made important contributions of a more applied nature to both economics and statistics. These were also motivated by practical difficulties and involved innovative solutions to the problems associated with the estimation of economic variables. The most important of Geary's economic contributions arose in the context of National Income Accounting, a field in which Geary can be regarded as a pioneer of approaches based on value added at constant prices. Geary's innovations included methods of estimating the trading gain from changes in the terms of trade which can influence the purchasing power of the incomes generated from domestic production. He also developed methods for dealing with the problem of using official exchange rates in international comparisons of flows expressed in different currencies. As Spencer indicates, both of these contributions had lasting impact and form part of the current guidance provided in the UN System of International Accounts. Other important contributions were the Stone–Geary utility function and techniques for updating input–output tables. Geary appears to have been the first to advocate and analyse the use of instrumental variables in econometric estimation. In papers delivered at the Statistical and Social Inquiry Society of Ireland, Geary also made important contributions to Irish demography and to the analysis of the problem of emigration.

Like Roy Geary, Terence Gorman emphasised the use of quantitative methods in economic reasoning but, unlike Geary, he believed in the value of economic theory as an engine of thought. One of Gorman's main interests was the relationship between individual behaviour and aggregate outcomes and he explored aspects of this in his very first paper published in *Econometrica* in 1953 in which he established necessary and sufficient conditions under which a society of utility maximising individuals behaved as if it were a single individual. In addition to the exploration of the relationship between micro and macro levels, Gorman was also interested in the modelling of individual behaviour. He believed that a good theory should be realistic and psychologically plausible. At the same time, he understood that the theoretical representations of individual actions had to be such that they were algebraically tractable. Much of Gorman's work on separability including his investigations of two-stage household budgeting were the product of his quest to provide credible representations of human behaviour in a framework of appropriate simplicity. Gorman also explored the use of characteristics-based models of demand. His work on this area was initially presented in 1956 as an exploration of quality differences in the egg market and eventually published in 1980. As Honohan and Neary show, Gorman's work on characteristics appeals to the same arbitrage logic as the option pricing models of Black, Scholes and Merton.

Policy and economic development – shifting economic paradigms

Whereas Part III focuses on the work of three major contributions to modern economic and statistical theory, Part IV provides a broader overview of the development and contribution of political economy in twentieth century Ireland. It has been suggested that, in decades following independence, Irish academic economists were conservative in both outlook and methodology and that innovations in both policy and methodology were largely the work of civil servants. This view is disputed by Brownlow who argues that, despite a lack of resources, economists such as George Duncan of Trinity and George O'Brien of University College displayed considerable originality and saw the importance of educating students in statistical and econometric techniques. Brownlow points to the importance of the *Journal of the Statistical and Social Inquiry Society of Ireland* and *Studies* as fora both for debate and the communication of ideas and research. These journals covered major policy-related issues such as the modernisation of agriculture, emigration, the relevance of Keynesianism in the Irish context, the role of planning in the post-war economy but surprisingly not the change in trade policy in the 1930s. Brownlow demonstrates that from the 1960s onwards, Irish economics increasingly came under American influence. The Ford Foundation supported the setting up of the Economic and Social Research Institute, and graduate students increasingly received their training at Schools in the United States. Brownlow suggests that the increase in the number of professional economists and the pattern of internationalisation and formalisation in Ireland followed the broad patterns identified earlier by Coats (2000). Brownlow also suggests that, in line with a pattern noted by Harry Johnson (1973), the economics profession in Ireland in the late twentieth century consists of a small elite group contributing to international journals with the bulk of the profession concerned with local problems and local outlets.

In the final chapter of the work, Frank Barry attempts to uncover the factors leading to Ireland's rapid development in the late twentieth century. Barry suggests that global increases in foreign direct investment in the second half of the twentieth century as well as the creation of the European single market created opportunities which were not available earlier. However, it was by no means automatic that Ireland would be able to take advantage of these opportunities. Barry shows that opening up to free trade and the removal of restrictions on foreign ownership were not enough. The development of the education system, the correction of malfunctions in the labour market, the overcoming of fiscal instability, policies to attract foreign direct investment, EC regional aid and the promotion of microeconomic reform were also important. Many of the reforms which, in retrospect, proved to be successful were initiated by public servants and presented as transcending party politics. However, it is also clear that major policy changes required a degree of political consensus which was usually achieved only following periods of severe crisis. This was the case with the 'Whitaker' reforms of the late 1950s and it was also the case with the fiscal and labour market reforms of the late 1980s and early 1990s. Barry also notes the importance of the political cover provided by external rules such as the restraints on national budgets introduced by the Maastricht Treaty. While economics may have contributed to policy innovation, it does not appear to have led it. Economics does not always provide clear or unique solutions. Even where it does, it is one thing to know what needs to be done, it is another to actually do it.

Conclusion

In summary, the contributions to this volume suggest that there is no distinctly national tradition in Irish political economy. Instead, individual Irish economists have made significant contributions to the wider discipline and debates centred upon specific Irish problems have influenced the nature of economists' concerns and have sometimes led to innovations in theory as well as wider economic vision. Present-day Irish economists work mainly on issues which have a bearing on the Irish economy and society though some contribute to the wider development of the discipline. Amongst Irish-based economists, Peter Neary, formerly of University College Dublin and presently at Oxford, has made important contributions in the field of international trade theory including pioneering work on Dutch Disease and strategic trade and industrial policy. Work by Philip Lane of Trinity College in the field of international macroeconomics is also widely cited as is that of Kevin O'Rourke, also of Trinity, in the field of globalisation. Morgan Kelly of UCD has contributed to the theory of growth and development while Patrick Honohan has made important contributions in applied macroeconomics. In terms of specific Irish economic issues, the work of Cormac Ó Gráda, particularly that on the Great Famine, has found a wide international audience.

In keeping with tradition, however, some of the most important work by Irish economists has been carried out in universities in the United States and the United Kingdom. Brian Arthur of Santa Fe Institute has made leading contributions to the understanding of increasing returns and the phenomenon of lock-in. His pioneering work has also contributed to the understanding of technological evolution and to the conception of the economy as an evolving complex system. John Sutton of the London School of Economics has made major contributions to the economics of industrial structure, to the understanding of the role of sunk costs and to non-cooperative bargaining theory. David Canning at Harvard has made important contributions on health and its relationship to development, while Canice Prendergast of the University of Chicago is a leading authority on the economics of bureaucracy and the role of economic incentives.

Note

1 Aspects of Burke's contributions to political economy are discussed in Considine (2002) and Prendergast (2000).

Bibliography

Black, R.D.C. (1960) *Economic Thought and the Irish Question, 1817–1870*, Cambridge: Cambridge University Press.

Boylan, T.A. and Foley, T.P. (1992) *Political Economy and Colonial Ireland*, London: Routledge.

Brewer, A. (1992) *Richard Cantillon: Pioneer of Economic Theory*, London: Routledge.

Cliffe Leslie, T.E. (1870) 'The Political Economy of Adam Smith', *Fortnightly Review*, 1 November.

Coats, A.W.B. (ed.) (2000) 'Introduction', *The Development of Economics in Western Europe since 1945*, London, Routledge.

Considine, J. (2002) 'Budgetary Institutions and Fiscal Discipline: Edmund Burke's Insightful Contribution', *European Journal of History of Economic Thought* 9.4: 591–607.

Daly, M.E. (1997) *The Spirit of Earnest Inquiry: The Statistical and Social Enquiry Society of Ireland 1847–1997*, Dublin: Statistical and Social Inquiry Society of Ireland.

Hutcheson, F. [1726] (2004) *An Inquiry into the Original of our Ideas of Beauty and Virtue in Two Treatises*, W. Leidhold (ed.), Indianapolis: Liberty Fund.

Johnson, H. (1973) 'National Styles in Economic Research: the United States, the United Kingdom, Canada and Various European Countries', *Daedalus* 102.2: 65–74.

Johnston, J. (1970) *Bishop Berkeley's* Querist *in Historical Perspective*, Dundalk, Dundalgan Press.

MacDonagh, O. (1962) 'Economic Thought and the Irish Question 1817–70 by R.D. Collison Black', *The Historical Journal* 5.2: 208–10.

Moss, L.S. (1976) *Mountifort Longfield: Ireland's First Professor of Political Economy*, Ottawa, IL: Green Hill Publishers.

Murphy, A.E. (ed.) (1983) *Economists and the Irish Economy from the Eighteenth Century to the Present Day*, Dublin: Irish Academic Press in association with *Hermathena*, Trinity College Dublin.

Murphy, A.E. (ed.) (1986) *Richard Cantillon: Entrepreneur and Economist*, Oxford: Clarendon Press.

Petty, W. (1899) *The Economic Writings of Sir William Petty*, C.H. Hull (ed.), Vol. I, Cambridge: Cambridge University Press.

O'Connor, A. (1998) *The State of Ireland*, J. Livesey (ed.), Dublin: Lilliput Press.

Prendergast, R. (2000) 'The Political Economy of Edmund Burke', A.E. Murphy and R. Prendergast (eds) *Contributions to the History of Economic Thought: Essays in Honour of R.D.C. Black*, London: Routledge, pp. 251–71.

Rashid, S. (1988) 'The Irish School of Economic Development: 1720–1750', *The Manchester School of Economic and Social Studies* 56.4: 345–69.

Sen, A.K. (1999) *Development as Freedom*, Oxford: Oxford University Press.

Senior, N.W. (1868) 'Ireland in 1843', *Journal, Conversations and Essays relating to Ireland*, Vol. 1, *London: Longmans, Green and Co.*

Smith, A. (1976) *The Theory of Moral Sentiments*, D.D. Raphael and A.L. MacFie (eds), Oxford: Oxford University Press.

Smith, A. (1976) *An Inquiry Into the Nature and Causes of the Wealth of Nations*, R. H. Campbell, A.S. Skinner and W.B. Todd (eds), 2 vols, Oxford: Oxford University Press.

Part I

Ireland and the birth of political economy

1 The Irish connection and the birth of political economy

Petty and Cantillon

Anthony Brewer

William Petty (1623–87) and Richard Cantillon (1680–1734) were perhaps the two most important figures in the development of economic thinking before about 1750. Both had strong Irish connections, though in quite different ways. Petty was not Irish, but wrote about Ireland and spent a substantial part of his adult life there. Cantillon, by contrast, was Irish by birth but spent most of his adult life in France. His writing was primarily theoretical, with no special reference to Ireland – the only specific reference to Ireland in his *Essay on the Nature of Commerce in General* was to Petty's work. Petty was a key point of reference for Cantillon, while Cantillon was in turn an important influence on Quesnay, Adam Smith, and the classical tradition in economics.

Petty in Ireland

Petty was the son of a small clothier in the south of England.[1] Like Cantillon two generations later, he was a self-made man, determined, ambitious, and remarkably able. He went to sea in his early teens, making money on the side by small-scale trade. Put ashore in France with a broken leg, he improved his education at a Jesuit college. Back in England, he was in the navy for a while but left the country to study medicine when the civil war broke out, and worked for a time with the great philosopher Thomas Hobbes in Paris. In England again, he started to take his place among the group which became the Royal Society – the founders of modern science. In 1650 he was appointed Professor of Anatomy at Oxford at the age of twenty-six and, soon after, Vice-Principal of Brasenose College, Oxford and Professor of Music at Gresham College, London. Achievement enough you might think for one who had been an uneducated cabin boy barely a dozen years before, but Petty was not satisfied.

In 1652 he took up a position as physician to the parliamentary army in Ireland. By then, Cromwell's bloody re-conquest was complete and Ireland was at the mercy of the Cromwellian regime. Petty had been angling for an opportunity to take part in (and profit from) the remaking of Ireland. He did indeed reorganise the army's medical provision with some success, but soon moved on to larger, more profitable, business.

The key issue in Ireland was the transfer of land from the defeated royalists to new owners. To finance the war, Parliament had, effectively, sold Irish land to English 'adventurers', to be delivered after the successful conquest, and had promised land to the soldiers to settle pay arrears. To carry out these promises, they had to identify particular pieces of land of known size and quality, and transfer ownership to identified people. This had to be done over a substantial part of the country, and done quickly. In 1652, they simply did not have the information to do it. A first attempt at a listing of estates, rather than a map, was proceeding slowly and did not fully meet the needs of the army.

Petty proposed a mapping of the confiscated lands (which covered much of Ireland) showing units as small as forty acres, with a less detailed survey of other lands in the counties concerned, all to be carried out in thirteen months. He divided the work so that the surveying on the ground was carried out mainly by soldiers, motivated by the fact that they expected to benefit personally from the division of lands, while their measurements were turned into a finished map by more skilled (and scarcer) personnel. All those involved had to be trained and supplied with simplified, mass-produced, instruments. It was a remarkable feat – perhaps the best map of any country at the time and 'a milestone in the history of cartography' (Strauss 1954: 71), despite being surveyed in haste by unskilled soldiers in a devastated and hostile country.

The Down Survey (as it came to be known) was done on time and under budget, leaving Petty with a substantial profit. He bought land cheaply, ending up with large holdings, particularly in County Kerry.[2] His Irish estates brought in rents of £4,100 p.a. in 1685 (Strauss 1954: 82), perhaps £500,000 in present-day purchasing power, though his huge estates in Kerry were relatively unprofitable, yielding only £1,100. His overall income, including non-agricultural enterprises in Kerry and property in England, was about £8,000 to £9,000 p.a. (equivalent to about £1 million now).

Not surprisingly, Petty's blatant self-enrichment came under fire and he faced a series of crises. He became personal secretary to Cromwell's son Henry, but the enemies of the Cromwell dynasty saw their chance to attack the regime through Petty. He was charged with corruption, and found himself dangerously exposed when (Oliver) Cromwell died in 1658. When the monarchy was restored in 1660, Irish royalists expected to get their estates back. In the event the king could not afford to challenge Cromwell's settlement head-on, but Petty had to yield some of his gains. When James II succeeded, Irish royalists and Catholics again saw the chance to pursue Petty in the courts. One way or another, Petty spent much of the rest of his life defending his gains.

He married a well-to-do widow, adding English properties to his portfolio, and made strenuous efforts to develop his Irish properties. From the late 1650s he divided his time between London, Dublin, and his various estates. His economic writings all date from this period. He died in 1687.

Political arithmetic

'Political arithmetic' was Petty's name for his distinctive approach to economic issues, influenced by Francis Bacon and the new physical sciences – the name 'political economy' had not yet come into general use.[3] He gave his own definition in 1676.

> The method I take ... is not yet very usual; for instead of using only comparative and superlative words, and intellectual arguments, I have taken the course ... to express my self in terms of *number, weight,* or *measure*; to use only arguments of sense, and to consider only such causes, as have visible foundations in nature; leaving those that depend upon the mutable minds, opinions, appetites, and passions of particular men, to the consideration of others.
>
> (Petty 1899: 244)[4]

Petty's political arithmetic was always aimed at current political issues and directed to policy makers. It was not quite economics in the modern sense, since there was then no clear division between economics, politics, demography, geography, and so on.

Few of his economic writings were published in his lifetime – publication was not the route to success or influence and could be dangerous, particularly since Petty relied on official support to defend his Irish holdings. His economic writings aimed to influence and impress the King and important royal officials, and were circulated privately. Many were posthumously published when the political situation had changed.

Ireland bulks large in Petty's writings. The *Political Anatomy of Ireland*, the *Treatise of Ireland*, and the two sets of *Observations on the Dublin Bills of Mortality* amount between them to about 40 per cent of Hull's (1899) collection of the economic writings, and Ireland also features in other items.

The *Political Anatomy of Ireland* (Petty 1899: 121–231), written in 1671–72 when Petty was based in Ireland, is among his most substantial works and demonstrates both his approach to economic issues and his view of Ireland. It starts by accounting for the lands of Ireland, measured in thousands of acres, classified by quality and by ownership, separating out the confiscated land and showing its redistribution, and estimating the total annual income generated from it – all this, presumaby, based on the Down Survey. The objective data is complemented by more partisan remarks: for example, those found innocent of rebellion could recover their lands, but 'of those adjudged innocents, not 1/20 were really so' (ibid.: 141).

Next, Petty estimated the number of people, classified by religion and national origin (Irish, English, Scots), and the number of houses, classified by the number of chimneys, which he used as an indicator of wealth (data was available from a tax on hearths). He also tried to divide the population by occupations and to estimate the amount of un- and under-employment. As an example of his

methods, consider alehouses: Dublin, he said, had a population of 4,000 families,[5] 1,180 alehouses and ninety-one 'public brew-houses'. Assuming the same
proportions throughout Ireland, he deduced that there were 180,000 people
employed in this trade, and that two-thirds could be spared 'even though the
same quantity of drink be sold', so 120,000 people could be reallocated to some
other trade (ibid.: 146–7). He applied much the same approach to priests of all
denominations. In the *Report of the Council of Trade in Ireland*, a sort of execu-
tive summary of the *Political Anatomy*, he proposed that 'the exorbitant number
of popish-priests and fryars, may be reduced to a bare competency, as also the
number of ale-houses' (ibid.: 223). The basic features of Petty's approach
emerge even from this brief summary. He was interested above all in numerical
totals, using whatever data came to hand coupled with heroic simplifying
assumptions when necessary. His proposals are often purely technocratic – a
certain task could be done by fewer people – with little consideration of the economic mechanisms involved but with a complete (Hobbesian) faith in the right
of the state to concern itself with the number of 'popish-priests', ale-houses, or
anything else.

The section dealing with Irish trade is a further example of the strengths and
weaknesses of his approach. He started with a division of the population into
16,000 families with houses with more than one chimney (the better off) and the
remainder (less well off). The latter are assumed to spend 52 shillings a year, so
their total income can be estimated (180,000 × 52 shillings), and similarly for
the better off, assumed to spend £10 p.a. The poor buy no imported goods, apart
from tobacco, while the better off spend 10 per cent of their income on imports.
These are very crude estimates, but they were better than anything else at the
time. Most previous economic writings focused on international trade and on
money. Petty did not ignore trade or money, but set them in the context of the
basic facts of resources, population, and so on. It was a critical step towards the
concept of the economy as a system.

A single page in the Hull edition (Petty 1899: 192), can serve to show why
Petty is seen as a founding influence in economics, but also how far he was from
realising the potential of the ideas he spun off in such profusion. The page starts
with a parenthetical remark that the Irish use turf (peat) rather than wood as fuel,
before commenting that most of the population have little use for trade, 'nor
scarce anything made outside their own village'. There follow two pregnant
digressions. First, Petty asked whether it would be better to restrain the luxury of
the rich or to 'beget a luxury' in the 950,000 poor 'so as to make them spend,
and consequently earn double what they presently do?' He answered, not surprisingly, that it would be better to increase 'the splendor, art and industry' of
the majority, and then dropped the subject. This brief comment could be read as
foreshadowing Keynes and effective demand or, more plausibly, as pointing to
the line of argument developed by Mandeville and Hume in which a taste for
luxury provides the incentive for development, but Petty never developed such a
potentially important insight. Second, he asked 'why should we forbid the use of
any foreign commodity … when we can employ our spare hands and lands upon

such exportable commodities as will purchase the same and more?' Again, he took an important argument no further. He then moved on to consider the size of the money stock relative to total spending (that is, implicitly, the velocity of circulation). All of this on one page (though not all his pages are quite so brilliant or so frustrating).

By the date of the *Political Anatomy of Ireland* the Irish economy had recovered substantially from its dreadful state in 1650. Petty argued that the poor people of Ireland were better clothed and had 'more Money and Freedom' than ever (ibid.: 203). Even so, incomes were lower than in England and there was widespread under-employment. He rejected the idea that this was due to laziness:

> Their lazing seems to me to proceed rather from want of employment and encouragement to work ... for what need they to work, who can content themselves with potatos, whereof the labour of one man can feed forty?... Why should they raise more commodities, since there are not merchants sufficiently stocked ... nor provided with other more pleasing foreign commodities, to give in exchange? And how should merchants have stock, since trade is prohibited and fettered by the statutes of England?
>
> (ibid.: 201–2)

This, and other passages suggest that Petty saw considerable potential in the Irish economy, provided trade restrictions were lifted. In the associated *Report of the Council of Trade in Ireland* he estimated that there might be 250,000 unemployed 'spare hands' who could earn £1 million per year in total if found employment, a measure of the potential for improvement (ibid.: 217). He went on to propose the removal of various restrictions on trade and the union of Ireland and England under a single legislative power.[6]

Political Arithmetic was probably started in about 1671, the same time as the *Political Anatomy of Ireland*, but not completed until around 1676. It is mainly concerned with England's wealth and potential military muscle, proposing a number of propositions such as:

> That a small country, and few people, may ... be equivalent in wealth and strength to a far greater people and territory. ... That France cannot ... be more powerful at sea than the English or Hollanders.... That the people and territories of the King of England are naturally near as considerable, for wealth and strength, as those of France.
>
> (Petty 1899: 247)

This was written during the reign of Charles II, when Louis XIV of France was bidding for hegemony in Europe and England was seen as a second rate power. Petty used his familiar method of building up numerical estimates of population, incomes, and so on, to argue that England had the capacity to match France. Within a generation he was proved right when Marlborough drove back Louis

XIV's generals using roughly the forces and revenues that Petty had argued were possible. This was a remarkable feat of prescience, and shows the practical strength of Petty's political arithmetic.

There is, however, what seems an odd reference to Ireland:

> And here I beg leave … to interpose a jocular, and perhaps ridiculous digression, and which I indeed desire men to look upon, rather as a dream or resvery, than a rational proposition; the which is, that if all the moveables and people of Ireland, and of the highlands of Scotland, were transported into the rest of Great Brittain; that then the King and his subjects, would thereby become more rich and strong.
>
> (Petty 1899: 285)

Can this have been intended seriously? To move the whole population of Ireland to England? As quoted above, Petty described it as 'perhaps ridiculous' and as a 'dream', but in 1687 he presented James II with a fully worked-out proposal to move three-quarters of the population of Ireland to England. Petty was dead within months, James was driven from his throne soon after, and nothing came of it.

Radical plans for Ireland were not new. Moving the Irish to England had been proposed before, in 1599 (Foster 1988: 35). Parliament had tried (with only moderate success) to move much of the Irish population of Munster, Leinster and Ulster to Connacht, and large 'plantations' of English incomers had been brought to Ireland. Large population movements were not ruled out of consideration.

Petty's basic argument was simple (Petty 1899: 554–74). Living standards in England were higher than in Ireland – the average person in Ireland spent £5 p.a., while in England the average person spent £6 13s 4d (£6.66), and might well earn more and save the difference. Each person transferred from Ireland to England would enjoy an increased income, while rents and tax revenues in England would increase (at least) in proportion to the increase in population. Petty wanted to move one million of the Irish population of 1.3 million, leaving 300,000 in Ireland, which would be converted to pasture for six million head of cattle. With free access to the English market for beef and a reduced workforce (paid at English rates), rents in Ireland would be half as high again.

The king would gain in revenue, landowners in both places would gain, as would the people transferred. Petty argued that the gains would greatly exceed the costs. The security situation would be transformed. The 300,000 remaining in Ireland would be too few and too scattered to be a threat, so the cost of policing Ireland would fall massively. The inflow of Catholics from Ireland would soon be absorbed into the much larger English population.

He considered the objection 'that this transplantation … amounts to an abolishment of the Irish nation: which will be odious to them and not compensable by any of the benefits' (ibid.: 577). He answered that his proposal was intended as a union of the two nations, 'which is a real blessing to both' (ibid.: 577), and that the Irish would be 'ingrafted and incorporated into a nation more rich, populous, splendid and renowned than themselves' (ibid.: 578). Not all will find this a convincing response, but Petty was confident enough to think that the transfer could be done on a voluntary basis.

From an economic point of view the key assumption was that a million Irish added to the labour force in England would add (at least) proportionately to output. Petty assumed that each Irishman or woman would be as productive individually as the English, given the same opportunities, since low productivity in Ireland was (he thought) due to a lack of incentives, and there would be advantages to increased population density, for example in improved communications and reduced transport costs. But he also implicitly assumed that there would be no scarcity of land or other resources in England, so that an enlarged labour force could be absorbed rapidly with no fall in productivity. This is more doubtful. Later (classical) writers treated population as endogenous, assuming that the population was limited by the land and/or the capital stock. In that case, there would be no jobs in England for a large influx from Ireland.

There is no sign that anyone (apart from Petty himself) took his proposal seriously, but it does point to an important aspect of his work. Petty treated population growth as an independent determinant of economic growth, rather than a result of it. He wrote about the rate and the determinants of population growth, for example in his papers on the Dublin bills of mortality (Petty 1899: 479–98), basing himself on Graunt's study of the London bills of mortality (Petty 1899: 314–435), now seen as the foundation of modern demography. Graunt and Petty were friends – it has been suggested that Petty collaborated with Graunt, and even (less plausibly) that he was the real author of the work published under his friend's name.

Petty explicitly rejected 'intellectual arguments' in favour of arguments based on 'number, weight or measure' in his definition of political arithmetic (cited above), but much discussion of his economics has focused on a number of 'intellectual arguments' which appear as digressions in his writings and point to ideas developed by later writers, if not by Petty himself.

Most prominent among these is the idea of surplus,[7] that is, the idea that a person or, more realistically, a number of people can produce more of the necessities of life than they themselves need to live on. The fraction of their output that they do not need themselves can support others – soldiers, landlords, priests, and so on. Petty's most quoted example, 'if there be 1000 men in a territory, and if 100 of them can raise necessary food and raiment for the whole 1000' (Petty 1899: 30), appears in a discussion of unemployment. The point is that if only 100 are required to produce necessities, while others are required for other activities (400, for example, produce luxuries and 200 are 'governors, divines, lawyers'), 100 might still be left without work.[8]

A different angle appears in a digression on rent. Petty imagined a man who raises corn, performing all the necessary operations himself.

> I say that when this man hath subtracted his seed out of the proceed of the harvest, and also what himself hath both eaten and given to others in

exchange for clothes and other natural necessaries, that the remainder of the corn is the natural and true rent of the land for that year.

(Petty 1899: 43)

Here the surplus over costs, including necessities for the worker/tenant, becomes the 'natural and true' rent, but whether this is meant as an explanation of actual rents is unclear. If it were combined with the numerical example given previously, it would seem to make rent nine-tenths of output, which is wildly unrealistic. In a discussion of Ireland, Petty gave a quite different account of rent, based on the fact that pasture predominated in Ireland but not in England. Here he assumed two acres of pasture grazed by a calf which adds a certain weight in a year, and argued that the value of this added weight – the produce of the land with no labour – constitutes rent (Petty 1899: 181). Any addition made by cultivation is attributable to labour and constitutes wages. The truth seems to be that Petty had many interesting ideas which undoubtedly inspired (or provoked) later writers, but that he did not have a consistent theory of rent, wages or prices.

Petty's involvement in Ireland was a major turning point in his life and in his intellectual focus. He was always a polymath with a wide range of interests, but before the Down Survey his focus was on medicine, the physical sciences, and mechanical inventions of various sorts (which he hoped would make him money). After the Down Survey, the focus shifted to political arithmetic, demography, and Irish affairs.[9] The survey itself may have been an important trigger. It was a survey of economic resources (land) with an eye to their profitability, and it was part of a transfer of ownership which had massive economic and political implications for Ireland. Given Petty's (hyper)active mind and his Baconian belief in quantification, it seems natural that he went on to look at the population that works the land, at the incomes generated from it, and so on.

Cantillon's Irish roots

The details of Richard Cantillon's birth and early life are uncertain, but he was probably born in the 1680s in Ballyronan in County Kerry.[10] His family came from the Anglo-Norman aristocracy, who had come to England with William the Conqueror and then joined Henry II's invasion of Ireland in the twelfth century, settling on land around Ballyheigue in Kerry. After supporting the Stuart monarchy against Cromwell in the 1650s, they lost to a conquering army what their ancestors had gained in the same way some five centuries earlier. Petty's survey was, of course, carried out precisely to locate and measure the land confiscated from Irish royalists like the Cantillons. As it happens, much of Petty's landholdings were also in Kerry, but I know of no indication that any of the Cantillons' land passed to him.

It seems that the Cantillon family remained on, or returned to, the land in the Ballyheigue area as tenant farmers. The future economist was the middle son of three. His older brother stayed in Ireland and leased land locally, while Richard went to France as a child or young adult. It would probably be wrong to think of him as a refugee – he was a younger son going out to seek his fortune.

Cantillon's homeland on the far western coast near the mouth of the Shannon may have seemed very remote seen from London, or even Dublin, but from the point of view of sea-borne trade with France, Spain and Portugal, it was not so remote. English policies restricted trade, but smuggling continued. There were merchants from Kerry and other parts of Ireland in the ports of western France and in Paris, including members of the Cantillon family and their relatives. In all, Kerry was not so bad as a starting point, but it was not a place for an ambitious young man to stay.[11]

It is not clear quite when Cantillon went to France, but by 1708 he was sufficiently established there to take out French nationality. He had relatives in France. Sir Daniel Arthur, a relative by marriage, was established as a banker on a large scale in Paris, in part by handling money taken from Ireland by aristocratic Catholic refugees. It was perhaps through Arthur that Cantillon met James Brydges, later Duke of Chandos. In 1711 Cantillon was working for Brydges, and the British Government, in Spain. After that, he was in Paris, working for his uncle, another Richard Cantillon, also a banker. His uncle's bank came close to failure in 1715, but our Richard Cantillon moved on, going into business for himself.

The basis of his fortune was laid during the years of John Law's 'system' in France. Law was a Scotsman who thought Scotland was poor because of a lack of circulating money and proposed a scheme to create paper money (Law 1705). He had been accused of murder in England following a duel and had to flee to the continent at the union of England and Scotland in 1707. He travelled around Europe offering his monetary schemes to different rulers while making a living as a professional gambler. He ended up in France, where he gained the support of the Regent.

The story of Law's system in France during the period 1716–20 is too complex to cover here,[12] but the essential fact is that Law engineered a massive speculative bubble in the shares of the Mississippi company, which he controlled. The company issued shares to the public, not for money but in return for state debt, *billets d'état*. The *billets* were then held by the company, which accepted a reduced interest rate, thus reducing the burden on state revenues. In return, the company got trading privileges in the French empire. Law provoked a speculative boom, to the point where almost all the upper class in France were competing to buy shares, but the bubble burst, the share price collapsed, and many were ruined.

Cantillon was closely involved, acting as Law's private banker as well as speculating on his own account. He recognised that the bubble could not last and got out in good time. He added to his fortune by speculating in South Sea Company shares in London, again riding the market up and selling out before the crash, and by speculating on the gyrations in exchange rates caused by Law's monetary manipulations in France. He came out of it all a very rich man, having made his fortune, essentially, by betting that Law's machinations would fail. His *Essay on the Nature of Commerce in General* can be seen, in part, as an explanation of why Law's scheme had to fail, though without any mention of Law's name.

Cantillon had made powerful enemies in France who pursued him with lawsuits of various sorts. He shifted his main base to London in the years after 1720. The *Essay* was probably written around 1730. He died in London in 1734. His death, like much about his life, is a mystery. His house burnt down, and a body was found in the ashes. What seemed a tragic accident looked more sinister as further evidence emerged and several of his servants were tried for murder. The evidence at the trial conflicted and they were acquitted, though suspicion remained about a cook who had fled abroad. Murphy (1986) even discusses the possibility that Cantillon had faked his own death to escape the burden of lawsuits.

Cantillon's essay on the nature of commerce in general

Cantillon is reported to have written a variety of pieces for himself and for circulation to friends, though he published nothing in his lifetime. Most of his papers were lost in the 1734 fire, but one or more copies of the *Essay on the Nature of Commerce in General* survived because they had been given or lent to friends. Our knowledge of Cantillon's economic thought comes from this single text. We do not know why he wrote it or whether he would have published it if he had lived longer. The Marquis de Mirabeau had a copy for many years but kept it to himself. It was finally published in 1755. Mirabeau drew on it in the first part of his *Ami des Hommes*, the most popular economic work of the period, written before he became Quesnay's collaborator and disciple, and it was without doubt a major influence on Quesnay and on other writers including Adam Smith.[13]

Cantillon's *Essay* is a work of pure theory, arguably the first attempt to explain the economy as an interconnected system and to build up, step-by-step, what would now be called a model of the economy. In contrast to Petty, Cantillon thought of population as endogenous: 'men multiply like mice in a barn if they have unlimited means of subsistence' (Cantillon 2001: 37). The main check on population, he thought, was that people would not marry unless they had the means to bring up children, so improved economic conditions would allow more to marry, and to do so younger, leading to population increase, whereas 'if [a] village continue in the same situation as regards employment, and derives its living from cultivating the same portion of land, it will not increase in population in a thousand years' (ibid.: 13). Capital plays no active role in the story, so land remains as the only limiting factor.

The owners of the land play a central role. Cantillon's starting point was a hypothetical estate which is assumed to be self-sufficient 'as if there were no other in the world' (ibid.: 27–8), that is, a miniature closed economy. The owner can 'follow his fancy' in the use of the land, but he will necessarily use part of it to feed and support the workers on the estate. If he wants horses, then land must be used to grow hay for them leaving less to grow food for humans, so he must make do with fewer servants. There is a very clear idea of opportunity cost here – land which is used for one purpose cannot be used for others.

Cantillon then argued that the owner need not manage the land himself, but can rent it to farmers and buy what he wants from them. The farmers will have to adapt their output to demand, as will artisans producing manufactured goods. The living standards and consumption of the mass of the people are assumed to be given by unchanging convention, so the decentralised estate produces the same outputs as before while the landowner is spared the 'care and trouble' of overseeing the estate personally and the farmers 'have more care and satisfaction in working on their own account' (ibid.: 28). In a full-sized economy with many landlords, the principle is the same – the tastes of the landlords (and of a few others with above-normal incomes) together with the conventional spending patterns of the rest determine the pattern of production. In this simple example, Cantillon sketched a model of a complete economy. No one had done anything like it before.

Landlords receive rent, others work for their living and earn 'wages' (French: *gages*), but Cantillon distinguished between those whose wage is fixed by agreement with the employer, and those (like farmers or independent artisans) whose income depends on the sale of their produce, and who therefore carry the risks inevitable in a decentralised market system. The risk takers are 'entrepreneurs' (in French – 'undertakers' in the standard Higgs translation). Cantillon recognised that entrepreneurs need capital to set up in production (Prendergast 1991), though he did not recognise capital scarcity as a significant limiting factor at the level of the whole economy. His treatment of entrepreneurship and capital pointed the way to later developments in economic theory.

What about prices? In his story about the introduction of markets into an imaginary isolated estate, Cantillon suggested that the owner could set prices so as to provide each producer with the necessary subsistence, but it soon becomes clear that there is no need for this. Cantillon distinguished between market prices, depending on the flux of events in the market, and what he called 'intrinsic values' or, in modern terms, long-run equilibrium prices. He sketched out the way prices would adjust to clear the market on any given day and described a longer-term adjustment process in which over- or under-supply in any particular trade leads people to move between occupations or places in a way which tends to restore equilibrium.

Equilibrium prices have to cover payments for the use of land and (conventional) subsistence costs for the labour required. Petty too had argued that the value of a good must depend on the land and labour required to produce it, and had puzzled over the 'par' or ratio which could be used to aggregate land and labour into a single price. Petty had made little progress – Cantillon referred rather scornfully to Petty's efforts as 'fanciful and remote from natural laws' (Cantillon 2001: 21). Cantillon had an answer: conventional standards of living for different types of labour can be converted to the land required to support a worker and family. The 'intrinsic value' of anything, then, is proportional to the land required to produce it, including the land needed to support the workforce. This fits with the analysis of what we would now call opportunity costs in terms of the allocation of land. No-one else has had a land theory of value like Cantillon's, because later writers from Adam Smith on included profit as a third category of income alongside wages and rent, and assumed that use of the land was constrained by the availability of capital.

Murphy has suggested that Part One of Cantillon's *Essay*, dealing with the real economy and centring on the role of the landlords, may have been inspired by 'the old feudal landlord world Cantillon was born into' in Ireland (Murphy 1986: 17). One could respond that Cantillon's city-based landlords, whose estates were a source of income and little more, were not quite traditional feudal lords, but one could say the same about Ireland at the time. Cantillon's background in Kerry may well have inspired his discussion of the low prices, low returns, and scarcity of circulating money in areas distant from city markets, whose products have to bear high transport costs before they can be sold at city prices (Cantillon 2001: 63–5).

The second part of Cantillon's *Essay* deals with the circulation of money between city and country. Like Petty, Cantillon saw the velocity of circulation as governed mainly by institutional factors, especially the frequency of rent payments. Money was little used in the countryside at that time, but rents had to be paid in cash. Farmers would sell their crops, less what was needed locally, to city merchants, and store the money up until rent payments were due. Once the money was paid to landlords it would be spent in the city, where it would pass from hand to hand fairly quickly and end up in the hands of merchants ready to buy the crops again. Cantillon's numerical examples of flows of money between sectors undoubtedly provided the basis for Quesnay's much better known '*tableau économique*'.

Cantillon's analysis of the circulation of money was the basis of his version of the quantity theory of money, written before Hume's definitive statement, but not published until after it. An increase in the quantity of money increases prices, which reduces international competitiveness and leads eventually to a money outflow, reversing the initial increase. Hume concluded that the money supply and the balance of trade would look after themselves and could safely be ignored.

Cantillon, however, emphasised the long lags involved. Much depends on the reason for the initial rise in the money supply. A discovery of gold or the issue of paper money (as in Law's system) will soon cause increased prices and imports because the money will be spent immediately.

> An abundance of fictitious and imaginary money causes the same disadvantages as an increase of real money in circulation, by raising the price of land and labour, or by making works and manufactures more expensive at the risk of subsequent loss. But this furtive abundance vanishes at the first gust of discredit and precipitates disorder.
>
> (Cantillon 2001: 125)

If, however, a successful manufacturing sector brings in money from abroad, the money will accrue first to merchants and manufacturers, who are likely to set it aside for future expansion or to purchase property. Prices will rise slowly and the trade surplus will only fall slowly since the underlying competitive strength remains. Cantillon thought it would take a long time for rival manufacturing centres to establish themselves, and thus that a successful manufacturing country could maintain a relatively high price level for a long time.

Manufacturing for export had a further advantage. Agriculture, and the corresponding rural population, are inherently immobile but (luxury) manufacturing can be located wherever is convenient. A country which exports, manufactures and imports food and raw materials can thus sustain a larger population than a country which lacks manufactures. Cantillon's example of a country weakened by importing manufactures was Poland, but it could equally have been Ireland.

Where Hume thought that the world system would reach equilibrium, Cantillon saw very long cycles in which one country after another would rise to prominence before sinking again as rivals with relatively low prices took over (after a long lag). Active policy could speed up the upswing and then postpone the downswing.

> It is by examining the results of each branch of commerce singly that foreign trade can be usefully regulated.... It will always be found by examining particular cases that the exportation of all manufactured articles is advantageous to the state,... that the best returns or payments imported are specie, and in default of specie the produce of foreign land into which there enters the least labour.
>
> (Cantillon 2001: 95)

A large population and a high price level, provided it can be sustained, are desirable primarily to maximise military power relative to other states. Cantillon's economic theory was a huge advance on anything that had gone before, but his view of the aims of policy was very much of his time.

Petty and Cantillon

Petty and Cantillon made contrasting but complementary contributions to the emerging discipline of economics. Petty's theoretical asides played only a minor role in his own writings but have been taken up and debated by later generations. The point for him was the use of quantitative data to throw light on practical questions. His estimates of population growth, of total population broken down by occupations and other characteristics, of incomes for different kinds of people and in total, of government revenues from different sources, of the money stock and the velocity of circulation, and so on, defined the national economy as an entity worth studying and potentially open to quantitative analysis.

Cantillon's *Essay*, by contrast, is an elegantly constructed work of pure theory, the first to analyse the economy as an integrated system, not just the sum of its parts. It includes many examples, but they are always chosen to illustrate a definite theoretical point, not for their own sake. It should be noted, though, that the contrast with Petty might be less striking if we had Cantillon's now lost 'supplement', which evidently contained empirical and quantitative material to fill out the material in the main text.

Notes

1 Biographical information is mainly drawn from Strauss (1954), Hull (1899), Fitzmaurice (1895) and Roncaglia (2004).
2 The full story, as you might expect, is more complicated. See Strauss (1954: 77–82).
3 It was used in French (*économie politique*) in the early seventeenth century. Petty himself used the phrase in English in passing. It first appeared in the title of a book on economics in English a century later with Steuart in 1767 (King 1948; Groenewegen 1987).
4 Most spelling and capitalisation have been modernised in quotations.
5 It may seem that 4,000 families in Dublin is rather few, but servants are included within the household.
6 He changed his policy proposals later.
7 For an interpretation of Petty which stresses the notion of surplus, see Roncaglia (1985, 1987: 854).
8 The numbers seem implausible for the seventeenth century, but they were only a hypothetical example.
9 Aspromourgos (2005) argues that Petty's involvement in the Hartlib group from the 1640s was important to the development of his ideas. I am sure he is right, but Petty's interest in the 1640s seems to have focused on technology rather than political arithmetic.
10 On Cantillon's life I rely heavily on the splendid biography by Antoin Murphy (1986).
11 Petty, like others before him, had noted that the upper class in Ireland knew French and Latin, but in Kerry even the lower classes often had some Latin.
12 On the 'system', and on Law's life and economics see Murphy (1997).
13 On Cantillon's economics see Brewer (1992, 2001).

References

Aspromourgos, T. (2005) 'The Invention of the Concept of Social Surplus: Petty in the Hartlib Circle', *European Journal of the History of Economic Thought* 12.1: 1–24.

Brewer, A. (1992) *Richard Cantillon: Pioneer of Economic Theory*, London: Routledge.

Brewer, A. (2001) 'Introduction', in R. Cantillon, *Essay on the Nature of Commerce in General*, H. Higgs (trans.), New Brunswick, NJ: Transaction Publishers.

Cantillon, R. (2001) *Essay on the Nature of Commerce in General*, H. Higgs (trans.), New Brunswick, NJ: Transaction Publishers.

Fitzmaurice, E. (1985) *The Life of Sir William Petty*, London: John Murray.

Foster, R. (1988) *Modern Ireland 1600–1972*, London: Allen Lane, the Penguin Press.

Groenewegen, P. (1987) '"Political Economy" and "Economics"', in J. Eatwell, M. Milgate and P. Newman (eds) *The New Palgrave: a Dictionary of Economics*, London: Macmillan, Vol. 3, pp. 904–7.

Hull, C. (1899) 'Introduction', in C. Hull (ed.), *The Economic Writings of Sir William Petty*, Cambridge: Cambridge University Press.

King, J. (1948) 'The Origin of the Term "Political Economy"', *Journal of Modern History* 20.3: 230–1.

Law, J. [1705] (1934) *Money and Trade Considered with a Proposal for Supplying the Nation with Money*, in P. Harsin (ed.) *Oeuvres Complètes*, 3 vols, Paris: Librarie du Recueil Sirey, pp. 2–164.

Murphy, A. (1986) *Richard Cantillon: Entrepreneur and Economist*, Oxford: Clarendon Press.

Murphy, A.E. (1997) *John Law: Economic Theorist and Policy Maker*, Oxford: Clarendon Press.

Petty, W. (1899) *The Economic Writings of Sir William Petty*, C. Hull (ed.), 2 vols, Cambridge: Cambridge University Press.

Prendergast, R. (1991) 'Cantillon and the Emergence of the Theory of Profit', *History of Political Economy* 23: 419–29.

Roncaglia, A. (1985) *Petty: the Origins of Political Economy*, Cardiff: University College Cardiff Press.

Roncaglia, A. (1987) 'Petty, William', in J. Eatwell, M. Milgate and P. Newman (eds) *The New Palgrave: a Dictionary of Economics*, London: Macmillan, Vol. 3, pp. 853–5.

Roncaglia, A. (2004) 'Petty, William (1623–87)', in D. Rutherford (ed.) *The Biographical Dictionary of British Economists*, Bristol: Thoemmes Continuum, pp. 927–31.

Strauss, E. (1954) *Sir William Petty: Portrait of a Genius*, London: The Bodley Head.

2 Swift and Berkeley on economic development

Edward McPhail and Salim Rashid

Introduction

The richly dense contributions of Ireland to the economic discourse of the early eighteenth century have yet to be adequately explored. Despite the persistence of Joseph Johnston and the additional efforts of T.W. Hutchison, almost all attention is given to the minutiae of Adam Smith and his circle. That the Irish, as the first colony of England (if not of Europe) initiated the field of development economics; that they were practitioners even as they theorized, who went into the countryside and actively encouraged economic activity, thus making them the first NGOs; that they believed in such theorizing and engagement as part of their Christianity; these are all facts that should have put them in the forefront of modern discussion. But the profession has seen fit to move differently. As attention is given to personalities in the first instance, we will focus here upon the two best known personalities of this age – Jonathan Swift and George Berkeley – in order to demonstrate the wider outlook and deeper grounding that motivated the activities of the Irish Anglican elite at this period. Examining only these two individuals is scarcely fair to Archbishop King, who also pioneered social analysis and social work (Fauske 2004), or to Thomas Prior and Samuel Madden, the stalwarts of the Dublin Society, on whom Berkeley relied so heavily, but one has to start somewhere.

That Swift and Berkeley knew and admired each other is well known but the extent of direct contact between them is uncertain. Their general philosophical and religious goals were alike – seeing Christianity in danger from the 'new learning' of their age they combated its science, its mathematics and its philosophy. Berkeley's efforts in multiple publications are well known, but Swift too did more than just mock science in *Gulliver's Travels* and political economy in the *Modest Proposal*. In his sermons Swift squarely tried to meet the challenge of heathen philosophy and he speculated on the causes of Irish wretchedness. While these general facts are easy to obtain from the literature, what is much less appreciated is the extent to which an appreciation of self-interest permeates the thought of both Swift and Berkeley. This is true of self-interest both in its narrow sense of selfishness and, more surprisingly, in the wider sense of sociability – both feelings were considered essential to human nature and the task of integrating them harmoniously was, to both men, an essential function of Christianity. To take a brief example of each: in the midst of a sermon on the superiority of Christianity Swift emphasizes the essential selfishness of Mankind by stopping to scoff at the idea of a people being motivated by the idea of virtue being its own reward (Swift 1790 2: 146); Berkeley began his career by emphasizing the social nature of Mankind to such an extent that he used the Newtonian image of social feelings as being the 'gravitational force' holding society together, and was constrained to mute his views only when Shaftesbury and his school started preaching that man was naturally good and preferred virtue on his own. Both Swift and Berkeley were vitally concerned to engage the social life of Ireland towards the building of a good society and both were well aware that this required more then individual virtues – social institutions had to be designed to encourage virtue and discourage vice, hence their insistence on social theorizing.

This paper focuses upon the depth of these social concerns in both Swift and Berkeley. The next section shows how well aware Swift was of the balancing act between private and public good needed to make social life thrive, particularly in paying attention to incentives. This is followed by a section dealing with Swift's one direct contribution to development institutions – his loan fund – which is an adumbration of modern microfinance. Later sections deal with the wider scope and goals set by Berkeley and examine how he envisaged their accomplishment in the first comprehensive plan for economic development. The penultimate section describes Berkeley's views on money and Irish monetary problems – the one issue where Swift and Berkeley may be said to have overlapped, with Swift opposing Wood's Halfpence and Berkeley working hard to achieve a national bank for Ireland. Swift's writings are largely only critique but Berkeley is amazingly original and positive. Furthermore, this is an issue where modern theory has cast a false light, so one should clarify why eighteenth century Ireland still needs more factual and more sympathetic study. The conclusion summarizes the discussion and suggests lines of further research.

Mutual subjection, doing good, and inalienable duties

Swift's sermons provide a window into his model of human action. Emanating from his Christianity, Swift's approach combines aspects of normative and positive egalitarianism. The author of *Mutual Subjection* and *Doing Good* is no armchair Christian. His Christianity translates into social policy and makes demands on both the social reformer and those to be reformed. While accepting a role for hierarchy in determining how the talents, circumstances, and stations of people play out in this world, his normative egalitarianism places everyone – from the Prince down to the 'meanest' – on the same footing before God:

> Christian wisdom is *without partiality*; it is not calculated for this or that nation or people, but the whole race of mankind: Not to the philosophical schemes which were narrow and confined, adapted to their peculiar towns, governments, or sects; but, in every nation, he that feareth God and worketh righteousness is accepted with him.
>
> (Swift 1790 2: 158)

Emphasizing a cosmopolitan Christianity of self-reflection, Swift's sermons ask the listener to think about their fellow human being and to realize 'There but for God's grace go I.' If God so willed it a person of high status with many talents could have occupied one of the 'meaner' stations in life. While people may differ according to their abilities the Irish poor were no different from the non-poor in the sense that all could contribute to the economic success of Ireland. All humans have the same potentiality to fulfill their role in the economic scheme of things. All people from the low to the high have a role to play in God's plan and that applies equally well to the workings of the economy.

Mutual subjection reconciles differences among equals. Although each person is different, all are equal before God. These differences play an important role in what might be called Swift's economic theodicy. Differences in talents, station, circumstance and fortune mean that we must rely upon one another. Hence, even Princes 'depend for every necessary of life upon the meanest of their people.' Indeed God so ordered the world that we ought 'to act, as far as our power reacheth, towards the good of the whole communit' (Swift 1790 1: 7). These bonds of 'subjection due from every man to every man' are due *because* we are human and 'cannot be made void by any power, pre-eminence, or authority whatever' (Swift 1790 1: 6).[1] Those 'who doth not perform that part assigned him, towards advancing the benefit of the whole, in proportion to his opportunities and abilities,' are guilty of free riding 'because he taketh his share of the profit, and yet leaveth his share of the burden to be borne by others, which is the true principal cause of most miseries and misfortunes in life' (Swift 1790 1: 7). It is free riding since talents and abilities are on loan from God and the degree of public spiritedness is effectively a public good.

Swift mentions the power of emulation when it comes to pursuing and reinforcing the good virtues:

> The very example of honesty and industry in a tradesman will sometimes spread through a neighborhood when others see how successful he is; and thus so many useful members are gained, for which the whole body of the public is the better.
>
> (Swift 1772 12: 241)

Similarly, Swift is well aware of what economists call 'the $1/n$ problem.' This arises when n individuals have to share out a task equally, so when n is large, each feels that by shirking they affect the outcome by $1/n$, or negligible fashion; since everyone thinks this way and shirks, the task fails to get done. What is individually rational can lead to a socially irrational outcome and the erosion of public spiritedness:

> But hence it clearly follows how necessary the love of our country or a public spirit is in every particular man, since the wicked have so many opportunities of doing public mischief. Every man is upon his guard for his private advantage; but where the public is concerned, he is apt to be

negligent, considering himself only as one among two or three millions, among whom the loss is equally shared, and thus he thinks he can be no great sufferer. Meanwhile the trader, the farmer, and the shopkeeper complain of the hardness and deadness of the times, and wonder whence it comes; while it is in a great measure owing to their own folly, for want of that love of their country, and public spirit and firm union among themselves, which are so necessary to the prosperity of every nation.

(Swift 1772 12: 244)

Under Swift's scheme the haves are obligated to assist the have nots. Yet this assistance is not mere gift giving or a permanent subsidy. Rather those who have should alter their tastes and preferences to include those less fortunate in their consumption calculus. It is not a problem if you are poor in a world where people fulfill their obligations under mutual subjection. The wealthy man should employ the poor and definitely should not spend his surplus on luxury goods from abroad. As we shall see again with George Berkeley, the responsible Christian is not free to choose whatever he prefers; faith directs choice. Swift is keenly aware of the incentives and motivations that can be used to spur on self-initiative. He wants assistance to lead to independence not dependence. In Sermon VII, *On the Causes of the Wretched Condition of Ireland*, Swift points to the destructive behavior that can lead to poverty: living beyond one's means, drunkenness, not providing for one's old age etc. While wishing to assist the elderly poor he does not wish to discourage people from making provisions for their old age. But since they are brothers and sisters, 'we ought to support him to the best of our power, without reflecting over seriously on the causes that brought him to misery' (Swift 1790 2: 27). While maintaining that a large number of poor are poor due to their own devices he nevertheless recognizes that through no fault of their own some are reduced to begging.

Swift understood that no serious account of human behavior could be built on the assumption that people are solely motivated by self-regarding preferences or that people ought to be only focused on their own well-being. Swift recognized that people do become different because of their environments. The environment affects their behaviors and even their cognitive abilities. Through his sermons he hoped to encourage his flock to act in the public interest and to thwart the

avarice or malice which, I am afraid are deeply rooted in too many breasts, and against which there can be no defence, but a firm resolution in all honest men, to be closely united and active in shewing their love to their country, by preferring the public interest to their present private advantage.

(Swift 1790 2: 123).

Swift also criticized selfishness as a guide to action realizing that it could undermine the very norms of behavior required for social cohesion and erode public spiritedness. Nevertheless, Swift recognized that self-regarding preferences are a powerful force and that they must play a role in any economic explanation:

> Now human nature is so constituted, that we can never pursue any thing heartily but upon hopes of a reward. If we run a race, it is in expectation of a prize, and the greater the prize the faster we run.
>
> (Swift 1790 2: 145)

But given 'that we can never pursue any thing heartily but upon hopes of a reward,' how are we to trade off self-interest against fulfilling our obligations to our brothers and sisters? Swift made two arguments. First, that pursuing the public interest is natural and second that our interests are sufficiently tied together that to neglect the public interest is to neglect our own:

> If a passenger, in a great storm at sea, should hide his goods that they might not be thrown over board to lighten the ship, what would be the consequence? The ship is cast away, and he loses his life and goods together.
>
> (Swift 1790 2: 123–4)

'Let us therefore preserve that public spirit, which God hath raised in us for our own temporal interest' (Swift 1790 2: 130).

His second argument set the limits to our assistance of another person. Swift argued that when we consider the good of another it is fundamental that we first ensure our own safety and then consider the safety of another. He implicitly tells his congregation to weigh the costs and benefits of taking action. As long as the cost is not so great as to endanger our own well-being we are compelled to help out a fellow human being. In this calculus we are to take action just short of 'blasting our own reputations' or 'losing our own lives.' Swift is reinforcing what those in his congregation already recognize as their duty – what they find to be compelling – 'that public spirit which God hath raised in us...' that we are not isolated freely floating atoms but that we are all in it together.

While Swift notes what is expected of good Christians he is under no delusion that people always act with other regarding motives. Indeed if they did there would be little point for Swift to give sermons encouraging his flock on to more Christ-like behavior or to point to bad actors whose actions have deleterious effects on the public interest as well as their own. Swift had little patience for systems that assumed away the problem of how to motivate people to pursue virtue. For Swift,

> to call virtue its own reward, and worthy to be followed only for itself: Whereas, if there be any thing in this more than the sound of the words, it is at least too abstracted to become an universal influencing principle in the world, and therefore could not be of general use.
>
> (Swift 1790 2: 146)

Incentives matter and any account of human improvement must rely on self-interest to help shape behavior. For Swift Christianity provides the reward to spur on improvement. Those who are pursing God's ends receive his blessings.

Those who actively attempt to thwart God's system condone evil and they will pay the consequences, if not in this life then in the next.

Swift the compassionate misanthrope: microfinance, humble friends, and the industrious poor

Putting his philosophy in action, Swift sought to promote the public interest. Using a sizable portion of his own wealth, he engaged in specific acts of charity and was one of the earliest practitioners of microfinance.[2] These activities are not mere ad hoc improvisations but are part and parcel of his views on mutual subjection. The form that aid took flows from his economic theodicy.

While Swift wished to promote the well-being of the poor he did not want assistance to diminish their work habits: 'He prudently thought, that to feed idleness tended only to propagate misery.' To that end Swift's practice of mutual subjection entailed 'debar[ring] himself of what he called superfluities of life, in order to administer to the necessities of the distressed ... When he dines alone, he drinks a pint of beer, and gives away the price of a pint of wine' (Sheridan 1787: 416). While out in his garden with Mrs Pilkington she observed that it was about to rain. 'I hope not for that will cost me six-pence for a coach for you. Come, haste; O how the tester trembles in my pocket!' Having made it home before the rainstorm Swift proclaimed 'Thank God, I have saved my money. Here, you fellow [to the servant] carry this six-pence to the lame old man that sells gingerbread at the corner, because he tries to do something, and does not beg' (Sheridan 1787: 415).

> [Swift] constantly lent out a large sum of money in small portions to honest, diligent, and necessitous tradesmen, who paid it with a small gratuity by way of interest to the person who kept account of the disbursements and weekly payments, for he received back these loans by a certain sum out of the weekly profit of borrowers trade, in such proportions as that the whole should be repaid in a year.
>
> (Swift 1754 1: 66)

According to one account, Swift gave

> about half of his yearly income in private pensions to decayed families; and [kept] five hundred pounds in the constant service of industrious poor, which he lent out five pounds at a time, and took the payment back at two shillings a-week...

This was believed to do the poor 'more service than if [Swift] gave it to them entirely' since 'it obliged them to work, and at the same time kept up this charitable fund for the assistance of many' (Sheridan 1787: 415). A number of recipients of the loans where 'poor tradesmen' without 'proper tools to carry on their work' (Sheridan 1787: 416).

While there are examples of earlier loan schemes none seemed to inspire others to take action as Swift's scheme did.[3] Early successes imitating Swift's model led to an explosion of independent charitably funded organizations for lending to the poor during the first part of the 1800s. These organizations began experimenting with accepting deposits, and fell under the regulation of the newly created 'Loan Fund Board' in 1837. By 1843, there were around 300 loan funds scattered through the entire island operating under the Board (Hollis and Sweetman 2003: 4).

Samuel Johnson claimed that Swift's loan program was a failure.

> [A] severe and punctilious temper is ill qualified for transactions with the poor; the day was often broken, and the loan was not repaid. This might have been easily foreseen; but for this Swift had made no provision of patience or pity.
>
> (Johnson 1793 3: 238; Sheridan 1787: 457)

Swift was 'forced to drop his scheme, and own the folly of expecting punctuality from the poor' (Johnson 1793 3: 238) and (Sheridan 1787: 457). Sheridan writes that Johnson's claim is 'utterly unsupported by any evidence' (Sheridan 1787: 456). Johnson finds fault with precisely those features that we see today in successful microfinance programs such as the Grameen bank.

> Swift addressed problems that remain ubiquitous in modern microcredit: asymmetric information in the screening of borrowers, moral hazard and enforcement. Four components of Swift's lending scheme endured: small loans, weekly repayments, cosignatories but not physical collateral, and the force of law to obtain repayment if necessary.
>
> (Hollis and Sweetman 2003: 4)

It should be clear that Swift was always keen to get the incentives right. Swift's widely known willingness to sue to ensure that a loan was paid in full and on time was an invaluable credible threat. Swift's actions made a credible commitment for enforcement helps to discipline participants to future agreements.

Without that commitment the scheme would not have succeeded and the circulating fund quickly diminished. 'What wise precautions Swift took to prevent any diminution of this fund; which were so effectual, that it held out entire to the last, and the circulation of it continued unimpaired, till he was deprived of his understanding...' (Sheridan 1787: 457). Swift guided by mutual subjection never forgot that people respond to rewards and punishments. He clearly understood that proper incentives would bring about a change in behavior.

From our discussion it should be clear that Swift's 'charity' is not merely giving away sums of money. His acts of goodwill are mediated by the market and have the disciplining effects that markets afford. When there is a market failure such as the case for the capital constrained 'poor tradesmen,' his solution is to provide the enabling conditions for just such a market. He helps to promote mutually beneficial exchange. Not only are both parties to the exchange better off but from his perspective the tradesman and the industrious poor are improved. Swift recognized that markets help to create people, that the characters of people are endogenous to the economic exchanges they make and that he could help to influence the kind of people they choose to become.[4] When Swift rails against luxuries purchased from abroad he has in mind the unfulfilled potential of the industrious Irish poor who go without. Those who are better situated whether by talent or circumstance are under Christian obligation to assist those in need, to enable them to become participating members in the economic life of the community and thereby help them to fulfill their own obligations under mutual subjection.[5]

Swift gives rise to strong feelings on the part of commentators. Mackintosh wrote about the 'masculine severity of Swift' (Mackintosh and Mackintosh 1850: 138). Hawkesworth remarked that '[a]s a member of civil society, he was a zealous advocate for liberty, the detector of fraud, and the scourge of oppression' (Swift 1754 1: 65). Robert Shiells noted

> [H]e had the most unbounded vanity to gratify, he was pleased with the servility and awe with which inferiors approached him. He may be resembled to an eastern monarch, who takes delight in surveying his slaves, trembling at his approach and kneeling with reverance at his feet.
>
> (Cibber *et al.* 1753 5: 99)

This stands in stark contrast to the accounts by Thomas Sheridan and John Hawkesworth. According to their accounts Swift's views on mutual subjection also governed his relations with his servants. He had a

> well known maxim, that a faithful servant should always be considered not as a *poor slave*, but an *humble friend* ... In his private capacity, he was not only charitable but generous; and whatever misanthropy may be found in his writings, there does not appear to have been any in his life.
>
> (Swift 1754 1: 65)

Swift paid them 'the full value of their work' at wages the 'highest rate then known' (Swift 1778 1: 137). He encouraged them to save and paid them interest to do so, but '[i]f ... their expences were greater than their income, it was judged a sufficient reason to discharge them...' (Swift 1778 1: 138). Swift had little patience with shoddy work and strove to promote industry in himself and others.[6]

Perhaps G.K. Chesterton who described Swift's 'inhuman humanity' best sums up these opposing views:

> Swift was much too harsh and disagreeable to be English ... [He] combin[ed] extravagant fancy with a curious sort of coldness ... Swift [has] that very quality which Thackeray said was impossible in an Irishman,

benevolent bullying, a pity touched with contempt, and a habit of knocking men down for their own good. Characters in novels are often described as so amiable that they hate to be thanked. It is not an amiable quality, and it is an extremely rare one; but Swift possessed it. When Swift was buried the Dublin poor came in crowds and wept by the grave of the broadest and most free-handed of their benefactors. Swift deserved the public tribute; but he might have writhed and kicked in his grave at the thought of receiving it.

(Chesterton 1989 11: 363)

Berkeley on human sociality

First, that as social inclinations are absolutely necessary to the well-being of the world, it is the duty and interest of each individual to cherish and improve them to the benefit of mankind (Berkeley 1901: 189).

Berkeley argued that fellow feeling and mutual benevolence were innate and necessary for human society: 'In a word, hence rises that diffusive sense of Humanity so unaccountable to the selfish man who is untouched with it, and is, indeed, a sort of monster or anomalous production.'[7] Amartya Sen made this very same point much later and to great effect in his celebrated *Rational Fools.* Berkeley recognized that people cooperate and express other regarding behaviors to a much greater degree than homo economicus alone can explain: 'if every man's heart was set to do all the mischief his appetite should prompt him to do, as often as opportunity and secrecy presented themselves, there could be no living in the world' (Berkeley 1752: 57).[8]

Berkeley's work sought to explain under what conditions economic prosperity could take hold and that required an explanation of the human actor. He not only had to be able to provide an account of the role of other regarding behavior in economic growth but also why individuals would be so motivated as to pursue the greater good. Why do individuals practice other regarding behaviors? What institutions can help support this other regarding behavior? What kind of behavior best supports the well-being of people? What of the claim that people pursue only their self-interest? Berkeley's work addresses these questions.

Berkeley argued that development policy should be based on the idea that the Irish poor were no different than the non-poor in the sense that they all could, and should, contribute to the economic success of Ireland. In Query 351 Berkeley asked, 'Whether all men have not faculties of mind or body which may be employed for the public benefit?'[9] He believed that a more equal distribution of income was not inconsistent with economic growth and rising living standards (Query 214). Indeed, he saw it as essential for the future prosperity of Ireland and as a necessary component of his project to promote human happiness. Berkeley assumed that all people respond to economic incentives and that no one was destined to be poor. Rather than blame the victims of the depressed Irish economy, Berkeley sought to lay bare the systemic failures that had brought it about. Economists consider people to be differentiated by their assets and their preferences. For fear of violating individual autonomy, to the economist, qua economist, all preferences are equivalent, or, as it is more commonly stated, preferences are exogenous. In common with most pre-modern social philosophers, Berkeley recognized that people do become different because of their environments. The environment affects their behaviors and even their cognitive abilities (Queries 60 and 61 are apt). 'People' are endogenous; they are in part the product of their economic environment. Berkeley saw this as a crucial aspect of his economics. At one level it means that it is possible to adapt demand by adopting new preferences, at another level it provides the means to address the problems posed by public goods and bads since collective action problems may be overcome with the aid of other regarding preferences.

Berkeley understood that no serious account of human behavior could be built on the assumption that people are motivated solely by self-regarding preferences or that people ought to be focused only on their own well-being. For example, experiments reveal that people participating in a Prisoner's Dilemma are prepared to take actions costly to themselves out of fairness. Their behavior is not consistent with a person who is entirely self-regarding. Berkeley took it for granted that properly socialized people are predisposed to cooperate and that they take into account the well-being of other people when they act.[10]

Berkeley saw human sociality not only as a means to achieving better economic performance but also as a means to promoting the well-being of the individual. Berkeley thought that to lead a fulfilling and rewarding life we need to appreciate certain goods and the institutions of the economy should be directed towards helping us develop the desires appropriate to achieving our potential as creatures made by God. Nevertheless, Berkeley recognized that self-regarding preferences are a powerful force and must play a role in any account of human motivation. He justifies faith in part by a rational self-interest argument. The anticipated future life acts to discipline the behavior of people in this life in part because it is in their interest. His argument justifying caring for one's community is similar: 'because the good of the whole is inseparable from that of the parts; in promoting therefore the common good, every one doth at the same time promote his own private interest.' Berkeley sees that belief in an afterlife acts as a disciplining device in this life and when that belief is absent then a plainly visible, credible threat of punishment here and now will be needed to induce the desired behavior (Queries 389–391). The fundamental issue, taken for granted by all thinkers in the Christian faith, is that Mankind is constantly capable of evil. Even though Berkeley preceded Shaftesbury in arguing for the importance of social affections; indeed, Berkeley used the Newtonian image of 'gravitational forces' in describing the pull of sociality, Berkeley had to sharply differentiate himself from the claim of Shaftesbury that human good-will is so strong and so reliable that neither incentives nor punishments are essential for a happy social life (Leary 1977).

Berkeley calls our propensity to seek community 'social inclinations.' All properly socialized people have these social inclinations, something that the 'Author of our being' so intended. Berkeley takes it from observation that 'social inclinations are absolutely necessary to the well-being of the world' that we have a 'duty and interest ... to cherish and improve them to the benefit of mankind'

(Berkeley 1901: 189). We are duty bound because God so intends it: he 'hath implanted the seeds of mutual benevolence in our souls' (Berkeley 1901: 189). It is in our interest 'because the good of the whole is inseparable from that of the parts; in promoting therefore the common good, every one doth at the same time promote his own private interest' (Berkeley 1901: 189). Berkeley argues 'that the main duty which [Christianity] inculcates above all others is charity ... [O]ur Lord's peculiar precept is, "Love thy neighbour as thyself. By this shall all men know that you are My disciples, if you love one another"' (Berkeley 1901: 189). This has several important implications for Berkeley's economic thought. His Christian theology and the way that he unpacks the practical implications of that theology imply certain moves for Berkeley to take developing his economics. Given his emphasis on brotherly love he proposes policies that address the condition of the mass in Ireland, the poor. For their benefit home trade ought to be developed, and economic policies pursued such as a national bank that help to promote industry and stimulate demand. The wealthy ought to redirect their conspicuous consumption to Irish produce and they ought to become good stewards: passing better laws, pursuing life-long learning, and promoting sound marriages.

Berkeley's understanding of mutual benevolence and the nature of the connectedness of humankind again has its counterpart in his various queries emphasizing that the health of the whole cannot be achieved without the health of the parts, e.g., Queries 343, 484, 579, 580, 581 on the 'natural body,' its 'extremities,' its 'health,' 'circulation,' etc. Comparing the state with the body and taking action with a 'remedy,' Berkeley queries '[w]hether it is not natural to wish for a benevolent physician' (Query 344)?

Berkeley notes that there are 'obstructions'[11] that can interfere with our natural fellow feeling and that 'private passions and motions of the soul do often obstruct the operation of that benevolent uniting instinct implanted in human nature' (Berkeley 1901: 188). His *Querist* details how in the economic sphere 'obstructions' can lead to a focus on private interest over public interest and how they help to make Ireland worse off. To help remedy the plight of Ireland Berkeley counsels that these obstructions which are the result of the artificial appetites, the vanities, and the passions, etc., need to be removed by state action if need be (e.g., 'speculation and other forms of passing money from hand to hand without industry' (Query 306, Part II: 115)) and when that is not feasible to be redirected so that they may be harnessed for the good of the community (Queries 115–125, 140–167): 'that benevolent uniting instinct implanted in human nature ... doth still exert, and will not fail to shew itself when those obstructions are taken away' (Berkeley 1901: 188).[12] Lest it be thought that Berkeley's mutualism, his emphasis on Christian charity and 'love thy neighbour' makes Berkeley a kind of proto Christian socialist who equates love with sentimental soft heartedness, his numerous queries on slavery and servitude as well as the role he sees for the state to redirect the appetites disabuses us of that notion. We are all equal before God, but before man what separates those who are equal from those who are not is whether they work. We all warrant equal treatment but we have a duty to contribute to the well-being of the nation through our industry.

This is how Berkeley can at one and the same time use the golden rule as a guide to policy and yet on the other hand be willing to force people to work. People are duty bound to contribute to society. The argument that each is equal before God and yet may have different roles to play in the economy implies that we are equally obliged to use our God given abilities to work. Berkeley's argument for mutuality implies that the whole can be greater than the sum of its parts because we are so constituted that we achieve our full potential only through society. Berkeley's spiritual economy concludes, 'in promoting therefore the common good, every one doth at the same time promote his own private interest' (Berkeley 1901: 189). How does Berkeley define 'own private interest?' Is it what a person guided by passions would think is in his interest? Is it what a sympathetic observer would think? Here interest is judged by the criteria that Berkeley has set forth that is truly in our interest. Berkeley notes, 'the sum of human happiness is supposed to consist in the goods of mind, body, and fortune...' (Johnston and Berkeley 1970: 124). *The Querist* 'offer[s] his mite towards improving the manners, health, and prosperity of his fellow-creatures' (Johnston and Berkeley 1970: 124). Hence Berkeley is not using interest in the sense of merely what we take to be the action that will maximize our present utility. Rather it includes an attempt to help shape and sculpt the human agent so that he is better fitted for this life and for the life to come. True interest is what one ought to pursue so that we become the person we ought to become. For Berkeley this is not pursued at the expense of this life for the next or of the individual for the community; rather it means playing one's role in the great drama since 'we are linked by an imperceptible chain to every individual of the human race' (Berkeley 1901: 189).[13]

The Querist: endogenous preferences and capabilities

The Querist provides the single best synthesis of Irish concerns and can well lay claim to one of the earliest if not the earliest treatment of the capabilities approach in economic theory. Amartya Sen points to Smith as an early proponent of the capabilities approach and has argued that a proper economic analysis should take Smith (and we will show Berkeley) at his word that economic arrangements ought to allow people to develop their capabilities so that they may lead choice worthy lives.

From the advertisement for *The Querist* Berkeley starts to lay the foundation for the economics of human development capabilities approach: 'the sum of human happiness is supposed to consist in the goods of mind, body, and fortune, I would fain make my studies of some use to mankind with regard to each of these three particulars...' (Johnston and Berkeley 1970: 124).[14]

Queries 1–5 set the message of *The Querist* in embryo.

Query 1: Whether there ever was, is, or will be, and industrious nation poor, or an idle rich?

Query 2: Whether a people can be called poor, where the common sort are well fed, clothed, and lodged?

Query 3: Whether the drift and aim of every wise State should not be, to encourage industry in its members? And whether those who employ neither heads nor hands for the common benefit deserve not to be expelled like drones out of a well-governed State?

Query 4: Whether the four elements, and man's labour therein, be not the true source of wealth?

Query 5: Whether money be not only so far useful, as it stirreth up industry, enabling men mutually to participate the fruits of each other's labour?

By Queries 1, 3 and 5 hard work makes a nation rich; the State should encourage all its members to work hard; a monetary economy is the most effective way to stir up industry and money is the most practical means to achieve that end; money is only valuable to society in as much as it continues to encourage industry. Query 4 helps to clarify the others: any increase in wealth must come from production – 'the four elements and man's labour therein.'

Berkeley demonstrates his considerable originality in Queries 2 and 3. He reorients the goals of economic policy away from the power or GDP of the nation towards the welfare of the common man when he defines the wealth of a nation in terms of properly distributed comforts of life. Indeed, Berkeley is one of the first economists who felt that economic development was really but one aspect of *human* development (Rashid 1988).[15]

Berkeley's account in *The Querist* stresses the role of human sociality in industry where cooperation and mutuality characterize exchange (Query 5). While recognizing the important role that money has to play in facilitating exchange,[16] Berkeley asks, 'Whether any other means, equally conducing to excite and circulate the industry of mankind, may not be as useful as money' (Query 6). Creating new wants 'produce[s] industry in a people' (Query 20) and less 'swiftly circulating' money can do the job of 'more money slowly circulating' (Query 22). The 'real end and aim of men' is 'power' (S.Q. 7).[17] By 'power' Berkeley not only means the ability to command goods and services but also the ability to take action expressing the will (Query 9). Power or the freedom to have control over one's own life 'according to … just pretensions and industry' (Query 8) ought to be 'the public aim in every well-governed State' (Query 8).

How the 'appetites' are formed play an integral part in the well-being of the population and in the development of preferences. Berkeley's analysis recognizes the importance of endogenous agents (Gintis 1972, 1974). The issue of preference formation cannot be ignored if one takes human sociality seriously. Berkeley's and Swift's arguments about frivolous tastes for fashions are not merely an expression of conservative religious views. Rather they are an integral part of their assessment of the Irish economy. Preferences inform the appetite. The appetites direct the actions of the people and this action is an expression of the power or freedom of the people. Once one agrees that some preferences are endogenously formed, it is no longer a violation of individual autonomy to interfere with the expression of those preferences.[18] For Berkeley and Swift the power to choose is a good thing but given the case of Ireland these appetites have what we would call today negative spillover effects.[19]

Berkeley likens the 'State or body politic' to the human body, which lives and moves under various indispositions, perfect health being seldom or never to be found' (Query 343). Even if nothing is 'perfect under the sun' (Query 343), 'men should ... aim at perfection' (Query 344). It would be 'natural to wish for a benevolent physician' (Query 344) and one such candidate is the legislature. The legislature ought to pursue 'public happiness' and 'such happiness doth ... contain that of the individuals' (Query 345). Because of the role that Berkeley envisions for a legislator they

> should be a person of reflexion and thought, who hath made it his study to understand the true nature and interest of mankind, how to guide men's humours and passions, how to incite their active powers, how to make their several talents co-operate to the mutual benefit of each other, and the general good of the whole.
>
> (Query 346)

Berkeley is not assuming that government direction is always best but is suggesting that the government step in to help address public goods (and 'bads') problems.

Berkeley emphasized the greatest happiness of the majority which entails the well-being of the whole (Queries 130, 131, 106) and combined with Queries 20, 107, 351, 352, and 353 that will promote economic prosperity. Working along the lines of a theory of the second best, Berkeley seeks to make the best of a difficult situation. Recognizing that some political and economic constraints are effectively given, he argues, for example, that lack of foreign trade need not hamper Ireland's attempt to achieve prosperity (Queries 106–108, 129): 'Be the restraining our trade well or ill advised in our neighbours, with respect to their own interest, yet whether it be not plainly ours to accommodate ourselves to it' (Q 136)?

Berkeley not only values the basic necessities but is aware of the role that freedom plays in making one's life better. In the context of the power of the people to exercise their ability to pursue their own ends he wonders about the tradeoff his policies entail: the reduction of freedom to choose whatever fashions the wealthy desire versus the implicit gain in freedom for the poor (Queries 14, 17, 18, 57, 140, 141). For Berkeley his policies directed towards the wealthy are an instance of 'when the root yieldeth insufficient nourishment men top the tree to make the lower branches thrive' (Query 158).

It is not that Berkeley is against trade or the wealthy living well. He is against the 'wrong' preferences in a depressed economy that mean that the poor do not have employment and are trapped in dire poverty. For example, the wealthy should not buy foreign fashions; instead they could purchase domestically produced fine furniture, nice homes, art, music, the fine arts, etc. Since the current preferences of the Irish landlords are being given to them by London society, why should this be better than having their preferences derive from a study of the needs of Ireland? Queries 395–417 make it clear that Berkeley sees this as a virtuous circle. If different towns could specialize in a particular manufacture taking advantage from the gains from specialization and the positive spillover effects from having a particular industry concentrated in a geographic location which would meet the desires of the upper classes, then the problem of absentees would be reduced and the poor classes would find employment helping to meet the wants of the wealthy. Berkeley's mechanism is that the preferences of the wealthy must be changed so that they will prefer to stay and spend in Ireland. By providing better living spaces the wealthy would be more inclined to reside in Ireland. If the wealthy see how the upper classes live in other countries then so too will the Irish gentry choose to reside on their estates in Ireland. Not only will this lead to a better life for the poor who will be engaged in the various industries satisfying the wants of the wealthy, but it will be good for the wealthy as well. Berkeley's normative stance is that it is the goods of 'mind, body, and fortune' that lead to human happiness. Queries 59–63 argue that Ireland will produce more goods under Berkeley's scheme and these benefits 'will shoot upwards into the branches, and cause the top to flourish.' This would lead to positive spillover effects. By Query 63 it would lead to the development of 'new arts and new branches of commerce,' all of which would benefit the people of Ireland and contribute to the growth of capabilities.

The problem in Ireland is that the wealthy spend a disproportionate amount of their income on goods produced outside of the country. A large portion of the income stream generated from agriculture in Ireland tends to go abroad and does not support domestic industry. But it is not only that the demand is the 'wrong' mix, it is also that the preferences are so shaped that the poor have become acclimated to their situation. Here the work of Sen is apt when considering the following queries:

> Query 19: Whether the bulk of our Irish natives are not kept from thriving, by that cynical content in dirt and beggary which they possess to a degree beyond any other people in Christendom?

> Query 20: Whether the creating of Wants be not the likeliest way to produce Industry in a People? And whether if our Peasants were accustomed to eat Beef, and wear Shoes, they would not be more Industrious?

> Query 61: Whether nastiness and beggary do not, on the contrary, extinguish all such ambition, making men listless, hopeless, and slothful?

Berkeley argues that to increase the happiness of Ireland the well-being of the mass of the population, the poor, must be addressed. Improving the lot of the poor makes the nation better off, not simply because it satisfies Berkeley's broad conception of well-being but also because of the positive economic benefits for the nation as a whole (Queries 59 and 60).

Berkeley argues that even without foreign trade remedying 'the dirt, and famine, and nakedness of the bulk of our people [Q 106]' would lead to wealth creation. Raising the standard of living will cause people to aspire to greater wealth: 'Whether there be any instance of a State wherein the people, living neatly and plentifully, did not aspire to wealth [Q 60]?' People become acclimated to 'comfortable living' that 'produce[s] wants, and wants industry, and industry wealth [Q 107].' Attacking the problem of poverty Berkeley likens to 'feeding the root, the substance whereof will shoot upwards into the branches, and cause the top to flourish [Q 59].' Just as people become acclimated to 'comfortable living' though 'nastiness and beggary ... on the contrary, extinguish all such ambition, making men listless, hopeless, and slothful' (Query 61). Preferences developed in such a state of the world should not carry the same kind of weight as those preferences formed in a situation that allows for the development of capabilities. For Berkeley not all preferences are equal and his early treatment of the capabilities approach makes that clear.

Providing for the poor has a twofold benefit; directly, the poor are better off and they are also more productive than they were before. Berkeley's program is effectively a redirection of economic demand away from foreign and towards domestic products. This is accomplished by a change in the preferences of the actors. This redistribution of demand though also has beneficial supply side effects that make the economic pie larger than before 'and cause the top to flourish.'

The enhancement of capabilities is at once a normative goal, something that ought to be pursued, and at the same time has positive economic effects. Having greater capabilities leads to a greater motivation to work and produce. Having more makes one want more. Once people have the basic capabilities satisfied then they will desire to develop more advanced capabilities (Queries 123–128), 'extending their industry to new arts and new branches of commerce' (Query 63). Moreover, having more makes one have more children and more children lead to a larger population helping to stimulate economic growth.[20] Population and 'industry' are the product of living well. Real wealth consists 'of all the necessaries and comforts of life' (Query 542). A Nation in which the 'People [are] well fed, cloathed, and lodged' will have a large and growing population and such a nation with 'a numerous Stock of People in such Circumstances' is 'flourishing' (Q 62). As Berkeley maintains, it is 'the numbers, the frugality, and the industry of the people' provide 'the real foundation for wealth' (Query 217).

For Berkeley the 'momentum of a state' is the 'sum of the faculties put into act' or what he refers to as the 'united action of a whole people' (S.Q. 582). Momentum of a state means the 'whole exertion of its faculties, intellectual and corporeal' (Query 585). The corporeal faculties could not act together without the intellectual (Query 585), 'the divided force of men, acting singly, would ... be a rope of sand' (Query 586). These intellectual and corporeal faculties ensure the attainment of capabilities for the individuals that make up the community. Capability achievement is limited in 'a country quite sunk in sloth or even fast asleep' (Query 591). Yet, capability enhancing effects take place 'upon the gradual awakening and exertion, first of the sensitive and locomotive faculties, next of reason and reflexion, then of justice and piety' (Query 591). Capability attaining faculties are like muscles that must be exercised and which strengthen with use. Hence, '[t]he momentum of ... [a] state ... become[s] still more and more considerable' with the gradual use and growth of capabilities (Query 591, omitted Part I). For Berkeley capability attainment begets more capabilities, not only in their number but in their quality since 'that which in the growth is last attained, and is the finishing perfection of a people, be not the first thing lost in their declension' (Query 592).

Berkeley's views on money

To achieve the economic abundance necessary for human flourishing, Berkeley argues that money plays an important role. A monetary economy provides the best mechanism to encourage industry and promote human development. Berkeley has numerous queries discussing his monetary views and their relation to industry: Queries 21–47, 218–254, 277–327, 424–450, 458–497, and 555–578 explain the roles of money, paper money and credit and how they could help to encourage the industry of both rich and poor in Ireland. Berkeley's point revolves around the functions of money. In Queries 46 and 47 Berkeley imagines a shipwrecked crew upon an island 'by degrees forming themselves to business and civil life, while industry begot credit, and credit moved to industry' (Query 46). Credit does not depend on gold or silver, but rather on industry whose source is the desire to consume. The crew 'subsists by the mutual participation of each other's industry' (Query 47). 'When one man had in his way procured more than he could consume, he would ... exchange his superfluities to supply his wants' (Query 47). This gives rise to credit and to 'facilitate these conveyances, to record and circulate this credit' (Query 47) a monetary unit is agreed upon. Hence, in a monetary economy money facilitates exchange by eliminating the double coincidence of wants problem, i.e., 'facilitates these conveyances.' Berkeley recognized that in an economy like Ireland's with an inadequate supply of money this important function of money is hampered. Resources are used up in trying to find an exchange partner rather than going towards more useful activities. Further, Berkeley saw circulating money promoting economic exchange. The wheels of commerce are lubricated, industry is promoted and a desire to consume grows. Not only does money close the circle of exchange it helps it to grow: 'whether comfortable living doth not produce wants, and wants industry, and industry wealth' (Query 107).

Sometimes Berkeley's views on money have been misinterpreted. For example, Mark Blaug lumps Berkeley in with John Law (of whose policies Berkeley was sharply critical):

> There is insufficient recognition in the writings of Law and Berkeley of the real problems of a dominantly agrarian economy, problems that cannot be

cured simply by cranking the monetary pump. Adam Smith and Ricardo may have overemphasized thrift and enterprise, but their skepticism about monetary panaceas was well taken in the circumstances of an economy suffering from scarcity of capital and chronic structural employment.

(Blaug 1985: 22)

A selection of queries were appended to Berkeley's *The Plan*. These queries make it clear that Berkeley saw money as facilitating exchange, that money need have no intrinsic value of its own, that fiat currency, if feasible, is the most advantageous money, that real wealth lies not in money, but rather the causes of that real wealth are 'fertile land and the industry of its inhabitants' (S.Q. 40). Berkeley argued that money is useful only in as much as it 'stirreth up industry' (Query 5) by promoting exchange. Query 4 makes it clear that Berkeley does not believe that 'cranking the monetary pump' generates wealth: 'Whether the four elements, and man's labour therein, be not the true source of wealth?'[21] Berkeley argues that money is essentially a 'token' or 'ticket' used 'to record and circulate' the exchange of the 'superfluities' (Query 47).

Berkeley's writings on the national bank scheme and government provided currency emphasize that the state has a role to play in addressing the ills of Ireland. He did not want a fiat currency in the modern sense of completely unbacked paper, rather, he believed that faith in the Government was such that paper money issued by a National Bank (with the safeguards he had provided) would be an effective financial instrument in Ireland.

> Whether, as public credit is greater than private, so the demands on a national bank would not be fewer than those on private banks? And therefore whether most of that money, which is now either shut up or trafficked with abroad would not appear publicly in our fairs, markets, and shops?
>
> (*The Irish Patriot*, Query 6)

Again relying on analogies from medicine he asks, 'whether it is not natural to wish for a benevolent physician' (Query 344). Yet, Berkeley is well aware of agency problems and does not assume that legislators are 'benevolent physician[s].' A perusal of the queries pertaining to the establishment of a national bank (the first edition of *The Querist* had a third of the queries on this topic), not to mention the whole corpus of Berkeley's writings, reveal that he is under no delusions when it comes to the motivations of people. He takes pains to recognize the problems with a private and a public banking system (see Queries S.Q. 210–233, Part I as well as *The Plan*) and attempts to develop a structure which would avoid the worst of each. He realizes that the human actor must be involved and so tries to provide appropriate incentives and to separate functions so as to minimize malfeasance. At the same time, he is unwilling to forego state action simply because all schemes require human agency. Berkeley's acerbic queries in *The Irish Patriot or Queries Upon Queries* are relevant:

No. 34: Whether it be possible to contrive any scheme for the public good which shall not suppose or require common honesty and common sense in the execution thereof; and whether this be not an unanswerable argument against all projectors?

No. 35: Whether therefore it be not vain to talk of schemes for bettering our affairs?

No. 36: Whether it be not more prudent to yield to our fate, and possess our poverty in peace?

Conclusion

The previous sections have attempted to reveal the abilities of both Swift and Berkeley to perceive and to solve economic problems. Swift gave attention to incentives and enforcement while Berkeley provided pioneering macro-monetary analyses of a poor economy. Berkeley's position on economic policy is that the most effective way to stimulate a people to hard work is through the use of a monetary economy. Money is merely a token or ticket and is a means to an end. Money is valuable to society only insofar as it continues to encourage industry. Any increase in wealth must come from production: 'the four elements and man's labour therein' (Query 4).

Why are Swift and Berkeley so neglected? Swift's angry brilliance was easy to ignore because it was both polemical and partisan. Even the content tended to lack a sense of proportion. His sermon on the causes of Irish wretchedness begins well with large concerns about liberty and the Irish absentee landlords, then spends the rest of the sermon complaining about servants and beggars. Such criticisms can scarcely be made about Berkeley, whose neglect requires a more nuanced approach. First, the style of *The Querist* is unusual. The matter was appreciated by many – Robert Wallace, S.T. Coleridge, Robert Southey, Lord Lauderdale, to name only a few – but the point is that all these men read seriously; they wanted to study the subject and not just be entertained by it. The concentrated wisdom of *The Querist* may well have reduced readership.

Second, consider its message. English readers could not fathom what it meant for an economy to be so radically different from that of England. Even in the 1820s, English MPs considered Ireland to be an exception to the laws of political economy. Among its novel claims, that of money as a counter was perhaps the most striking. Berkeley was an advocate of paper money and understood the role of credit but the major economists of the succeeding generation including both Turgot and Smith were conservative on financial matters and generally hostile to financial innovation (Murphy 2009).

Modern theorists only compound the difficulties of the situation with their portrayals of past economic history. In an acclaimed recent book, Sargent and Velde (2002) claim to deal with the shortage of coin – a situation the Irish complained of on more than one occasion. But the theoretical economic model created by Sargent and Velde have people who are all alike, who can calculate economic consequences into the indefinite future, where agents control completely their ability to create money substitutes and where equilibrium is readily reached! It is no wonder that the central conclusion of Sargent and Velde, that copper coins should fall in value relative to gold and silver, is clearly denied by Irish observers such as Thomas Prior. Unless modern theorists are willing to address questions of development differently they are unlikely to illuminate the problems of eighteenth-century Ireland.

Finally, one cannot discount the role of party politics and religion. Party politics placed Swift and Berkeley in Ireland – both were, in different ways, considered too troublesome to be close to London – and thus politics unwittingly contributed to the formation of an Irish School of development economics. But partisan politics extracted a severe price in that all of Swift's and much of Berkeley's social efforts were placed under a cloud of suspicion. The extensive lobbying that Berkeley did for a national bank led to nought and even seems to have embittered Berkeley. Archbishop King too engaged in such analyses but his clear Whig sympathies meant that more explicit coordination of these social reform minded Christians never took root. Swift's charity knew no sect bounds and Catholics benefitted, while Berkeley explicitly tried to involve the Catholics in his program of social development. The farsightedness of both Swift and Berkeley led them to see that the real enemy to their social philosophy lay in the new 'Enlightenment.' For their part, Swift and Berkeley then tried to infuse Christianity with a strong sense of social responsibility.

One can only speculate about the reasons why the Irish did not achieve more lasting fame. Connections between Ireland and Scotland were strong at this time and this is particularly the case with Francis Hutcheson, who became Professor at Glasgow after his stay in Ireland, and went on to influence Scotland considerably. Since Hutcheson had lived and taught in Ireland for many years, particularly as part of Molesworth's circle, it is practically unthinkable that he would not have been fully aware of the thoughts and activities of Swift, Berkeley and the Dublin Society. Why did Hutcheson not give them any prominence? We know that there were many members of the elite who thought of doctrines of hellfire to be 'vulgar' stuff and Hutcheson might well have sympathized with them. How he survived questioning by church elders about his 'new light' one can only guess, but the doctrinal emphasis of Hutcheson's Christianity is entirely different from that of either Swift or Berkeley. This did not mean that the thoughts of the Irish school were not known in Scotland in the 1740s. One has only to read Robert Wallace to see an ardent admirer of Berkeley. But as time went by, the school of Hutcheson gave rise to the school of Adam Smith; the party of Adam Smith carefully sided with the elite and against the 'Popular party in the church in Scotland – sending off John Witherspoon to the presidency of Princeton – and one has to note the strong whiff of populism in the economic program of the Irish school; Culloden made the entire reading public careful about praising anyone with a Tory affiliation for fear that this be taken to mean Jacobite sympathies [most unfair to Berkeley who even tried to train bands to fight off such a revolt]. A series of historical accidents may have served to keep the Irish out of sight. Joseph Johnston dreamt of seeing a work on the 'perennial relevance' of the social philosophy of *The Querist* – perhaps it is time to have an exposition of the current relevance of the Irish school of economics.

Notes

1 While we are familiar with inalienable rights these thoughts spread the idea of 'inalienable duties.'

2 The accounts put his charitable giving at one-third to one-half of his yearly income.

3 John Kendrick, a draper in London who died in 1624, provided five hundred pounds in his will to be lent to particular persons and to be paid in full in seven years. At that time it would be lent again 'fifty pounds a piece, gratis, for three years' to ten 'honest, industrious poor clothiers' (Ashmole 1719 2: 528).

4 Swift's emphasis on the linkage between economic and moral improvement via his lending scheme was not lost on the authors of a 1787 handbook for 'Intelligent Servants.' A certain Lord Alton in the book pursues a Swiftian scheme but on a much grander scale with 'forty thousand pounds … thus continually kept afloat, at a higher interest than the most productive commerce ever afforded, the inestimable satisfaction of knowing that by the same act he is perpetually improving the morals and circumstances of the persons relieved' (Anon. 1787: 123).

5 Echoing Swift's use of Saint Paul's analogy between the human body and the social body, Hawkesworth describes Swift's bounty

> … [as] the instrument of equal happiness: to feed idleness is to propagate misery, and discourage virtue; but to insure the reward of industry is to bestow a benefit at once upon the individual and the publick; it is to preserve from despair those who struggle with difficulty and disappointment, it is to supply food and rest to that labour which alone can make food tasteful and rest sweet, and to invigorate the community by the full use of those members which would otherwise become not only useless but hurtful, as a limb which the vital fluid ceases to circulate will not only wither but corrupt.
>
> (Swift 1754 1: 67)

6 > When the masons were building [my wall], (as most tradesmen are rogues), I watched them very close, and as often as they could, they put in a rotten stone; of which however I took no notice, until they had built three or four perches beyond it. Now, as I am an absolute Monarch in the Liberties, and King of the Rabble, my way with them was, to have the wall thrown down to the place where I observed the rotten stone; and, by doing so five or six times, the workmen were at last convinced it was their interest to be honest.
>
> (Sheridan 1787: 414)

7 'It is not the result of education, law, or fashion; but is a principle originally ingrafted in the very first formation of the soul by the Author of our nature' (Berkeley 1901: 188).

8 This is a common theme among Christian commentators on politics e.g., Bishop Warburton.

9 All Queries are from Johnston and Berkeley (1970).

10 Social preferences, reciprocity, other regarding preferences, context dependent behavior among others are discussed in Chapter 3 of Bowles (2004).

11 Berkeley appears to use a medical term. In Query 580 he writes about obstructions in 'capillary vessels,' in *Moral Attraction* he makes an analogy between physical bodies and the social body. With respect to the social body he writes of 'passions and motions' that can obstruct. When writing about circulation he discusses obstructions

and the disorder of the body. When writing about bodily maladies he often uses the word 'obstructions.'

12 He argues that legislators ought to know 'how to guide men's humours and passions' (Query 346).

13 See Arthur O. Lovejoy's seminal work *The Great Chain of Being: A Study of the History of an Idea* (Lovejoy 1936).

14 Rashid (1988) makes the case that Berkeley is an early proponent of the view that economic development should not come at the expense of the Irish poor but ought to promote the well-being of all of the Irish.

15 Another early proponent of this view is Ludwig Carl (McPhail and Rashid, current research).

16 Query 481 is relevant: 'Whether, without the proper means of circulation, it be not vain to hope for thriving manufacturers and a busy people?'

17 Johnston uses S.Q. to denote 'selected queries printed in the pamphlet ... prefixed to the *Plan or Sketch of a National Bank*' (Johnston and Berkeley 1970: 125).

18   There is a tendency in economics to relegate discussions about preferences to moral philosophy. During the heyday of the neoclassical model, economics was limited to 'positive' economics, the economics of what 'is' not what ought to be. From this perspective, economics could predict the consequences of different policies but should leave normative concerns up to the political process. Abba Lerner put this position succinctly 'As a social critic, I may try to change some desires to others of which I approve more, but as an economist I must be concerned with the mechanisms for getting people what they want, no matter how these wants were acquired.

(Lerner 1972: 258)

Defending the sanctity of individual preferences, in his Nobel lecture Paul Samuelson argued for the 'notion of giving people what they want' (Samuelson 1972: 261). Yet taking preferences as given ignores the important role that economic arrangements play, fostering behaviors and disseminating beliefs. If economic institutions help to shape people, then that opens the door to ethical concerns about the nature of those institutions. And if people act upon ethical and religious beliefs, then normative concerns play an important role in predictive economics (McPhail 2009: 286).

19 Frank (1999), George (2001), and Schor (2004) have addressed the theme of preference pollution and how preferences may thwart the achievement of human happiness.

20 Query 217: Whether the real foundation for wealth must not be laid in the numbers, the frugality, and the industry of the people? And whether all attempts to enrich a nation by other means, be laid in the numbers, the frugality, and the industry of the people? And whether all attempts to enrich a nation by other means, as raising the coin, stock-jobbing, and such arts are not vain?

21 As Rashid (1990) points out with respect to Query 4:

In his *Inquiry into the Nature and Origin of Public Wealth*, Lord Lauderdale notes that, among the several views held by Adam Smith of the sources of wealth, when Smith considers the real wealth of a country to consist in the annual produce of its land and labor, 'this opinion ... coincides with that of the Bishop of Cloyne.'

(Lauderdale 1804: 118)

Bibliography

Anon. (1787) *The Contrast: Or the Opposite Consequences of Good and Evil Habits, Exhibited in the Lowest Ranks of Rural Life. For the Benefit of Intelligent Servants, and the Best Proficients in Sunday Schools*, London: printed for T. Longman, G.G.J. & J. Robinson, J. Johnson, and T. Cadell.

Ashmole, E. (1719) *The Antiquities of Berkshire By Elias Ashmole, Esq; With a Large Appendix ... and a Particular Account of the Castle, College, and Town of Windsor*, 3 vols, London: printed for E. Curll.

Berkeley, G. (1752) *A Miscellany, Containing Several Tracts on Various Subjects. By the Bishop of Cloyne*, Dublin: George Faulkner.

Berkeley, G. (1901) *The Works of George Berkeley*, Vol. 4, A.C. Fraser (ed.), Oxford: Clarendon Press.

Blaug, M. (1985) *Economic Theory in Retrospect*, Cambridge: Cambridge University Press.

Bowles, S. (2004) *Microeconomics: Behavior, Institutions, and Evolution*, The Roundtable Series in Behavioral Economics, New York: Russell Sage.

Chesterton, G.K. (1989) 'Plays and Chesterton on Shaw,' in D.J. Conlon (ed.) *The Collected Works of G. K. Chesterton*, 11, San Francisco, CA: Ignatius Press.

Cibber, T., Shiells, R., and Coxter, T. (1753) *The Lives of the Poets of Great Britain and Ireland, to the Time of Dean Swift*, London: R. Griffiths.

Fauske, J. (ed.) (2004) *Archbishop William King and the Anglican Irish Context, 1688–1729*, Dublin; Portland, OR: Four Courts.

Fox, C. (2003) *The Cambridge Companion to Jonathan Swift*, Cambridge: Cambridge University Press.

Frank, R.H. (1999) *Luxury Fever: Why Money Fails to Satisfy in an Era of Excess*, New York: Free Press.

Frank, R.H. and Cook, P.J. (1995) *The Winner-take-all Society: How More and More Americans Compete for Ever Fewer and Bigger Prizes, Encouraging Economic Waste, Income Inequality, and an Impoverished Cultural Life*, New York: Free Press.

George, D. (2001) *Preference Pollution: How Markets Create the Desires we Dislike*, Ann Arbor, MI: University of Michigan Press.

Gintis, H. (1972) 'A Radical Analysis of Welfare Economics and Individual Development,' *Quarterly Journal of Economics* 86: 572–99.

Gintis, H. (1974) 'Welfare Criteria with Endogenous Preferences: The Economics of Education,' *International Economic Review* 15: 415–30.

Hollis, A. and Sweetman, A. (1997) *Complementarity, Competition and Institutional Development: the Irish Loan Funds through Three Centuries*, Calgary: University of Calgary, Dept of Economics.

Hollis, A. and Sweetman, A. (2003) *Microfinance and Famine: the Irish Loan Funds during the Great Famine*, Calgary: University of Calgary, Dept of Economics.

Johnson, S. (1793) *The Lives of the Most Eminent English Poets with Critical Observations on their Works*, 4 vols, London: printed for J. Buckland, C. Bathurst, and T. Davies.

Johnston, J. and Berkeley, G. (1970) *Bishop Berkeley's Querist in Historical Perspective*, Dundalk: Dundalgan Press (W. Tempest).

Lauderdale, J. M. (1804) *An Inquiry into the Nature and Origin of Public Wealth, and into the Means and Causes of its Increase*, Edinburgh: Arch. Constable & Co.

Leary, D.E. (1977) 'Berkeley's Social Theory: Context and Development,' *Journal of the History of Ideas* 38.4: 635–49.

Lerner, A.P. (1972) 'The Economics and Politics of Consumer Sovereignty,' *American Economic Review* 62: 258–66.

Lovejoy, A.O. (1936) *The Great Chain of Being: a Study of the History of an Idea*, Cambridge, MA: Harvard University Press.

Mackintosh, J. and Mackintosh, R.J. (1850) *The Miscellaneous Works of the Right Honourable Sir James Mackintosh*, 3 vols complete in 1, Philadelphia, PA: Carey and Hart.

McPhail, E. (2009) 'Socialism after Hayek and Human Sociality,' *Review of Austrian Economics* 22: 285–88.

Murphy, A.E. (2009) *The Genesis of Macroeconomics: New Ideas from William Petty to Henry Thornton*, Oxford: Oxford University Press.

Rashid, S. (1988) 'The Irish School of Economic Development: 1720–1750,' *Manchester School of Economic and Social Studies* 56: 345–69.

Rashid, S. (1990) 'Berkeley's *Querist* and its influence,' *Journal of the History of Economic Thought* 12: 38–60.

Samuelson, P.A. (1972) 'Maximum Principles in Analytical Economics,' *American Economic Review* 62: 249–62.

Sargent, T.J. and Velde, F.R. (2002) 'The big problem of small change,' *Princeton Economic History of the Western World*, Princeton, NJ: Princeton University Press.

Schor, J. (2004) *Born to Buy: the Commercialized Child and the New Consumer Culture*, New York: Scribner.

Sheridan, T. (1787) *The Life of the Rev. Dr Jonathan Swift, Dean of St Patrick's, Dublin*, London: J.F. and C. Rivington [*et al.*].

Swift, J. (1772) *The Works of the Reverend Dr Jonathan Swift Dean of St Patrick's, Dublin*, 20 vols, Dublin: George Faulkner.

Swift, J. (1754) *The Works of Jonathan Swift, D.D. Dean of St Patrick's, Dublin, accurately revised in twelve volumes, adorned with copper-plates; with some account of the author's life, and notes historical and explanatory*, J. Hawkesworth (ed.), London: Printed for C. Bathurst, C. Davis, C. Hitch, L. Hawes, J. Hodges, R. and J. Dodsley, and W. Bowyer.

Swift, J. (1778) *The Works of Jonathan Swift, D.D: D.S.P.D. accurately revised in eighteen volumes, with notes historical and critical*, J. Hawkesworth (ed.), L.L.D. and others.

Swift, J. (1790) *The Sermons of Dr J. Swift Dean of St Patrick's, Dublin. To which is prefixed the author's life: together with his prayer for Stella, his thoughts on, and project for the advancement of religion*, London: sold by R. Dampier, J. Thompson, W. Manson, T. Davidson, and P. Watson.

3   The contested origins of 'economic man'

Hutcheson, Berkeley and Swift's engagement with Bernard Mandeville

Renee Prendergast[1]

Introduction

Economic man is generally regarded as self-interested and rational. While most economists allow that people are neither entirely self-interested nor entirely rational, they argue that the concept of economic man is a useful abstraction with tractable analytical and predictive properties. The dominant conception is not, however, uncontroversial. Ariel Rubinstein (2006) has expressed concern that economic training distorts behaviour and causes people to act in more selfish ways. Deirdre McCloskey (2007) has argued that economists have focused excessively on prudence to the neglect of other virtues which are equally important for the health of bourgeois life. In several papers over three decades, Amartya Sen has engaged with the assumptions underlying the conception of rational economic man. Among the aspects to which he has drawn specific attention are: (i) consequentialism, the judging of acts by their consequences; (ii) the focus on act evaluation rather than rule evaluation; and (iii) the focus on the effects on the individual. Concerns of the type expressed by McCloskey, Rubinstein and Sen go back a long way. They were at their most intense in the early eighteenth century as the conception of the market economy emerged in the writings of Mandeville, Hutcheson and Hume. Bernard Mandeville's provocative espousal of consequentialism, arguing that private vices could lead to public benefits, suggested that the traditional virtues had no relevance in the modern world. Mandeville's intentional provoking of his critics succeeded magnificently and his views were widely condemned as dangerous and immoral. Amongst Mandeville's best known critics were Francis Hutcheson and Bishop Berkeley both of whom lived in Dublin in the 1720s. Less well known as a critic of Mandeville but perhaps the most effective of all, was the Dean of St Patrick's Cathedral, Jonathan Swift.

Bernard Mandeville

Bernard Mandeville was born in the Netherlands where he studied philosophy and medicine. In 1693, he came to London where he began to practise as a physician (Cook 1999: 119). He quickly acquired an excellent command of English and began the literary career which was to make him known throughout the western world. In 1705, Mandeville published a poem *The Grumbling Hive: or, Knaves turn'd Honest.* The poem told the story of a prosperous hive which fell into decay when the bees tried to live virtuously. It argued that the attempt to achieve prosperity without great vices was 'a vain eutopia seated in the brain'. On the contrary, Mandeville concluded:

> ...vice is beneficial found,
> when it's by justice lopt and bound;
> Nay, where the people would be great,
> As necessary to the state,
> As hunger is to make 'em eat.
>   (Mandeville 1924 edn I: 37)

Almost a decade later the poem re-appeared accompanied by a prose commentary on the origins of moral virtue and a series of remarks on lines of the original poem under the title *The Fable of the Bees: or, Private Vices, Public Benefits.* The book did not attract immediate attention but when, in a later edition, 1723, Mandeville included an essay attacking the charity schools, the book was denounced as a public nuisance. A second volume of the *Fable* containing six dialogues and an introduction was published in 1729.

The argument that luxury rather than necessity was the main spur to industry and trade which is often associated with Mandeville had, in fact, been made earlier by Colbert and his followers in France and by the English writers Barbon [1690] (1905) and North [1691] (1907). Had Mandeville simply re-iterated their position, it is unlikely that his work would have attracted much controversy. Mandeville, however, took pains to embellish his case and to exploit its potential as a paradox. This he did by describing as luxury anything that went beyond bare necessity and which had been improved upon by man. This view of luxury was that employed by Fenelon in his *Aventures de Telemaque* (1699) in which he criticised the debilitating effects of luxury on the moral fabric of the French nation and advocated the type of frugal and wholesome utopia which Mandeville criticised in the *Grumbling Hive* (Hont 2006). In addition to his austere definition of luxury, Mandeville also adopted a stringent definition of virtue according to which no practice, action or good quality, however beneficial in itself, could count as virtue unless it involved self-denial (Mandeville 1924 *Fable*: I.48–9). To imagine that men could be virtuous without self-denial, Mandeville argued, was a vast inlet to hypocrisy. As Frances Hutcheson and, subsequently, Adam Smith noted, Mandeville's characterisation of virtue was made plausible by some popular ascetic doctrines which were current at the time 'which placed virtue in the entire extirpation and annihilation of all our passions' (Smith 1776b *Theory of Moral Sentiments* (*TMS*): VII.ii.4.12). It was then easy for Mandeville to prove that 'the entire conquest never actually took place' and that, if it did, it would undermine society by putting an end to all industry and commerce (ibid.).

Having so defined luxury and virtue that most ordinary acts of consumption counted as vices, Mandeville argued that private vices were necessary for the continued existence of industry and commerce and, as such, should be regarded as public benefits. In making this argument, Mandeville simultaneously employed two different moral standards (*Fable*: I.xlix). He evaluated the public results of private actions according to consequentialist standards but used non-consequentialist standards in judging the morality of individual actions. Thus Mandeville argued: 'when we pronounce actions good or evil, we only regard the hurt or benefit the society receives from them, and not the person who commits them' (*Fable*: I.244). However, referring to individual actions, he also maintained: 'If I have shown the way to worldly greatness, I have always without hesitation preferred the road that leads to virtue' (*Fable*: I.131). While Mandeville employed two different moral standards for the purpose of generating his paradoxical claims, there is strong evidence that his real commitment was to consequentialist standards. For example, in his *Modest Defence of Public Stews* published in 1724 he wrote:

> it is the grossest absurdity, and a perfect contradiction in terms, to assert, that a government may not commit evil that good may come of it; for, if a public act, taking in all its consequences, really produces a greater quantity of good, it must, and ought to be termed a good act ... no sinful laws can be beneficial and vice versa, no beneficial laws can be sinful.

(A Modest Defence: 68–9)

This judgement of acts by their consequences went back at least to Epicurus but whereas Epicurus saw the traditional virtues as instrumental goods valuable for the sake of the ends they promoted, Mandeville was willing to claim that the right action is that productive of the best consequences no matter how wrong it might otherwise appear.

It is important to recognise that, while there was a strong polemical element to Mandeville's attack on moral approaches to the evaluation of human actions, his wider argument was based on a profound understanding of the emerging commercial society. Mandeville was the first person to use the term 'division' of labour though the concept itself and the importance of specialisation in facilitating invention and increases in productivity had been discussed somewhat earlier by William Petty and Henry Martin. In a passage from which Adam Smith later borrowed freely (Smith 1776a *Wealth of Nations* (*WN*): I.I.i.ii), Mandeville brought out more clearly than anyone before him that once the division of labour had thoroughly taken hold, the satisfaction of even the simplest needs required the contribution of innumerable independent branches of labour distributed throughout the globe (*Fable*: I.356–8). He argued that if we were acquainted with the entire process of production and the toil, hardship and risk involved in some of its aspects, it would be hard to imagine that even a tyrant would exact such services from his slaves and admit that he had done it for the sake of a piece of crimson cloth. Things are different, however, when looked at from a different point of view.

[I]f we turn the prospect, and look at all those labours as so many voluntary actions, belonging to different callings and occupations ... and in which every one works for himself, how much soever he may seem to labour for others ... we shall find that the labour of the poor is so far from being a burden and an imposition upon them; that to have employment is a blessing, which in their addresses to heaven they pray for....

(*Fable*: I.358)

The whole superstructure of civil society is 'made up of the reciprocal services men do to each other'. How to get these services performed for us by others when we have need of them is a constant preoccupation in the life of every individual. It would be unreasonable to expect others to perform these services for nothing. If you want something, no matter how great your need, the seller will only part with it for a consideration he likes better than the thing you want (*Fable*: II.349). Consumers and other participants in the global division of labour are not generally in a position to evaluate the morality of the processes in which they are involved. In any case, the market has its own mechanisms for evaluation, voluntary exchanges will only happen when people perceive them to be beneficial.

Mandeville argued against the views of those such as Lord Shaftesbury who found the basis for society and all its achievements in man's innate sociability. On the contrary, almost all of the qualities that enable us to pronounce man a sociable creature beyond other animals, were historically acquired through interaction within a wider and evolving social environment. Every grape, he said, contains a small quantity of juice which by skilful management can be made into wine when great heaps of them are joined together, but it would be wrong to say that in every grape there was wine (*Fable*: II.189). Likewise, although men became sociable by living together in society, their sociability was not attributable to any one quality but rather the concurrence of several things. Among these was man's capacity to acquire and accumulate knowledge which was itself facilitated by the length of the life span and the significant proportion of it during which he had the capacity to learn (*Fable*: II.182 and 191). Other aspects included the development of language, submission to the rule of law and the development of social practices and institutions more generally.

Mandeville emphasised that, in contrast with most writers, his approach was to describe human beings as they are and not as they ought to be (*Fable*: I.39).[2] Untaught human beings, he wrote, were creatures of their passions and followed their own inclinations without regard to other people. Others who had taken this view argued that it was the duty of men to enquire into their passions in order to govern them (Hundert 1994: 585), but Mandeville disputed the capacity of reason to control passions for the common good. The only way to overcome the passions was to offer something more gratifying in return. This Mandeville found in the individual's relationship to this historically evolved society: 'the greediness we have after the esteem of others' which 'are equivalents that overpay the conquest of the strongest passions' (*Fable*: I.68). As Kaye, editor of the definitive edition of the *Fable* put it, for Mandeville 'the passion of pride is the great bulwark of morality, the instigator of all action for the good of others which seems contrary to the interests and instincts of the performer' (*Fable*: I.xci).[3]

Mandeville thus asserted not only that private vices could give rise to public benefits but also that actions which had the appearance of altruism were fundamentally selfish in their motivation. The passion of pride meant that we sought the approbation of others but this did not require that actions be genuinely meritorious (Hundert 1994: 126). People sometimes appeared to act altruistically but, in such cases, the actions were selfishly motivated either by pride or compassion. Altruistic acts motivated by the desire for the esteem of others were not virtuous. Neither were natural acts such as when a savage saves a child being attacked by an animal because the rescuer was acting according to his instincts to relieve his own compassion (*Fable*: I.255–6).

Given that he was writing in a period in which most Europeans were still practising Christians despite increasing challenges from sceptics and atheists, Mandeville's claim that private vices give rise to public benefits was calculated to cause widespread offence. Likewise, his claim that seemingly moral behaviour involved hypocrisy and self-deception caused alarm even amongst secular moralists. Counterattacks of varying degrees of effectiveness were forthcoming from many quarters. Two of the most notable were by George Berkeley and Francis Hutcheson. In Berkeley's *Alciphron*, a defence of the Christian religion against free-thinkers, the second dialogue was devoted to an attack on Mandeville. This Mandeville responded to in *A Letter to Dion* (Mandeville 1732a). Mandeville's *An Enquiry into the Origin of Honour* also published in 1732 (Mandeville 1732b) acknowledged the general usefulness of religion in making people governable but it also contained a critique of theological utilitarianism which as we shall see was an important feature of Berkeley's defence of Christianity. Hutcheson's criticisms of Mandeville permeate his work but the main arguments are contained in his *Inquiry into the Original of our Ideas on Duty and Virtue* and his *Dublin Weekly Journal* letters. Mandeville ironically referred to Hutcheson's attempts to weigh and measure quantities of affection and benevolence in the second volume of the *Fable* (345–6). However, his main criticisms of Hutcheson's views are implicit in his critique of Shaftesbury both in the essay 'A Search into the Nature of Society' which was first included in the 1723 edition of the *Fable* and in the extensive discussion of the evolution of society in Volume II of the *Fable*. The most effective criticism of all came from a third Irish clergyman, Jonathan Swift, who when it came to satire could beat Mandeville at his own game.

Francis Hutcheson

Francis Hutcheson was born in 1694 into a dissenter family of Scottish origin in Saintfield, Co. Down. Debarred by his religion from entering Trinity College in Dublin, he pursued his studies at the University of Glasgow where he came under the influence of the 'New Light' thinkers who were seeking to moderate and modernise the Church of Scotland's Calvinist traditions. On returning to Ulster, he aligned himself with the liberal wing of Presbyterianism and became involved in the setting up of a dissenting academy in Dublin where he taught for ten years. While there, he became associated with the circle around Molesworth, a follower of Shaftesbury. His main philosophical works: *Inquiry into the Original of our Ideas of Beauty and Virtue, Essay on the Nature and the Conduct of the Passions,* and *Illustrations upon the Moral Sense* all date from his Dublin period. In 1730 Hutcheson took up the chair in Moral Philosophy in Glasgow University where he remained for the rest of his life and where he acted as an important liberalising influence (Scott 1900).

The first edition of the Hutcheson's *Inquiry* contained a subtitle referring to the work as a defence of Shaftesbury's system against Mandeville. Many of the arguments in the second treatise of the *Inquiry* are indeed identifiable as responses to Mandeville's *Fable* but it is clear that Hutcheson's target was not just Mandeville but the wider system of the Epicureans and Hobbes. Hutcheson's most specific critique of Mandeville's *Fable* was published in the form of three letters in the *Dublin Weekly Journal* in 1725. The letters were subsequently published in a volume edited by James Arbuckle in 1729.

The Dublin Weekly *critique*

In the first of the *Dublin Journal* letters, Hutcheson criticised Mandeville for his wilful ambiguity and noted that 'Private vices public benefits' could signify any of five different propositions all of which could be supported by citations from Mandeville's *Fable*. Having enumerated and criticised these interpretations, Hutcheson acknowledged that people had basic human needs which had to be satisfied before they could be happy. They also had desires above necessity which could neither be fully suppressed nor fully satisfied. The solution was to regulate desires by forming just opinions of the real value of their several objects (Hutcheson 1750: 2). This correction of desires would allow a person to be satisfied with the ordinary but it would not prevent him from enjoying superior pleasures of life or from recognising that the true pleasures of life consisted in the kind affections of our fellow creatures (ibid.). Hutcheson concluded his letter with the statement that, apart from the Epicureans, all moralists accepted that kind affections were natural to men and that consulting the greatest good of the whole was the surest way for men to be happy. Even the Epicureans accepted that the pursuit of the good of the whole society was the surest way to happiness though they denied any affection as distinct from self-love (ibid.)

Hutcheson's second letter focused on the issue of the extent to which luxurious consumption was necessary to promote the industry and power of a country. He accepted that consumption and production necessarily went hand in hand but disputed the view that great consumption necessarily entailed vice. It was true that drunkards consumed more wine than the sober at any given point in time but, given that they lived longer, the lifetime consumption of the sober was likely to be at least as great (Hutcheson 1750: 6). It was also the case that money saved by cutting back on excess was available for more wholesome expenditure such as on clothes and improved habitations. Unless mankind was fully provided with necessaries and innocent conveniences, there was plenty of scope for great consumption without any whiff of vice. Hutcheson also pointed to Mandeville's use of the terms luxury, intemperance and pride not just in contexts where they referred to vices but also in contexts in which they referred to innocent, even virtuous behaviour. All sects, including the Stoics, recommended the regulation of desire beyond necessity but they did not object to consumption consistent with the offices of life. Provided someone had sufficient wealth to allow for sumptuous dress, habitation and so forth while at the same time discharging offices of humanity at a proportionate rate, there was no question of vice because the consumption plainly tended to the public good and injured no one (Hutcheson 1750: 7). Christianity recommended diligence in providing for ourselves and our families but nowhere did it condemn the rich and powerful for being so (Hutcheson 1750: 5).

Hutcheson's third letter provided a critique of the strategies employed by Mandeville to impress and confuse the reader. Following a long list of complaints about Mandeville's ambiguities, contradictions and misuse of words, Hutcheson suggested a possible explanation for Mandeville's rigid definition of virtue:

> He has probably been struck with some old fanatic sermon upon self-denial in his youth, and can never get it out of his head since. It is absolutely impossible on his scheme, that God himself can make a being naturally disposed to virtue: for virtue is self-denial and acting against the impulse of nature.
>
> (Hutcheson 1750: 3)

It may have given Hutcheson considerable satisfaction to associate Mandeville, the rumoured unbeliever, with the most dogmatic trend of Calvinist theology to which he, himself, was strongly opposed.

The natural sociability of man

Whilst the letters in the *Dublin Journal* focused on establishing that virtue and prosperity could go hand in hand, Hutcheson's reply to Mandeville's critique of morality is to be found in his philosophical writings. In these, Hutcheson endeavoured to show that man was naturally sociable and that virtue consisted in benevolent behaviour which was recommended to us by a moral sense rather than either by self-love or reason. This argument was a development of the position put forward by Lord Shaftesbury in his multi-volume work, the *Characteristics* in the first decade of the eighteenth century. It is not known when Hutcheson first became familiar with Shaftesbury's work but his engagement with it must have been strengthened when he became part of a group of young intellectuals who gathered at the home of Robert Molesworth in Brackdenstown, Co. Dublin

(Brown 2002). The group included James Arbuckle, a dissenter and graduate of Glasgow University and Edward Synge, a graduate of Trinity College Dublin and friend of George Berkeley who was later to precede him as Bishop of Cloyne. Molesworth, a prominent member of Dublin society, was a former merchant, diplomat and author of a number of works including his *Account of Denmark*, 1693 and *Some Considerations for the Promoting of Agriculture and Employing the Poor*. Although he produced no writings in philosophy, Molesworth was a keen student of the subject and counted Locke, Shaftesbury and Toland as friends and correspondents.

Shaftesbury's major work, the *Characteristics*, was intended to combat Puritan asceticism on the one hand and Hobbesian egotism on the other. In it, Shaftesbury was strongly critical of Hobbes' depiction of human beings as wholly governed by self-love and moral only on account of their fear of punishment by the state. He was also critical of churchmen who believed that men were moral because of their dread of eternal punishment. In their zeal to promote God, these churchmen were pronouncing mankind to be essentially vile (Scott 1900: 154). The keynote of Shaftesbury's work was the classical conception of the harmony of nature in which everything was ordered and governed for the best. Human passions were conceived of as being of three kinds: natural affections which lead to the good of the public; self-affections which lead to the good of the individual; and unnatural affections which lead to the injury of both the individual and the public. A proper balance between the natural affections and the self-affections were necessary for a virtuous existence. This balance ought to be such that the self-affections made the individual as efficient as possible in the service of the whole community (Scott 1900: 165). Each individual was endowed with a moral sense, an 'inward eye', which enabled him to discern the correct, harmonious course of action without recourse to reason. However, like any other aesthetic sense, this moral sense could be refined by cultivation.

Mandeville launched a robust attack on Shaftesbury's position in the essay entitled 'A Search into the Nature of Society' which was added to the second edition of the *Fable*, 1723. He disputed Shaftesbury's assertion that men were naturally sociable creatures. He also disputed Shaftesbury's claim that men were able to discern and agree on the real worth and excellency of things both in morality and in works of art and nature (*Fable*: I.324–5). Mandeville argued that Shaftesbury's belief that men could be virtuous without self-denial was a vast inlet to hypocrisy. Moreover, the middle way – the calm virtues – recommended in the *Characteristics* was incompatible with progress and good for nothing but to breed drones (ibid.: 333). Society could not be explained by the friendly qualities of man or the real virtues that he was capable of acquiring. On the contrary, the origin of society and of all arts and sciences was to be found in the moral and natural evils that human beings faced (ibid.: 369). In denying that men were naturally sociable beyond other animals and that this provided the basis for society, Mandeville also seems to have been implicitly criticising the second of our Irish thinkers, George Berkeley who, in an anonymous article in the *Guardian* of 5 August 1713,[4] had argued that the reciprocal attraction in the minds of men implanted in them by the Author of our nature was the basis of moral action.[5] According to Berkeley, this natural sociability was always present and asserted itself when not rendered inconspicuous by the more powerful attraction towards those closely related.

Hutcheson's Inquiry

As noted earlier, Hutcheson's *Inquiry* was initially conceived as a defence of Shaftesbury's system against the criticisms that had been levelled against him by Mandeville. While Shaftesbury had treated ethics and aesthetics together, Hutcheson separated them, devoting the first treatise of his *Inquiry* to the sense of beauty and the second to the sense of virtue (Hutcheson 2004: x–xi). In the introduction to the second treatise of the *Inquiry*, Hutcheson informed the reader that his main objective was to show that 'human nature was not left quite indifferent in the affair of virtue'. 'The author of nature had much better furnished us for virtuous conduct, than our moralists seem to imagine' and 'had made virtue a lovely form to excite our pursuit of it' (Hutcheson 2004: 9). Hutcheson defined moral goodness as a quality apprehended in actions by means of a moral sense which procures approbation and love from a disinterested observer. This sense of goodness was distinct from advantage and antecedent to it (*Inquiry*: II.Intro.).

Hutcheson argued that people's opinions about actions were independent of any advantage or disadvantage they might obtain from them. This was shown by the fact that choosing an action as advantageous did not prevent a person from being conscious that the action was in itself either good or evil (*Inquiry*: II.I.V.3).[6] While utility or interest might explain our feelings towards spacious living accommodation or a fruitful field, it could not explain our admiration for a noble character (*Inquiry*: II.I.I; II.I.IV.1). Hutcheson accepted that actions we approve are generally useful to mankind but he argued that this merely showed that 'reason and calm reflection may recommend to us, from self-interest, those actions, which at first view our moral sense determines us to admire, without considering this interest (*Inquiry*: II.I.VI). Hutcheson considered the objection that there was no need to suppose a sense of morality since reflection and instruction would recommend the same actions on the grounds of self-love (*Inquiry*: II.VII. III). He allowed that there was some truth in this but argued that the processes of human reason were too slow and too full of doubt and hesitation to enable us to always judge correctly what was for our own good or the good of the whole (ibid.). He also argued that those who deduced all ideas of good and evil from the private advantage of the actor or from the relation to a law and its sanctions were perpetually recurring to the moral sense which they denied (*Inquiry*: II.VII.IV). That our ideas of moral good did not depend on laws was evident from the fact that we constantly inquired into the justice of laws themselves. In any case, there was a big difference between the sense of obligation arising from the desire to do what was right and good and the sense of obligation or rather constraint which arises from threatening and presenting some evil, in order to make us act in a certain manner arising from self-interest (*Inquiry*: II.VII.V).

Hutcheson also disputed Mandeville's contention that people were moved to engage in actions beneficial to the public by their love of honour; that is, they would undertake a good action out of pride. If this were true, men would never be fond of such actions in solitude nor ever love anyone for practising them in solitude. Neither would they be dissatisfied with themselves when they act other than virtuously in solitude (*Inquiry*: II.V.V). For Hutcheson, virtuous actions could be motivated by benevolence or jointly by self-love and benevolence and he took considerable pains to argue that benevolence was not due to the love of the esteem that inevitably went along with it (*Inquiry*: II.II.III). He also denied that we choose to love others as a means of procuring bounty (*Inquiry*: II.II.VI). It could be argued that virtue is pursued because of the concomitant pleasure but this implies that from the frame of our nature, we were determined to perceive pleasure in the practice of virtue and to approve it when practised by ourselves and others (*Inquiry*: II.II.VIII).

Actions which were benevolent towards some persons but not pernicious to others were approved of by the observer and morally good (*Inquiry*: II.III.I). Actions which flowed from self-love were not necessarily immoral as long as they had no harmful effects on others. In some cases, the pursuit of private good was necessary for the good of the whole. Where a person pursued his private interest with a view to promoting the general good, this action could be considered virtuous (*Inquiry*: II.III.V).

Although Hutcheson was clear that approbation or otherwise of actions did not depend on reason, he was an instrumental rationalist in that he held that moral sense needed the assistance of cognitive powers when it came to choosing one action as opposed to another (Frankena 1955: 358; Hutcheson 1994: xxviii):

> In comparing the moral quality of actions, in order to regulate our election among various actions proposed, or to find which of them has the greatest moral excellency, we are led by our moral sense of virtue to judge thus: that in equal degrees of happiness, expected to proceed from the action, the virtue is in proportion to the number of persons to whom the happiness extend … that action is best which produces the greatest happiness for the greatest numbers.
>
> (*Inquiry*: II.III.VIII)

Thus, it seems that, in spite of the moral sense, the actual choice of actions is to be determined largely by utilitarian methods. Hutcheson, himself, put the matter thus: 'Men have reason given to them to judge the tendencies of their actions, that they may not stupidly follow the first appearance of public good; but it is still some appearance of good which they pursue' (*Inquiry*: II.IV.III).

In his critique of Shaftesbury, Bernard Mandeville had pointed to the diversity of moral opinion in different countries' different ages. Hutcheson acknowledged that the diversity of moral principles in various nations and ages was a good argument against innate ideas or principles but he argued that it was not evidence against a moral sense (*Inquiry*: II.IV.III). This was because men are often mistaken in computing the consequences of actions and thus their desire to promote the public good might result in the approval of different actions at different times and places (ibid.). While Hutcheson was of the opinion that the perception of moral good was not derived from custom, education, example or study, he also insisted that the moral sense did not imply innate ideas or propositions, merely a 'determination of our minds to receive amiable or disagreeable ideas of actions' (*Inquiry*: II.I.VIII).

In the early editions of the *Inquiry*, the moral sense appeared to have the role of both approving and motivating particular actions (Raphael 1947: 22–3; Bishop 1997: 281). This conflation was rectified in the work containing *An Essay on the Nature and Conduct of the Passions* and *Illustrations on the Moral Sense* which was published in 1728 in which Hutcheson put forward a more complete system of morality incorporating a theory of motivation (Hutcheson 1999: vii). In *Passions*, Hutcheson distinguished between passions on the one hand and the calm affections on the other. Passion was used to denote 'a strong and brutal impulse of the will'. The affections, on the other hand, referred to desire or aversion. According to Hutcheson, calm self-love and calm benevolence were the most important of the affections and he saw them as governing and restraining the particular passions (Jensen 1971: 13). These affections could never be excited by reason alone but Hutcheson saw them as being directed by reason towards long-term goals (ibid.). In the case of self-love, the long-range goal is the happiness of the agent and, in the case of benevolence, 'it is the greatest good of the greatest number'. Both calm self-love and benevolence have the capacity to govern and restrain other appetites and passions (ibid.).

Whereas the passions and affections were related to motives for action or exciting reasons, the moral sense was related to justifying reasons. The moral sense was rooted in our nature and there was 'no avoiding these desires and perceptions of morality' (*Passions*: 60). However, 'a vigorous use of our reason' was necessary 'to discern what actions really tend to the public good in the *whole*' (ibid.). Hutcheson concluded: 'When the moral sense is thus assisted by a sound understanding and application, our own actions may be a constant source of solid pleasure, along with the pleasures of benevolence, in the highest degree which our nature will admit...' (*Passions*: 61).

In *Illustrations upon the Moral Sense*, Hutcheson's main purpose was to argue against the view that the morality of actions consists in conformity to reason in opposition to the rationalist views of authors such as Burnet, Clarke and Wollaston. Having reiterated the view that the qualities moving to election or exciting to action were different from those moving to approbation, Hutcheson argued that reason could neither provide a motive to action nor a basis for approbation. Desire was necessary in order for an agent to aim at any object, and all desire was traceable in the end to desire for one's own happiness or that of others and these in turn could be aroused only by the affection of self-love or benevolence (Hutcheson 1999: xii, 115). As far as approbation was concerned, Hutcheson argued that the ultimate ends we pursue cannot be shown to be justified by conformity to truth or reason because whatever the relations reason discovers with regard to actions to be justified must equally be discoverable with regard to actions agreed not to be justified (Hutcheson 1999: 111–12).

After taking up the chair in Moral Philosophy in Glasgow in 1730, Hutcheson concentrated primarily on teaching and administration. In his inaugural lecture at Glasgow University in 1730, he sought to defend his view that men were naturally sociable against those such as Puffendorf who regarded social life as being natural to man only in the sense that it was necessary in order to avoid evil and obtain advantages. Hutcheson accepted that Puffendorf's thesis was partially true but he argued that men were driven to society not just by external factors but by sublimer pleasures prompted by no external sense (Hutcheson 1730: 10–11). Hutcheson's *A Short Introduction to Moral Philosophy* was published in Glasgow in 1747 and his *System of Moral Philosophy*, which was begun in 1734–35, was published posthumously in 1755 (Scott 1900: 113). One noteworthy difference between the *System* and Hutcheson's earlier work is that an emphasis on excellence of function displaces good as the end of action (Jensen 1971: 107; Scott 1900: 220). Another is an expansion of the function of the moral sense which becomes a faculty for perceiving moral excellence 'designed for regulating and controlling all our powers' (Hutcheson 1755: I.61). Scott (1900: 211–12) linked this change to Hutcheson's embrace of the Hellenic revival which was taking place at the University of Glasgow around the time of his return. Bishop (1997: 284–5), on the other hand, linked the new emphasis on excellence and perfection to Hutcheson's need to develop a non-hedonistic theory of motivation so that something approved because it is morally good is not also self-interested. Both Scott (1900) and more recently Moore (2000) have suggested that Irish influences contributed to Hutcheson's mature work. While Moore (2000: 255) argues that Hutcheson's *System* contains a number of distinctive features also present in Berkeley's *Alciphron*, it remains the case that there were important differences between these authors as is outlined below.

George Berkeley

George Berkeley's background was quite different to that of Hutcheson. He was an Anglican, a high Tory and a defender of the principle of passive obedience. He was born into an Anglo-Irish ascendancy family in County Kilkenny in 1685. He was educated in Kilkenny College and at Trinity College Dublin where he eventually obtained a fellowship. Berkeley was ordained as an Anglican deacon in 1709 and as a priest in 1710 (Leary 1977: 640). Berkeley is best known for his immaterialist philosophy which he developed in the period 1705–09 and published in a series of works between 1709 and 1713. His *Passive Obedience* also dates from this early period. In 1713, Berkeley left Ireland for London where he became acquainted with leading literary figures including Pope, Addison, Steele[7] and his fellow countryman Swift. He contributed a number of essays to Steele's short-lived *Guardian* newspaper. One of the most important of these now known by the title 'The Bond of Society' argues that there is a principle of attraction in the minds of men whereby they are drawn together into various forms of social organisation. In 1721, in the aftermath of the South Sea Bubble, Berkeley published *An Essay towards Preventing the Ruin of Great Britain*. The main message of this work has been summed up by Kelly (2005: 342) as being that a well-ordered society should provide for moderate wants through individual industry and frugality. The more methods there were in a state to acquire riches without industry or merit, the more likely that the result would be moral and political ruin (Berkeley 1953: VI.71).

Having lost confidence in the Old World, Berkeley turned his attention to the New and conceived a project to set up a seminary in Bermuda to ground both native and settler Americans in religion and morality with 'a good tincture of other learning' (Berkeley 1955: 345–56). With this in mind, he left for Rhode Island in 1728. In the end, the government failed to provide promised support for the Bermuda project and it had to be abandoned. However, while in Rhode Island, Berkeley wrote *Alciphron, or the Minute Philosopher*, a defence of natural religion and Christianity in seven dialogues (Berman 2005: 15). The second dialogue was directed against Mandeville's *Fable* while the third offered a critique of Shaftesbury and by implication also of Hutcheson, though the latter is nowhere mentioned by name. Berkeley returned to London in 1731 and remained there until 1734 when he returned to Ireland as Bishop of Cloyne. Part I of Berkeley's main economic work, *The Querist* was published in 1735. Further parts were published in 1736 and in 1937.

The critique of Mandeville

Berkeley's criticism of Mandeville in the second dialogue of *Alciphron* is not always fair or to the point but 'it is exceptional for meeting Mandeville in the bantering language of his own discourse' (Lamprecht 1926: 561). Its main focus is on refuting the proposition that great prosperity and vice go hand in hand. Like Hutcheson, Berkeley argued that a virtuous life was no less beneficial to the public than one involving vice because, over a lifetime, a sober and healthy person could circulate more money by eating and drinking than a glutton or drunkard in a short one (*Alciphron*: II.5). He also agreed that the things a man did for his convenience and pleasure were not vices provided they were in proportion to his fortune (ibid.). In *Alciphron* Berkeley presents Mandeville as claiming that men like other animals naturally tended to pursue sensual pleasure which was their true end and happiness (*Alciphron*: II.15). Against this, Berkeley argued that those who judge pleasure by sense are unable to take account of future pleasures and of pleasures of the understanding (*Works*: II.101). Mandeville is also presented as arguing that only weak men regarded rules and systems as being necessary in life and in government and that, by contrast, men of spirit delighted 'in the noble experiment of blowing up systems and dissolving governments, to mould them anew upon other principles and in another shape' (*Alciphron*: II.107).[8] Noting that according to the principles of the minute philosophers, a wise man will make his own particular individual interest in this present life the rule and measure of all his actions, Berkeley argued that such a man is like 'a ball bandied about by appetites and passions' (*Alciphron*: II.115). Throughout the second dialogue, the charge of freethinking is levelled against Mandeville and his followers. In this instance, Berkeley's conjecture seems plausible although Mandeville was always careful to represent himself in print as a believer.

The fact that the opinions which Berkeley put into the mouths of 'freethinkers' were not opinions that were actually held by anyone was noted by nineteenth century commentators such as John Stuart Mill and Leslie Stephens. Luce and Jessop, however, argue that while the opinions Berkeley attributed to freethinkers were not actually written they were staple fare in the drawing rooms of the *beau monde*. In his *Letter to Dion* published in 1732, Mandeville argued that Dion (Berkeley) had not read the *Fable* because it was impossible to believe that a man of sense and penetration who had done so could have misrepresented it in such an atrocious manner. Mandeville suggested that the reason for the undeserved disrepute of his book was the fact that it exposed vice and luxury and pulled off the disguises of artful men (Mandeville [1732a] 1954: 8). In saying that societies cannot be raised to wealth and power without vices, he was not encouraging people to be vicious (Mandeville [1732a] 1954: 16). On the contrary, he had always without hesitation encouraged virtue. The reason why people did not believe that he was earnest was that they were unwilling to countenance giving up the luxuries they enjoyed (Mandeville [1732a] 1954: 31). Mandeville then broached the question of whether a positive evil may be justified that good may come of it. He used the example of pardons that were granted to felons who impeached two or more of their accomplices to argue that this was already the practice and that it brought clear benefits to the public (Mandeville [1732a] 1954: 41–5). Contrasting his own and Berkeley's views of mankind, Mandeville noted that Berkeley's design was to make men copy after the beautiful original while his own was to enforce the necessity of education. As noted earlier, the importance of education for the transmission of mankind's accumulated wisdom was discussed in dialogue IV of volume II of the *Fable* in the context of a critique of Shaftesbury's (and hence Hutcheson's) system. Mandeville emphasised that rather than being natural to mankind, many of the attributes that made people sociable were the fruit of care and industry.[9]

Berkeley's critique of Shaftesbury

Whereas the second dialogue of *Alciphron* was directed against Mandeville, the main target of the third was Shaftesbury's *Characteristics*. Shaftesbury was perceived by Berkeley as promoting freethinking by arguing that virtuous atheism was possible (a position also held by Hutcheson). Alciphron, who is intended to represent Shaftesbury's position, argues that true virtue could not be promoted by scaring men into practices contrary to the natural bent of their souls with threats of future rewards and punishments. The true basis of virtue and duty was an idea of beauty natural to the mind of man which 'all men desire ... purely from an instinct of nature' which 'strikes at first sight, and attracts without a reason' (*Alciphron*: III.3). Berkeley's spokesman, answers that the passions implanted in the human soul 'seem a very uncertain guide in morals' and would 'infallibly lead different men different ways, according to the prevalency of this or that appetite or passion' (*Alciphron*: III.5).[10] Berkeley also makes the point that the natural reactions to good and evil which Shaftesbury attributes to moral sense could equally be accounted for by conscience, affection, passion, education, reason, custom and religion (*Alciphron*: III.6). Moreover, he argues that by 'recommending morals on the same foot with manners' and 'under the pretence of making men heroically virtuous' Shaftesbury was destroying 'the means of making them reasonably and humanely so' (*Alciphron*: III.13).

Berkeley's comments on Shaftesbury show that while he may have failed to subscribe to Mandeville's view relating to the true meanness of human nature, his own view was hardly rose-tinted. This might seem surprising given the views expressed in the *Guardian* article of 5 August 1713, 'The Bond of Society', to the effect that people were endowed with a social appetite that 'inclined each individual to an intercourse with his species and models everyone to that behaviour which best suits with the common well-being'. However, in an earlier *Guardian* essay of 14 May 1713, Berkeley had made it clear that he fully understood that men were far from being heroically virtuous. There, he argued that anyone who imagined that mere beauty and fortitude were enough to cause people to resist the temptations of present profit and sensuality must be destitute of passion (Berkeley 1955: 198–201). He then went on to suggest that it would be foolish of a man who believed in no future state to be thoroughly honest and it would be just as foolish to expect him to be honest. On the other hand, a Christian who forewent some present advantage for the sake of his conscience acted accountably because it was with a view of obtaining some greater good. It was also the case that a Christian had to break through stronger engagements and suffered more remorse when s/he engaged in criminal acts. Berkeley concluded that although there was nothing more lovely than virtue and the practice of it was the surest way to happiness, 'titles, estates and fantastical pleasures' were more ardently sought after by most men. Where people believed that existence terminates in this life, they were more likely to focus on temporary and selfish ends. The wise heathens of antiquity had understood this and endeavoured by fables, conjectures and other means to possess the minds of men with the belief of a future state (*Works*: IV.162). This position that it was impossible for those who did not believe in an afterlife to sacrifice their particular interests and passions for the public good was re-interated in *An Essay Towards Preventing the Ruin of Great Britain* and in section 11 of the fifth dialogue in *Alciphron*.

It is clear from this that Berkeley's opposition to Mandeville related not so much to his utilitarianism but to his hedonism and his suspected freethinking and scepticism. It is also clear that his opposition to Shaftesbury related not to the issue of natural sociability but to the issue of whether or not religion had a role in cherishing and improving the social inclinations which were necessary for the well-being of the world. Leary argues that Berkeley's critique of Shaftesbury involves an amplification of the social theory presented in 1713 to the effect that social appetite alone was insufficient to motivate men to proper behaviour in the presence of private passions (Leary 1977: 645). Social appetite was still seen as natural but on its own unequal to the task of promoting the public good. Religious training in the social virtues and religious beliefs in the afterlife and in punishment provided essential supports to social appetite in the maintenance of social order (Leary 1977: 646).

In his philosophical works, Berkeley identified the source of scepticism in the view that things existed independently of our perception of them (Luce 1963: 145–6). His general solution to the problem of scepticism was the doctrine 'to be (*esse*) is to be perceived (*percipi*)' which implied a refutation of the doctrine of material substance and a denial that there was a gap between ideas and things (Grayling 2005: 169).[11] The specific arguments for the existence of God were developed in dialogue IV of *Alciphron* where Berkeley represented the visible world as 'a Divine Language, which contains all the signs of a perpetually present God' (*Alciphron*: IV.14). The general rules according to which ideas are caused in us by God, Berkeley called laws of nature. These laws which were learnt by experience indicated what would happen in the normal course of things and, on this basis, enabled us to regulate our conduct in ways that promoted general well-being (Darwall 2005: 321).

Rule versus act utilitarianism

There were two ways in which the general well-being of mankind might be pursued. The first, nowadays termed act utilitarianism, required that each individual consult the public good and to act in the manner most conducive to promoting it. The other, nowadays termed rule utilitarianism, was by observing some 'determinate, established laws, which, if universally practiced' would generally promote the well-being of mankind although they might occasionally fail to do so (*Passive Obedience* (*PB*): 8). A problem with the first method was that the lack of information about the circumstances and hidden consequences of actions meant that it was either impossible to calculate their effects or too time-consuming to make it practical to do so (*PB*: 9). Besides, there would be no sure standard according to which actions could be pronounced good or bad because men could differ in their opinions as to what was conducive to the public good according to their particular views or circumstances. If instead of attempting to work out the consequences of actions, the individual were to compare the proposed action with some particular precept, it would be far easier to judge with certainty whether or not the action was appropriate. Berkeley argued that the *laws of nature* or *eternal rules of reason* should be observed by all men in all times and places even on those occasions when they were accidental causes of misery because if we allowed that they could be transgressed whenever the public good seemed to require it, we would in effect be leaving everyone to be guided by his own judgement (*PB*: 27). Since laws of nature were to be discovered by reason and argumentation in which every man necessarily judged for himself, Berkeley was aware that it might be argued that men were still left to their own private judgements. Against this, he argued that while men might differ as to what was beneficial or otherwise on particular occasions, there would not be much difference between them 'in general conclusions, drawn from an equal and enlarged view of things' (*PB*: 29).

While Berkeley's rule utilitarian arguments have universal application, the context in which they were originated was entirely political. According to Berkeley himself, the aim of *Passive Obedience* was to argue against the pernicious view that subjects might lawfully resist the supreme authority where the public good seemed to require it. The issue of whether the pamphlet had pro- (Berman 1986) or anti-Jacobite (Ross 2005) intentions is a matter of dispute. What is clear, however, is that Berkeley's view that it was wrong to seek to overthrow the sovereign power placed him in conflict with leading Irish thinkers such as Molesworth and Archbishop King. As might be expected, Hutcheson also differed from Berkeley on rule utilitarianism and commented specifically on the issue of passive obedience in the *Inquiry* (II.III.III). Here he made it abundantly clear that, in his view, 'what tended in the whole to the public natural good, was also morally good'. Hutcheson believed that a right to resistance existed when inalienable rights were invaded. Restraints of a moral kind in this instance existed only where it was anticipated that the force available was insufficient to accomplish the objective of removing the corrupt authority or where the transgression was too small to overbalance the advantages of the administration (*Inquiry*: II.VII.X.). As Berman (1986: 316) notes, Hutcheson's defence of resistance was explicit in its act utilitarianism and more progressive in its use of natural rights theory than that of Archbishop King. Berkeley is a theological rule utilitarian whereas Hutcheson, on this matter at least, is a secular act utilitarian (ibid.).

Berkeley and Hutcheson

Berkeley's rule utilitarianism can be viewed as a means of demonstrating that there were general moral standards, adherence to which was consistent with and would promote the general public good. Hutcheson also sought to demonstrate that virtuous behaviour was consistent with the public good though in his case, there was recognition that people might be good in different ways. For Berkeley, the good life was not possible without a belief in God and an afterlife. Hutcheson, on the other hand, believed that God had furnished people well for virtuous conduct but he was also clear that the moral sense was not founded on religion and explicitly criticised the view that good actions were promoted by the expectation of rewards from the Deity (*Inquiry*: II.I.5 and II.7).

Hutcheson and Berkeley both accepted Mandeville's proposition that individual consumption drove production but both also argued that moderate consumption patterns were consistent with substantial demand. They also disagreed with Mandeville's ascetic definition of luxury arguing that consumption appropriate to one's station in life was quite acceptable as long as it was within one's means. Berkeley's engagement with Mandeville on the relationship between the structure and level of demand and the wider productive structure is likely to have been an important influence on his views on economic development as set out in his *Querist*. There, Berkeley argued for a reformation of demand involving control of fashion among the rich (Kelly 2005: 349) and an expansion of the wants of the poor. Like Mandeville, Berkeley was convinced that content was the 'bane of industry' (*Fable*: I. Remark V) and he argued that in order to encourage industriousness amongst the poor, it was necessary to develop their wants (*Querist*: Q20, 107, 128).[12] In addition to his advocacy of sumptuary laws, Berkeley differed from Mandeville in advocating controls on foreign trade. With the British and Dutch models in mind, Mandeville believed that with a wise administration 'people may swim in as much foreign luxury as their product can purchase without being impoverished by it'. Berkeley, whose main focus was Ireland, saw the country as being impoverished by its foreign trade which consisted in the export of agricultural raw materials and the import of expensive foreign luxuries. Consequently, he constructed a model of development which emphasised the substitution of domestically produced goods for foreign imports (*Querist*: Q63–175).

For all his emphasis on benevolence, Hutcheson later echoed Mandeville and indeed Berkeley in recognising the limitations of natural sociability. As he put it in his Inaugural Oration at the University of Glasgow:

> It is not the general kinship of human nature and the universal affection which embraces however feebly the whole human race which we should take note of, to illustrate our sociability. For most of the ties between human beings are narrower, and because of them some persons become far dearer to us than others.
>
> (Hutcheson 1730: 12)[13]

Consistent with this view, in a later work on moral philosophy, Hutcheson wrote: 'diligence will never be universal, unless man's own necessities, and the love of families and friends excite them' (*System of Moral Philosophy*: I.321).

> Now nothing can so effectively excite men to constant patience and diligence in all sorts of useful industry, as the hopes of future wealth, ease, and pleasure to themselves, their offspring and all who are dear to them, and of some honour too to themselves on account of their ingenuity, and activity, and liberality. All these hopes are presented to men by securing to everyone the fruits of his own labours.... If they are not thus secured, one has no other motive to labour than the general affection to his kind, which is commonly much weaker than the narrower affections to our friends and relations....
>
> (*System*: I.321)

Hutcheson fully understood that, in a society with an advanced division of labour, the mutual dependence of human beings was mediated through commerce and contract (*Inquiry*: II.VII.VIII) and he argued that such allocations were likely to be superior to distribution by magistrates. This was on the grounds that the former would provide greater incentives for effort and that people would be rightly concerned about just treatment if all were left to the pleasure of magistrates (*System*: I.322–3).

While the above statements seem to point to a fairly restricted role for Hutcheson's moral theory and to support to the view that Hutcheson's moral and political theories are differently grounded, Haakonssen (1996: 77–81) has argued that this is not the case. Haakonssen shows that Hutcheson's theory of rights is derivative from his concept of the common good which is itself a motive judged to be morally good by the moral sense. This may explain how notions of rights arise from the moral sense of right and wrong. Yet, it does not change the fact that, even for Hutcheson, the role of benevolence in economic life is a restricted one. In this, the parallel between Hutcheson and his student Adam Smith is worth noting. In his *Theory of Moral Sentiments*, Smith saw benevolence as being a feature of private relationships – 'an ornament which embellishes, not the foundation which supports' society (*TMS*: II.ii.3.4). Benevolence, therefore, was less essential to the existence of society than justice without which society could not subsist.[14]

Swift's critique of utilitarian evaluation

In their different ways, both Berkeley and Hutcheson can be regarded as answering Mandeville's paradox by showing that virtue was consistent with the public good. In doing so, both were driven in the direction of accepting the validity of the utilitarian evaluations of outcomes. In so far as they criticised utilitarian evaluation, it was mainly because of lack of information, uncertainty about outcomes and the weaknesses and slowness of reasoning processes. Only one of Mandeville's Irish critics could be said to have provided a critique of utilitarian evaluation in itself. This was in 1729 when Jonathan Swift, Dean of St Patrick's Cathedral in Dublin, published *A Modest Proposal for Preventing the Children of Poor People in Ireland, from Being a Burthen to their Parents or Country, and for Making Them Beneficial to the Public*. In part, Swift's satire is despair at what English (and particularly Whig) policy was doing to Ireland, but it is also one of the most effective critiques of the consequentialist approach to ethics that has ever been written. Although Mandeville is nowhere mentioned in Swift's pamphlet, it is generally accepted that the 'Modest' in the title echoed Mandeville's[15] use of the term in *A Modest Defence of Public Stews or an Essay Upon Whoring* which had been published five years earlier. There Mandeville argued the case for the setting up of state-run brothels on strictly utilitarian grounds thereby scandalising conventional morality and sealing his reputation as a preacher of the immoral. Mandeville concluded that 'if a public act, taking in all its consequences, really produces a greater quantity of good, it must, and ought to be termed a good act; although the bare act considered in itself without the consequent good, should be in the highest degree wicked and unjust (*A Modest*

Defence: 68–9). Emulating Mandeville's utilitarian analysis, Swift, in his *Modest Proposal*, enumerated the costs and benefits to themselves and the public generally which would result from killing the children of the poor and using their flesh as food. He then considered and rejected some possible modifications of the proposal, examined the compatability of incentives and concluded that the benefits greatly exceeded costs. Finally, Swift argued that the proposal was more humane than the status quo. The conclusion is made all the more chilling by the measured tone of the writing. The proposal is left to speak for itself and no attempt is made to articulate its implications for Mandeville's consequentualist arguments.

Anscombe (1958) noted that English utilitarians such as Mill had taken it for granted that certain things such as the killing of an innocent were forbidden regardless of the consequences. This, she regarded, as an important part of the Hebrew–Christian heritage which had disappeared in more modern times. Mandeville had been provocative in choosing to apply consequentialist reasoning in the case of prostitution which it was generally accepted should be forbidden but, at least, he could convincingly argue that the prohibition had been entirely ineffective. Swift took things a step further and showed that consequentialist reasoning could justify anything even the killing of innocents which was accepted as an absolute taboo.

From Irish to Scottish enlightenment

Both Berkeley and Hutcheson's encounter with Mandeville crystallised the challenges the evolving capitalist society posed for them as theologians and social philosophers. According to George Davie, Scottish philosophy found its central problems in the tension between their two contrasting positions. In the Berkeleyian system, the interest is in reconciling progress with traditional standards. For Hutcheson, the aim also is to reconcile material advance with intellectual principles but of a more secular and progressive variety (Davie 1994: 41–2). Though Berkeley was a defender of traditional standards and his philosophical writings were an important part of his project to undermine scepticism, his immaterialist philosophy was much misunderstood and its early reception was almost uniformly hostile (Bracken 1965). In Scotland, he received more attention than elsewhere although this was by no means sympathetic. Nonetheless, it is accepted that, directly or indirectly, Berkeley influenced Hume. At the same time, Reid's Common Sense philosophy was in large part a reaction against Berkeley's idealism and perceived scepticism (Graham 2009).

In the case of Hutcheson, the influence on Scottish thinkers was much more immediate and clear-cut. Hutcheson was a significant influence on the intellectual development of Hume and Adam Smith both of whom developed theories of morals which built on the naturalistic foundations he had provided. Both regarded individuals as being equipped with moral sentiments which enabled them to distinguish virtue from vice. Hume was sensible to the criticism made by both Mandeville and Berkeley that subjective feelings were a very arbitrary basis on which to found a system of morals and consequently emphasised the necessity to fix on a general point of view, to reflect on our own behaviour and see ourselves as others see us. While thus accepting Mandeville's proposition relating to the formative and regulative function of other people's views, Hume argued that we could derive no pleasure from undeserved praise (Bracken 1977–78; Russell 2007).

In the *Wealth of Nations*, Adam Smith did Mandeville the honour of appropriating his account of the division of labour without reference to its (disreputable) source. In *The Theory of Moral Sentiments*, he provided a critique of Mandeville's licentious system at the conclusion of which he noted that the system could not have imposed upon so many 'had it not in some respects bordered upon the truth' (*TMS*: VII.ii.4.14). Like Hutcheson and Berkeley before him, Smith took issue with Mandeville's stringent definition of luxury (*TMS*: VII.ii.4.11), but his main difference with Mandeville seems to revolve around the issue of social recognition. Smith accepted that men sought the approbation and esteem of their fellow men but, unlike Mandeville, he did not regard the desire for approbation as sufficient to render man fit for society. Like Hume, he argued that 'Nature had endowed [mankind], not only with the desire of being approved of, but with a desire of being what ought to be approved of; or of being what he himself approves of in other men' (*TMS*: III.2.7). The first would be sufficient to make man wish to appear fit for society; the second would make him wish to be really fit.

On the face of it, Smith's ethical position appears to be much stronger than that adopted by Mandeville but it is not as robust as it appears at first sight. For Mandeville, the tribunal is other people's opinion of our actions and, since others may lack information, appearances are all that count. For Smith, the tribunal is the judgement of the 'impartial' spectator who although not handicapped by the same information problems is likely to be more partial than real external spectators might be expected to be (Raphael and MacFie 1976: 16). Hundert (1994: 235–6) also argues that, in the *Wealth of Nations* especially, Smith subsumed the passions promoting the need for recognition under the pursuit of economic advantage. All non-economic drives are translated into economic ones and the individual's unending struggle to better his condition serves his need for recognition. As Mandeville predicted, a moral vocabulary is no longer relevant to the description or understanding of such a society.

To conclude, as Hutcheson and, before him, Berkeley realised, the effective ties binding human beings are narrow. Benevolence diminishes when extended to mankind in general and is thus less relevant to economic transactions in a society with a developed division of labour. Given these considerations, Berkeley relied on the discipline imposed by the belief of punishment in an after-life. Mandeville relied on education, on reputation and social regulation by means of evolved institutions. Although Hutcheson's position was to stress the individual's innate sociability and desire to pursue the social good, he too had to progressively qualify this assumption. At the same time Hutcheson continued to be strongly opposed to Berkeley's theological rule utilitarianism. In terms of the moral regulation of economic activity, Hutcheson's innate but limited human benevolence had little to offer and there was little to distinguish his arguments in favour of property and other institutions on the basis of the common good from those of the Epicureans he so despised. In *Theory of Moral Sentiments* and *Wealth of Nations*, Adam Smith acknowledged the restricted role of human benevolence but built a theory of the evolution of justice on the basis of moral sentiments. He combined this with Mandeville's dynamic vision of the beneficial outcome of an advanced division of labour but without Mandeville's perspective on the role of historically evolved social institutions. Instead Smith invoked the 'hidden hand', a powerful though mysterious metaphor, which evaded the earlier dilemmas. However, as Sen and others were later to point out, it remained an evasion nonetheless.

Roughly a century after the publication of the final version of *The Fable of the Bees*, the controversy which it occasioned about the compatibility of the virtuous life and economic growth had faded completely. Reflecting on the earlier controversy in his *Lectures on Political Economy*, Richard Whately, who was soon to be Anglican Archbishop of Dublin, singled out Mandeville for praise and argued that his originality consisted in bringing into juxtaposition, notions, which separately, had long been current but whose inconsistency had escaped detection. Whately argued that, contrary to popular belief, Mandeville did not seek to encourage vice but showed hypothetically, that if the notions then current respecting the character of virtue and vice and the causes and consequences of wealth were admitted, national virtue and national wealth must be irreconcilable (Whately 1832: II.16). Whately went on to argue that the dangers attendant on the acquisition or possession of wealth referred chiefly to individuals and that national wealth presented nothing of such dangers to counteract its advantages. Consequently, no choice had to be made between wealth and virtue.

Notes

1 I am grateful to John Foster for comments on earlier drafts of this chapter.
2 Mandeville's determination to examine human beings as they were and not as we would like them to be has been compared to the naturalistic anthropology of Spinoza (see den Uyl 1987; Israel 2001; Klever n.d.).
3 In the *Fable* Mandeville took pride and shame to be two distinct passions but he later substituted the term 'self-liking' to cover both. When moderate and well regulated, self-liking excited in us the desire to be thought well of and stirred us up to good actions. When self-liking was excessive, it rendered us odious to others and was called pride (Mandeville 1732b, dialogue I).
4 The article has been given the title 'The Bond of Society' by Luce and Jessop (Berkeley 1955: VII.225).
5 Berkeley is not specifically mentioned by Mandeville but there are strong similarities between the example used by Berkeley to support his position and that used by Mandeville to refute it. Berkeley had argued that two Englishmen meeting in Rome or Constantinople would soon run into familiarity and that, in Japan or China, Europeans would soon run into conversation. For Berkeley this showed that the benevolent uniting instinct implanted in human nature was always present and would show itself as long as it was not obstructed by passions and motions. In 'A Search into the Nature of Society', Mandeville referred to the French, English and Dutch meeting in China

and feeling a natural propensity to love one another if no passion intervened. Mandeville held that this merely showed that man loved company for 'his own sake' or because it was beneficial to him (*Fable*: I.343). He also poked fun at the notion of natural sociability by retailing his own amusement on reflecting on the sociability of shoals of herring and other fish (*Fable*: I.337).

6 In what follows, the first Roman numeral refers to Treatise II, the second to the section of Treatise II and the third the sub-section. Arabic numbers refer to the number of the paragraph in the sub-section.

7 Addison and Steele's attempts to reform manners and to equate cultivation with the dictates of morality were satirised by Mandeville in his early writings in *The Female Tatler* (Hundert 1994: 119–21).

8 This is hardly a fair representation of Mandeville's position given the emphasis he placed on the importance of evolved institutions (Bianchi 1993). However, it is possible that Berkeley was unaware of Mandeville's second volume when he wrote *Alciphron*.

9 For an extended discussion of the development and transmission of both tacit and codified forms of knowledge in Mandeville, see Prendergast 2009.

10 This point was also made by Mandeville in *A Search into the Nature of Society*.

11 The precise interpretation of Berkeley's philosophy is a matter of some controversy. Some see Berkeley as reducing all things to ideas in the mind whereas other e.g. Ferrier and Luce argue that Berkeley merely denied the distinction between things and their appearances.

12 See also *A Word to the Wise* in which Berkeley bemoans the wretched state of his fellow countrymen but lays the blame for their poverty on their own idleness and lack of industry.

13 Mandeville did not deny that people had natural affections which amongst other things prompted them to care for their children. However, he argued that natural affection was 'neither instrumental to the erecting of societies, not ever trusted too in our prudent commerce with another' (*Fable*: II.183–9).

14 For a useful overview of this problem, see R. Teichgraeber III (1981: 106–23).

15 Phil-Porney, the author of *A Modest Defence* is generally considered to be Mandeville.

Bibliography

Albee, E. (1902) *A History of English Utilitarianism*, London: Swan, Sonnenschein and Co.

Anscombe, G.E.M. (1958) 'Modern Moral Philosophy', *Philosophy* 33.124: 1–19.

Arbuckle, J. (1729) *A Collection of Letters and Essays on Several Subjects*, London: J. Osborn.

Barbon, N. [1690] (1905) *A Discourse of Trade*, Baltimore, MD: Baltimore Press.

Berkeley, G. [1712] (1953) *Passive Obedience*, in A.A. Luce and T.E. Jessop (eds) *The Works of George Berkeley Bishop of Cloyne* VI: 15–46, London: Thomas Nelson and Sons Ltd.

Berkeley, G. [1713] (1953) 'The Bonds of Society', The *Guardian*, Wednesday 5 August, in A.A. Luce and T.E. Jessop (eds) *The Works of George Berkeley Bishop of Cloyne*, VII: 198–201, London: Thomas Nelson and Sons Ltd.

Berkeley, G. [1713] (1955) 'The Sanctions of Religion', The *Guardian*, 14 May in A.A. Luce and T.E. Jessop (eds) *The Works of George Berkeley Bishop of Cloyne*, VII: 198–201, London: Thomas Nelson and Sons Ltd.

Berkeley, G. [1721]) (1953) *An Essay Towards Preventing the Ruin of Great Britain*, in A.A. Luce and T.E. Jessop (eds) *The Works of George Berkeley Bishop of Cloyne*, VI: 69–85, London: Thomas Nelson and Sons Ltd.

Berkeley, G. [1732] (1950) *Alciphron; or the Minute Philosopher*, in A.A. Luce and T.E. Jessop (eds) *The Works of George Berkeley Bishop of Cloyne*, III, London: Thomas Nelson and Sons Ltd.

Berman, D. (1986) The Jacobitism of Berkeley's Passive Obedience, *Journal of the History of Ideas* 47.2: 309–19.

Berman, D. (1993) *George Berkeley, Alciphron, or the Minute Philosopher in Focus*, London and New York: Routledge.

Berman, D. (2005) 'Berkeley's Life and Works', in K. Winkler (ed.) *The Cambridge Companion to Berkeley*, Cambridge: Cambridge University Press.

Bianchi, M. (1993) 'True and False Solutions to Mandeville's Problem', *History of Political Economy* 25.2: 209–40.

Bishop, J.D. (1997) 'Moral Motivation and the Development of Francis Hutcheson's Philosophy', *Journal of the History of Ideas* 57: 277–95.

Bracken, H.M. (1965) *The Early Reception of Berkeley's Immaterialism 1710–1733*, The Hague: Martinus Nijhoff.

Bracken, H.M. (1977–78) 'Bayle, Berkeley, and Hume', *Eighteenth Century Studies* 11.2: 227–45.

Brown, M. (2002) *Francis Hutcheson in Dublin – The Crucible of his Thought*, Dublin: Four Courts Press.

Cook, H.J. (1999) 'Bernard Mandeville and the Therapy of "The Clever Politician"', *Journal of the History of Ideas* 60.1: 101–24.

Darwall, S. (2005) 'Berkeley's Moral and Political Philosophy', in K.P. Winkler (ed.) *The Cambridge Companion to Berkeley*, Cambridge: Cambridge University Press.

Davie, G. (1978) 'Berkeley, Hume and the Central Problem of Classical Scottish Philosophy', in D.F. Norton, N. Capaldi and W. Robinson (eds) *McGill Hume Studies*, San Diego, CA: Austin Hill Press.

Davie, G. (1994) *A Passion for Ideas: Essays on the Scottish Enlightenment*, Vol. II, Edinburgh: Polygon.

Frankena, W. (1955) 'Hutcheson's Moral Theory', *Journal of the History of Ideas* 16: 356–75.

Fraser, A.C. (1901) *The Works of George Berkeley*, 4 vols, Oxford: Clarendon Press.

Graham, G. (2009) 'Scottish Philosophy in the 19th Century', *Stanford Encyclopaedia of Philosophy*. Online. Available at http://plato.stanford.edu/entries/scottish-19th/13 (accessed April 2010).

Grayling, A.C. (2005) 'Berkeley's Argument for Immaterialism', in K.P. Winkler (ed.) *The Cambridge Companion to Berkeley*, Cambridge: Cambridge University Press.

Haakonssen, K. (1996) *Natural Law and Moral Philosophy*, Cambridge: Cambridge University Press.

Hont, Istvan (2006) 'The Early Enlightenment Debate on Commerce and Luxury', in Mark Goldie and Robert Wokler (eds) *The Cambridge History of Eighteenth-Century Political Thought*, Cambridge: Cambridge University Press.

Horne, T.A. (1978) *The Social Thought of Bernard Mandeville*, London: Macmillan.

Hundert, E.G. (1994) *The Enlightenment's Fable, Bernard Mandeville and the Discovery of Society*, Cambridge: Cambridge University Press.

Hutcheson, F. [1726] (2004) *An Inquiry into the Original of our Ideas of Beauty and Virtue in Two Treatises*, W. Leidhold (ed.), Indianapolis: Liberty Fund.

Hutcheson, F. [1728] (1999) *An Essay On the Nature and Conduct of the Passions with Illustrations on the Moral Sense*, A. Ward (ed.), Manchester: Clinamen Press.

Hutcheson, F. [1730] (2006) 'On the Natural Sociability of Mankind, Inaugural Oration', in James Moore and Michael Silverthorne (eds) *Logic, Metaphysics, and the Natural Sociability of Mankind*, texts translated from the Latin by Michael Silverthorne, introduction by James Moore, Indianapolis: Liberty Fund.

Hutcheson, F. (1747) *A Short Introduction to Moral Philosophy*, Glasgow: Robert Foulis.

Hutcheson, F. (1750) 'Remarks upon the *Fable of the Bees*'. Online. Available at http:// socserv.mcmaster.ca/econ/ugcm/3113/hutcheson/remarks.htm (accessed 13 April 2010).

Hutcheson, F. (1755) *A System of Moral Philosophy*, Vol. 1 of 3, Glasgow: R. & A. Foulis, 430 pp.

Hutcheson, F. (1994) *Philosophical Wrtings*, R.S. Downie (ed.), London: J.M. Dent; Vermont: Charles E. Tuttle.

Israel, J. (2001) *Radical Enlightenment – Philosophy and the Making of Modernity 1650–1750*, Oxford: Oxford University Press.

Jensen, H. (1971) *Motivation and the Moral Sense in Francis Hutcheson's Ethical Theory*, The Hague: Martinus Nijhoff.

Johnston, J. (1970) *Bishop Berkeley's Querist in Historical Perspective*, Dundalk: Dundalgan Press.

Kelly, P. (2005) 'Berkeley's Economic Writings', in K.P. Winkler (ed.) *The Cambridge Companion to Berkeley*, Cambridge: Cambridge University Press.

Klever, W. (n.d) 'Bernard Mandeville and his Spinozistic Appraisal of Vices', No. 20, *foglio Spinozi*. Available at www.foglio Spinozi.it (accessed 9 December 2009).

Lamprecht, S.P. (1926) 'The Fable of the Bees', *Journal of Philosophy* 23.21: 561–79.

Leary, D.E. (1977) 'Berkeley's Social Theory: Context and Development', *Journal of the History of Ideas* 38.4: 635–49.

Luce, A.A. (1963) *The Dialectic of Immaterialism*, London: Hodder and Stoughton.

McCloskey, D. (2007) *The Bourgeois Virtues – Ethics for an Age of Commerce*, Chigago: University of Chigago Press.

Mandeville, B. [1724] (1973) *A Modest Defence of Public Stews*, Intro. R.I. Cook, Los Angelos: William Andrews Clark Memorial Library.

Mandeville, B. [1732a] (1954) *A Letter to Dion*, B. Dobree (ed.), Liverpool: University Press of Liverpool.

Mandeville, B. (1732b) *An Inquiry into the Origins of Honour and the Usefulness of Christianity in War*, London: Printed for J. Brotherton.

Mandeville, B. (1924) *The Fable of the Bees*, 2 vols, F.B. Kaye (ed.), Oxford: The Clarendon Press.

Mautner, T. (ed.) (1993) *Francis Hutcheson on Human Nature*, Cambridge: Cambridge University Press.

Moore, J. (2000) 'Hutcheson's Theodicy: The Argument and Contexts of *A Sytem of Moral Philosophy*', in P. Wood (ed.) *The Scottish Enlightenment: Essays in Re-Interpretation*, Rochester: The University of Rochester Press, pp. 239–66.

North, N. (1907) *Discourses Upon Trade*, Baltimore, MD: Baltimore Press.

Popkin, Richard H. (1979) *The History of Scepticism from Erasmus to Spinoza*, Berkeley, CA: University of California Press.

Prendergast, R. (2009) 'Accumulation of Knowledge and Accumulation of Capital in Early "Theories" of Growth and Development', *Cambridge Journal of Economics*. Advance access published 31 March. http://cje.oxfordjournals.org/cgi/reprint/bep009 (accessed 23 January 2010).

Raphael, D.D. (1947) *The Moral Sense*, Oxford: Oxford University Press.

Raphael, D.D. and MacFie, A.L. (eds) (1976) 'Introduction', *The Theory of Moral Sentiments*, Oxford: Oxford University Press.

Ross, I.C. (2005) 'Was Berkeley a Jacobite? *Passive Obedience* Revisited', *Eighteenth Century Ireland* 20: 17–30.

Rubinstein, A. (2006) ' A Sceptic's Comment on the Study of Economics', *Economic Journal* 116.510: C1–C9.

Russell, P. (2007) 'Hume's Treatise and the Problem of Virtuous Atheism', *Nowa Krytyka* 20.21: 333–80.

Scott, W.R. (1900) *Francis Hutcheson*, Cambridge: Cambridge University Press.

Seth, A. (1885) *Scottish Philosophy*, Edinburgh and London: William Blackwood and Sons.

Skinner, A.S. (1987) *Francis Hutcheson*, in J. Eatwell, M. Milgate and P. Newman (eds) *The New Palgrave Dictionary of Economics*, London: Macmillan.

Skinner, A.S. (2006) *Frances Hutcheson – 1694–1746*, in A. Dow and S. Dow (eds) *A History of Scottish Economic Thought*, London: Routledge.

Smith, A. (1776a) *An Inquiry into the Nature and Causes of the Wealth of Nations*, 2 vols, R.H. Campbell, A.S. Skinner and W.B. Todd (eds), Oxford: Oxford University Press.

Smith, A. (1776b) *The Theory of Moral Sentiments*, D.D. Raphael and A.L. MacFie (eds), Oxford: Oxford University Press.

Swift, J. (1730) *A Modest Proposal for Preventing the Children of Poor People in Ireland from Being a Burthen to their Parents or Country, and for Making them Beneficial to the Publick*, Dublin, London: printed and re-printed in London for Weaver Bickerton.

Teichgraeber III, R. (1981) 'Rethinking Das Adam Smith Problem, *The Journal of British Studies* 20.2: 106–23.

Uyl den D.J. (1987) 'Passion. State and Progress: Spinoza and Mandeville on the Nature of Human Association', *Journal of History of Philosophy* 25: 369–95.

Whately, R. (1832) *Introductory Lectures on Political Economy*, London: B Fellowes.

Winkler, K.P. (2005) *The Cambridge Companion to Berkeley*, Cambridge: Cambridge University Press.

4 Economic thought in Arthur O'Connor's *The State of Ireland*

Reducing politics to science

Daniel Blackshields and John Considine[1]

Introduction

Published on 1 February 1798, *The State of Ireland* was one of the last pamphlets to go into circulation before the United Irishman rebellion of that summer. Its author Arthur O'Connor (1763–1852) was a prominent member of the United Irishmen. He was also a follower of the work of Adam Smith having read *The Wealth of Nations* in his teenage years.[2] Despite being a pamphlet, *The State of Ireland* contains enough economic thought to be of interest to scholars of the subject. Although the work draws heavily on the *Wealth of Nations* it is worth examining as an application of the principles in that tome. In particular, O'Connor's attempt to use the principle of self-interest to explain the governance of Ireland and the implications for the economic conditions of its people is worthy of greater attention. The purpose of this paper is to present the economic thought in O'Connor's pamphlet. The authors believe that there is enough of the economic method in the work for it to be considered a forerunner of public choice and institutional economics.

The next section provides a biographical sketch of Arthur O'Connor. The third section gives a brief overview of the intellectual environment of the time by presenting Irish political thought in the late eighteenth century. The fourth section presents the economic thought in *The State of Ireland* and highlights the similarities with various aspects of the *Wealth of Nations*. O'Connor's work is then located by reference to Adam Smith and Edmund Burke. The sixth section explains how O'Connor's legacy was more biological and spiritual than intellectual as illustrated by the life and works of his illegitimate son William Conner and his nephew Feargus O'Connor. The relevance of O'Connor's work for twenty-first century economics is introduced in the concluding section.

Who was Arthur O'Connor?

Arthur Conner was born 4 July 1763 near Bandon in County Cork. He was one of nine children, and the youngest of five boys, born to Roger Conner and Anne Longfield. Arthur changed his name to O'Connor in an effort to claim kinship with ancient Irish nobility via the O'Connor–Kerrys clan. Introduced to the writing of philosophers and moralists by his mother, he attended two Munster boarding schools, and read *The Wealth of Nations* before registering for a Bachelor of Arts in Trinity College at the age of sixteen.[3] He gained his BA in 1782 and returned home that year to find his mother dying. He remained in West Cork for the remainder of the year and joined the Volunteers under the guidance of Appolos Morris.[4]

The following year O'Connor enrolled to study Law in Lincoln's Inn, London. Here he read Montesquieu's *The Spirit of the Law* and took a keen interest in the political debates that resulted in treaties with America and France. He was in London again for the impeachment of Warren Hastings in 1787 before returning to serve as High Sherriff for County Cork in 1791.

With the help of his mother's brother, Lord Longueville, he was to sit in the House of Commons as member for Philipstown from 1790 to 1795. In May 1795 O'Connor spoke on Grattan's bill to admit Catholics to parliament. While receiving critical acclaim from the opposition Whigs, his speech cost him his seat and his uncle's favour. During his time representing Philipstown he fathered an illegitimate son – William Conner – whom John Stuart Mill later referred to as 'the earliest, most enthusiastic, and most indefatigable apostle' of land reform.[5]

It was at this juncture that O'Connor took the revolutionary route. French victories in the war with England in 1794 and 1795, and the Fitzwilliam affair,[6] seem to have heavily influenced his decision to secure a French invasion of Ireland. While there is little doubt that O'Connor's direction became more radical and revolutionary from 1795, it is difficult to establish the exact weight of intellectual conviction and personal ambition in his motivation.[7] Not surprisingly, O'Connor claims that his ideas on these matters were the result of his lifelong reading and experience. Sympathetic authors like Hayter Hames (2001) tend to side with O'Connor. Towards the other end of the spectrum is W.E.H. Lecky (1903), one of the foremost authorities on eighteenth-century Ireland.[8] A more balanced assessment is found in MacDermot (1967: 63) where he quotes with approval the Swiss intellectual Benjamin Constant, who came to know O'Connor, as saying that O'Connor was '[m]ore ambitious than a friend of liberty, and yet a friend of liberty, because to be so is the refuge of ambitious men who have missed success.'[9]

In the summer of 1796 he travelled to the continent where he met General Hoche.[10] A subsequent unsuccessful invasion departed from France on 15 December. The landing at Bantry Bay failed due to bad weather and a lack of local support.

After his meeting with Hoche, O'Connor returned to Ireland in October 1796. He decided to reside in Belfast and announced his intention to represent the people of Antrim at the next election. It is widely assumed that his motivation for doing so was to provide a pretext for subversive propaganda in an area of the country that was ripe for such material.[11] It is also possible he was attempting to generate suitable conditions for the proposed French invasion. His inaugural address appeared a number of times in the *Northern Star* – a newspaper with a print run of 4,000 that was estimated to reach 40,000 individuals[12] and probably the most influential channel for the United Irishmen in their attempt to influence popular political culture. In late January 1797, O'Connor's *Address to the Electors of the County of Antrim* was published and he questioned the opposition to the unsuccessful French invasion 1796 in the *Northern Star*. William Drennan's sister, Martha, said of the *Address*, '[h]is paper will indeed be a touchstone, and must have effects of importance.'[13] One effect was the arrest of O'Connor on 2 February.

O'Connor was released untried in August 1797. During his period in jail the *Northern Star* had been repressed by the authorities. On his release O'Connor was amongst those who started *The Press* newspaper. The prosecution of the nominal publisher of *The Press* for seditious libel in December lead to O'Connor announcing that he was the actual publisher, and he departed for London on 30 December 1797.

On 1 February 1798 he published *The State of Ireland*, accompanied by his 'Address to the Electors of the County of Antrim' claiming that it was a year since he promised such an account of the Irish conditions but that persecution and suppression made it difficult. At the end of the month, O'Connor and others attempted to sail for France but were captured, tried and imprisoned. He was spared hanging by the intervention of the Whig leaders.

O'Connor was in jail for the United Irishmen rebellion during the summer of 1798. In exchange for their lives O'Connor and the leadership of the United Irishmen provided details on their dealing with France.[14] O'Connor and other United Irishmen were imprisoned in Scotland until the peace of Amiens in 1802, at which point they were deported to the continent.

Banned from Ireland, O'Connor made his way to Paris. He integrated himself into French ideologues in the salon of the Marquise de Condorcet, widow of the mathematician-philosopher-politician, sister of General Gouchy, and translator of Adam Smith. In 1807 O'Connor married her daughter, Eliza, and they settled in Le Bignon seventy miles south of Paris where they raised their family. On the intervention of a General Dalton, Napoleon agreed to give him the rank of *general de division* – a position he held with varying success during the changes of power in France during the next four decades.

He was refused his repeated requests to visit Ireland until 1834 when a Whig government held power in London. During this time O'Connor settled a conflict between himself and his brother Roger over his estate. By the end of 1834 the Tories had returned to power and O'Connor was again returned to France where he remained for the rest of his life. In 1848 he wrote *Monopoly: The Cause of All Evil* and four years later, at the age of eighty-eight, he died.

In what context did O'Connor write *The State of Ireland*?: late eighteenth century Irish political thought

The State of Ireland, like much of the work produced by the United Irishmen 'served to define an alternative culture designed to supplant traditional mentalities' (Curtin 1994: 8). Part of this work involved relaying the ideas and events from revolutionary America and France via newspapers such as the *Northern Star* and *The Press*. And, part of the efforts of the United Irishmen involved transforming these ideas to fit the Irish context via pamphlets such as *The State of Ireland*. All was part of an effort to 'make everyman a politician' through engagement in popular political culture.[15]

By the time *The State of Ireland* was published, the reaction of the authorities to these newspapers and pamphlets had moved from surveillance to suppression. Dated 1 February 1798, it was published while O'Connor was in London – having fled Ireland after the *Northern Star* was suppressed and the nominal publisher of its successor, *The Press*, was prosecuted for seditious libel. The change in the reaction of the authorities was a natural response to change in the ideas and events to which they were reacting. The patriotism of the 1770s was replaced by radicalism in the 1780s and by revolutionary republicanism in the 1790s (Small 2002).

When considering O'Connor's arguments, and the expression of these arguments, in *The State of Ireland* it is important to remember that they are presented towards the end of the evolution of Irish political thought from patriotism to republicanism. The evolution and expression of Irish political thought during the period was constructed out of a number of political traditions and languages.[16] The variety of these languages and traditions, combined with the political environment of repression, meant that Irish '[l]ate eighteenth-century political writing was often messy' (Small 2002: 8). This applied to the writings of the United Irishmen and was exaggerated by the fact that the 'United Irish movement was riddled with contradictions' (Curtin 1994: 10). Moreover, the same language and ideas were being used by revolutionary and counter-revolutionary alike.[17]

Internationally writers like Burke and Paine clashed at the level of ideas involving the rights and responsibilities of citizens and rulers. Paine expounded the Rights of Man whilst Burke defended the appropriateness of rule by aristocracy. However, for O'Connor and other Irish thinkers, the implications of enlightenment ideas took a far more radical hue in Ireland than they did in England because the context was different. Connolly (2000: 14) argues that, before the latter third of the eighteenth century, enlightenment appeals to liberty had less traction in England (and Ireland) because contemporary writing in Britain (and Ireland) celebrated British liberty based on either the ancient constitution or the Glorious Revolution. Problems arose when Englishmen living in Ireland claimed the same liberties, or when Irishmen claimed liberties and rights based on appeals to the Kingdom of Ireland,[18] or when the issue of the admission of Catholics to the political nation arose. The Fitzwilliam affair had demonstrated that a public-interested enlightened elite did not exist in Ireland. Lord Fitzwilliam upon his appointment as Lord Lieutenant had dismissed John Beresford and supported Gratton's call for Catholic emancipation. Beresford lobbied Pitt and Fitzwilliam was ordered to return from Ireland. He was replaced by Earl Camden and Beresford (a noted anti-Catholic emancipation advocate) resumed his former position. Such problems contributed to the rise of Irish patriotism and its subsequent evolution to republicanism via radicalism. For O'Connor this demonstrated the abuse of a monopoly power by self-interested individuals.

The result is that O'Connor's work can be distinguished from 'the bulk of eighteenth-century thinkers on the mutual distortions of politics and economics ... [by] his argument that the solution to these problems would be a democratic republic' (O'Connor 1998: 17). O'Connor rejected civic humanism or classical republicanism because it did not work given the practicalities of the Irish political system. Whereas other writers in other contexts rejected democracy because of events in France, O'Connor rejected the alternatives to democracy because of events in Ireland. It was in this cacophony that O'Connor produced *The State of Ireland*. In doing so he constructed his political arguments using the ideas and methods of Adam Smith.

It is the combination of method and context that distinguishes *The State of Ireland*. O'Connor applies the method of economics to politics in a manner similar to late twentieth century public choice writers or institutional economists. The application of this method to the Irish context produced the conclusion that only democracy could provide the solution to Ireland's political and economic woes.

Economic thought in *The State of Ireland* – O'Connor and the influence of Smith

There are two parts to *The State of Ireland*. The first, and larger, part is titled *To the Irish Nation*. In this part O'Connor presents his analysis of the economic conditions of Ireland. The second part is titled *Defence of the United People of Ireland* and it is here that O'Connor justifies the activities of the United Irishmen. In *To the Irish Nation* O'Connor presents his analysis of the sources of prosperity and how these are constrained by the governance of Ireland. Governance is also cited as the source of an inappropriate and excessive cost of the State. According to O'Connor the problems with the governance of Ireland can be traced to primogeniture. He explains: why, in practice, the self-interest of the governing class moved out of line with the public interest; why, in principle, self-interest should be used to evaluate any system of governance; and, why primogeniture produced a governing elite with an interest that differs from the public at large.

As a pamphleteer he sets out his task in rhetorical questions, sometimes in the form of a paradox. The content of these questions are usually economic, e.g. if the Irish are idle then why do they emigrate to seek employment? His main question is: Why has the Irish economy not performed as well as countries of similar size but with fewer natural advantages?[19] It is around these types of questions the pamphlet is structured. It is possible to trace the development and structure of O'Connor's pamphlet by the type of questions he asks. Consider the following sample of questions: Does the produce of the lands of Ireland go to supply the fund for the employment of its People?; How, then, shall a country, subject to such a code as the Revenue Laws of Ireland, become commercial?; How shall the People of Ireland become a manufacturing nation, whose materials and provisions are exported without any return?; But what will be your indignation on being informed that this sacred fund has been embezzled by the already exorbitantly endowed Protestant Clergy?; If this bounty is thus injurious, how has it been the subject of the praise of both tenant and landlord?; Whether the great revolution in property has not effectually destroyed the constitutional power of the Lords?

The sources of wealth accumulation

O'Connor begins his analysis by saying:

> Industry is the source of human prosperity, and the wages of industry is its excitement. In every civilized country, the wealth garnered by industry forms a fund for the employment of the industrious; and as the existence of this fund is the great discriminating mark between civilization and barbarism, so the state of this fund is what regulates the condition and character of every people upon earth.
>
> (O'Connor 1998: 34)

The important phrase here is 'every civilized country'. He later returns to this theme when he explain why capital flows into France when there is a shortage of capital but it actually flows out of Ireland despite there being a shortage of capital. The key determinant of whether capital flows into a country is the extent to which that country is 'civilized'. He attacks the claim that the war with France has only damaged French capital. He points out that the reduction in capital in France will mean a higher return is available to capital in that country and as a result capital will flow from England to France. The question for O'Connor is: Why is this 'sacred fund' dissipated in Ireland?

O'Connor argues that this fund 'for the employment of the industrious' only exists 'if the Government and the Legislature protect the people in their national rights' (O'Connor 1998: 34). Where the government and legislature do not perform this role then this fund is squandered. He proceeded to examine if the government and legislature aided the accumulation or squandering of capital in agriculture, trade, manufacturing, fisheries, and savings in turn. His argument is that there is little incentive to accumulate capital primarily due to the fact that it is extracted from agriculture by absentee landlords, extracted from commerce by the State in the form of taxation,[20] and regulated out of existence by the Revenue officials that determine where and when fishing can take place.

There are similarities here between O'Connor's account and that provided by Smith in Book II, Chapter III in the *Wealth of Nations*. In that chapter Smith explained how there is a fund available for employment of productive labour (capital accumulation) or unproductive labour. This fund amounts to what is left after capital employed is maintained. According to Smith this fund could be used for productive or unproductive labour. He says that '[t]his proportion is very different in rich and poor countries' (Smith 1981 [1776] *WoN*: II.iii.8) and that 'in present times the funds destined for the maintenance of industry, are much greater in proportion to those which are likely to be employed in the maintenance of idleness, than they were two or three centuries ago' (Smith 1981 [1776] *WoN*: II.iii.10). Smith explains this difference between rich and poor countries at a point in time, or between the wealth of countries over time, as resulting from the employment of productive or unproductive labour. In particular he highlights the role of the State when he says 'nations are never impoverished by private, though they sometimes are by publick prodigality and misconduct' (Smith 1981 [1776] *WoN*: II.iii.30). Smith explains that the employment of unproductive labour, such as the employment of public servants of various kinds, can diminish the incentive for the employment of productive labour and the accumulation of capital when he says

> [t]he idleness of the greater part of the people who are maintained by the expense of revenue, corrupts, it is probable, the industry of those who ought to be maintained be the employment of capital, and renders it less advantageous to employ a capital there than in other places.
>
> (Smith 1981 [1776] *WoN*: II.iii.12)

This idea formed the kernel of O'Connor's argument. The actions of the government and legislature resulted in diminishing the incentive to accumulate capital.

O'Connor links the lack of incentives to accumulate capital with the prodigality and misconduct of the government when he says that it

> is not enough that you should know the manner by which you have been deprived of the means of acquiring wealth: You should, also, be informed of the various ways by which the pittance of wealth your industry has acquired under its mutilated means, has been robbed and plundered under a system of Corruption and Treason.
>
> (O'Connor 1998: 40)

Here O'Connor advises the people to consult the data on Irish public finances published in the Court Calendar. His complaints revolve around the level and type of public expenditure (and taxation to finance it). He exclaims, 'O ill-fated country! where the crime of wasting the public money merges into insignificance compared with the mischief its expenditure creates!' (O'Connor 1998: 39). Public expenditure is directed toward the benefit of vested interests with a monopoly on power. O'Connor claims that the large increase in the price of a parliamentary seat plus the increase in tax revenue is clear evidence of the value of rent-seeking.[21]

Deductions for religious instruction and education

He begins his examination of public expenditure by examining the discriminatory and ineffective expenditure on religious instruction for Protestants. He has two major problems with the sixty-fold larger expenditure per capita on Protestant religious instruction compared to that spent on other religions. The first difficulty he has is with its objective. He believes it a folly to force beliefs on others given the diversity of religious beliefs: 'Can the human mind conceive a greater absurdity than that one man should direct what another should believe?' (O'Connor 1998: 40). His second difficulty is, in essence, a critique of State-provided services.

> If those of what are called the learned professions, physicians and lawyers, were paid regular annual stipends, like these Protestant clergy, independent of any exertions they made to deserve them, in vain would you look for the present competition, and unwearied attention to patient and clients.
>
> (O'Connor 1998: 43)

He traces the history of religious movements to illustrate his point noting that they prosper where the clergy is devoted to the aims of the flock rather than when devoted to the State as their paymasters – 'the larger his stipend, the greater his temptation, and his means, to desert his parishioners' (O'Connor 1998: 41).

A related complaint by O'Connor is on the funding of education. He claims that if the fund devoted to education were properly allocated

> it would have been ample for the establishment of parish schools throughout the whole nation, where the poor might be instructed in reading, in writing, and in keeping accounts, paying each master for the number of scholars he really taught; also for the establishment of barony schools, for teaching mathematics, geometry and such other practical sciences are essential to national industry, county schools for those who had shown genius in the graduate schools, and provincial universities for all sorts of instruction – where, by instituting public examinations, and making the higher seminaries judges how far the junior teachers had earned their salaries – by discriminating those schools who had been instructed, from those who had been neglected – the diligence and exertions of the public teachers would have been called forth, by making their industry and their interest go hand in hand.
>
> (O'Connor 1998: 47)

O'Connor's account captures some of the key points made by Smith in Book V, Chapter I in the *Wealth of Nations*. What O'Connor called religious instruction Smith dealt with under the heading *Of the Expense of the Institutions for the Instruction of People of All Ages*. O'Connor's account is not far removed from Smith's account of the disadvantages of paying religions from the public purse in terms of who the clergy serve. Smith says of those funded from the public purse 'while they pay their court in this manner to the higher ranks of life, are very apt to neglect altogether the means of maintaining their influence and authority with the lower' (Smith 1981 [1776] *WoN*: V.I.g.34). Similarities also exist in terms of their views on education as can be seen from the following quotation from Smith.

The teachers of the doctrine which contains this instruction, in the same manner as other teachers, may either depend altogether for their subsistence upon the voluntary contributions of their hearers; or they may derive it from some other fund to which the law of their country may entitle them; such as landed estate, a tythe or lane tax, an established salary or stipend. Their exertion, their zeal and industry, are likely to be much greater in the former situation than in the latter.

(Smith 1981 [1776] *WoN*: V.i.g.1)

Both Smith and O'Connor made a distinction between religious instruction and education but both acknowledged an overlap in coverage. Again, it is clear that O'Connor was influenced by Smith's work. There is little difference between the quotation taken from *The State of Ireland* dealing with stipends to the Protestant clergy and Smith's claims that '[i]n every profession, the exertion of the greater part of those who exercise it, is always in proportion to the necessity they are under of making that exertion' (Smith 1981 [1776] *WoN*: V.i.f.4). Later in Book V Smith asks what can be done to ensure education is provided where it is funded by the public purse. He suggests co-payment, badges for those who achieve a certain standard, and examinations or probations (Smith 1981 [1776] *WoN*: V.i.f.55–7). O'Connor approved of these sentiments.

Defence

O'Connor also complains about the cost of administering the Irish legal system that enforces a law that retards investment and productivity, promotes rent-seeking and by being against the wishes of the majority, is more difficult and expensive to enforce. He claims that public expenditure on law and order within Ireland is the funding of 'sanguinary laws and military outrage, the expense of which are endless, have been substituted for justice, whose expenses are nothing' (O'Connor 1998: 55). He makes a similar claim for the defence of the nation.

With the strongest pretensions to cheap government, with compactness of territory, with insular strength, and without a single act of injustice on our part against any nation upon earth, where is there a country whose expenses are more enormous from such mutilated means, or whose progress in debt is more rapid?

(O'Connor 1998: 58)

Bounties for agricultural produce

The complaints about the contrary nature of public expenditure in *The State of Ireland* also apply to the subsidies for agricultural produce. He claims that they distort the market producing only short-term gains for the landlord and tenant but losses for the consumer and taxpayer. He examines the implication: for the import and export of corn; the resulting distribution of land between tillage and pasture with the associated changes in quantities produced and prices; and, for the welfare effects on landlord, tenant, consumer and taxpayer. His conclusion on the subsidy is that

> the only advantage that could have accrued from this bounty, was a temporary benefit to those tenants whose leases were unexpired when the bounty was granted; whilst the tenants who had to renew, the entire classes of labourers and manufacturers, and the rest of the nation, as producers and consumers, have been, both really and relatively, grievously injured, and the seeds of such mischief have been sown, that the longer they are suffered to grow, the more difficult it will be to destroy them hereafter.
>
> (O'Connor 1998: 51)

Another interesting aspect of O'Connor's analysis of this subsidy is that he is aware of the information problems for individuals in understanding the policy. These information problems allow the introduction of inefficient policies. He describes the subsidy as 'ill-understood' and the result of a 'popular error'. He understood that information problems could cause both market and government failure.

There are parallels between O'Connor's treatment and that in Book V, Chapter IV of the *Wealth of Nations*. Where Smith argues that using a bounty to encourage production by increasing the price is questionable because the 'real value of every other commodity is finally measured and determined by the proportion which its average money price bears to the average money price of corn' (Smith 1981 [1776] *WoN*: IV.v.a.23), O'Connor argues that 'it is impossible to raise the price of corn without raising the price of all the other produce of land, as well pasture as tillage, in alike proportions' (O'Connor 1998: 49). Both argue that the Corn Laws were unlikely to have the desired effect.[22]

The governance problem

According to O'Connor the underlying problem is one of governance. It is the governance of Ireland that reduces the incentives to accumulate capital. It is the governance of Ireland that requires and sanctions wasteful, ineffective and rent-seeking public expenditure. And, it is governance of Ireland that hinders effective solution to these problems. As O'Connor puts it when talking about the lack of incentive for production, 'Creative as this evil has been of the misery and wretchedness of the People of Ireland – destructive as it has proved to their industry – I ask, why have the Government and Legislature of Ireland resisted every attempt to correct or to prevent it?' (O'Connor 1998: 36). His answer to this apparent paradox is that it is not in the interests of those who govern. This is clear from his 'remedy for the evils of our political state' (O'Connor 1998: 66) where he seeks a remedy that will ensure that the interests of the nation are in line with the interests of those who govern. His remedy is democracy. He sought a political system that achieved this end rather than any solution that sought to encourage the rulers to consider the interests of the nation. For O'Connor popular representation was the appropriate solution because it is the only system that is based on self-interest of those who comprise the nation.[23]

His explanation has two parts to it. In the first part he justifies democracy by appeals to the science of 'true political principles' (O'Connor 1998: 67). In the second stage he uses historical analysis to provide empirical support for his contention regarding the superiority of democracy and his claim that self-interest is among the 'primordial principles of human nature' (O'Connor 1998: 68). It is instructive to examine each of these elements in turn.

A governance based on the principle of self-interest

When seeking to justify his remedy 'by establishing the true political principles only' (O'Connor 1998: 67), O'Connor argues that

> as self-interest, tempered by sympathy, is the acknowledged principle which regulates and governs the existence and movements of human action and society, why should we not account for the phenomena which have appeared in one science, as well as those which appear in another, by strict adherence to principle?
>
> (O'Connor 1998: 68)

Here he is clearly invoking the work of Adam Smith. O'Connor advocated the presumption of self-interest in the analysis of politics just as in economics because consistency demanded it. From this basis he claimed that if

> the existing institutions are consonant to the self-interest of the bulk of mankind, in their present advanced stage of knowledge, independence and industry, they will stand: But, if they are repugnant to their self-interest, no force, no device, can uphold them. Convinced of this truth, I will judge of their validity, or fall, by the standard of self-interest of mankind.
>
> (O'Connor 1998: 69)

O'Connor's analysis of the problem and solution to the Irish economic problems follows from this assumption. It was the institutions that required changing because all of mankind is motivated by self-interest and 'a change of men could never cure diseases which require a change of system' (O'Connor 1998: 79). Laws relating to property ownership, transfer and economic use must be judged 'by the standard of the self-interest of mankind' (O'Connor 1998: 69). Laws that promote monopoly ownership of property he judges to be subversive and destructive to the nation because they militate against the self-interest of the vast majority.

O'Connor's analysis applied to specific policies as it did to the whole system of governance. For example, in evaluating the policy of funding specific infrastructure projects by a tax on land, O'Connor explained how the tax was not based on the principles of taxation because it was not based on ability to pay as no account was taken of the quality of the land. O'Connor did not leave his analysis of the tax on this point; rather, he explained why the tax was not based on the ability to pay. He says 'why should we be surprised' (O'Connor 1998: 49) when the grand-jury that decides the tax is selected by the sheriff and that the sheriff is appointed by the wealth landowners.

O'Connor is in no doubt but that his pamphlet was based on what was to become known as *homo-economicus*. In his conclusion to *The State of Ireland* O'Connor says,

> If I have succeeded in demonstrating that self-interest is the governing principle in politics, as well as of all human action; that we are the creature of our wants and desires, and those who possess the means of satisfying those wants and desires must possess the means of influencing the actions and commanding the services of mankind; that those who possess property are possessed of those means, and that those laws which monopolize property invest a few with the power of dictating to the many, which is invariably abused, and a necessity on the part of the many of yielding to such a dictation; I trust I have impressed on the minds of my countrymen that all Reform which would leave the monopoly of property untouched, must prove insufficient, and that the only reformation by which their liberties can be secured is that which destroys the dependence, and establishes the independence of the whole CONSTITUENT BODY.
>
> (O'Connor 1998: 118)

The implication is clear. The economic policies decided upon will be those that are in the self-interest of the polity deciding the policy and, therefore, the solution is to have a polity that serves the bulk of mankind.

The problem of the primogeniture – an evolutionary or revolutionary solution?

In O'Connor's historical analysis he states that traditionally the interests of those who owned and worked the land were aligned.[24] They were aligned by economic circumstance when land was the only *effective* property. However, O'Connor believed circumstances were now changed. New forms of property brought about by new production techniques and the capital markets, and the sale of lands by those occupying positions in the Lords meant that they now held less than a one-hundredth part of property. Hence, there was a need to reform the political structure.

The interests of the people and the ruler were also aligned by the people who imposed political constraints on rulers as the Anglo-Saxons did on Alfred. These constraints were based on the division of power – what O'Connor calls a *vital principle*. He says that the true definition of the constitution will be found that a total disconnection between the Crown and the Commons, and between the Lords and the Commons, together with a never-ceasing distrust and jealousy of both Crown and Lords on the part of the Commons, was the *vital principle* by which the Constitution was *originally generated, afterwards nurtured, and finally established at the Revolution*.

(O'Connor 1998: 88, emphasis in the original)

However, he argues that the traditional balance of power was destroyed by 'the great Revolution in property and in mind' (O'Connor (1998: 89),[25] the result being that 'the gigantic growth of Democracy has totally subverted those ancient relations between the parts of the constitution by which it was formerly balanced' (O'Connor 1998: 91). The Lords no longer represented all propertied interests and many of the seats in the Commons were corruptly purchased.

For O'Connor the increasing extent of the market due to trade, the associated division of labour, and the spread of ideas was crucial to the evolution of political power.

Behold how the Marnier's Compass has encouraged the industry of nations, by enabling the most distant to exchange their surplus produce, one with the other. See how the same quantity of labour produces so much more of the necessaries and conveniences of life now, than before those machines and engines for the abridgment of labour were known, or the present vast division of labour had been established. See what numerous ingenious classes have been introduced into society, and how the condition of the ancient classes have been improved.

(O'Connor 1998: 121)

O'Connor's analysis seems to owe much to Book III the *Wealth of Nations* – 'Of the different Progress of Opulence in different Nations'. In the first chapter Smith talks about the natural inclination towards progress. He argues that if these natural human inclinations were not thwarted by human institutions then 'the progressive wealth and increase of the towns would, in every political society, be consequential, and in proportion to the improvement and cultivation of the territory or country' (Smith 1981 [1776] *WoN*: III.i.4). Smith then traces the discouragement of agriculture throughout history. He explained how the introduction of primogeniture and entails prevented land being broken into smaller and smaller parcels of unproductive land. Smith argued that when 'land was considered as the means, not of subsistence merely, but of power and protection, it was thought better that it should descend undivided to one' (Smith 1981 [1776] *WoN*: III.ii.3) but the conditions that made primogeniture and entails reasonable were past – '[l]aws frequently continue in force long after the circumstances, which first gave occasion to them, and which could alone render them reasonable, are no more' (Smith 1981 [1776] *WoN*: III.ii.4). Smith was in little doubt that primogeniture and entails diminished the productivity of the agriculture even though they were partly offset by the laws that favoured the yeomanry. These latter laws 'contributed more to the present grandeur of England than all their boasted regulations of commerce taken together' (Smith 1981 [1776] *WoN*: III.ii.14).

O'Connor's reference to the source of change being 'the Marnier's Compass' and 'the industry of nations' are the same as Smith's 'commerce' and 'manufactures'. 'But what all the violence of the feudal institutions could never have effected, the silent and insensible operation of foreign commerce and manufactures gradually brought about' (Smith 1981 [1776] *WoN*: III.ii.10). Both agree on the implications of this increased commerce and manufactures. Smith says that 'for the gratification of the most childish, the meanest and the most sordid of all vanities, they gradually bartered their whole power and authority' (Smith 1981 [1776] *WoN*: III.iv.10), whereas O'Connor says 'when from the introduction of luxuries and vanities, those great proprietors have been tempted to part with their lands' (O'Connor 1998: 90). The difference between Smith and O'Connor was that while Smith argued his case against primogeniture O'Connor was not willing to wait for the evolutionary solution but, instead, sought a revolutionary solution.

The last section of *The State of Ireland* is titled *Defence of the United People of Ireland*. Here, within the constraints of a pamphleteer in late eighteenth-century Ireland, he justifies the move towards revolution. He does this with a series of claims designed to lay the blame for the conflict at the door of Pitt and those who have sought to monopolise power. By contrast he supports the behaviour of the United Irishmen by references to Camden, Selden and Locke, and to the willingness of their predecessors to impose constraints on their rulers.[26]

O'Connor, Smith and Burke

There can be little doubt but that *The State of Ireland* is heavily influenced by the *Wealth of Nations*. O'Connor had read Smith and the previous section demonstrated some clear parallels between the works. It would have been unthinkable for O'Connor to lay claim to explaining the economic conditions of Ireland without some explicit or implicit nod in the direction of Smith. Equally, it would not have been possible for O'Connor to raise the issues of democracy and revolution without reference to the Irish author of *Reflections on the Revolution in France* – Edmund Burke.

It is useful to briefly locate Burke relative to Smith before locating O'Connor relative to them both. A detailed account of the similarities between Smith and Burke can be found in Winch (1996).[27] Winch (1996) claims that Burke and Smith are closest in their views on the practical governance issues faced by Britain – although the underlying reasons for the similarities of these views differed. Both rejected the contractarian view of government being presented by Locke and others. Both saw very limited circumstances where the rights of resistance and revolution were justified. Both believed that 'the loss of regal government' was potentially not in the interests of both America and Ireland. Smith viewed the issue on America in a manner akin to cost-benefit analysis whilst Burke's views on Ireland were based on the perceived behaviour of the Irish parliament.

Burke and Smith differed most in terms of their views on primogeniture and entail. It is difficult to reconcile Burke's views, particularly those expressed in *Reflections on the Revolution in France*, with those of Smith outlined above. Although Burke was far from blind to the questionable origins of the power and prosperity of the aristocracy, as presented in *A Letter to a Nobel Lord*, his defence of existing property rights and laws overrode everything else (Canavan 1995). Burke's reverence for the past lies in stark contrast to Smith's preference for the present.

> They [Entails] are founded upon the most absurd of all suppositions, the supposition that every successive generation of men have not an equal right to the earth, and to all that it possesses; but that the property of the present generation should be restrained and regulated according to the fancy of those who died perhaps five hundred years ago.
>
> (Smith 1981 [1776] *WoN*: III.ii.6)

On matters of economics there are certainly some similarities between Burke and Smith. Whilst Burke's economics is woven into most of his writings; he contributes two pieces that could be said to deal explicitly with economic issues as their primary focus. Towards the end of his life he wrote *Thoughts and Details on Scarcity*. This dealt with the issues surrounding the shortages in corn. Prendergast (2000: 270) argues that '[o]ne outstanding feature of *Thoughts and Details on Scarcity* is the emphasis it placed on the amount of information required for effective intervention in the market'. Smith had expressed similar views as outlined above in Section IV and explained in greater detail in Prendergast (1987). Interestingly O'Connor discusses the information problems individuals had in understanding the Corn Laws, however, there is no suggestion that this came from Burke.

Burke's other foray into explicitly economic matters came in his *On Economical Reform* speech in 1780. Like Smith, Burke was aware of the damage that could be done by inappropriate and corrupt public expenditure. Unlike Smith, Burke was concerned primarily with the damage done to the political system whereas Smith was primarily concerned with the damage done to the incentives to accumulate capital. Burke was more explicit in his suggested remedies for such an eventuality than Smith (see Considine 2002 and 2006a). In detailing the corrupt expenditure O'Connor was closer to his countryman than to Smith.

The remaining area of interest for any location of O'Connor relative to Burke and Smith is on religious matters. It is only a slight exaggeration to say that Burke saw the natural order of human interaction to be divinely ordained while Smith saw the natural order arising from the desires and inclinations of the being of this world. While both supported tolerance for minority beliefs they did so for different reasons. Smith was critical of State support for, or suppression of, religion because of the incentives it distorted for its human practitioners. Burke's views on religion were like Smith's views on liberty – he was not concerned with governance provided the idea of divinity (liberty) was accepted.

The similarities between *The State of Ireland* and the *Wealth of Nations* are presented in the fourth section. It is, therefore, not surprising to find O'Connor is located closer to Smith than Burke on many issues. O'Connor agrees with Smith on primogeniture but goes further than Smith, or Burke, in recommending revolution.[28] O'Connor takes Burke to task for his criticism of the French Revolution when he says 'I am aware that the public mind has been dragooned and deluded by a man notorious for the total abandonment of every principle which has recommended him to the public confidence' (O'Connor 1998: 67). He is also closer to Smith when he appeals to present interests rather than institutions rooted in time when he holds 'in contempt and detestation every institution, however rooted in time, or supported by force or corruption, which is incompatible with the liberty, happiness and interests of Man' (O'Connor 1998: 75).

O'Connor is probably closest to Burke in the manner in which both of them detail the damage done to the governance of a country by inefficient, inappropriate and corrupt public expenditure. Where Burke complained about the undue influence of the Crown driven by his concern for the power of the landowning Whigs, O'Connor complained about its implications for prosperity in a manner similar to Smith. However, Burke was concerned with the danger of revolution and sought to promote measures to avoid it, whereas O'Connor advocated revolution. It is important to bear witness to their targeted audiences when considering their views. Essentially Burke was writing for the English to convince them to keep Ireland happy, whilst O'Connor was writing for the Irish not so as to pacify them but to instigate revolt.

O'Connor is probably located somewhere between Burke and Smith on religion. As was outlined earlier, he used similar arguments to Smith against State support of religion. Like Burke he advocated equality for Catholics. However, he argued that Catholic emancipation 'must prove wholly inadequate to establishment of our National Liberty' (O'Connor 1998: 67).

To summarise, O'Connor was closer to Smith in his analysis but the Irish context meant that his application of Smith's thinking and methods brought him closer to Burke on the applications – if not the solutions. Burke has been criticised for his failure to follow his arguments in support of the American colonists to the logical conclusion of separation. O'Connor could not be criticised on these grounds.

O'Connor's spiritual legacy of radical reform

It is probably fair to say that the ideas of Arthur O'Connor as presented in *The State of Ireland* were forgotten following the failure of the United Irishmen in 1798 and the Act of Union in 1801. Black (1950) makes the point that the economic grievances that were the root of the commercial complaints of the Irish during the last quarter of the eighteenth century became less of an issue of governance towards the end of the century. It might be also pointed out that many of the complaints of O'Connor and Burke involved the activities of the Irish parliament. Union removed many of these complaints. The failure of 1798 plus the ongoing antagonism between Britain and France effectively ruled out further talk of independence or revolution. This effectively left Catholic emancipation the only cause around which the Irish, under the leadership of Daniel O'Connell, could gather and the Whigs could offer united support (Dudley Edwards 1975). It was only after 1815 that repeal of the Union and economic issues could make their way back to the table but by that time Catholic emancipation was the burning issue. Economic issues remained important to Irish affairs during the nineteenth century but they were almost always overshadowed by political issues. O'Connell and Catholic emancipation dominated the first third of the century. Parnell and home rule dominated the latter third. While O'Connell moved on from emancipation to repeal after 1830, his failure to achieve this objective plus his lack of thought on economic issue resulted in his failure in the 1840s (Dudley Edwards 1975). Parnell might have surfed the wave of agrarian discontent but as time passed his primary focus was home rule (Lyons 1977).

In this context the legacy of Arthur O'Connor was his radicalism on economic issues as perhaps best personified by his illegitimate son William Conner and his nephew Feargus O'Connor. William and Feargus sought reform on economic issues and both proved a thorn in the side of O'Connell. Feargus was the son of Roger and he inherited much of the ancestral lands in County Cork from his uncle Robert. He seems to have engaged in a less than intensive study of the law at Gray's Inn, London during the 1820s and applied successfully for admission to the Irish Bar in 1831 (Read and Glasgow 1961: 22). In 1822 Feargus printed a pamphlet with the same title as that of his uncle. Feargus's attempt has been described as 'a series of disjointed and unoriginal though stringent observations upon landlords and clergy' (Read and Glasgow 1961: 25). Little is known about his political activity until he campaigned for election following the Reform Act of 1832 and the groundswell of support for O'Connell. His success in the election, and his membership of the Repeal party, was short-lived. Within months of his electoral success he quarrelled with O'Connell on the issue of repeal and by 1835 was removed as an MP following a complaint about his financial eligibility for the position.

The career of Feargus bore many of the hallmarks of his uncle's career. After the loss of his seat Feargus became involved in radical politics. He moved to England and became a radical agitator. He started up a newspaper which he called the *Northern Star* and used it to gain support for his cause and that of the Chartists.[29] From his base in Manchester, Feargus made a number of attempts to unite the Irish and British working class but to little avail due to the hold O'Connell had on the Irish tenant farmer.[30] The concerns of the British working class with industrial wages were different to the Irish concern with agrarian issues. The difficulties aligning the interests of both groups can be seen in the opposition to the Corn Laws. In so far as he was interested in economic issues,[31] O'Connell supported the Anti-Corn Law League whereas Feargus opposed the Anti-Corn Law League for much of the time on the grounds that manufacturers might reduce wages further if corn prices fell. It was only in the mid-1840s that Feargus changed his mind on the corn laws after seeing this course pursued by Richard Cobden.

In July 1847 Feargus was returned as the second Member of Parliament for Nottingham. His return coincided with a downturn in economic fortunes in Britain and renewed popularity of the Chartists. With famine in Ireland and revolution in Europe, tensions increased in Britain. Circulation of the *Northern Star* increased in England and 'Marx and Engels promised to extend the circulation of the *Northern Star* on the continent and to have extracts translated in as many continental newspapers as possible' (Read and Glasgow 1961: 128). In the excitement Feargus and the Chartists organised a demonstration for Kennington Common intended as the highpoint of a new campaign. As the people gathered the authorities approached Feargus and it appears he lost his nerve and called off the demonstration. With the loss of nerve came a loss of credibility and a swift deterioration of his physical and mental health so that by the 1850 he lost his seat and it seems his mind.[32]

During his time as an MP for Cork and during the late 1840s Feargus attempted schemes at improving the lot of the tenant farmer. Arthur's illegitimate son, William Conner, did likewise on his lands in County Kildare. William Conner's focus was on agrarian concerns and to that end he followed his father's lead by producing a series of pamphlets.[33] He came to public attention in 1832 when he published *The Speech of William Conner Esq. Against Rackrents, etc.* in which he argued that the principle of regulating the price of monopoly articles should be extended to land. In 1840 he published another pamphlet titled *The Axe Laid at the Root of Irish Oppression* which, when delivered as a speech in 1842 in Mountmellick, brought prosecution for sedition and a six-month jail sentence. It would appear that incarceration was a good O'Connor family tradition! On his release from jail he addressed a letter to the 1843 Devon Commission titled *A Letter to the Right Honourable the Earl of Devon on the Rackrent System.*

The central arguments of these pamphlets are that because land was in limited supply it should be regulated like any other monopoly article. This monopoly power gave landowners the power to extract most of the surplus earned by labour. O'Brien (1923: 284) makes the point that William sought the regulation of private property because the abuse of the institution would undermine it. As a supporter of private property William Conner clashed with James Fintan Lalor and others among the group of Young Irelanders who favoured revolution. His proposed system of valuation was later adopted by the Tenants' League and 'was the foundation of Gladstone's legislation' (O'Brien 1923: 287).

William also clashed with O'Connell. Whereas Feargus clashed with O'Connell over the political loyalty and organisation of the Irish, and the appropriate political strategy, William confronted O'Connell on his lack of commitment to agrarian reform. In September 1843 William confronted O'Connell at a Dublin Repeal Association meeting on the issue. O'Connell sought to gain approval for his political/legal strategy but William Conner wanted a complete rent strike. William warned that if O'Connell persisted then the following year 'millions of men, women and children will be starved for the want of crops' (Bew 2007: 162). However, William was removed from the meeting and

O'Connell carried the day. It seemed that it was to be William's fate to have his ideas ignored and when others later came up with similar solutions to the agrarian concerns he was seldom credited. O'Brien says that

> his name was not even once mentioned in the whole course of the proceedings of the Bessborough Commission, whose recommendations, hailed as a masterpiece of wisdom and enlightenment at the time, were nothing more or less than the suggestions which Conner had put forward precisely half a century before.
>
> (O'Brien 1923: 289)

Both William Conner and Feargus O'Connor inherited the spirit of radicalism that had characterised Arthur O'Connor. Feargus maintained the symbols of Arthur's political campaigning via his production of his version of *The State of Ireland*, his election to parliament, and his establishment of another *Northern Star* newspaper. William inherited Arthur's attraction for producing pamphlets on economic issues. Like Arthur he focused attention on the monopoly aspects of land. Arthur saw the monopoly ownership of land conveying monopoly political power and resulting in economic decline. William saw the limited supply of land as conveying monopoly power resulting in the owners extracting the surplus from labour. Given the earlier quotation from John Stuart Mill, and the analysis of the similarities between *The State of Ireland* and the *Wealth of Nations*, it would seem that there was greater originality in the work of William.

Governance and growth: the relevance of *The State of Ireland*

The relevance of Arthur O'Connor for twenty-first century economics can be gleamed from an examination of the evolution of a widely used graduate macroeconomic textbook – David Romer's *Advanced Macroeconomics*. In his preface to the second edition in 2001 Romer writes

> [t]he second half of Chapter 3, which examines cross-country income differences, bears no resemblance to the corresponding material in the first edition: the evidence and ideas developed in the five years since I wrote the first edition have cause me to completely rethink my views on that subject.
>
> (Romer 2001: xix)

The biggest difference was the inclusion of a section on Social Infrastructure that 'tells us about the roles of physical-capital accumulation, human-capital accumulation, and output for given quantities of capital in cross-country income differences' (Romer 2001: 143). Romer (2001: 144) argues that growth is enhanced by: fiscal policies that encourage capital accumulation; institutions, legal systems and policies that encourage competition and limit monopoly power; and, a system that limits rent-seeking including that by the government itself. O'Connor could not have agreed more. A new sub-section is added to the Social Infrastructure section in the third edition of *Advanced Macroeconomics* and it is titled 'Empirical Applications: Geography, Colonialism, and Economic Development'. Drawing on the work of 2005 John Bates Clark medal winner, Daron Acemoglu and others, Romer discusses the issues of absentee owners of the factors of production and the extent to which the institutions of the enlightenment were transferred to the colonies as key determinants of economic performance. These issues are central to *The State of Ireland*.

Broadly speaking, the social infrastructure literature arose as a response to difficulties explaining differences in the economic performance in different countries. Standard growth theory as captured in the Solow growth model, and its various upgrades, has difficulty explaining the lack of convergence between countries. The theory suggests that capital should flow from countries with high amounts of capital per person and high income per person to poor countries. This does not happen as often or as quickly as theory might suggest.

Romer (2006) describes social infrastructure as institutions that bring private return into line with social return. Where there is a difference between private and social returns then individuals are more likely to engage in consumption rather than investment and more likely to engage in rent-seeking rather than productive activities. The empirical evidence on social infrastructure is usually derived by one of three methods: large-scale econometric studies (Acemoglu and Robinson 2000); historical studies (North and Thomas 1973; Olson 1982); and natural experiments (Olson 1996). O'Connor used a version of the natural experiment approach when he compared the Irish situation to countries of similar size but with different governance.

The literature suggests that the determinants of social infrastructure are the distribution of political power, beliefs and ideas, and culture. The importance of the distribution of political power is explained in Olson (1993). In this paper Mancur Olson uses the industrial organisation structures like monopoly and perfect competition to examine the structure of political power. Monopoly is aligned with dictatorship. Democracy is aligned with perfect competition. Autocracy is closer to the monopoly end of the spectrum. This is exactly what O'Connor did 200 years earlier.[34] Whereas the conclusions in Olson (1993) were deduced from economic theory, North and Thomas (1973) came to a similar conclusion based on a comparison of the economic performances of the absolute monarchies of Spain and France and the more democratic regimes of Britain and the Netherlands.[35] O'Connor presented an eighteenth century version of economic theory and empirical evidence.

There are also some parallels between O'Connor's work and that of DeSoto (2001). Both argue that the inability of individuals to access capital is due to an inefficient set of institutions that govern the transfer of property rights.

To summarise, the authors know of no work pre-dating *The State of Ireland* that evaluates, using the self-interested individual from economic theory, the governance of a country and the implications of that governance for the economic performance of the country. If the authors are correct then O'Connor's work deserves greater attention in the history of economic thought.

Conclusion

The State of Ireland is a pamphlet explaining the economic conditions of Ireland at the end of the eighteenth century using the framework provided by Adam Smith. At times its revolutionary purpose detracts from its economic analysis. This economic analysis is unique in the conclusions drawn from application to the Irish situation. O'Connor's emphasis on the relationship between governance and economic growth is worth re-examining especially given the recent upsurge in interest in this relationship in the macroeconomic literature.

Notes

1 The authors are grateful to Professor Luke Gibbons (University of Notre Dame) for directing them towards O'Connor's work and for the comments of Dr Renee Prendergast (Queens University, Belfast) on earlier drafts.

2 Livesey (O'Connor 1998: 9) suggests O'Connor was obsessed with Smith and quotes correspondence between Lord Wycombe and Lady Holland where Wycombe says that O'Connor 'talks a few pages out of Adam Smith in lieu of conversation'.

3 Hayter Hames (2001: 35) says that he 'had read *The Wealth of Nations* by Adam Smith before he went to college and was so impressed by "economical science", its lucid exposition by Smith, that he returned to it again and again, determined to master all it contained'.

4 This limited experience was to form the bases of his later claims to military experience in discussions with the French.

5 Quoted in O'Brien (1923: 289).

6 The French Revolution threatened Pitt's parliamentary support and to divide the Whigs. In 1794 conservative Whigs opened negotiations on a coalition with Pitt. As part of the agreement the Whigs gained control of Irish affairs with Earl Fitzwilliam becoming Lord Lieutenant. Fitzwilliam's attempted reforms led to his being recalled to London. The result was the alienation of Irish reformers.

7 Connolly (2000: 2–21) explains how it is difficult to separate the influence of ideas and more personal ambition in the general context of eighteenth century Ireland.

8 Lecky (1903: 255) says that O'Connor was 'rash, obstinate and arrogant, very incapable of waiving his personal pretensions for a public end'.

9 A similar view of Tone as a person who turned revolutionary after their desire to serve the administration was rebutted is presented in Bew (2007: 3).

10 Wolfe Tone was also in France at the time seeking French help.

11 The counties of Antrim and Down were opposition Whig counties and also east Ulster had exceptionally high literary levels.

12 Whelan (1996: 66).

13 Agnew (1999: 298).

14 The behaviour of O'Connor and his colleagues in the plea-bargaining process can be interpreted in their favour or against them. Regardless, O'Connor's involvement embarrassed Fox and the English Whigs given their testimony for him after his capture in Margate in February.

15 See Curtin (1994) and Whelan (1996) for a more general discussion of the United Irishmen's involvement in popular political culture. Whelan (1996) argues that the use of newspapers and pamphlets brought the debate beyond the elites by making the material more accessible in terms of language and price.

16 Small (2002: 1) lists five languages and traditions: 'Protestant superiority, ancient constitutionalism, commercial grievance, classical republicanism, and natural rights'.

Connolly (2000: 14–20) lists civic humanism or classical republicanism, British constitutionalism, and protestant patriotism and corporatism.

17 The biggest difference was that the revolutionaries put nationalism before religion and the counter-revolutionaries did the reverse Whelan (1996: 108).

18 The writings of Charles O'Conor contributed to this strand of argument.

19 Olson (1996) uses this natural experiment approach when he asks why countries divided for political reasons faired so differently after the division, e.g. East and West Germany, North and South Korea.

20 He describes Ireland as 'a country where its most important branches are made to bend under the weight of the fees and exactions of the Officers of the Revenue' (O'Connor 1998: 36). He also notes the lack of political representation for that taxation in a manner similar to that used in the American revolution.

21 An Irish seat in the House of Commons for life could be had for £500 prior to the establishment of the Irish parliament. Yet, a seat in the Irish parliament cost £3,000 for eight years (O'Connor 1998: 58).

22 While Smith's treatment is far more comprehensive and includes a digression on both the Corn Trade and Corn Laws, Smith's account is not without its problems as was pointed out at the time by James Anderson (see Prendergast 1987).

23 He also argued that the Fitzwilliam affair proved that bringing the interests of those with a monopoly in property and political power into line with the rest of the nation was not possible (O'Connor 1998: 109).

24 O'Connor discusses the political structure of England rather than Ireland because he claims that even that superior structure is in need of reform.

25 The source of the revolution in 'the state of property, and knowledge, arising from the arts, from education and commerce, which have made such rapid progress since the invention of the marnier's compass and the press' (O'Connor 1998: 77).

26 'It is to OURSELVES that we must be indebted for whatever freedom we have, or shall ever possess' (O'Connor 1998: 113).

27 Accounts of Burke's political economy can be found in Prendergast (2000) and Canavan (1995). Considine (2002, 2006a and 2006b) explain Burke's views on how the State should be constrained by constitutional means including fiscal rules.

28 Although it has been suggested that Burke 'verged on complicity' with O'Connor and Tone (Bew 2007: 22).

29 The *Northern Star* printed accounts of the lives of famous radicals including Arthur O'Connor. Its contents had Feargus jailed for sedition.

30 His publication of *A Series of Letters from Feargus O'Connor to Daniel O'Connell* in 1936–1937 probably contributed to O'Connell's ire with him.

31 Dudley Edwards (1975: 75–6) claims that O'Connell's obsession with politics prevented him from acting responsibly on economic issues.

32 It is perhaps poignant to note that neither man's revolutionary vision was achieved though perhaps it could be said that the Chartist 'revolution' of 1848 was more of a failure than that of the United Irishmen some half a century earlier.

33 This section is based on O'Brien (1923).

34 Interestingly, both Olson and O'Connor use the 'bandit' in their analogies.

35 A similar conclusion was reached by DeLong and Shleifer (1993) and DeLong (2000).

Bibliography

Acemoglu, D. and Robinson, J.A. (2000) 'Political Losers as a Barrier to Economic Development', *American Economic Review* 90 (May): 126–30.

Acemoglu, D. and Robinson, J.A. (2006) *Economic Origins of Dictatorship and Democracy*, New York: Cambridge University Press.

Agnew, J. (ed.) (1999) *The Drennan – McTier Letters, 1794–1801*, Dublin: Irish Manuscripts Commission.

Bew, P. (2007) *Ireland: The Politics of Enmity 1789–2006*, London: Oxford University Press.

Black, R.D.C. (1950) 'Theory and Policy in Anglo-Irish Trade Relations 1775–1800', *Journal of the Statistical and Social Inquiry Society of Ireland* (April): 312–26.

Canavan, F. (1995) *The Political Economy of Edmund Burke*, New York: Fordham University Press.

Connolly, S.J. (ed.) (2000) *Political Ideas in Eighteenth-Century Ireland*, Dublin: Four Courts Press.

Considine, J. (2002) 'Budgetary Institutions and Fiscal Discipline: Edmund Burke's Insightful Contribution', *The European Journal of History of Economic Thought* 9(4): 591–607.

Considine, J. (2006a) James M. Buchanan and Edmund Burke: Opposite Sides of the Same Fiscal Constitutional Coin', *Journal of History of Economic Thought* 28(2): 243–57.

Considine, J. (2006b) 'Constitutional Interpretation: Edmund Burke and James Buchanan and their 18th Century Intellectual Roots', *Constitutional Political Economy* 17 (June): 71–85.

Curtin, N.J. (1994) *The United Irishmen: Popular Politics in Ulster and Dublin, 1791–1798*, Oxford: Clarendon Press.

De Long, J. Bradford (2000) 'Overstrong Against Thyself: War, the State, and Growth in Europe on the Eve of the Industrial Revolution', in Mancur Olson Jr and Satu Kahkonen (eds) *A Not-So-Dismal Science*, Oxford: Oxford University Press, Ch. 5.

De Long, J. Bradford and Shleifer, A. (1993) 'Princes and Merchants: European City Growth before the Industrial Revolution', *Journal of Law and Economics* 30(2): 671–702.

De Soto, H. (2001) *The Mystery of Capital*, London: Black Swan.

Duddy, T. (2002) *A History of Irish Thought*, London: Routledge.

Dudley Edwards, R. (1975) *Daniel O'Connell and his World*, London: Thames and Hudson.

Gibbons, L. (2003) *Edmund Burke and Ireland*, London: Cambridge University Press.

Hayter Hames, J. (2001) *Arthur O'Connor United Irishman*, Cork: The Collins Press.

Lecky, W.E.H. (1903) *A History of Ireland in the Eighteenth Century*, Volume IV, London: Longmans, Green and Co.

Lyons, F.S.L. (1977) *Charles Stuart Parnell*, London: Collins.

MacDermot, F. (1967) 'Arthur O'Connor', *Irish Historical Studies* XV: 48–69.

Madden, R.R. (1858) *The United Irishmen, their Lives and Times*, Dublin: J.Madden.

North, D. and Thomas, R.P. (1973) *The Rise of the Western World*, Cambridge: Cambridge University Press.

O'Brien, G. (1923) 'William Conner', *Studies* XII: 279–89.

O'Connor, A. [1798] (1998) *The State of Ireland*, J. Livesey (ed.), Dublin: Lilliput Press.

Olson, M. Jr (1982) *The Rise and Decline of Nations*, New Haven, CT: Yale University Press.

Olson, M. Jr (1993) 'Dictatorship, Democracy, and Development', *American Political Science Review* 87 (September): 567–76.

Olson, M. Jr (1996) 'Big Bills Left on the Sidewalk: Why Some Nations Are Rich, and Others Poor', *Journal of Economic Perspectives* 10(2): 3–24.

Persson, T. and Tabellini, G. (2005) *The Economic Effect of Constitutions*, London: MIT Press.

Prendergast, R. (1987) 'James Anderson's Political Economy – his Influence on Smith and Malthus', *Scottish Journal of Political Economy* 34(4): 388–409.

Prendergast, R. (2000) 'The Political Economy of Edmund Burke', in Antoin E. Murphy and Renee Prendergast (eds) *Contributions to the History of Economic Thought: Essays in Honour of R.D.C. Black*, London: Routledge, Ch. 13.

Read, D. and Glasgow, E. (1961) *Feargus O'Connor: Irishman and Chartist*, London: Edward Arnold Ltd.

Romer, D. (1996) *Advanced Macroeconomics*, London: McGraw-Hill.

Romer, D. (2001) *Advanced Macroeconomics*, 2nd edn, London: McGraw-Hill.

Romer, D. (2006) *Advanced Macroeconomics*, 3rd edn, London: McGraw-Hill.

Small, S. (2003) *Political Thought in Ireland, 1776–1798: Republicanism, Patriotism, and Radicalism*, Oxford: Clarendon Press.

Smith, A. [1776] (1981) *An Inquiry into the Nature and Causes of the Wealth of Nations*, R.H. Campbell and A.S. Skinner (eds), London: Liberty Classics.

Tillyard, S. (1997) *Citizen Lord: Edward Fitzgerald 1763–1798*, London: Chatto & Windus.

Whelan, K. (1996) *The Tree of Liberty*, Cork: Cork University Press.

Winch, D. (1996) *Riches and Poverty: An Intellectual History of Political Economy in Britain 1750–1834*, Cambridge: Cambridge University Press.

Part II

The classical era

The rise and fall of laissez-faire

5 Value and distribution theory at Trinity College Dublin, 1831–1844

Laurence Moss

In this chapter, I argue that between 1831 and 1844, at Trinity College Dublin (TCD), an articulate and original series of young Irish lawyers took to the lectern to explain the basic principles of the new discipline of political economy. The selection of the successive holders of what I shall call the "Whately chair" of political economy were made by the Board of Trinity College and required the applicants to sit for a written examination (Murphy 1984). Young lawyers awaiting their call to the bar were allowed to teach while waiting. Some of the best minds applied and received this appointment. Starting with Mountifort Longfield and followed by Isaac Butt and James Anthony Lawson, a sequence of lawyer economists pushed the boundaries of British economic reasoning quite a distance and pointed towards a genuine "market process approach" to the problems surrounding value theory and the determination of the distributive shares among the three great classes in society. Each was paid to deliver no less than nine lectures each year and published at least one of these lectures each year of his tenure. The appointment as Professor of Political Economy was limited to one five-year term.

We have the published lectures but not too much else. Still, based on this limited evidence, it is possible to make out the contours of what their thinking was on many issues and at the same time to extrapolate the direction of their thinking. Most excitingly, they were committed to the discipline of economics and they shared the point of view of Richard Whately, the remarkable Anglican archbishop to Dublin, that political economy was an important science and deserved a place in the modern university (Murphy 1984).

Richard Whately (1786–1863) was the catalyst, entrepreneur, and energizer behind these fruitful developments at TCD. He came to Dublin from Oxford with a number of projects in mind. As far as economics was concerned, the late 1820s and early 1830s were tumultuous times. The First Reform Bill in England of 1832 and subsequent bills extended the franchise to the middle class. The lower working class remained disenfranchised but hardly without a voice. Their behavior and welfare were hotly debated, especially in the months leading up to the 1834 New Poor Law for Ireland, which transferred responsibility for the poor from the parishes to the workhouses. And there was the constant fear that the workers might resort to violent revolution as the landowners and established families worried might happen and believed had already happened in France decades earlier. Indeed, in 1834, as Longfield was completing his first set of lectures, a group of farm workers in Dorset were arrested for "combining" and sentenced to seven years in jail amidst much controversy and discussion. The fear of machine breaking and general worker unrest was real and a constant topic for discussion in Britain (Berg 1980: 1–19). In order to smooth things in Ireland, Whately supported the creation of a regular chair of Political Economy at TCD.

One important purpose of political economy was to promote social stability by correcting errors and misunderstandings that had "crept" into the discipline and by drawing out implications that might help guide both public policy and public understanding. That was Whately's aspiration for the chairholders. The teaching of economics was tied directly to the need to address arguments about the fairness of capitalism and the restoration of social order. Before I offer an interpretation of the substantive content of their economics, it is important to distinguish the Whately group of university professors from what Salim Rashid and others have named the "Dublin School of development economics."

The older Dublin school of economics

The study of economic ideas and especially ideas about economic development had a long and rich development in Ireland *before the 1830s*. There was the towering George Berkeley, Bishop of Cloyne, who in the first part of the eighteenth century set out to sketch a program to eliminate poverty in his diocese (Waterman 2004). Other writers in Ireland included Jonathan Swift—the inspiration for the school—and Thomas Prior, Samuel Madden, and Arthur Dobbs (Rashid 1988: 348). According to Professor Rashid, "[these] Irish economists were a *school*, in that the major economists were personally known to each other and they tried to tackle the same set of problems within a common framework" (Rashid 1988: 362). Those issues included strategies to elevate living standards in Ireland so that it no longer would rank as one of the poorest of all civilized countries in Europe.

One hundred years later, in 1830, Ireland remained pitifully poor. My thesis is that at TCD, between 1833 and 1844, a *second* Dublin school took root. This was a development that took place entirely within the old walls of this venerable university, not entirely without precedent. The situation is analogous perhaps to the remarkable University of Salamanca that existed in Spain after the great theologian Vitoria began lecturing in 1534 on matters of money and commerce to the educated Spanish merchants trading with the new world (Grice-Hutchinson 1952: 42). Vitoria was followed by a number of important theologians who tackled ideas about commerce, property rights, and value theory. Value theory and the pricing of the roads and bridges was at the heart of the later discovery of the engineers at the celebrated École Nationale des Ponts et Chaussées who in conversation with each other (and in numerous articles and government reports) molded the essential ideas of Marshallian price theory, especially after 1815, during the Restoration period in France (Ekelund, Jr and

Hebert 1999). And finally, I mention the Vienna school of economics that centered around the brilliant work of Carl Menger, Eugen von Boehm-Bawerk, Friedrich von Wieser, Ludwig von Mises, and others that lasted at the University of Vienna for decades, until the advent of National Socialism in Austria (Mises 1969). As with these other university situations, the occupants of the Whately chair knew each other, read each other's published work, and tried to tackle a common set of problems with a common framework of analysis. By Rashid's definition, we have a definite school of thought. Furthermore, it is a school of thought within a particular university, TCD. The context in which this development took place needs to be understood.

In England, the remarkable advances in economics, especially in the writings of Thomas Malthus and David Ricardo, stirred up a firestorm of protest among the theologians. The fledgling study of "political economy" had earned a reputation among theologians as "hostile to religion" (Waterman 2004: 113, 118). In the first version of his population theory (1798), Malthus suggested that God made human misery and tragedy *necessary* for social order. Later theologians, friendlier to economics, would sketch several intellectual arguments to calm matters down and show that the major teachings of the new field of political economy could be made compatible with theology and that the hysterical responses of many theologians were out of order. Among these theological peacemakers was Whately.

Richard Whately

Whately first arrived in Dublin in 1831 from Oxford University. At Oxford, Whately earned his degrees and stayed on as a lecturer of great stature, earning a reputation as the foremost teacher in a Socratic mold (MacMahon 2005: 11). When he was appointed Archbishop of Dublin in 1831, Whately was immersed in the study of political economy and had just completed the delivery of his first and only set of lectures as the Drummond Professor of Political Economy at Oxford University that Spring semester (Whately 1966 [1832]). He was already well into the second set of his Oxford lectures when he was suddenly called to service in Dublin. This was as complete a surprise to the orthodox faculty at Oxford as it was to Whately himself. He graciously accepted this call to duty and the new lifestyle in Dublin that it would require.

Once in Dublin, Whately used his influence and part of his salary to fund a chair at Trinity College Dublin. The conditions of the chair were similar to the Drummond chair at Oxford. The first occupant of the Drummond chair at Oxford had been Whately's own pupil, Nassau Senior, in 1826. It is possible that Whately had some influence on this appointment as he would have on the later appointments in Dublin. This is significant because Senior's ideas about value and distribution are consistent with the ideas of the TCD group and Senior is often cited by the TCD group.

There is no evidence of any correspondence between the TCD group and Senior. It is reasonable to assume that Whately was the intermediary between Senior and the Dublin group of economists, perhaps promulgating Senior's ideas and perhaps circulating the texts of Senior's lectures as well (cf. Bowley 1967 [1937]: 94, 109, 185). The Senior–Longfield connection is of great interest because an early variant of Senior's abstinence theory of profit did assume pride of place in Longfield's lectures and by this route made its way into the lectures of several subsequent occupants of the Whately chair at TCD. S. Leon Levy insists that the germ of Senior's profit theory first appeared in print in 1826 in the *Encyclopedia Metropolitana* essay "Some Ambiguous Terms Used in Political Economy" (Levy 1970). Whately included Senior's essay in his *Elements of Logic* as one of the several appendixes (Whately 1875 [1826]: 230–239).

Whately's *Elements of Logic* was republished at least nine times in Whately's lifetime and remained one of his most influential works. Senior's major treatise on political economy was published in 1836, but the major advances in the "waiting" or "abstinence" theory of profits in the writing of Longfield and Isaac Butt at TCD were already in print by 1834. Senior somewhat mysteriously never mentioned the work in Ireland and the seminal improvements to his theory that were made by the TCD group (Senior 1836; Bowley 1967 [1937]: 185). Had Senior done this, I suspect that the TCD group's contributions would have been better known among historians.

Whately's main interest was in theology and the prospects for genuine educational reform in Ireland (McKerrow 1981: 167). His interest in the purely technical questions of economics was fairly limited. As far as economics was concerned, he was determined to show that there is no inherent contradiction between theological teachings based on the scriptures and a systematic understanding of wealth based on scientific theories and facts. As a physician can study disease without approving of disease or even welcoming it, so a theologian can study wealth with the aid of science. But the field of "natural theology" would also benefit from the study of political economy. It often happens that man, acting in his own interest, ends up "undesignedly" promoting the good of the entire community under the guidance of Providence (Whately 1966 [1832]: 103). The division of labor, that amazing process by which specialization proceeds, had been described in the eighteenth century by Bernard Mandeville, David Hume, and, of course, Adam Smith. To a student of natural theology, the division of labor is a marvelous process. It is propelled forward by the self-interested actions of men and women but ends up producing a remarkable and beneficial social order. Even private spending works to put others to work.

The miser once could do damage in society by hoarding food and coins. In modern times, things are quite different. The avaricious miser does better by divesting his hoards and purchasing financial assets, and this helps free up private capital for productive investment in both trade and agriculture. And Whately saw the corn-dealers who speculate during a famine as starting from a desire to make money but at the same time promoting a system that allows an "enormous population [to be] fed from day to day" (Whately 1966 [1832]: 98). Thus in "the wise arrangements of Providence, not only self-interest, but in some instances the most sordid selfishness, are made, in an advanced state of society, to conduce to public prosperity" (Whately 1966 [1832]: 158).

Whately also took sides in the ongoing debate about the "labour theory of value" that engaged most writers since Adam Smith's classic presentation of the problem. The critics' general attitude was that anything can be made a "measure of value," and labor is probably one such measure because just about everything that is produced by man involves the expenditure of labor. Still, just because labor has been expended in the past does not mean that labor is what causally determines exchange value in markets today and tomorrow. As a general matter, the cost of production, however measured, can only affect market prices indirectly (if at all) through its effects on the supply. Whately put the matter as succinctly as possible when he wrote about pearls and their enormous market value: "it is not that pearls fetch a high price because men have dived for them; but on the contrary, men dive for them because they fetch a high price" (Whately 1966 [1832]: 253).

According to Whately, the discipline of economics is all about exchange, and he proposed that the subject be renamed *Catallactics* or "the science of exchanges." This idea had been expressed by J.B. Say and later was taken up by Senior and others. It may have been the source of the "utility tradition" in Ireland, although Longfield was ambivalent about the role of utility, preferring instead a supply-and-demand explanation, as I argue below.

Mountifort Longfield (1832–1836)

Mountifort Longfield (1802–1884) was the first to be appointed to the Whately chair of Political Economy. He was chosen as a result of a competitive examination administered by Archbishop Whately himself but the final selection was made by the Board of Trinity College (Fitzpatrick 1864: 184–186; McDowell and Webb 1982: 168; Moss 1976: 14–16). The circumstances of this appointment were not without controversy inside Trinity College, but the general verdict was that Longfield really was the most qualified of all the candidates for the job (Murphy 1984). Longfield served from 1832–1836 and published three excellent collections of lectures (nineteen lectures in all) that made seminal contributions to the classical theory of value and exchange in the fruitful period in British economic thought between David Ricardo and John Stuart Mill. These lectures also set a common framework within which the subsequent Whately professors made their respective contributions.

Since our principal interest is in the theoretical originality of Longfield and his immediate successors to the Whately chair, two sets of lectures stand out for their theoretical acumen and overall expository brilliance. The first is Longfield's *Lectures on Political Economy* (*LPE*), published in 1834, which is a faithful transcription of the actual lectures that he delivered one year earlier of the course of two semesters. The second set of lectures was published in 1835 under the title *Lectures on Commerce and One on Absenteeism* (*LCA*), representing what he said about commercial policy and the international financial mechanism at TCD. In both sets of lectures, Longfield broke new ground. In between these two sets of conceptually remarkable presentations of economic analysis, Longfield delivered and published a more policy-oriented set of lectures on the controversial poor laws, delivered in 1834 and published that same year under the title *Four Lectures on Poor Laws.*

Longfield's lectures might have had more direct influence on economics had either John Elliot Cairnes or John Stuart Mill referred to them in some meaningful way. Cairnes and Mill corresponded with Judge Longfield after his elevation to the Landed Estates Court in Ireland in 1858 (Dowling 2005). Longfield succeeded from the Whately chair to the Regius Professorship in Feudal and English Law (also at TCD) and played a major role in the land reform debates of the second half of the nineteenth century. These debates culminated in major legislative reform under Gladstone starting in 1870, when the tenant rights custom that provided limited compensation for tenant improvements to farmland was passed into law (Bull 1996: 195). Curiously, although Longfield is mentioned in John Stuart Mill's *Principles*, it is not for any of his theoretical contributions. Rather, he is identified as the source for Mill's understanding of the land tenure situation in Ireland. That information was sent to Mill by Cairnes, who contacted Longfield about preparing the report and arranged to have it sent to Mill (cf. Boylan and Foley 1984: 96–119).

Longfield's scientific bent of mind could not keep him entirely away from analytic ideas in economics and finance, even decades after his tenure as the Whately professor. Perhaps his most puzzling work is the terse collection of mathematical results about series and their sums. It is a mathematic manual of formulae under the title *An Elementary Treatise on Series* (Longfield 1872a). Certain of these formal mathematical theorems are critical when evaluating sums of terms that differ from each other in some systematic way. Such sums are needed when calculating the present value of an annuity or a farm. Longfield's many years of service on the Landed Estates Court in Ireland may have required that he make such present value calculations when evaluating real estate and determining the proper allowance for tenant improvements and related calculations. I also mention Longfield's celebrated essay on "The Tenure of Land in Ireland," which still ranks as the definitive historical source for information about the state of tenant–landlord contracting in Ireland in the nineteenth century (Longfield 1870).

Longfield published his four-part article on "Banking and Currency" in the *Dublin University Magazine* (Longfield 1971 [1840]). There he anticipated Lord Overstone's support of the "currency principle" of banking reform and also presented the view that trade fluctuations were actually a cycle of some sort, with periods of prosperity followed by distrust and bankruptcy. Longfield hammered home this point by actually drawing a large circle (similar to the one that Overstone presented) to illustrate the course of what we today call the business cycle (Longfield 1971 [1840]: 44). In addition, he worked out an ingenious numerical example to illustrate how competitive banking ("free banking") might lead to an over-issuance of the currency because one single bank of issue may impose an external cost on the other banks that it itself does not recognize (Moss 1976: 161–164). Longfield's mature thoughts about the role of the government intervention in the economy were presented before the Statistical and Social Inquiry Society of Ireland in 1872 and published that year under the title "The Limits of State Interference with the Distribution of Wealth in Applying Taxation to the Assistance of the Public" (Longfield 1971 [1872b]: 133–148). In that essay, Longfield endorsed a variant of liberalism such as we can find in John Stuart Mill's work, in which there is a general presumption in favor of leaving markets alone that can be overruled when conditions require.

The rediscovery of Longfield in 1903

Contemporary scholarship on Longfield's analytic contributions as well as the contributions of Isaac Butt, Robert Torrens, and a large group of talented economists dates to 1903, when E.R.A. Seligman published his essay "On Some Neglected British Economists" in the *Economic Journal* (Seligman 1903). Seligman's intent was to call attention to a broader British literature that had been unduly neglected and held many surprises for historians looking for "firsts." Toward the end of his long article he devoted an entire section to "the Marginalists," by which he meant the Whately group, that is, Whately, Longfield, and Butt. Lawson is not mentioned. In these eleven pages of text, Seligman touches on Longfield's main technical contributions in both value and distribution theory with precision and accuracy. He emphasizes not only the originality of the contribution but also how it mimics the latest developments in "contemporary" economic theory, especially the production and interest theory that was discussed at that time. Longfield is correctly portrayed as a non-Ricardian because he was opposed to the "agricultural theory of profits." Seligman's presentation of Longfield's thought received Joseph A. Schumpeter's endorsement in 1950 (Schumpeter 1954: 464–465) and inspired two dissertations on Longfield, the first by R.D. Collison Black in 1942 and the second by me in 1975, which was published one year later (Black 1942; Moss 1976). Other historians have contributed magnificently to our understanding of Longfield, the most significant member of this group being O'Brien (O'Brien 2004). Today, there is hardly a textbook in the history of economic thought that does not take some notice of Longfield. Seligman succeeded quite well: Longfield is no longer a "neglected economist."

Longfield's credentials as a non-Ricardian

Longfield's credentials as a non-Ricardian are only as secure as our understanding of what Ricardianism is all about, which is an enormously important and complex topic. For many decades the common understanding was that Ricardo's value theory was a cost of production theory with labor theory of relative value overtones (Stigler 1965 [1958]). The prevailing view, thanks to the archival work of Piero Sraffa and Maurice Dobb during the 1950s and 1960s, was that Ricardo's distribution theory was all about "getting rid of rent" by way of the differential theory of land rent and then explaining the division of the remainder portion of the net national product by positing a "subsistence wage" and an agricultural theory of the profit rate (Sraffa 1966). The rational reconstruction of this alleged Ricardian model of how the distributive shares are determined is known as the "corn model" (Baumol 1964: 13–21). But with the publication of Samuel Hollander's close readings of the entire body of literature and correspondence, Ricardianism has turned out to be a moving target, and a slippery one as well (Hollander 1979, 1997).

Most sensationally, Hollander insisted that the "corn model" interpretation of Ricardianism is better found in Malthus's writings and is really not part of Ricardo's *Principles*, although it may have played a part in his earlier "Essay on Profits" (Hollander 1997: 447). Ricardianism includes the following claim and the implications of that claim: that in the absence of an increase in the money supply, a general all-around rise in nominal wages must lower profits and not raise prices. This and a related idea about the dynamic paths of wages and profits constituted the Hollanderian reinterpretation of Ricardo. This interpretation was later endorsed by Paul Samuelson (Samuelson 1978).

Agree or disagree with Hollander, our appreciation of Longfield's originality should not rise or fall with the changing meanings of Ricardianism, although this really cannot be avoided. It is impossible to discuss economics during the first part of the nineteenth century without saying something about Ricardo's seminal contributions to analytic economics. Ricardo has become the benchmark against which the analytic achievement of most other British writers is compared. I shall offer an alternative appreciation linking Longfield more closely to the context of the economic discussions in Dublin during the 1830s. We start with Longfield's interest and contribution to the natural theology of Whately.

Longfield and natural theology

As Anthony Waterman has explained, the *Wealth of Nations* can be read as natural theology. As such, it provides "putative knowledge of God arrived at by the study of nature alone, without any reliance on 'revelation' ... [and again] the whole point of natural theology is to show by means of a scrupulously positive ... inquiry that knowledge of God may be had *without any resort to revelation whatsoever*" (Waterman 2004: 105–106). And so it is that in Lecture 11 of *LPE*, Longfield summarizes what has been accomplished. The main subject of economics is to investigate what laws and customs impact the great sources of social revenue, namely, rent, profits, and wages. And the results have been pleasing. According to Longfield: "The laws according to which wealth is created, distributed, and consumed, have been framed by the Great Author of our being, with the same regard to our happiness which is manifested by the laws that govern the material world" (Longfield 1971 [1834a]: 223). Longfield goes on to warn (as had Adam Smith) about the folly of human laws and institutions and how the natural course of things can be interfered with. But the general tendency is for the three classes to prosper together, and that is what we learn from our study of political economy.

Natural theology peppers the *LPE* at various places throughout. Longfield covers a few of the topics that Whately covered in his *Introductory Lectures*, but similar ideas can be found in Adam Smith's *Wealth of Nations* as well (Whately

1966 [1832]). In Lecture 3, Longfield explains how by a "wise provision of nature" the more indispensable any commodity is to life, the more likely a rich person will exchange it and not hoard it. All exchanges of equivalents in the market are actually "advantageous to both parties," and by this wonderful mechanism the rich end up divesting themselves of any surplus food they might accumulate, thereby serving others even though this altruism is not part of their intention (Longfield 1971 [1834a]: 44–45). Elsewhere in the same lecture, we learn that high prices during a famine are a wonderful thing because they help regulate consumption and work through the self-interest of speculators who, when they are successful and make profits, actually reallocate supply from less urgent to more urgent uses, helping to mitigate suffering. The more the speculators—the corn-dealers—consult their self-interest and maneuver the meager supply for greatest gains, the more "benefit the public derives from them" (Longfield 1971 [1834a]: 60). In Lecture 4, Longfield treats the division of labor and the magnitudes of the benefits it produces in enhancing productivity. He explains that the poor derive the greatest benefit from the progress in the division of labor (Longfield 1971 [1834a]: 106).

Finally, I mention that the workers must be dissuaded from violence and taught the importance of industry, intelligence, and frugality. Bad laws that encourage improvident behavior must be repealed or defeated in the legislature. A welfare system that pays the able-bodied not to work must be avoided (Longfield 1971 [1834b]). Property rights must be protected and respected to provide individuals with the "security" that they need to engage in creative economic enterprise (Longfield 1971 [1834a]: 4, 18, 19, 20, 139, 236, 239, 242).

The market mechanism

As I have remarked, the benevolent trends that Longfield cited in his lectures were not inevitable. In addition to the benevolent tendencies already outlined, the legislators must allow "mutual competition" to establish wage rates and profit rates and must not try to raise wages by artificial means, such as by lowering profits. The workers must be taught that their interests will best be served by their "prudence and industry" (Longfield 1971 [1834a]: 18). Most importantly, they must be taught that laws are formed for the good of all, and not for the benefit of a single order or a single individual (Longfield 1971 [1834a]: 20).

By speaking up for the benevolent nature of the market process, Longfield joined forces with Whately and produced a "correct" political economy that would counter the rantings of the radicals and machine breakers. Indeed, as I shall show below, his major contribution to production and distribution theory had the effect of solving the great problem of the age: If labor produces all or nearly all of the GDP, why did labor have to share it with the landlords and the capitalists? Were not landlords' and capitalists' shares a *deduction* from what should have been paid over to labor in the form of wages? In Longfield's view, the capitalist cannot take without at the same time improving the situation of the laborer. I shall return to this central theme of the *LPE* after I have said something about the theory of price in Longfield's work.

The theory of price and the wage of labor

Again, following Whately's lead, Longfield was not too impressed with what has been called the "labor theory of value." Quite early in his lectures he denied that labor is the only "real" measure, since measurement was largely a matter of convenience; there is no such thing as an "invariable measure" of value. In his *Principles*, Ricardo made some strong assumptions about the money commodity always and everywhere requiring the same amount of labor to be produced along with an average amount of capital. If that were true, then of course all changes in price when measured in units of this "invariable measure" must occur on the *goods* side of the market and not on the money side. But the "invariable measure" was invariable only in the examination of abstract tendencies and not in any practical applications. This was something that Longfield emphasized and with which Ricardo would most probably have agreed (cf. Longfield 1971 [1934a]: 267).

Certainly, labor was the most convenient measure because it entered into the manufacture or harvest of most of the items bought and sold. It was also true that "no permanent change in relative prices would happen without a change in relative amount of labour" in the commodities. In these matters, Longfield seemed to be contributing to the general line of thought among the classical school writers linking market prices to the amounts of labor-time embodied in the traded goods (Stigler 1965 [1958]). Nothing terribly original here.

In stark contrast to what he had to say about the labor measure, Longfield offered a profoundly original account of how demand and supply worked to establish market prices. I have offered a rational reconstruction of that model elsewhere, and so here I shall repeat only the salient points about his supply and demand framework (Moss 1976: 29–49).

Let us recount Longfield's remarkable theory of demand that builds upon an earlier distinction that can be found in Malthus's *Principles of Political Economy* (Malthus 1986 [1820, 1836], vol. 5: 57). In Adam Smith's account of what happens when the supply brought to market falls short of the "effectual demand," a competition begins and the market price rises above what Smith called the commodity's "natural price." It was Longfield's genius to insist that the competition does not simply begin when quantity demanded does not equal quantity supplied. Rather, there is a "mutual competition" at work at all times in the market. The "effectual demand" is not a single extensive magnitude but varies from individual to individual and even within the same individual, as can be readily seen at an auction. According to Longfield, it makes better sense to speak of a "series" of demands of different degrees of intensity that exist in the market, although not easily visible to the untrained eye. Much like Scottish chemist Joseph Black's development of the concept of heat, demand, like some forms of heat, can exist in a "latent" form.

Many individuals have a more intense demand for the objects that they purchase but happily pay the going market price rather than volunteer to pay more than that price. Their more intense demand exists "latently," waiting to show its face. It would show its face in the case of a famine, for example, where some individuals consent to pay the higher price rather than do without the commodity whose supply has been sadly diminished. Those individuals who drop out when the price rises have a lower intensity of demand. At any moment in time, the individual who would leave the market if the price were a bit higher has the *least intensive demand*, and his demand is exactly measured by the market price. This is a clear and equivocal recognition of what we recognize as the concept of "marginal demand."

I wish to emphasize two things about Longfield's presentation of this idea. First, the theory is brilliantly presented and carefully stated at different places in the *LPE* (Longfield 1971 [1834a]: 115, 194). This was not a passing insight or a reference to a supplementary idea that perhaps had come to him in a flash of insight. Rather, this was to him a central organizing idea in analytic economics. He would use the very same idea in his most important account of the determination of the profit rate, which he separated from the agricultural profit theory that is identified with the writings of Ricardo, Malthus, and West.

Second, Longfield realized that what he had stated about demand involves a "species of reasoning" in political economy that he will have reason to use again in other contexts (Longfield 1971 [1834a]: 194). This pattern of explanation is evident enough in the writings of Longfield and his immediate successor, Isaac Butt, for us to correctly declare a definite analytic tradition at TCD. I shall return to this point below.

Longfield declared himself part of a larger group of economists that adhered to a supply and demand explanation of price formation. Several important writers have tried to link Longfield to the "utility tradition" in economics. Certainly, Longfield's gloss on the enigmatic Aristotelian claim that exchange is about "equivalents" being exchanged remarks that the equivalents that are exchanged are "mutually advantageous" to the trading parties. A similar reference to the "equivalents" idea is addressed later in the writings of James Anthony Lawson (Lawson 1844: 84). Does this mean that the subjective gain that each receives is "equal"? Longfield does not say, nor would such a claim be credible.

Still, the concept of the "least intensive demand," being one of a series of demands that many individuals have when they participate in market activity, is not a marginal utility theory. It may be close or consistent with the marginal utility approach, but sometimes what seems "close" with the aid of hindsight is not supported by the textual evidence at all. I have insisted on this in my earlier work (Moss 1976: 44–48; but cf. Black 1984).

Now let us turn our attention to the notion of "cost of production." According to Longfield, some of the commodities brought to market have a cost of production associated with them. By "cost of production," Longfield meant the sum of the wage expense and profits associated with bringing a unit of supply to market. Since Ricardo's presentation of the agricultural theory of rent, it was well established that the most costly portion of the required food supply sets the price that must be paid for all units of supply. Thus, the marginal cost of producing the requisite food supply sets the price of food and generates differential land rent on the more fertile plots of land. As Seligman pointed out in his précis of Long-field's *LPE*, Longfield certainly extended that idea of marginal cost pricing to manufacturing as well as agriculture at at least one place in *LPE*, although the same idea can be found in Nassau Senior's writings as well (Seligman 1903).

It is also clear that Longfield was opposed to the cost of production theory of value. Longfield identified the cost of production theory with Ricardo's writings at one point, confidently insisting that Ricardo has a cost of production theory and not a supply and demand theory. According to Longfield, this was a tragic error on Ricardo's part because it led him to a fallacious theory of how the wage rate of labor was determined in the market settings. Ricardo adhered to the illusion that "men first determined what they should consume and then had the goods made according to order, and paid the cost of production, because on such terms only would the goods be produced for them" (Longfield 1971 [1834a]: 257). This is a false account of the market process in most cases. According to Longfield, producers produce supply with an eye towards the future and calculate as to what they can expect to sell as a remunerative price (Longfield 1971 [1834a]: 257). Cost of production enters into the future-oriented calculation and operates to affect supply but, almost always and everywhere, supply in relation with demand leads to the formation of the market price.

Ricardo and others stated that the wages of labor depended on the worker's "mode of living," that is, his "customary standard" of living. According to Long-field, nothing could be further from the truth. The pure and simple truth of the matter is that the mode of living of the worker depends on his wages. It is certainly not the other way around. His wages depend on the rate of profit and the productiveness of labor itself in producing output. At one place, Longfield clearly reasons that the entire demand for any category of labor depends on the utility or value of the work that labor can do. Other numerical examples in *LPE* clearly indicate that Longfield had an imputation theory of wages, in which the current pricing of labor is affected by expectations of what the labor services are worth later on when the product of labor is sold in the market (Longfield 1971 [1834a]: 166–167].

The policy implications of Longfield's wage theory are plain: If the legislature wishes to ameliorate the condition of the workers, its best strategy is to encourage the market process by protecting property rights and encouraging habits of industry, thrift, and knowledge in the market. Longfield is quite emphatic about this. Logically, he wrote that there are only two ways in the abstract that wages can be raised. One way is to lower the profit rate. The second way is to enhance the productiveness of labor. Since (according to Longfield) the legislator cannot lower the profit rate, that leaves only policies to increase the productiveness of labor, to which we now turn our attention (Longfield 1971 [1834a]: 200, 218).

The productiveness of labor

In the theory of land rent, the fact that there are less fertile agricultural investments out there, which can be utilized when the price of food rises, keeps the price of food from rising as quickly as it otherwise would. It is not the less fertile land that *causes* food prices and rents to rise; rather, the existence of less fertile land operates to make the supply of food more elastic than it otherwise might be, and this happily keeps food prices from rising as quickly as they otherwise might. While this is a small point, it was not an obvious one. This important insight can also be found in Malthus's *Principles of Political Economy* (Malthus, 1986 [1820] vol. 5: 113). When we keep in mind the natural theology theme in Longfield's *LPE*, it is an important point to make.

Elsewhere, I have characterized Longfield as a "population optimist," in the sense that he did not think that a large population and sizeable working class had to be a problem at all. In a society with security of property and a well-mannered workforce, there was no reason whatsoever that wealth creation and population growth might not proceed together in a mutually supportive way (Longfield 1971 [1834a]: 237; Moss 2005: 216–217). This, despite Malthus's claim that there was a "tendency" for population to grow in size geometrically and another "tendency" for the food supply to grow arithmetically (Whately 1966 [1832]: 250). The subsequent lectures of Butt and Lawson continued the theme of population optimism, as I mention below.

Certainly, a larger population means a larger market. As Adam Smith and others explained, larger markets make possible a more advanced division of labor with all of its gains in labor productivity that contribute to rising living standards. Yes, of course, a rising population might require a large harvest and, in the absence of technological improvements in agriculture, higher food prices (Longfield 1971 [1834a]: 130; cf. Longfield 1870: 68–75). But as a matter of historical fact, the higher food prices are in practice offset by innovations that are slowly introduced into agriculture (Longfield 1971 [1834a]: 253). Historically, food prices have not risen dramatically along with population growth. This positive optimistic result may again be evidence of a benevolence that far exceeds our scientific efforts to understand certain tendencies at work.

Finally, even if food prices did somehow manage to rise with the growth of the population, the average worker does not spend his entire family budget on food and food alone! The average worker also consumes manufactured goods, and their prices tend to fall with the accumulation of capital and the introduction of improvements. The net impact of these price changes on real income is anything but clear. It is, however, clear that the wages of labor do not depend on the price of food or on the customary habits of the workers.

The profit deduction

In the "corn model" variant of the classical theory of distribution, the productivity of the marginal investment in agriculture determines the rate of return on capital throughout the economy. According to some presentations of the corn model, (1) as the productivity of the marginal investment in agriculture declines due to diminishing returns in agriculture (and the added assumption that agricultural innovations are slow in coming), (2) with the wage rate set by the habits and customs of the workers (the "subsistence wage" theory), (3) then the residual amount left to the farmer after he pays the wages is profit. That residual amount is continually falling as the margin of cultivation is extended because of diminishing returns. This drives down the rate of profit on capital that is invested in farming and propels the economic system toward the "stationary state." Profits in manufacturing fall along with the agricultural profit rate in agriculture due to competition that constantly and effectively arbitrages away any difference in the two rates. In an extreme version of the "corn model," the productivity of investments in agriculture "rules the roost" and determines the rate of profit. Longfield attributed this more uncompromising version of the profit theory to Sir Edward West, not Ricardo or Malthus as is more customary today, especially in the textbook accounts of the classical theory (Longfield 1971 [1834a]: 182; Baumol 1964; Vance 1848).

Hollander's successful challenge to the simple-minded expositions of Ricardo's economics did not put the "corn model" entirely to rest (Hollander 1979). It is now well accepted that many of the economists of the day interpreted Ricardo as holding to a "corn model" theory of the determination of the profit rate. Certainly, Robert Torrens, whose *Essay on the External Corn Trade* influenced the entire TCD group, used the "corn-ratio" profit theory tacitly attributing the idea of a corn model to Ricardo. That was already in 1820 (cf. de Vivo 1985)! In his treatise on Malthus, Hollander admitted that the corn-ratio theory of profit is important to Malthus's work, admitting that the story of the development of classical economic thought cannot be told without this important model (Hollander 1997).

Certainly, although the marginal productivity of investment in agriculture was only one factor that *might* explain a decline in the profit rate, Ricardo was persistent in his belief that no permanent fall in the profit rate could occur without a rise in wages. This is called the "inverse wage–profit theorem" of Ricardian economics (Moss 2001: 299). According to Hollander, it is the essential idea of Ricardian economics and thus the litmus test to decide if a classical economist can be dubbed "Ricardian." By this test, Hollander insisted, Longfield was a "Ricardian." I am not convinced.

Longfield prided himself on destroying this Ricardian claim. He did this on two different levels. First, he pointed out that if you begin by claiming that wages and profits added together determine the cost of production of, say, food and, furthermore, if you assume that this cost of production is constant in amount when measured in units of the imaginary money commodity produced with a constant amount of labor and a standard amount of capital, then, when measured in this monetary unit, a rise in wages has to lower profits. It is obviously a matter of algebra and has nothing much to do with human behavior. If A + B = C and C is constant while A increases, then B has to decline. It cannot be otherwise. We can agree with Longfield that such a presentation of the "inverse profit–wage theorem" is often a matter of definition or tautology.

But the "inverse profit–wage theorem" is in error for an entirely different reason: It does not *logically* follow at all from the basic model of capital accumulation that Ricardo presented in his *Principles*. Consider the case where society is "progressing" and population and capital are increasing together. In this situation, the wage rate is rising and certainly rises above the "cost of pro-duction" value or "customary wage" hypothesized by some of the *cost-of-production-determines-value* writers. Under these circumstances, a rise in the price of food can occur without changing nominal wages at all. The higher food prices will eat into the wage premium (the amount by which actual real wages exceed the "cost of production" amount). Since the wages are already above the cost of production amount, the real wage rate can take a "hit" without cutting into profits or affecting the profit rate at all.

This proves that in a progressing economy, food prices can rise and real wages can fall *without requiring a rise in nominal wages and a lowering of the profit rate*. Ricardo's model permits such a deduction. As such, it proves that real wages can fall when food prices rise, without affecting the profit rate. Long-field's presentation of this refutation has turned out to be one of his important but unappreciated analytic contributions.

Still, we wonder about the profit rate itself. What principles of economics regulate its amount? Again, we need to return to fundamentals.

The profit rate

Longfield, along with Senior, was an adherent of what is called in the literature the "abstinence" or "waiting" theory of profit. The basic idea that is so often overlooked in economic analysis is that production takes time. The time-consuming nature of production was featured by Adam Smith in his celebrated account of the division of labor. The capitalist accumulates "stock" to allow him to set up that division of labor that, once it is set up and maintained, operates to advance the productivity of labor. Indeed, in the *LPE*, Longfield offered a gloss on these ideas along with numerical calculations to highlight the sources of the productivity gains that accompany that division of labor.

For example, if production takes time and the workers are getting paid on a regular basis before any final product is coming forth, someone must have *advanced* these wages to the workers (Longfield 1971 [1834a]: 90). After all, the current wages are being paid based on the expectation that the product produced will be valuable when it is produced and marketed in the future. There is no doubt of this in Longfield's mind, and he repeats at various places throughout *LPE* that the capitalist advances wages to the workman before anything has been sold (Longfield 1971 [1834a]: 187). The capitalist advances the wages, and this is costly to the capitalist and involves a "sacrifice" on his or her part (Longfield 1971 [1834a]: 196, 249).

The capitalist forgoes present consumption opportunities, and this sacrifice requires compensation (Longfield 1971 [1834a]: 196). The capitalist must also be compensated for the risks he assumes. There also is always the risk that the goods-in-process cannot be sold later at an economic price. The profit is that compensation, and it technically is a *deduction* from the *future* wages imputed to the workers. According to Longfield, the wages of the workers are discounted when they are paid out. The size of this discount varies directly with the time-consuming nature of production. In other words, the discount from the workers' wages will be larger in the case where the period of production is two years compared with one year.

Now, in a labor market based on competition and free contracting, this discount from wages is tacitly agreed to by the workers. They "consent" to the discount by not quitting and finding another job. They willingly agree to the discount so they can enjoy prompt payment of a fraction of their future value productivity.

In the face of these brute facts about production, it is a short move to the radical conclusion that the workers are not paid in full for their labor power. Many agitators and troublemakers have reached that conclusion. They claim that part of the workers' productivity has been hijacked by the capitalists! Such rhetoric stirs up trouble in society. It infuriates labor and propels the worker towards violence. Violence begets insecurity as to life and property, and these in turn propel the economy into decline. The lessons of natural theology are soon forgotten.

The wage discounts are consented to. If a worker can produce, say, 100 units of output later sold in the market for a certain amount, working with his bare hands and utilizing a method of production that is short in duration, he expects that his wage rate in a factory will certainly never be less than this minimum amount. If he were offered less than this amount, he would quit and live by his own wits. Clearly, what the laborer can earn on his own without using any capital at all establishes the lower "limit" on his factory wage rate.

But what determines the upper limit? The first point to note is that the capitalist must be paid some profits. The ones who make these advances to the workers are only induced to make this sacrifice by the prospect of making profits (Longfield 1971 [1834a]: 162, 196). But, assuming that they desire more profits rather than less, what principles of economics will establish the maximum amount that can be deducted from wages? In Longfield's spirit we ask, "What are the principles that regulate this contract between the workers and the capitalists?" This, Longfield concluded, is the "most important subject in political economy" (Longfield 1971 [1834a]: 200).

To explain this division, Longfield asks his listeners to think of capital goods as simply "machines." According to Longfield, the use of the term "machines" is shorthand for "instruments, tools and machinery" (Longfield 1971 [1834a]: 187). In a market system, machines are employed with varying degrees of efficiency. The "least efficient [unit of] capital" sets the maximum amount the capitalists can deduct from the workers' wages in the market system. This cannot be more than the yield on the least efficient unit of capital, or other capitalists will see a profit opportunity and bid away the relatively underpaid workers by offering to employ them at a lower discount (that is, at a higher net wage).

Longfield offers an elaborate analysis of why it is that successive applications of machinery tend to experience lower levels of efficiency. He does not claim that the mere ratio of capital to labor accounts for this varying physical productivity, as would later become a common theory in neoclassical economics, underscored by the famous neoclassical production function that allows factor substitutions even in the face of constant returns to scale (Vickrey 1964: 168–169). Despite Longfield's interest in mathematical ideas and proficiency with quantitative reasoning, there is no evidence that he anticipated the "neoclassical production function".

Longfield's reasoning had more to do with the behavior of the workers chosen to work the machines and pecuniary difficulties of selling large amounts of products in markets where population may not be increasing quickly. Again, Longfield's theory of intensity of demand led him to the conclusion that when population is not increasing, any general increase in the supply of commodities requires a drop in prices to attract additional demand. Those with lower than the least-intensive demand—the latent demand—must be drawn into the market as buyers. So, as the number of machines multiplies, it is the "least efficient machine" that is "leased" to the worker that sets the size of the wage deduction. As the productivity of the machines declines, so does the profit rate "deduction," leaving a larger real wage for the workers. It is an "inverse wage–profit" theory but established on foundations that are not the same as those of Ricardo and his followers.

Of course, it could also happen that population grows more rapidly than the accumulation of capital and knowledge. This would lower the profit rate. Still, the lowering of the profit rate is not a bad thing at all. Lower profits (and presumably lower interest rates) make projects that only yield economic benefits in the distant future appear to be excellent investments. Bridges, canals, and other transportation improvements become profitable and worth undertaking at a lower discount rate (Longfield 1971 [1834a]: 239–240). Importantly, Longfield pointed to the role that worker education would play in enhancing the quality of the workforce. Lower interest rates make borrowing to construct human capital more attractive, again promoting a rise in living standards.

In the end we are left with the impression that regardless of whether profit rises or falls, the future prospects of capitalist production and distribution operate to the economic advantage of all. This is part of the overall natural theological framework of Longfield's *LPE*. The economic reasoning helps us appreciate the benevolent nature of the capitalist economy when it is permitted to operate under a rule of law that protects property rights and capitalist profits. The capital-using economy encourages industry, honesty, and frugality on the part of the workers.

Theory of rent

And this brings us to the landlords. What kind words can be said about this class, who claim a share—a sizeable and increasing share—of the national output merely by virtue of the fact that they own the farmland? Their remuneration many times bears no relationship at all to how hard they have worked the land. Often they reap where they have not sowed. It is difficult to deny that the classical theory of land rent established the basis for a long line of radical thinking in economics about how the legislature might tap into this "unearned" return for the good of the entire society. For John Stuart Mill and later for the American reformer Henry George, the taxation of land rents seemed to be an ideal way of financing public goods because it imposed little "excess burden" on the whole of society.

As will come as no surprise, Longfield was a staunch defender of the land-owners. He found it useful to have a class or order of men who spend their days honing their good manners and high culture, which demonstrates to the lower order what manners should be like. Without such role models in society, who knows what surly hooligan behavior might come to plague human affairs?

Longfield accepted the West–Ricardo–Malthus theory of differential land rent. Indeed, he was a major exponent of the analysis and in 1834 offered one of the best summary expositions of that theory (Longfield 1972 [1834a]: 180–181). The landlords want to maximize their rent collections. The tenant wishes to pay as little rent as possible for the use of the best quality lands possible. The out-comes or the array of rent contracts is the result of "mutual competition" and (therefore) the legislature is best advised to leave those contracts alone. What-ever rent agreements follow as a result of mutual competition are in the public interest. In his later years, after serving on the Landed Estates Courts and study-ing firsthand the abuses in Irish agriculture, Longfield would become considera-bly more interventionist on the land question and on the problem of securing tenure and financial returns for tenant improvements on the land (Longfield 1870). But in *LPE* we find Longfield quite complacent about the landlords.

With a rising population and diminishing returns to agricultural investment on land, the tendency is that the price of food will rise and, with that rise, so will the land rents paid over by the farmers. The land rents must rise because, as Longfield shows using counterfactual reasoning, if the land rents did not rise, certain farmers would be making a greater return on their investments than others, a situation that would lead to a mutual competition between the farmers to obtain leases over the better lands. Already established landlords would benefit by this competition when lease rents come up for renewal. Differential land rents persist because of competition, but they serve an important function. They keep the profit rates equal to each other throughout the agricultural sector. Here Longfield closely follows the standard classical school presentation such as can be found in Ricardo's *Principles* or Malthus's *Principles* (cf. Malthus 1986 [1820, 1836], vol. 5: 113–116).

Again, while there is a tendency for land rents to rise with population growth, this scenario may not at all be probable. Improvements in agriculture, which include drainage innovations, harvesting tools and equipment, and so on, can offset this rise in rents (cf. Malthus, 1986 [1820, 1836], vol. 5: 130–131). One can conduct a thought experiment as follows. Suppose a series of agricultural improvements were introduced overnight. Assume also that all rental contracts were instantly and costlessly renegotiated so as to keep the rate of profit on all the farms in line with each other. Under these imaginary circumstances, the land rents would *fall*. In a world where inventions are instantly employed, the landlord class might lose and become staunch opponents of agricultural improvements. They might indeed lobby for legislation to retard this sort of technological progress.

Fortunately, agricultural improvements are never introduced suddenly and completely. Their advent is gradual and steady, making their introduction less controversial and hardly noticed. As a result, land rents do not rise as much as they would otherwise, despite the progress in population growth.

Finally, Longfield shared two important insights that should be emphasized. As I pointed our earlier: First, the supply and demand model revealed that the existence of lands with varying degrees of fertility actually kept land rents from rising as quickly as they might otherwise have. The existence of less fertile lands actually keeps the price of food and rents from rising as quickly as they otherwise might. Stated in modern terms, the higher elasticity of farmland keeps the price of farm products from rising very quickly.

Second, the fact that rents are rising does *not* imply that the relative share of output paid over to the landlords is rising as well. Since relative rental shares are ratios, if the denominator were rising more quickly than the numerator, the share of the national income paid over to the landlord class might actually diminish (Longfield 1971 [1834a]: 155–156). Longfield insisted that this was indeed the case. There were more landlords investing in agriculture every day. Longfield's analytic acumen in the area of the classical theory of rents has been appreciated by several commentators and has been praised in the literature (Moss 1976: 50–64).

Longfield's lectures on commerce

According to Jacob Viner, Longfield was the first to claim that the effect of absentee landlords living outside Ireland was to depress Irish prices and (therefore) require Irish tenants to offer more Irish goods to remit their rents and other debts (Viner 1964 [1937]: 322). This is known as a "worsening" of the Irish terms of trade: more exports have to be offered for a unit of foreign imports. Longfield insisted that "absenteeism is most prejudicial to the welfare of a community" and offered several other arguments in support of his position (Longfield 1971 [1835]: 73). He concluded that the additional exportation of Irish goods that was needed to remit farmers' rents to the absentee landlords was a consequence of the diminished demand for commodities in Ireland. To restore a balance, local Irish prices had to fall to encourage additional exports, and that is why the Irish terms of trade worsened as a result of the absentees.

I have argued that in these same lectures, Longfield anticipated Abba Lerner's remarkable symmetry theorem about the similar impact of a tax on imports or exports (Moss 1976: 138–147). To understand why it makes no essential difference to the pattern of international trade whether a nation puts its tax on its own exports to foreigners or instead puts a tax of similar magnitude on the foreigner's imports, Longfield explained how trade is motivated in an international context by the algebraic difference between the pre-trade price ratios in the two regions.

So while each form of a tax on international commerce effects a different market price, the absolute difference between the pre-trade price ratios narrows in the same way regardless of which form of taxation is used. This is a subtle and sophisticated understanding of the logical implications of the classical theory of international trade (Moss 1976: 138–147).

To date, the texts do not credit Longfield for this brilliant analysis and, unfortunately, much of the novelty of Longfield's analytic approach has gone unnoticed over the years. At TCD, however, there were some who took notice. It is now time to say something about the second occupant of the Whately chair at TCD, Isaac Butt.

Isaac Butt (1836–1841)

Isaac Butt (1813–1879) was the second holder of the Whately chair, succeeding Longfield in 1836 and serving until 1841. In his later years, Butt would establish his reputation as a celebrated Irish lawyer defending the Fenians at mid-century in Ireland, and he later became an articulate advocate of "home rule" and the founder of a reforming party in Ireland with that same name. He expanded the skepticism about the impact of absenteeism on the Irish economy by moving farther away from free trade, towards advocating protectionism for Irish industry in at least two lectures that were delivered before the University of Dublin in 1840 under the title *Protection to Home Industry: Some Cases of Its Advantages Considered* (Butt 1846). The name Isaac Butt appears in the index of nearly every book on nineteenth-century Irish history. He was a significant activist in the long struggle for justice in Ireland.

While Isaac Butt does not need a long introduction to students of Irish history, his contributions to theoretical economics are seldom mentioned and often are overlooked by historians. Butt published two of his lectures at the University of Dublin as part of the requirements of the Whately chair. The first was entitled *Introductory Lecture* (Butt 1837) (hereafter *IL*) and the second had the title, *Rent, Profits, and Labour* (Butt 1838) (hereafter referred to as *RPL*).

In *RPL*, Butt credited Longfield with having rendered a service to the science of political economy that is of such importance that it rivaled the differential theory of rent in its importance and stands with Adam Smith's contributions as seminal (Butt 1838: 23). That principle is one about which "no educated person should remain in entire ignorance" because it is part of the common body of knowledge that "[regulates] the distribution and production of wealth" (Butt 1838: 11–12, 32). It is one of the "elementary abstract propositions" of the new science of political economy. What was this single economic principle to which Butt devoted so much praise?

It was the principle that explained the exchange ratio between "the powers of capital" and labor (Butt 1838: 26). Let us digress a short while in order to highlight the main theoretical import of Butt's discussion.

Butt is first and foremost a "utility theorist." By that I mean not only that he recognized, as did Longfield, that production is really the production of "utility" but also that he hammered away at the distinction between "productive" and "unproductive" labor by arguing essentially that all well-planned labor was "productive." As Butt explained in this lecture and in his earlier lectures, the retailer is also a producer because he or she brings goods nearer to the consumer and in so doing "creates" utility. The declaration that services provided by what was so often called "unproductive labor" is really "productive" of utility is a major theoretical platform of the utility tradition in economics. Butt declared himself at one with J.B. Say, who defined production to be the "creation of utility" (Butt 1837: 6). Classical liberalism has long considered the roles of the speculators and middleman as valuable. They were not parasites and bloodsuckers but, like the speculators and the corn-dealers, performed valuable functions (cf. Whately 1966 [1832]: 98; Smith 1976 [1776]: I, p. 532).

Still, Butt's credentials as a utility theorist placed him far from the Austrian school notion of the "entrepreneur" who creates value by discovering profit opportunities. The expenditure of labor (measured in "time") was still at the core of the exchange process. Just as Longfield before him, Butt held to the notion that as a first approximation, prices varied in markets in direct proportion to the labor-time expended on their production. Of course, not all labor was of equal value, and some professions involved more risk and uncertainty and therefore exchanged for larger amounts of unskilled labor, but despite these qualifications, it was basically labor that put the difference in value on all final goods and services.

The problem that Butt wished to highlight did not have to do with the prices of final goods and services. Rather, it had to do with the subtle problem of when labor and capital are employed together in the production of certain things, "what is it that will regulate the exchange between things both produced by the joint operation of labour and capital?, or, between things produced by labour and those produced by capital?" (Butt 1838: 21). Later on in his lectures, the problem is stated somewhat differently. Butt wishes to explain what "regulates the relation in exchange between the powers of capital and labour" (Butt 1838: 26).

The problem of breaking out the separate contributions of labor and capital when labor and capital are employed together in the production of some item can easily be solved based on Longfield's principles.

As machines are successively employed in the economy, the productivities of successively employed machines *decreases*. When all the capital is employed in the economy, the "relative value of labour and capital will be determined by that point in the scale at which all the capital in the country can be employed" (Butt 1838: 23). That will be the productivity provided by the "least" efficiently employed machine.

Suppose the least efficient machine increases the productivity of the employer's laborer by ten units. The machine owner cannot claim more than the value equivalent of these ten units as his profit. If he does claim more, the worker will quit and find another job. The wages paid to labor cannot be less than the competitive wage. Butt emphasized the "competition" between the capitalists, but the idea can be just as easily explained by job searching by the laborers. As

Longfield pointed out, the competition is always "mutual" or on both sides of the market. Longfield's remarkable discussion of the profit rate determination is at the core of Butt's presentation.

At this point, Butt tries to dissolve the classical theory of rent by attempting to prove that Longfield's same principle of the "least efficiently employed" resource, which explains the return to all units of that resource, can also explain land rent. In other words, both the theory of land rent and the theory of the profit rate on capital are simply logical implications of one seamless economic principle. Butt explains that the theory of land rent is really a theory about how to price "natural agents." Some natural agents supersede labor, but other agents do what no man or team of workers can accomplish. The classic example for Ricardo, Longfield, and the other economists of the day was the "vegetative powers of the soil" (Butt 1838: 28). Butt's text is not entirely clear about how this same economic principle can be applied to the pricing of natural agents but he was confident that the principle could be applied.

Butt's efforts at political economy were aimed at pleasing Archbishop Whately, to whom his first published lecture was dedicated (Butt 1837). Whately's commitment to natural theology is reflected in Butt's work. He wrote that the

> all wise Creator has placed [man] in such a relation to the external world that many things possess the power of gratifying his wishes and ministering to his wants. This power which is a relation of things to our nature we call utility.
>
> (Butt 1838: 13–14)

The final paragraphs of *IL* are reminiscent of what we have seen in both Whately's *Elements* and Longfield's *LPE*. According to Butt, the study of political economy is important even if it never leads to any legislation or practical results:

> [I]t is still well worth our while to explore this wonderful system—even to contemplate the beauty of its arrangement, and see in every curious contrivance of its mechanism, another manifestation of the wisdom that has alike arranged the natural laws which confine the worlds in their orbits, and those which combine the apparently changeable passions and propensities of men to produce the result which the Creator of men and the Constitutor of society has designed.
>
> (Butt 1837: 48)

James Anthony Lawson (1841–1846)

Lawson (1817–1887) like his two predecessors was a graduate of TCD and an attorney. Also like Longfield and Butt, he went on to enjoy a celebrated career in law. He was a tough law-and-order judge admitted to the Queen's Bench in Ireland and presided over notorious trials involving political prisoners during the agitation for a separate Irish state. Our interest in Lawson is mostly due to his *Five Lectures on Political Economy*, which were delivered at the University of Dublin in 1843 (Lawson 1844). These lectures bear evidence of Whately's influence, which Lawson graciously and lavishly acknowledges in the early (unnumbered) opening pages of the published edition.

The five collected lectures are published more or less exactly as they were delivered publicly; an appendix of some length was appended to these lectures on commercial policy and the tariff question. This appendix contains an attempted refutation of some policy recommendations of Robert Torrens and represents the most theoretical of Lawson's published writings. Lawson's theoretical acumen seems to be far below the standard set by Longfield and Butt, although it is still possible to discern the direction of his thinking on a variety of issues.

There are some links to Longfield's *LPE* and *LC* that are worth simply noting. First, Lawson dismisses the claim that the wage of labor will vary with the price of food. The fact is that wages do not vary with the price of food, and to think that they would do so is simply a "misapplication of the principle of population" (Lawson 1844: 8 note).

Second, Lawson examined the incidence of a tax on the supply of any commodity. Following Longfield, he explained that the tax will raise the price of the commodity and lower the amount demanded of that commodity in the market. This falling-off in demand will have an impact on the supply situation as well. In the case of agricultural products, a tax on food is often said to fall on rent and (therefore) to not lower the worker's real wage. Lawson took issue with these conventional views, since there is no such thing as a "customary wage" that limits market-determined wages. Longfield's battle against the "customary wage" theory is still underway.

Third, in obvious references to natural theology, Lawson points to the unintended consequences of self-interested behavior as leading to overall general results that produce *harmony* in society (Lawson 1844: 21). In one notable part of the 1844 lectures, Lawson (following Robert Torrens) praises the "territorial division of labour" as being what separates us from savage, barbaric life. Indeed, machinery itself is like specialization because it raises the productiveness of labor and allows the cultivation of the arts and especially inventions to occur. Such radical changes do produce problems, such as the crowding of workers in the towns and the awful factory work environments, but these sources of distress can best be handled by appropriate legal statutes.

Fourth, Lawson defines profit as the reward to the capitalist for allowing his stored-up wealth to be used to help produce other people's wealth rather than consuming it himself (Lawson 1844: 27). This is a clear restatement of the Senior–Longfield "waiting" or "abstinence" of profit.

The fifth and last theme of Lawson's lectures that directly harks back to Whately and also Longfield's published lectures has to do with Malthusian theories about population. His discussion makes mention of Whately's gloss on the word "tendency" and how it can be misunderstood in the social sciences as implying a forecast about things about to happen in the future. The fear that the growth rate of the population will outdistance the growth rate of the food supply and lead to famines is, according to Lawson, a "groundless" fear (Lawson 1844: 66).

The remaining parts of Lawson's published lectures parallel many of the ideas that Longfield presented in his *Lectures on Commerce*. I have remarked that some credit must be given not only for the originality of the idea but also for the excellent way the idea is explained and presented. Lawson's restatement of the basic principles of free trade liberalism is also not without merit. Whether he was directly influenced by Longfield, Senior, Torrens, or all three is difficult to state with any certainty. Longfield, Senior, and Torrens must each have helped shape his thinking about trade and exchange. It is sufficient to point to the excellent teaching of free trade liberal principles in the early years of the Whately chair at Trinity College Dublin in the period under study.

Lawson is particularly tough on government intervention. We learn that governments "cannot increase the production of wealth, their power is confined to altering its distribution, and the effect of such alterations is generally … to diminish production" (Lawson 1844: 109). Governments redistribute wealth, rather than providing a net additional demand for labor and thereby increasing jobs. In a nutshell, government spending only redistributes labor.

Lawson sounds "libertarian" to the modern ear. This bias in his thinking was especially apparent in his gloss on the 1842 *Edinburgh Review* debate between Senior and Torrens. The issue was whether commercial policy should encourage unilateral tariff reduction rather than reciprocity. A little bit of background might be useful to modern readers.

Torrens took the view quite early in his economic writings that a nation can gain a trade advantage by placing a tax on another nation's exports. Similarly, it is unwise for a nation to remove its tariffs *unilaterally* because that will lower its people's economic welfare. Torrens insisted that continuing protectionism is better than unilateral tariff reduction. His apostasy became especially evident after the publication of his budget series during the 1830s (Robbins 1958: 182–225). Nassau Senior, who was long associated with the Whigs and a diehard advocate of unilateral tariff reduction, took no pleasure in Torrens's claims and penned a long reply to Torrens's article in the *Edinburgh Review*. Lawson took up the Torrens–Senior debate in the appendix to his *Lectures* at TCD.

Lawson sided with Senior against Torrens. Lawson tried to show that the fundamentals of relative price determination were not permanently affected by the imposition of tariffs and, in these cases, there could be no alteration of the money supplies of the two areas and (therefore) no permanent decline in the terms of trade for the nation that unilaterally removes its tariffs. Lawson also held that the absentee landlords could not affect the Irish terms of trade, despite the fact that these landlords consumed their rents while living abroad (mostly in England). Here Longfield is politely criticized for holding opposite views (Lawson 1844: 95; Longfield 1971 [1835]: 72–80).

There were in addition a complicated array of arguments adduced to throw light on this debate about commercial policy. Torrens argued (against Senior) that international exchange rates are regulated not by local cost-of-production but by demand and supply. Lawson then tried to clear up the matter by indentifying the singular principle that regulates the exchangeable value of *all things*, whether domestically produced and sold or else sold in foreign markets. According to Lawson, "the exchangeable value of all articles depends upon their utility," that is, that value of all articles depends upon their utility, or upon their power to gratify the wants and wishes of mankind. This principle applies to everything: to monopolized and unmonopolized articles, equally in a siege or in a famine. Lawson explains that it is all about utility:

> It appears to me, therefore, that the simple and obvious statement is, that the value of articles is governed by their utility, and if the labour of an Englishman for one day, can produce an article possessing double the utility in the market of the world, that an article produced by the day's labour of a Frenchman possesses, a day's labour in England will procure double the quantity of gold or any other commodity, in the market of the world, that the day's labour of a Frenchman will, and will always continue to do so until the productiveness is diminished; and unless the imposition or removal of duties affects that productiveness, it can never permanently affect the supply of the precious metals. Of this we may as well be assured, as we are of any conclusion in Physical Science.
>
> (Lawson 1844: 147)

Our entire understanding of Lawson's value and distribution theory is admittedly sketchy. He refers to lectures he has given as part of his service at TCD that he did not publish. One of them defines political economy as the "science which treats of the nature and production of value, and the laws which regulate the distribution of wealth among the different orders of the community" (Lawson 1844: 26). Lawson is quite an optimist and a believer in the harmony between all classes in a progressing society with capital accumulation. His natural theology is neatly expressed in this conclusion: "The conclusion, then, to which I come … is that in examining the connection between wealth and the increase in [population] it is impossible to discover any hostility between the growth of the population and the growth of wealth" (Lawson 1844: 76).

By way of summary, I conclude that Lawson's credentials as part of the TCD school turn on his commitment to natural theology, his commitment to the productivity theory of wages, his rejection of the cost-of-production theory of value, and an uncompromising belief in market institutions in installing utility as part of the ultimate measure of the productiveness of labor. This last idea was also proposed by Butt and mentioned by Longfield. However, in Lawson's published lectures, the idea becomes an all-encompassing principle and establishes grounds for declaring the TCD group part of the "utility tradition" in economic thought (Black 1971).

Conclusion

The Trinity College Dublin group explored at least three important topics in a reasonably consistent manner.

First, they contributed to the "natural theology" tradition in economics. The idea is that the historical processes described by economics, for example, Torrens's territorial division of labor, were cited as examples of how Providence wisely provided for the welfare of humans. References to Providence or the benevolence of the Creator are quite common in the published writings of this group. This natural theology tradition would make an appearance in certain presentations of the idea of "spontaneous social formations," although much ink has been spilled in explaining the subtle ways in which the Austrian school has made use of the idea and supposedly avoided theological speculation. Still, there is an uncomfortable resemblance in certain Austrian school writings of the twentieth century. Here the Austrian emphasis is not on proving the benevolence of God but rather highlighting how interesting spontaneous social formations can be (on occasion but never without exception) at promoting social welfare.

Second, the entire TCD group expressed their differences with the cost of production theory of market value. They wanted a more inclusive theory that would include anything that was subject to exchange. Their focus was mutually advantageous exchange conducted under competitive conditions. Longfield's ingenious description of demand as consisting of a "series of demands of varying intensity" that interact to help form a market price is a major analytic contribution of this group. Longfield extended the idea to the pricing of machines, insisting that machines exist with varying degrees of efficiency (that is, their ability to enhance the productivity of labor) and that the least efficiently employed machine set the limit as to what the other machine owners could "charge" the workers. Isaac Butt saw this particular idea as the key to unifying distribution theory and sketched out an approach that even included the determination of land rents on the basis of this same principle.

In Lawson's lectures, the efficiency idea is interpreted as meaning efficient at producing "utility" and, by the end of the period, the TCD group had clearly paved the way towards a marginal utility theory of input pricing as can be found among the later Austrian school writers such as Carl Menger, Friedrich von Wieser, Eugen von Boehm Bawerk, Friedrich A. Hayek, and Ludwig von Mises (Mises 1969; Kirzner 1994: I, pp. ix–xxx, II, pp. vii–xx).

Third, there is a curious market process emphasis in their work. By "market process emphasis" I mean that the valuation of objects subject to exchange is always "future oriented." It is not a matter of how much labor was expended in the past or how much labor is presently needed to reproduce the object in the future. The valuation of scarce factors, and especially labor, is based on how much they can yield in the future since all production takes time. The wage rate is linked to labor productivity, and the worker tacitly consents to be paid a fraction of that productivity today rather than wait to be paid tomorrow. The discount from his wages is much less than he is able and willing to pay for prompt payment, precisely because markets are competitive and capitalists have a lower time preference than workers. This is spelled out quite exactly in Longfield's lectures but admittedly receives less emphasis in Butt and Lawson. (Or, more precisely, it receives less emphasis in the lectures they chose to publish— they may have said more about these problems in their oral lectures at TCD.)

And so I make my case for a fledging "school of thought" at TCD from 1831 to 1844. Subsequent Whately professors would turn their attention to the historical condition surrounding Irish economic life and how could it have been otherwise in the wake of the horrific famine and its tumultuous aftermath. Butt would become the leader of the home rule movement in Ireland. Longfield (never really losing his interest in abstract economic matters) would turn his attention to policy reform in both banking and land reform, where his seminal insights about Irish land reform were recognized by both Cairnes and Mill. He would advocate a prominent role for government in helping the economy meet important social welfare objectives, especially in his later writings (Longfield 1971 [1872b]). Lawson returned to economic issues in his lifetime in a lecture entitled *Duties and Obligations involved in Mercantile Relations*, published in 1855 after his term as Whately professor had expired (see Boase 2004).

My case for this school of thought at TCD has been based on what written evidence there is available, especially the published lectures I have cited and examined. Surely, however, the published sources are not the whole story. There may have been an active oral tradition among and between the professors. Butt and Lawson presented several more lectures delivered at TCD, but they were not published and so far have not been found. The lectures that were published were selected by their authors for publication, but what criteria they used to publish one set of lectures rather than another remains a matter for speculation.

Did Butt and Lawson specifically select the lectures so as not to duplicate what Longfield had already covered? If so, then the presence of a school of thought would be more firmly established—but we do not know if this was the case. A skeptic might just as well argue that rather than have a head-to-head confrontation, the Whately professors only published what was not very controversial at all. In this way, they met their moral and legal obligations under their contract with the university but avoided offending their predecessors.

The historian looking back nearly two centuries later has to take a stand and make a choice. My choice is that there was indeed a TCD "school" of thought. The Whately chair holders all knew Whately and his many published works and had a clear idea of his major interests and topic of discussion in economics. Their interests in natural theology did in some fundamentals derive from Whately's and perhaps may have been offered to compliment Whately—a nod in his direction from the lecture lectern. Longfield's influence was great. His *LPE* were important and authoritative. His subsequent two sets of lectures on the poor laws and on commerce were also important and timely. Clearly, there was a network of interaction and conversation in Dublin that should not be neglected any longer. All told and by way of summary, there was indeed a value and distribution theory tradition at TCD that anticipated the "market process emphasis" of the later Austrian school and embraced important elements of the broader "utility tradition" in neoclassical economics.

Bibliography

Baumol, William (1964) *Economic Dynamics: An Introduction*, New York: Macmillan.

Berg, Maxine (1980) *The Machinery Question and the Making of Political Economy, 1815–1848*, Cambridge: Cambridge University Press.

Black, R.D.C. (1942) "Mountifort Longfield: His Economic Thought and Writings Reviewed in Relation to the Theories of His Times and the Present Day," Ph.D. dissertation, Trinity College Dublin.

Black, R.D.C. (1960) *Economic Thought and the Irish Question: 1817–1870*, Cambridge: Cambridge University Press.

Black, R.D.C. (1971) "Introduction," in Mountifort Longfield, *Economic Writings of Mountifort Longfield*, Clifton, NY: Augustus M. Kelley.

Black, R.D.C. (1984) "The Irish Dissenters and Nineteenth-Century Political Economy," in Antoin Murphy (ed.) *Economists and the Irish Economy: From the Eighteenth Century to the Present Day*, Dublin: Irish Academic Press, pp. 120–137.

Boase, G.C. (2004) "Lawson, James Anthony (1817–1887)," rev. Sinéad Agnew, *Oxford Dictionary of National Biography*, Oxford University Press. Online. Available at www.oxford.com/view/article/16201 (accessed 13 April 2010).

Bowley, Marian (1967) [1937] *Nassau Senior and Classical Economics*, New York: Octagon Books.

Boylan, T.A. and Foley, T.P. (1984) "John Elliot Cairnes, John Stuart Mill and Ireland: Some Problems for Political Economy," in Antoin Murphy (ed.) *Economists and the Irish Economy: From the Eighteenth Century to the Present Day*, Dublin: Irish Academic Press, pp. 96–119.

Bull, Philip (1996) *Land, Politics & Nationalism: A Study of the Irish Land Question*, Dublin: Gill & Macmillan.

Butt, Isaac (1837) *Introductory Lecture Delivered Before the University of Dublin*, Dublin: William Curry, Jun. and Company.

Butt, Isaac (1838) *Rent, Profits, and Labour: A Lecture Delivered before the University of Dublin*, London: William Curry, Jun. and Company.

Butt, Isaac (1846) *Protection to Home Industry: Some Cases of its Advantages Considered*, Dublin: Hodges & Smith.

Corry, B.A. (1987) "Robert Torrens," in J. Eatwell, M. Milgate and P. Newman (eds) *The New Palgrave*, London: Macmillan.

de Vivo, Giancarlo (1985) "Robert Torrens and Ricardo's 'corn-ratio' Theory of Profits," *Cambridge Journal of Economics* 9: 89–92.

Dowling, J.A. (2005) "The Landed Estates Court, Ireland," *Journal of Legal History* 26 (August): 143–182.

Ekelund, Robert B. Jr and Hebert, Robert F. (1999) "The Dupuit–Marshall Theory of Competitive Equilibrium," *Economica* 66(262): 225–240.

Fitzpatrick, W.J. (1864) *Memoirs of Richard Whately*, 2 vols, London: Richard Bentley.

Grice-Hutchinson, Marjorie (1952) *The School of Salamanca. Readings in Spanish Monetary Theory 1544–1605*, Oxford: Clarendon Press.

Hollander, Samuel (1979) *The Economics of David Ricardo*, Toronto: University of Toronto Press.

Hollander, Samuel (1997) *The Economics of Thomas Robert Malthus*, Toronto: University of Toronto Press.

Johnson, Dennis A. (1999) "Paradox Lost: Mountifort Longfield and the Poor," *History of Political Economy* 31(4): 675–697.

Kirzner, Israel (1994) "Introduction[s]," in I. Kirzner (ed.) *Classics in Austrian Economics*, 3 vols, London: Pickering, I: ix–xxx; II: vii–xx.

Lawson, James Anthony (1844) *Five Lectures on Political Economy*, London: John W. Parker.

Levy, S. Leon (1970) *Nassau W. Senior 1790–1864*, London: David and Charles Pub.

Longfield, Mountifort (1834a) *Lectures on Political Economy Delivered in Trinity and Michaelmas Terms, 1833*, Dublin: Richard Milliken. Reprinted *in idem*, 1971. *The Economic Writings of Mountifort Longfield*, R.D. Collison Black (ed.) New York: Augustus M. Kelley.

Longfield, Mountifort (1834b) *Four Lectures on Poor Laws, Delivered in the Trinity Term 1834*, Dublin: Richard Milliken. Reprinted *in idem*, 1971. *The Economic Writings of Mountifort Longfield*, R.D. Collison Black (ed.) New York: Augustus M. Kelley.

Longfield, Mountifort (1835) *Three Lectures on Commerce and one on Absenteeism, Delivered in the Michaelmas Term, 1834*, Dublin: William Curry, Jun. and Company. Reprinted *in idem*, 1971. *The Economic Writings of Mountifort Longfield*, R.D. Collison Black (ed.) New York: Augustus M. Kelley.

Longfield, Mountifort (1840) "Banking and Currency," *Dublin University Magazine*, 15 (January): 3–15, etc. Reprinted *in idem*, 1971. *The Economic Writings of Mountifort Longfield*, R.D. Collison Black (ed.) New York: Augustus M. Kelley.

Longfield, Mountifort (1870) "The Tenure of Land in Ireland," in Cobden Club *Systems of Land Tenure in Various Countries*, London: Macmillan and Co., pp. 1–94.

Longfield, Mountifort (1872a) *An Elementary Treatise on Series*, Dublin: Hodges, Forster, and Co.

Longfield, Mountifort (1872b) "The Limits of State Interference with the Distribution of Wealth in Applying Taxation to the Assistance of the Public," *Journal of the Statistical and Social Inquiry Society of Ireland* 42 (November): 105–114. Reprinted *in idem*, 1971. *The Economic Writings of Mountifort Longfield*, R.D. Collison Black (ed.) New York: Augustus M. Kelley.

MacMahon, B. (2005) *Eccentric Archbishop: Richard Whately of Redesdale*, Kilmacud: Stillorgan Local History Society.

McDowell, R.B. and Webb, D.A. (1982) *Trinity College Dublin 1592–1952*, Cambridge University Press.

McKerrow, Ray E. (1981) "Archbishop Whately: Human Nature and Christian Assistance," *Church History* 50 (June): 166–181.

Malthus, T.R. (1826) [1798] *An Essay on the Principle of Population*, London: John Murray.

Malthus, Thomas Robert (1986) [1820, 1836] *Principles of Political Economy*, in E.A. Wrigley and David Souden (eds) *The Works of Thomas Robert Malthus*, 8 vols, London: William Pickering.

Mises, Ludwig von (1969) *The Historical Setting of the Austrian School of Economics*, New York: Arlington House.

Moss, Laurence (1976) *Mountifort Longfield: Ireland's First Professor of Political Economy*, Ottawa, IL: Green Hill Publishers.

Moss, Laurence (2001) "Ricardian Economics: Reasoning about Counter-intuitive Tendencies When System Constraints are Present," in Evelyn L. Forget and Sandra Peart (eds) *Reflections on the Classical Canon in Economics: Essays in Honor of Samuel Hollander*, London: Routledge, pp. 290–317.

Moss, Laurence (2005) "Playing Fast and Loose with the Facts About the Writings of Malthus and the Classical School," *History of Political Economy* 37 (Summer): 211–218.

Murphy, Antoin E. (1984) "Mountifort Longfield's Appointment to the Chair of Political Economy in Trinity College, Dublin, 1832," *Economists and the Irish Economy: From the Eighteenth Century to the Present Day*, Dublin: Irish Academic Press.

O'Brien, D.P.O. (2004) [1975] *The Classical Economists Revisited*, Princeton, NJ: Princeton University Press.

Rashid, Salim (1988) "The Irish School of Economic Development: 1720–1750," *Manchester School* 56 (December): 345–369.

Robbins, Lionel (1958) *Robert Torrens and the Evolution of Classical Economics*, London: Macmillan.

Samuelson, Paul A. (1978) "The Canonical Classical Model of Political Economy," *Journal of Economic Literature* 16: 1415–1434.

Schumpeter, Joseph A. (1954) *History of Economic Analysis*, New York: Oxford University Press.

Seligman, E.R.A. (1903) "On Some Neglected British Economists I & II," *The Economic Journal* 13(51): 335–363 and 511–535.

Senior, Nassau W. (1965) [1836] *An Outline of the Science of Political Economy*, New York: Augustus M. Kelley.

Senior, Nassau W. (2002) [1827–1852] *Selected Writings on Economics*, Honolulu, HI: University Press of the Pacific.

Smith, Adam (1976) [1776] *An Inquiry into the Nature and Causes of the Wealth of Nations*, 2 vols, Indianapolis: Liberty Classics.

Sraffa, Piero (1966) "Introduction," in David Ricardo, *The Works and Correspondence of David Ricardo*, P. Sraffa and M.H. Dobb (eds) 10 vols, Cambridge: Cambridge University Press: I: xiii–lxii.

Stigler, George J. (1965) [1958] "Ricardo and the 93 Per Cent Labour Theory of Value," in idem, *Essays in the History of Economics*, Chicago: University of Chicago Press, pp. 326–342.

Vance, Robert (1848) *The English and Irish Analyses or Wages and Profits*, Dublin: Hodges and Smith.

Vickrey, William S. (1964) *Microstatics*, New York: Harcourt Brace & World.

Viner, Jacob 1964 [1937] *Studies in the Theory of International Trade*, London: George Allen & Unwin.

Waterman, A.M.C. (2004) *Political Economy and Christian Theology since the Enlightenment*, New York: Palgrave Macmillan.

Whately, Richard (1875) [1826] *Elements of Logic*, 9th edition, London: Longmans, Green and Co.

Whately, Richard (1966) [1832] *Introductory Lectures on Political Economy*, New York: Augustus M. Kelley.

6 The classical economist perspective on landed-property reform

Charles Hickson

Introduction

Many classical economists were prominent participants in the political controversies that led up to a sequence of land-law legislative initiatives introduced from the mid-nineteenth to the turn of the twentieth century. An important dimension of the ongoing debate related to demands to dramatically alter long-standing inheritance rules, which acted to make it difficult for sitting tenants, that is, the family member in possession, to dispose of entailed property. Another dimension was the call to extend to Irish farm tenants greater security in their farm holdings, generally at the expense of landlords.

A primary interest of this chapter is to weigh to what extent the attitudes of prominent classical economists regarding changes in land law were either normative, that is redistributional, rather than positive in the sense of Pareto improving. Indeed, Pareto improvement may itself be construed as a normative criterion. In our discussion this realisation may be important because we are dealing with a reassignment of property rights, leading to wealth redistribution and thereby to the possibility of a different Pareto efficient outcome. Nevertheless, as is discussed below, reassigning property rights to existing assets comes at a substantial additional cost, which may arise from a badly instituted policy that imposes any new badly specified property-right reforms.

Normative tendencies among classical economists may have arisen due to close relationships with financial and mercantile interests. Many early economists also had legal training and anti-landed-wealth sentiment was typical of many lawyers of the period, as well as a commonly held opinion of many of the liberal elite. Particular hostility was directed against the House of Lords, which was the forum through which the dominant families of landed wealth advanced their interest. Moreover, anti-landed-wealth political sentiment became more acute after the extension of the franchise in the 1860s.[1]

Both entail and tenant rights issues were fuelled particularly in the Irish context. For example, John Stuart Mill clearly realised both issues were closely intertwined with the "Irish Question". Furthermore, significant legislative changes that were at first applied to Ireland, served later as a model for national legislation. For example, many of the features of the Encumbrances Act were later adopted in England, and many characteristics of Irish tenant legislation were later extended into parts of Scotland.

We are interested in the change in inheritance laws in general, and in legislation favouring Irish tenant farmers. The political controversies surrounding each included both redistributional and social efficiency aspects. Opposition to existing inheritance laws centred on the elimination of the strict-settlement system which worked to reduce the potential mal-incentives of a sitting tenant to squander family wealth to the detriment of future generations and current family members. The latter typically received life-long annuities. The parental mal-incentive aspects of the system were apparently largely discounted by classical economists. As will be elaborated below, many classical economists believed that strict settlement was an impediment to the free transfer of land, reducing the supply available to meet the increasing demand for land for urban or industrial uses. Since its establishment at the end of the seventeenth century, the strict-settlement system acted to perpetuate the aristocratic ownership of large landed estates. The system declined from the mid-nineteenth century, but was not effectively eliminated until the first quarter of the twentieth century.

Arising from the long-term political trend aimed at improving the welfare of Irish tenants, a second controversy arose. In part, this was motivated by the belief that land reforms would improve agricultural productivity.[2] However, pro-agricultural tenant sentiment was also based on the belief that somehow large landholdings had a somewhat illegitimate origin. As is elaborated below, this was clearly the view of many of later classicists and particularly that of the institutional classicists. As noted previously, Irish-style legislation was soon used as a model applicable to fringe areas of Scotland, where the population was also alleged to have a different property-right tradition. Eventually, at the turn of the twentieth century some of its features, such as compensation for tenants for "unjust" eviction, were extended to England.

The story of Irish tenant-right legislation marks an unprecedented and remarkable trend in Britain in the erosion of traditional rights over property for the individual, reflecting a dramatic transformation in the psychology of the political elites of the period. For example, the Deasy Act passed during the 1860s aimed to improve tenant welfare through more clearly defining the traditional rights and obligations of both tenants and landlords. Nevertheless, that approach was abandoned in subsequent acts. Ostensively to promote investment, in the early 1870s the Gladstone government granted Irish tenants greater protection against eviction if in good standing, and the right to compensation for "improvements". Subsequent legislation in the early 1880s, also passed under a Gladstone government, set up a new Land Commission to administer "fair rents", which required that Irish tenants be granted fixity of rent and fixity of tenure.

Fixity of tenure and fixity of rent extended to the Irish tenant farmer de facto co-ownership (Solow 1971: 23). Consequently, the provisions of the Act were considered to violate for the first time the traditional private property maxim of the individual having the right to dispose of his property as he saw fit. Later legislation extended to the Irish tenant farmer the legal right to sell his "ownership interest" thereby enabling him to also capitalise on his co-ownership. Arguably this additional legislative step encouraged Irish farm tenants to invest further in political bargaining. In retrospect, it is unsurprising that subsequent legislation at the end of the century subsidised eventual full ownership for sitting tenants.

Regarding their general view on *all* property ownership, classical economists, at least up to John Stuart Mill and John Elliot Cairnes, followed the lead of Adam Smith in the belief that the pursuit of self-interest led to the common good. This led them to the *laissez-faire* conclusion that an individual should be left free to use his property and to freely contract as he saw fit. The classical theory of rent, which was apparently independently developed by Torrens, Malthus and Ricardo, may have reinforced leading economists in opposing the Corn Laws (Seligman 1903). It can be argued that classical economists saw correctly that, in a well-defined property right system, rents were generated by the scarcity of land, and were independent of who received them. The classical theory of rent should in fact have reinforced the traditional hostility to landed property redistribution. Consequently, classical economists writing in the early nineteenth century followed Smith in accepting Locke's natural-law view of property rights, whereby the role of the state was limited to the protection of existing property rights.[3]

It is interesting to contrast a Lockian inspired state system to that of a Hobbesian. The latter argues that the existence of government is a necessary precondition in order to avoid the costly and therefore welfare-reducing condition where each individual is inclined to predate against his neighbours' property. Significantly, the role of the Hobbesian state is to both assign as well as to enforce its preferred bundle of property rights. Nevertheless, *ceteris paribus*, an obvious advantage of a Lockian over a Hobbesian property-right system is that the former acts as a better prophylactic against the prospect of any state-inspired property redistribution in future periods, arising out of political realignments or new technology. While it may be always important for the law to adapt to new problems, successful economies invariably always extend strong protection to existing property rights in order to avoid substantial costs generated by time inconsistency problems.

It is important to note that it was through the perspective of Benthamite utilitarianism that many lawyers and elements of the growing bureaucratic establishment became convinced of the classical economic approach to resolving property and contractual problems (Atiyah 1979: 293).[4] Benthamism was in basic agreement with the other classical economists regarding traditional property rights, but differed from the Smithian notion that the pursuit of self-interest naturally leads to the public good. Indeed, Bentham argued that the public good had to be protected against the excessive pursuit of self-interest. Thus his approach to government intervention is wholly consistent with Lockian principles.

The influence of Benthamite doctrine over nineteenth-century legal and other elites was replaced during the late 1860s and early 1870s by historicist ideology, particular the work of Henry Maine. Maine's approach to jurisprudence was greatly influenced by the evolutionary approach of Savigny and other German historicists (Atyiah 1979: 603). The important aspect of the new historicist hegemony in the legal profession is that it served as a rationale for the weakening of traditional landed property rights, particularly in regard to non-English contexts such as Ireland, where claims of customary tenant privileges, resting on natural law sentiments, generated greater political resonance. Significantly, historicist relativism also gained influence among economists organised around the Oxford–Dublin School. Prominent Irish economists such as Leslie and Ingram were well-known historicists who to varying degrees influenced nineteenth-century Irish land law (Black 1953: 118).

The rest of this chapter is organised as follows. The next section discusses the political arguments of classical economists regarding the strict-settlement system with the aim of attempting to identify the reasons underlying their inherent dislike of the system. We will conclude our discussion on the strict-settlement system by identifying some of its potential social advantages, which were seemingly overlooked by nineteenth-century economists. The following section contrasts the property-right approach relating to farm tenancies of early classical economists, such as Nassau Senior and James McCulloch with the more redistributional approach of John Stuart Mill and John Elliot Cairnes. The latter discussion concludes by comparing the views of the latter with subsequent legislation.

The classical economist preference for alienable over inalienable rights

The strict-settlement trust system arose during the late seventeenth century. The nature of the trust was designed as a device that acted as a legal shield in order to protect large landowners against a common law trend threatening perpetuities (Berman 2003: 335).[5] Over the same period, law was evolving to facilitate the sale of land, which required that trust law could distinguish between equity and legal title. Lawyers representing the large landed families were able to respond to the common law threat through a clever application of the above distinction. The strict-settlement trust allowed the father to bequeath the estate to his eldest son with a tie that the estate would then be passed on to his grandson or in the absence of a grandson to the next male heir.

Strict settlements were not administered by the Common Law Court, but rather by the Chancery Court. The device prevented the sitting tenant from becoming vested in his property until his heir was twenty-one years of age, by which time he was thought to be beyond the period in his life when he was most likely to be a spendthrift. Consequently the device worked to prevent a sitting tenant from selling property or from incurring high levels of debt beyond the present value of his expected income derived from the property (Habakkuk 1995: 75–6).

Permanent perpetuities were not permitted in England, having been abolished in the late seventeenth century, but the Common Law courts continued to be hostile to even less permanent forms of entail. This hostility carried over to the newly independent United States, where entail was nationally abolished by a statute passed by the Continental Congress in 1776. Thomas Jefferson famously declared at the time that "the dead hand of the past should not hold sway over the present". However, perpetuities persisted in some European nations, including Scotland, where the practice was sanctioned by Parliament as late as 1685 (Habakkuk 1995: 6).

Adam Smith was against all forms of entail, including its Civil Law form called *fedeicommissum*. The latter Civil Law device had been adopted by European aristocracy in the early sixteenth century as a dynastic defence against potential property alienation. Such a threat had become much greater at the end of the fifteenth century with the elimination of remaining feudal forms of property, which tended to occur in Western Europe after the reception of Roman law.

Adam Smith also thought that entail was based on the absurd notion that "the property of the present generation should be restrained and regulated according to the fancy of those who died perhaps five hundred years ago" (Smith 1939: 363). Smith here seems to be particularly objecting to the restriction imposed by entail on the free transfer of land. He further argued that entail was an obsolete custom, having only been useful when landownership was necessary in order to raise a feudal army. Moreover, he argued that its continued existence was more due to the desire of the aristocracy to maintain the custom of primogeniture, which was necessary for a family to maintain its influence in the House of Lords. The latter chamber was generally regarded as the primary means through which the landed aristocracy maintained their political power (Smith 1939: 363). Smith broadly agreed with the sentiments of the physiocrats who had also opposed perpetuities (Samuels 1962).[6] Smith's anti-entail or anti-perpetuity sentiments were more strongly and consistently expressed by Ricardo and other classical economists writing in the early part of the nineteenth century (for example, see Ricardo 1973: 386).

The view of the early classical economists on entail is consistent with the growing legal trend toward individualism and away from older ideas of collectivism. According to Atiyah this trend strengthened from the beginning in the last quarter of the eighteenth century (Atiyah 1979: 226–37). We know for example, that economists typically received formal legal training and for the first forty years of the nineteenth century there was a particularly close relationship between law, economics and social sciences (Atiyah 1979: 293).

Despite the expression of such strong opposition, the strict-settlement system remained secure until the mid-nineteenth century, when it suffered its first blow in the aftermath of the Irish famine. As is well known, among the liberal and Whig political elite of the period, Irish landlords were particularly disliked, in large part due to the impoverishment of their tenants. Irish landlords were seen as less legitimate and such sentiments found expression in the written opinions of leading economists. For example, in his *Essays on England, Ireland and the Empire*, Mill argues that the landlord class in Ireland were somehow less legitimate as they were perceived by the native Irish as members of an alien culture, who had seized and held their land under an alien legal system (Mill 1982: 513). Cairnes expresses similar sentiments, and goes on to criticise the larger landlords for becoming disinterested absentee rent collectors, who had resorted to employing a hierarchy of middlemen to run their estates (Cairnes 2004: 167). Nassau Senior stated that "Providence had ordained the existence of landlords – a class of persons whose interests it is that land should produce as large as possible an amount of surplus produce", but he, nevertheless, hastened to chastise absentee landlords (Senior 1928: 309–16).

The legal form of the strict-settlement trust was such that it prevented creditors from pursuing debt claims beyond the life interest of the sitting tenant. In regard to Irish landlords, this safeguard proved ineffective when in 1848, Landed Estates Courts were established to oversee the forced liquidation of encumbered estates in order at least in part to satisfy creditors. The interesting aspect of the Encumbrances Act was that for the first time, despite the previously understood practice that limited liability to a sitting tenant's interest only, claims were made against the interests of heirs and other family claimants (Habakkuk 1994: 636–8). Cairnes notes that by 1858, when the Estates Court was replaced by the Landed Estates Court, which continued in the same vein, a seventh by area of landed property changed hands, and by 1865, under both Courts one eighth of Irish land by value had changed hands. Cairnes on the whole saw this process as a good thing as it replaced "greedy, reckless and pernicious landlords as well as landlords who were insolvent with those having a more mercantile instinct" (Cairnes 2004: 171–91).[7]

The Irish Encumbrances Act formed a basis for later reforms in England. The Cardwell Act made it easier for English landlords to raise debt ostensibly for agricultural improvement. However, increasingly debt was also used for "conspicuous consumption buildings and gambling debts", and correspondingly trustees acquired more power to sell property to pay off encumbrances (Habakkuk 1994: 636–8). Subsequently, the Settled Estates Act of 1856 eased the sale of tied land as long as it was approved by Court of Chancery. Chancery approval became easier over time, until finally, under the Settled Land Act of 1882, a sitting tenant was permitted to sell settled land of his own free will (Habakkuk 1994: 645). The above legislative trend is consistent with the growing liberal influence in the House of Commons, which became increasingly paramount after the mid-nineteenth century. For example, Gladstone was known to be an enemy of entail (Habakkuk 1994: 636–8).

One of the claims against the practice of entail is that it worked to lock up land and to limit the use of its produce. But there are a number of difficulties with this charge. First, each settlement agreement tied family property for approximately twenty years, after which time the family was able to reassess its options when a new settlement was drawn up. Second, any strict-settlement agreement could always be altered if all the family members agreed. Consequently, in this aspect the strict-settlement contract was not unlike any common law fixed-term contract. Therefore, if land was becoming more valuable than before for industrial or urban use, then the opportunity cost borne by the family of continuing as before must rise substantially. Given this, it is difficult to see why the family would not optimally respond to changes to the economic environment. Finally, recent evidence indicates that land values in England, as measured by years of purchase, fell for three decades after the demise of entail. Offer (1991) notes that this pattern follows agricultural incomes, suggesting that land prices were not greatly influenced by the rapid urbanisation characteristic of the period. While it may be argued that the non-responsiveness of land prices to urbanisation factors may be due to the fact that entail made such land unavailable for that purpose, this view does not explain why land prices actually fell during the 1880s when legislation had made it easier for the sitting tenant to release entailed land. Furthermore, during this period there is little evidence of any great surge to dissolve and sell family property (Offer 1991). Consequently, one can conjecture that much of the opposition to entail may be attributed to political rather than economic motives.

Freedom of property verses feuding over property

An existing substantive body of research outlines the conflicting opinions among nineteenth-century economists on the best way forward to improve the welfare of the Irish farm tenant (e.g. see Black 1960; Dewey 1974; Kinser 1984). The typical approach of the existing literature is to partition the early classical econo-mists as being *laissez-faire* in orientation, and later classical economists, particu-larly John Stuart Mill and John Elliot Cairnes as more interventionist.[8] This chronological distinction also conforms to the early classicists having a stricter positive approach, and the latter acquiring a more normative approach, favouring redistribution in favour of Irish tenant farmers.

According to R.D.C. Black, the relatively *laissez-faire* approach to Irish poverty of the classical economists, writing before the famine, was in large part forged by their theory of distribution, particularly the Classical Theory of Rent and the Wage Fund analysis, combined with a belief in the Malthusian doctrine of population (Black 1953). Consequently, they concluded that the Irish popula-tion had outstripped the available land, although investment and reclamation might temporarily ameliorate this imbalance. Classicists also proposed, as a longer-term remedy against impoverishment, a reduction in the population through emigration. While the above analysis has much to offer in terms of understanding the policy perspective of early classical economists, it neglects their views on the role of property rights.

The views of Senior

It is widely accepted that Senior, who is known to have had intimate knowledge of rural Ireland, did not agree with the Malthusian doctrine. In large part this may be attributed to his belief that landlords were

> a class of persons whose interest it is that land should produce as large as possible an amount of surplus produce, and for that purpose should be occu-pied by only the number of persons necessary to enable it to produce the largest possible amount beyond its own subsistence.
>
> (Senior 1928: 309)

Senior's argument rests on what Hardin in the 1960s termed the "Tragedy of the Commons", but the problem of the over-exploitation of common ownership was well known even to the ancients. For example, the problem is clearly expressed in the works of Aristotle and Thucydides, but the first mention of it is most likely of more ancient origin.

In the language of modern economics, Senior's comments above seem to express the idea that it is in the landlord's interest to limit the employment of labour on his property up to the point where the "bounty" of the land is maximised. Consequently, Senior argues that landowners should be legally empowered to limit entry into their property, and that the landlord's interest is consistent with the social welfare of the nation.

Senior's insightful comment recognises that, if the exploitation of a parcel of land is freely available to all, entry will continue up to where the value of the average product equals the last entering tenant farmer's opportunity cost. Consequently, given diminishing returns to labour in farm-production technology, the level of agricultural output would far outstrip the level at which land value is maximised. By extension Senior's argument implies that, *ceteris paribus* and where the supply of arable land is fixed, well-defined property rights can prevent excess population growth.[9]

Senior took issue with the prevailing English public opinion, which increasingly tended to blame Irish landlords for creating rural poverty. He warned of the dangers of excessive subdivision of the land, going as far as to defend a "clearance" because it was the lesser evil to an inevitable over-exhaustion of the soil. Thus, Senior argued that laws introduced to prevent landlords from ejecting sub-tenants would, in fact, end up increasing rural poverty.

Nevertheless, Senior criticises Irish landlords for being inattentive and disinclined to invest in their property (Senior 1928: 312–13). He in fact attributes much of rural Irish poverty to inadequate levels of investment, and compares low investment in Ireland with levels in Yorkshire, which was at the time more prosperous. Senior fails to extend his argument to suggest that landlord under-investment may be a natural consequence of the property-right failure that he had clearly identified.

Senior also places responsibility for incidences of subdivision on landlord negligence. He quotes in detail from a report to the Devon Commission relating to Donegal. According to Senior, the report described the county as one where the population was left to fend for themselves, and where rents were low and rarely raised. Senior adds that the report also described in detail the practice of sub-tenanting in the parish of Kilmacrenan. Senior admitted that Kilmacrenan was an extreme case, but he argued that it served to make a general point. He quotes the report as describing a practice where primary tenants subdivide their tenancy, which is in turn subdivided by their tenant. The extent of the severity of subdivision was illustrated by one case mentioned in the Devon report where one small patch was held by twenty-two individuals. Senior also noted that from the same source many cases were recorded whereby "land was hired not by the acre, but by a cow's graze, and even by a cow's foot (cosbo), the fourth of a cow's graze, varying in value according to the quality of the soil, from 1s.8d to 17s.6d" (Senior 1928: 313).

The views of McCulloch

Regarding the agricultural industry, McCulloch's approach is in the same *laissez-faire* spirit as that of Senior. However, McCulloch concentrates more on the peculiarities of landlord–tenant property relationships due to their customary nature. McCulloch argues that the customary and thereby informal relationship existing between landlords and tenants, created many contractual problems, as elaborated below. Consequently, he believed strongly that agriculture should adopt the same contractual form existing in other industries. McCulloch points out that the overwhelming majority of Irish tenants, and anywhere from two-thirds to three-quarters of English farmers, operated without a lease. This was true in the latter case even in advanced areas. McCulloch argued that this did not imply that they were on at will notice, but operated under a custom whereby tenancies were expected to be permanent and pass through generations.

McCulloch noted that the customary leasing system remained popular with farm tenants because rents were seldom increased. Furthermore, landlords often found it difficult to evict tenants in good standing, a problem aggravated by the fact that the customary tenancy rights extended to the practice that leases were typically passed from father to son. McCulloch believed that agriculture would be more efficient if this system was replaced with one where leases had fixed terms as well as containing clearly specified conditions (McCulloch 1967: 167–8). Obviously McCulloch is of the opinion that a more market-friendly leasing system would assure that the land would be allocated more efficiently to the highest valued tenant.

McCulloch goes on to specify what should be the optimal term for farm leases. He argues that the shorter the lease, the more likely it will be that the tenant will use the land in an overly intensive manner. Similarly, he argued that leases tying the landlord but leaving the tenant free to quit, would also lead to over-exhaustion of the land. Consequently, the optimal lease should not only include a fixed-rent over its lifetime, but also be of sufficient duration to allow proper husbandry to allow proper crop rotation and to assure tenants the fruits from their improvements. He further realised that short-duration leases should impose restrictions in order to guard against abuse of the resource. Consequently, the shorter the lease, the more carefully the farm tenant would need to be monitored. McCulloch also agreed with Senior that subletting was a curse (McCulloch 1967: 190–6).

McCulloch concurs with Senior that it is always in the interests of landlords to ensure that the farm is always in good working order, but he clearly sees that there are inherent problems with any fixed-term lease. He notes that farm tenants will always have a tendency to leave the holding impoverished, and he stresses that any owner who fails to recognise the inherent mal-incentives of fixed-term contracts is not fit to be a landlord. Thus, the landlord should always monitor. To stress this point McCulloch cites the English folk saying "he that havocks may sit; he that improves must flit". McCulloch interprets the saying to mean that, under a fixed-term contract, the landlord would be inclined to seize all the gains from any improvement. However, he later cites an Italian expression, "*lascia podera*", which translates to mean adieu farm. This expression has a slightly different interpretation in that it refers to the tendency of the leaving tenant to ruin the vineyard at the end of his lease. Indeed, McCulloch also refers to a phrase from the ancient Greek author Theophrastus, who noted that fixed-term leases were common on the island of Thasos, and so proprietors there were on guard against abuse at the end of a lease. Thus McCulloch clearly recognises what modern economists refer to as the last period problem (McCulloch 1967: 199–200).

A prescient McCulloch identifies many of the bargaining problems that would be generated by forthcoming landlord–tenant legislation, when he argued against the customary practice, such as under the Ulster system, allowing farm tenants to claim for "unexhausted improvements". His argument against the latter is based on his realisation of problems due to the bargaining costs associated with ex post opportunism. The practice, which is generally termed tenant's right, was common in Ulster, and according to McCulloch was also common in parts of Yorkshire and Kent (McCulloch 1967: 215–16). McCulloch argued that claims for improvements were subject to all sorts of fraud and abuse, which everyone who was familiar with the practice was well aware of. McCulloch argues that where the practice was observed, landlords typically claimed that it was a fiction that payments for improvements were necessary in order to prevent eviction. Furthermore, after a lease signing, it was impossible to get tenants to spend on any improvements. McCulloch goes on to claim that it was common knowledge that everywhere it was practised, farms were in a worse state. This led McCulloch to conclude that it was the old tenant's fault if he had not exhausted his improvements before his lease had expired.

The views of John E. Cairnes and John Stuart Mill

To summarise our discussion above, classical economists such as Senior stressed more the importance of having well-defined and enforceable property rights. On the other hand, McCulloch focused on the need for landlord and tenant relations to be placed on the same contractual terms as that existing in other industries so that farms would end up in the hands of the highest-valued users. He also specified many of the contractual problems that can arise due to ex post hold-up and bargaining costs and last period problems. Both Senior and McCulloch's perspectives are consistent with a *laissez-faire* approach to welfare.

Despite the insights expressed by the early classical economists as to the efficiency of well-defined property rights, during the 1860s, later economists, including many leading classical economists, increasingly argued in favour of polices that would give rise to unclear property-right claims with regard to landed property. Such arguments were motivated by a strong tendency by later economists to redistribute in favour of tenant farmers. We take as examples of the above trend the arguments of the classical economists, John Elliot Cairnes and John Stuart Mill. Both men were significant contributors to the political debates on landlord–tenant issues. For example, the Irish economist Cairnes argued in favour of regulation in order to fix the rents of Irish tenants and to impose fixity of tenure. John Stuart Mill also called for fixity of Irish tenant rents. While at first Mill was reluctant to also call for fixity of tenure on the basis that this would imply expropriation of landlords, he eventually did so, apparently in response to the threat to English rule posed by the Fenian movement during the 1860s (Kinser 1984).

The stance of Cairnes is particularly interesting, given his favourable account of the rapid transformation of Irish agriculture within a few years after the famine, from being a cereal-dominated to a pasture-dominant industry, which he attributes to the elimination of the Corn Laws, which enabled a return by Irish agriculture to its comparative advantage. This transformation, he noted, is associated with a decline in population of about one-third within a few decades, and a dramatic corresponding decline in the cottier class of farmers on small potato-patch lots, replaced by a class of "farmers holding 15 to 20–40 acres" (Cairnes 2004: III: 181–6, 228). There was also a corresponding decline in the practice of subdivision, which encouraged Cairnes to state optimistically that the median size of tenancies, though still comparatively smaller than other parts of Britain, had increased sufficiently to permit profitable larger scale investment. But perhaps more significantly, Cairnes also noted that the forced sell-off of land due to the Encumbrances Act had transferred land "from listless and bankrupt to solvent and enterprising hands" (Cairnes 2004: III: 143, 179). He notes that that farm incomes had risen by 1865 by as much as much as 40 per cent (Cairnes 2004: III: 228).

Nevertheless, Cairnes, writing in 1865, believed that short-term leases were still a major problem in Irish agriculture (Cairnes 2004: VI: 217). In fact, as late as the 1860s, only approximately 20 per cent of tenants had leases. While most tenants held only by the year, it was understood by custom that the tenancy would be renewed year by year, and the tenant was to be evicted only for just cause, such as rent arrears, and only through legal process (Cairnes 2004: VI: 217).

Cairnes believed that even in the 1860s, rackrenting was still common, as indeed was absentee landlordism (Cairnes 2004: VI: 231). Consequently, he believed that the earlier classical economist had been wrong in treating agriculture as similar to other industries. He noted that in many European countries, such as in Prussia after the Stein reforms, and in nineteenth-century France, tenants enjoyed fixed rents and fixity of tenure (Cairnes 2004: VI: 231). Consistently, he also supported so-called tenant rights, but only insofar as the scheme was a fair compensation to tenants for improvements. Significantly, he states that "if improvements were only allowed that landlords approved no improvements would be approved" (Cairnes 2004: VI: 241). He also seemed aware that any such scheme would produce substantial bargaining costs. For example, he objected to a cost-based approach as it would work to favour landlords, as it was they who would gain from any added value stemming from investment. On the other hand, he conceded that landlords should not be asked to indemnify every improvement made by tenants. He suspected that the latter approach was the one favoured at the time by the land court (Cairnes 2004: VI: 241).

John Stuart Mill in general was a strong advocate of proprietary farming, and believed that land belonged to the people of the nation. His opinion appears in part to be based on a moral aversion to the large landlord class, which he believed were mere idle rent collectors, and whose interest in holding their estates stemmed solely from their dynastic political ambitions. He expressed particular moral aversion for the Irish landlords, among whom there were a high proportion of absentee owners.

Mill also argued that proprietor ownership was more efficient as farmers would have a better incentive to make improvements leading to increased productivity. In Parliament he proposed that the government should establish a scheme to assist tenants to purchase their holdings. Mill, consistent with the classical tradition, argued against expropriation. However, he argued that compensation to landlords should deduct from the market value that component attributable to the expected growth in the overall economy or due to any improvements made by tenants. Mill's recommendations required detailed information on the value of all Irish landholdings. This recommendation faced the difficulties of accounting for variations in the price of parcels of agricultural land across a region in accordance with their productivity, ease of access to markets and the changing relative price of crops etc. Nevertheless, the Griffith land valuation surveys undertaken in 1826, 1846 and 1852 were intended to collect such information. However, even accepting that the surveys were able to overcome the difficulties noted above, Mill's proposal carried the danger of double discounting due to the fact that land prices would immediately decline once such a policy was announced. Furthermore, it is paradoxical that Mill called only for a rent-adjusted reduction in the price for agricultural land, since many other fixed-supply durable assets also earn rents, such as art works, jewellery and even residential housing.

Unlike Senior, Mill was not particularly well informed on Irish agricultural developments, and to become better informed he corresponded with Cairnes. Mill expressed his mature ideas on the political solution for Ireland in the late 1860s in a pamphlet entitled *England and Ireland*, which of course was written during the Fenian uprising. In this article he argued that Irish landlords were particularly neglectful of their estates, and that this was a major factor underlying Irish rebelliousness. In this pamphlet he states that the rebellion is in large part a natural reaction by the Irish people against a landlord class, which was alien in culture, having an illegitimate claim to their possessions as it was gained through armed invasion (Mill 1982: VI: 513).

As stated above, Mill was at first reluctant to call for proprietary farming in Ireland, because he believed that many farms were still too small and that Irish tenants at the time had neither sufficient knowledge nor experience to become successful market farmers. Consequently, his early policy was to suggest a fixed rent system, which was to be set at a rate sufficient to compensate owners for the value of their estate valued at the current market price, but appropriately discounted to exclude the expected discounted value attributable to growth in the overall economy. As stated above, due to the heterogeneity of land parcels and to the fact that rents were generally determined by custom and not the market, there were obvious difficulties in determining the particular from the general components of rents. However, ignoring this difficulty, it is clear that Mill's fixed-rent scheme, due to the rent-discount adjustment, would operate as a price floor.

As noted above, Mill was not at first in favour of fixity of tenure, which leaves open the effectiveness of his original scheme in terms of both efficiency and maximising the net welfare gain to sitting tenants. For example, Mill makes no mention of a government tax scheme equal to the amount of the rent. However, he preferred that landowners should be reduced to receiving an annuity determined by the amortised market value of their estate according to the formula described above. If we assume that landlords were to remain in managerial control of their property, allowing them to freely contract (for any length of time) with any one of a large number of potential tenants would mean that even though nominal rent levels may be fixed, real rents would tend to rise. For example, landlords would select higher quality tenants than before, and landlords would spend less on estate-wide improvements such as drainage. Moreover, prospective tenants would be inclined to offer landlords side-payments.

The above scheme would tend to eventually reallocate the higher quality tenant with the higher quality landlord. On the other hand if the sitting tenant had the default right to remain in his holding, that is given fixity of tenure, and was unable to capitalise on it, then the lower quality tenants would have no incentive to quit, and would have even less incentive to improve, while landlords would be more inclined to offer less estate-wide improvements. Mill's reluctance to embrace fixity of tenure on the grounds that it would lead to expropriation of landlords' property seems to have been based on his cognition of this process. Nevertheless, if the tenant is granted the right to sell, he would then acquire a de facto co-ownership in the property. Given a right to sell, we expect, that while as before the landlord would have the same reduced incentive to improve his estate, the tenant would have an increased incentive to improve his holding or to sell to an individual who would. Consequently, the best property would be eventually allocated to higher quality tenants.

Nevertheless, overall welfare improvement in farming depends on the trade-off between the decline in public good or estate-wide investments and the extent of the aggregate farm-level improvements. Thus much of the net social welfare effect would depend on such details, and unfortunately there are few clues in Mill's writings on the subject.

It is interesting to compare Mill's policy prescriptions with later legislation. Both the 1871 and 1881 acts were designed to improve the welfare of Irish tenants. As noted above, the earlier legislation granted sitting tenants the right to claim, under arbitration, compensation for "improvements". The objective was to encourage greater investment. The value of such claims, as we noted above, would have been difficult to determine due to overall economy and local market changes. Consequently, the provision of the legislation also would give rise to substantial hold-up problems, which would have produced substantial bargaining costs. The later legislation having the aim of fair rents, granting tenants fixity of tenure and fixity of rents would have created substantial quasi rents. Thus bargaining costs over their distribution would have been high.

In contrast to Cairnes, Mill seems unaware that compensation claims for improvements would have generated substantial bargaining costs. The evidence indicates that the land courts, which had been established to adjudicate disputes between landlord and tenant, had quickly become clogged with demands for compensation and petitions to lower rents.

Mill also seemed to have had little appreciation of the potential political bargaining costs that would naturally arise from his policies outlined above.[10] For example, the 1871 Act included what was called the Bright clause, which introduced a scheme to encourage Irish tenants to convert to owners. Even though the scheme included a substantial subsidy from the tax-payer, few tenants took up the offer (Solow 1971: 186). However, the 1871 and 1881 legislation would have operated to substantially reduce property values during the 1880s, which were at the time also suffering from an agricultural recession (Solow 1971: 189). The legislation had also made it difficult to evict tenants, thus it may have added to the effectiveness of the rent strike organised by Davitt (Solow 1971: 189). Consequently, by the late 1880s, landlords requested that a new scheme be introduced that was attractive enough to encourage tenants to purchase their holdings.

The 1891 Ashburn Act offered tenants purchase terms with greatly subsidised interest payments. Under this Act, landlords were offered annuities that were substantially lower than their rental incomes. Thus only encumbered landlords would be better off (Solow 1971: 191–2). Unsurprisingly, substantial purchase of farms by tenants did not occur until the Wyndham Act was passed in 1903. This legislation carried a huge subsidy of £150 million, enabling tenants to purchase on very favourable terms. Mortgage repayments rates were offered at levels that were between 20 and 40 per cent below first-term rents (Solow 1971: 192). Moreover, the size of the subsidy was such that the position of landlords was also improved.

Conclusion

The object of this chapter was to analyse the contributions of classical economists to the nineteenth-century political debates over landownership rights as to whether they were positive or redistributive in orientation, and it was noted that the classical economists appear to have heavily discounted obvious social efficiency aspects of the strict-settlement system. It was argued that the system acted to discourage parental mal-incentives as well as other anti-family behaviour and that there were no identifiable analytical market inefficiencies as the family and the sitting tenant internalised all the opportunity costs and gains from maintaining an entailed estate.

Both the early and later classical economists consistently argued against the strict-settlement system on the basis that it impeded the transfer of land to its highest valued use. They also applied a political economy rationale, in that entail was essential in order for the aristocracy to maintain its collective political influence as expressed thought the House of Lords. They argued that this influence acted to prevent economic progress. This charge was levelled with particular force by classical economists against Irish landlords, and most probably influenced the Encumbrance Acts passed immediately after the famine.

As was noted above, the early classical economists argued in favour of replacing the customary landlord–tenant relationships existing in Irish agriculture and elsewhere, with a clearly defined contractual system. A contract system which clearly specified the contract duration and rights and obligations of both parties would have allowed the land to be applied by its owner to its most productive use. As was argued above, Senior stressed that landlord rights were essential to prevent land overuse, particularly through the practice of subdivision. On the other hand, much of McCulloch's work related to inefficiencies arising from poorly defined rental (including implicit) contracts. He was particularly critical of customary rental agreements that passed through the generations. Interestingly, McCulloch seemed particularly interested in ex post contractual problems, such as contractual costs associated with claims for "un-exhausted improvements", and the overuse of land due to last-period problems.

The discussion concluded by considering the work of later classical economists such as Cairnes and J.S. Mill, both of whom expressed moral sentiments in favour of the Irish tenant. Both of the above economists deviated from the position of the early classicists and argued in favour of fixity of tenure and rents, as well as compensation for "un-exhausted improvements". These policy recommendations led to a blurring of property rights in Irish agriculture that lead to substantial costs arising from time inconsistency problems, but also to substantially increased bargaining costs borne in part by tenant, landlord and the society at large.

Notes

1 It is often argued that anti-landed-wealth sentiment, which was characteristic of the period, was a product of increasing industrialisation and urban growth, but this view does not explain similar anti-landlord trends in pre-industrial societies such as late-eighteenth-century France. Paradoxically, land reform was also introduced in landlord-dominated Napoleonic era Prussia. Thompson and Hickson alternatively argue that greater sympathy toward the masses came due to a change in military technology favouring mass citizen armies (Thompson and Hickson 2001: 182–8).

2 As will be expanded below, John Stuart Mill's views supporting peasant proprietorship rested on the basis that it would lead to increased efficiency, and on the basis that landlords were not entitled to gains generated by improvements (Kinser 1984).

3 As Armen Alchian points out, the Lockian view also precludes the use of any asset such that it interferes with the rights of other asset owners (Alchian 1977: 105). Alchian's comment implies that even though classical economists accepted the existing property structure, non-optimal uses of assets leading to externalities was implicitly

recognised by them. The advent of the modern property-right theory began with the publication in 1960 of R.H. Coase's "The Problem of Social Cost" (Demsetz 1967). On the basis of Coase's seminal article, property-right theory evolved to stress the importance on a clear specification of limits on usufruct rights in order to minimise social costs generated through potential rent seeking.

4 Significantly, it was a Bentham disciple who is accredited with first advancing the concept of externality. In a Sanitary Report to the Poor Law Commission in 1834, the lawyer identified the considerable cost to the Commission due to the actions of third parties who were not called upon to carry the burden (Atiyah 1979: 293).

5 The Long Parliament had previously expressed its dislike of perpetuities. However, during the Restoration, the so-called "rule against perpetuities" was first enunciated by Lord Nottingham in 1681 in the Duke of Norfolk's case, and it was later elaborated by successive eighteenth-century chancellors This law placed restrictions on perpetuities, which were defined as grants of land that perpetuated ownership for more than twenty-one years beyond the death of any one person named in the grant (Berman 2003: 500). A clear distinction between equity and legal ownership is also credited to the same Lord Nottingham (Berman 2003: 336–7).

6 According to Warren Samuels the physiocrats, particularly Turgot, opposed *foundations*, which were the French equivalent of Anglo-Saxon perpetuities (Samuels 1962: 101).

7 Cairnes was aware that forced sales of so many estates in a short time would generate a fire sale effect whereby land prices would be depressed at a time when other legislation was placing burdens on landed property (Cairnes 2004: 173).

8 A third group of nineteenth-century economists referred to as the Oxford–Dublin School were more interventionist and much more redistributive. However in this article we will restrict our discussion to classical economists.

9 In the case where we have industrialisation, restricted entry to the point where the value of the marginal product equals the opportunity wage, would not be the same as the number of firms can expand as long as it is profitable to do so.

10 That both Cairnes and Mill called for both fixity of rent combined with fixity of tenure is interesting from a social welfare and redistribution perspective. For example the ensuing legislative provisions made it difficult to evict sitting tenants. This was crucial to ensure that tenants would not end up bearing most of the welfare cost from rent control. For example, while land was in fixed supply and inelastic, the supply of farm leases can be expected to fall after the imposition of a below-market level of rent. Furthermore, the elasticity of supply would also increase over time as owners shift into products requiring less individual attention e.g. into pasture rather than grain. Thus, if realistically we assume that the demand for farm leases remained constant after rent control regulation, and if the fall in the supply of farm leases was sufficiently large, then the welfare loss to tenants would dominate any welfare gain generated by fixed rents. Hence the necessity to prevent landlords removing sitting tenants through provisions of fixity of tenure for long periods, and substantial compensation to evicted tenants in good standing. From a social welfare perspective, restricting conversion to owner-managed farms would have been Pareto-improving if it had prevented a shift into less profitable crops. However, paradoxically, many economists such as Cairnes and Leslie, for example, argued that this was the natural comparative advantage of Irish agriculture anyway.

Bibliography

Alchian, A. (1977) *Economic Forces at Work*, Indianapolis: Liberty Press.

Atiyah, P.S. (1979) *The Rise and Fall of Freedom of Contract*, Oxford: Clarendon Press.

Berman, H.J. (2003) *Law and Revolution, Vol. 2*, Cambridge, MA: Belknap Press of Harvard University Press.

Black, R.D.C. (ed.) (1947) *The Statistical and Social Inquiry of Ireland, Century Volume: 1847–1947*, Dublin: Eason.

Black, R.D.C. (1953) "Classical Economics and the Irish Problem", *Oxford Economic Papers, New Series* 5: 26–40.

Black, R.D.C. (1960) *Economic Thought and the Irish Question, 1817–1870*, London: Cambridge University Press.

Blaug, Mark (1996) *Economic Theory in Retrospect*, 5th edn, Cambridge: Cambridge University Press.

Cairnes, J.E. (2004) *Collected Works*, Tom Boylan and Tadhg Foley (eds) III–IV, VI, London: Routledge.

Demsetz, Harold (1967) "Towards a Theory of Property Rights", *American Economic Review, Papers and Proceedings* 7: 347–59.

Dewey, Clive (1974) "The Celtic Agrarian Legislation and the Celtic Revival", *Past and Present* 64: 30–70.

Habakkuk, John (1994) *Marriage, Debt and the Estates System – English Landowner-ship: 1650–1950*, Oxford: Clarendon Press.

Kinser, Bruce (1984) "J.S. Mill and Irish Land", *The Historical Journal* 27: 111–27.

McCulloch, John R. (ed.) (1967) *Treatises and Essays on Subjects Connected with Economic Policy: with Biographical Sketches of Quesnay, Adam Smith and Ricardo*, New York: Augustus Kelley.

Mill, John S. (1982) "Essays on England, Ireland and the Empire", *Collected Works of John Stuart Mill*, John Robinson and Joseph Hamburger (eds) VI, Toronto: University of Toronto Press, Routledge.

Offer, Avner (1991) "Farm Tenure and Land Values in England, c.1750–1958", *Economic History Review, New Series* 44: 1–20.

Ricardo, David (1973) *The Principles of Political Economy*, New York: Everyman's Library.

Samuels, Warren J. (1962) "The Physiocratic Theory of the State", *The Quarterly Journal of Economics* 75: 96–110.

Seligman, Edwin R.A. (1903) "On Some Neglected British Economists", *The Economic Journal* 13: 335–63.

Senior, Nassau (1928) *Industrial Efficiency and Social Economy*, 1 and 2, London: P.S. King and Son.

Smith, Adam (1939) *An Inquiry into the Nature and Causes of the Wealth of Nations*, New York: Random House.

Solow, Barbara (1971) *The Land Question and the Irish Economy, 1870–1903*, Cambridge, MA: Harvard University Press.

Steel, E.D. (1970) "J.S. Mill and the Irish Question: Reform, and the Integrity of the Empire, 1865–1870", *The Historical Journal* 13: 419–50.

Thompson, E.A. and Hickson, C.R. (2001) *Ideology and the Evolution of Vital Institutions: Guilds, the Gold Standard and Modern International Cooperation*, Boston: Kluwer Academic Publications.

7 John Elliot Cairnes

Land, *laissez-faire* and Ireland

Tom Boylan and Tadhg Foley[1]

The meeting of John Elliot Cairnes (1823–75) and John Stuart Mill at the Political Economy Club in London in 1859 initiated a deep and enduring friendship that generated an extensive correspondence, making Cairnes 'perhaps the most highly valued' of all of Mill's later correspondents (Mineka and Lindley 1972: xxxviii). In the course of his review of Cairnes's *The Slave Power* in the *Westminster Review* in 1862, Mill described Cairnes as 'one of the ablest of the distinguished men who have given lustre to the much-calumniated Irish colleges, as well as the chair of Political Economy that Ireland owes to the enlightened public spirit of Archbishop Whately' (Mill 1862: 489–90). This accolade from Mill, delivered in his characteristically modulated manner, was indeed warranted given Cairnes's standing in 1862. But it was particularly prescient when account is taken of Cairnes's standing at the time of his death in 1875, at the early age of fifty-two.

Cairnes was born at Castlebellingham, County Louth in 1823. He received the BA degree from Dublin University in 1848 and the MA in 1854. In 1856 he competed successfully for the Whately professorship of political economy at Trinity College Dublin and held this position for the full five-year tenure. In 1859 he was appointed to the chair of jurisprudence and political economy at Queen's College Galway, a position he held until 1870. In 1866 he was appointed to the professorship of political economy at University College London. Thus he held joint-professorships in Dublin and Galway between 1859 and 1861, and in Galway and London between 1866 and 1870. He resigned the London professorship in 1872 on health grounds, having vacated his Galway chair two years previously. Like many of his compatriots who held the Whately Chair, Cairnes also trained as a lawyer, having been called to the bar in 1857, but he never seriously practised law or engaged in any other occupation. He was from the outset a full-time academic economist and was one of the first professional economists in Great Britain and Ireland.

Cairnes's theoretical work ranged over a number of areas which included methodology, monetary economics, and economic theory, where he made a number of important contributions. In general, however, Cairnes's reputation rests largely on his two major works, *The Character and Logical Method of Political Economy* (1857, 2nd expanded edition 1875), and *Some Leading*

Principles of Political Economy Newly Expounded (1874). In particular, his *Leading Principles* is seen as the final restatement of classical political economy within the broad Ricardo–Mill tradition, which has earned him the enduring title of the 'last of the classical economists'. But the assignment of labels to Cairnes, whether Ricardian or Millian, should be carried out in a qualified and nuanced manner. While Cairnes certainly worked within the broad church of the Ricardo–Mill framework, his 'Ricardianism' requires careful decipherment; and while his commitment to the Millian paradigm was hardly in question, he differed sharply from Mill in a number of areas, both methodologically and in terms of economic theory. Thus he provided his own distinctive contribution, which has been recognized by a number of discerning scholars (Schumpeter 1954; Hands 2001).

We have elsewhere surveyed and evaluated Cairnes's contribution to political economy, both theoretical and applied (Boylan and Foley 1983, 1984a, 1984b, 1985, 2004). While Schumpeter called Cairnes 'a born theorist', he went on to remind his readers that 'we must not forget however […] that the bulk of his working hours went into practical problems and that it was his "factual" contribution (in particular his *Slave Power* 1862), which accounts for his reputation with the English public of his time' (Schumpeter 1954: 534). Further writings in this 'factual' domain, or what we could call the area of economic policy, were collected in his *Essays in Political Economy, Theoretical and Applied* and *Political Essays*, both published in 1873. Central to his 'factual contribution' was his long-standing concern with Irish affairs, more specifically his preoccupation with the pivotal issue of nineteenth-century Irish politics and economic policy, namely, the ownership and tenancy of land. The major outcome from this concern was Cairnes's stringent critique of *laissez-faire*, the presiding doctrine of British political and economic discourse during the nineteenth century. In this chapter we consider Cairnes's writings on both of these intimately related topics, which are among the dominant themes in nineteenth-century Irish economic thought. When Cairnes addressed these topics, he was not merely adding, we would argue, to what Schumpeter chose to call his 'factual contribution'. Much more was at stake. Underlying these topics were such fundamental issues as: the rights of property, the philosophical basis of liberalism, the status and limitations of the 'science' of political economy (especially when applied to Irish circumstances), and the role of the state in relation to the operation of the free market. An analysis of Cairnes's writings suggests that Irish land played an ideological role in British political discourse quite disproportionate to its economic significance. Part of our objective in this paper will be to outline Cairnes's thinking on, for him, the intimately related subjects of land and *laissez-faire*. In more general terms, we will indicate that solutions to the perennial problem of Irish land were widely perceived of in Britain as infringing on sacrosanct property rights, the doctrine of *laissez-faire*, and even on the laws of political economy itself.

John Maynard Keynes stated that Cairnes 'was perhaps the first orthodox economist to deliver a frontal attack upon *laissez-faire* in general' (Keynes 1926: 26). In a previous paper we suggested that it was no accident that such an attack came out of Ireland and we remarked on the widespread hostility towards political economy in Ireland. We noted the mischief wrought by Ireland, with its different socio-economic arrangements and ideas, to that quintessentially English discourse – political economy (Boylan and Foley 1983, 1984a: 111–15). It was widely felt that the laws of political economy, though universal in their application, somehow contrived not to have relevance to Ireland. Ireland was a sort of 'liberty' where the writs of political economy did not run. As R.E. Thompson, the American commentator, stated,

> Gladstone and Robert Lowe have held fast to every letter of the old shibboleths, except when it comes to legislation about Ireland. The laws of economics which govern the rest of the world are not in force on the western shore of St. George's Channel.
>
> (Thompson 1874: 638)

English theory, according to Cairnes, was notably at variance with 'Irish ideas' but it did not explain Irish 'fact' (Cairnes 2004: VI, 231–2). The terms 'Ireland' and 'land' were closely linked in the nineteenth century. When economists wrote on land, Ireland was never far from their attention. Land retained its centrality as a source of wealth in Ireland, though it was becoming increasingly peripheral in England, and it is a considerable historical irony that, as we shall maintain, 'Ireland' and 'land', marginal to English concerns, should contribute to subverting some of the very central tenets of the sovereign public discourse in nineteenth-century Britain, political economy. We will discuss these debates in the first part of our paper, while in the second we will consider Cairnes's important contributions to them.

Predictably, it was in the analysis of land that Ireland wielded greatest influence on political economy. In late 1846 and early 1847, when the famine was raging, Mill suspended work on his *Principles of Political Economy* for some months to write a total of forty-three leading articles on Ireland for the *Morning Chronicle*. So it is hardly surprising that a later economist, J. Shield Nicholson, opposing Mill's views on land, should observe that 'no doubt Mill's views were affected by the condition of Ireland when he wrote, and by its history' and he proceeded to admonish Mill for arguing from 'a particular case' (Nicholson 1909: 113). As Goldwin Smith observed, 'the whole subject of the relation of landlord and tenant has been opened by the questions raised upon it in Ireland' (quoted in Finlason 1870: iv). Gunnar Myrdal has stated that the Benthamites (who dominated English economic thinking) 'were radical in all respects, except in their views on property' (Myrdal 1953: 118). Commenting on this statement, Professor R.D. Collison Black has said that 'such a combination of attitudes was particularly unfortunate when applied to the Irish problem, whose solution primarily called for radical thinking on the issue of property relations' (Black 1960: 246). The conventional English wisdom was that its agricultural model was appropriate to Ireland as was a political economy based on English experience. It is hardly to be wondered at, wrote Black, that by 1868 or 1870, 'the majority of Irishmen had come to fear the application of classical political economy in

Irish land policy'; for the Irish, 'political economy meant *laissez-faire* and freedom of contract, not the doctrines of Mill and Cairnes' (Black 1960: 71, 70). By the middle and late 1860s, it was no longer assumed that English conditions had any necessary relevance to Ireland's position and there was a concomitant questioning of central tenets of political economy on private property in land and the role of the state in economic affairs.

Oliver MacDonagh, in his book *States of Mind*, argued that the Act of Union subjected Irish land, as well as all other Irish affairs, 'directly to a Parliament where English (I do not even say British) concepts and presuppositions predominated. Initially, this meant the gradual transference of the notions of political economy to the sister island' (MacDonagh 1983: 35). There was increasing friction between an imported and a native notion of property, the one absolutist, individualist, and contractual, the other a communal concept of Irish land. From 1801–65, stated MacDonagh, 'the official view of land in Ireland [...] was English derived' (McDonagh 1983: 36). The aim of the Encumbered Estates Court had been described as attempting to establish free trade in Irish land, to establish free contract, as against traditional status and custom. But the Irish tenants' views remained stubbornly recalcitrant to such notions. As Barbara Solow has said about the 'three Fs' (fair rent, fixity of tenure, and free sale), the

> correct interpretation of the tenant demands is not about divided property rights between owner and tenant [...] but rather concerns a different concept of property altogether, and the issue between landlord and tenant in Ireland was whether property was to be thought of as private or as in some sense communal.
>
> (Solow 1981: 303)

MacDonagh added that '[m]uch nineteenth-century Irish history then needs an appreciation of the subterranean challenge to the formally dominant theory of property, which the communal vision presented, to be fully understood' (MacDonagh 1983: 39). Gladstone's Land Act of 1870 'was presented as wholly orthodox, that is, as upholding the accepted rights of property; and as such, its passage through both Houses was quite smooth'. But, MacDonagh insisted, 'the ineffectuality of the measure should not lead us to miss the revolution in principles which it set off'. The right to compensation for improvements made without the landlord's consent; 'the qualification of his powers to evict; and the statutory endowment of a tenant's right to sell an "interest" in his land, all contradicted the shibboleths of unbridled landlord control over his own property' (MacDonagh 1983: 47–8). The 1881 Act, fully conceding the 'three Fs', was, according to MacDonagh, an 'undisguised acceptance of co-ownership', while free contract was 'wholly abandoned, to be replaced essentially by status; and the state was to be permanently involved in the conflict between the wrangling partners through the institution of the land courts, enjoined to fix "judicial rents"' (MacDonagh 1983: 48). Co-ownership proved to be an unstable condition and the eventual move was 'towards the elimination of landlordism altogether'. MacDonagh claimed that just as they had been 'elevated and inspired' in the earlier nineteenth century by English political economy and law, 'so now the Irish proprietors were being rejected and (as they would have said) betrayed by the turnabout in both, for which the Irish peasant offensive could largely claim the credit' (MacDonagh 1983: 49).

There was widespread anxiety in England in the 1860s that what was often described as the 'pacification' of Ireland, especially the final settlement of the Irish land question, might have to involve interference with private property in land. There were fears that these radical ideas might make their way to England and subvert property relations there, not only on the question of land (which most middle-class radicals would not be too perturbed about), but also might unsettle other forms of private property. One could give countless examples of economists, politicians, journalists, publicists, and pundits of all kinds warning the British public that the sacred rights of property were in danger if Britain capitulated to Irish ideas on the question of landlord–tenant relations. A letter to the *Pall Mall Gazette* (19 June 1867) spoke of the 'purely Fenian view of confiscation and division, which we need not discuss'. The letter went on to remark that the Irishman believed that he had a right of some sort 'as indefeasible as the right of his landlord to the land he occupies. If we are to content the Irish people, if we are to legislate in conformity with Irish ideas we must legislate thus.' To describe an idea as Irish was, of course, to condemn it for the very notion of an Irish idea was a contradiction in terms. The author of the letter could not comprehend how the idea of 'absolute property in landed estates' never 'penetrated the Irish mind'. The previous year, 1866, saw the introduction of Fortescue's Landlord and Tenant (Ireland) Bill. In the course of the debate Lord Naas said he believed that

> anything which involved so great a departure from the principle that has been for so many years adopted by Parliament and which involved also so great a departure from the almost sacred rights of property would be destructive to the ultimate settlement of the question, and greatly detrimental to the interests of the tenants
>
> (*Daily News*, 12 July 1866)

Commenting on Bright's oration in Dublin, *The Times* wrote, in an editorial, defending the right of the landlord, as owner of land in Ireland, to make whatever contract he pleased with regard to the letting of it. Land in Ireland should be treated 'precisely in the same manner as land in Scotland, England, and America, and as every other kind of property'. It added that the

> free right to contract lies at the bottom of all individual and national prosperity, and the man who invades this may be a leveller, but is not a Liberal. The same may be said with regard to the complaints against absenteeism, and of the accumulation of large properties in few hands. These things are the result of unrestricted personal liberty, of acquisitions by the provident and of alienations by the reckless, and the cry that is raised against them in

the name of Liberalism is really a cry for the restriction of the rights now enjoyed by the individual citizen, and for pushing the dictation of the State into the management of everyman's private affairs. The tendency of liberty is towards inequality and it naturally follows that those who wish to create equality can only do so by striking a series of deadly blows against liberty itself.

(*The Times*, 2 November 1866)

Even liberal supporters of the amelioration of the lot of Irish tenants were anxious not to interfere with the rights of property. The *Northern Whig*, a liberal paper for which Cairnes occasionally wrote, felt that a 'just scheme of Tenant-Right' was desirable, not only for the occupier's sake but as a means of 'counteracting the wild and semi-socialistic theories'. 'Monopoly and spoliation are', it continued, 'sowing the seeds of communism in Ireland.' Sir John Gray, the Member for Kilkenny and owner of the *Freeman's Journal*, said with regard to the measure proposed by Maguire and his colleagues (Maguire Motion, 10 March 1868):

> practically no other thought entered into the minds of members but this, that every clause should aim at one principle – the saving the rights of property; first that there would be no attempt to indicate a socialistic desire to deprive the landlord of that which is his rightful property; secondly, that the same care which was shown to protect the property of the landlord from communistic or socialistic distribution should be applied to protect the property of the tenant, the property created by the tenant in the same manner as the landlord's property is protected for the landlord.

The *Northern Whig* concluded that 'Tenant-right and landlord-right, properly understood, are the same; and landlord-wrong is even more directly and seriously tenant-wrong also' (*Northern Whig*, 5 January 1866).

Land legislation for Ireland was frequently accused of breaking the laws of political economy. Speaking of the new ideas on property in land, freedom of contract, *laissez-faire* and the relevance of English agricultural models to Ireland by Mill, Cairnes and W.T. Thornton, Professor Black has written that even with the influence of such a 'widely known and respected figure' as Mill, it took some considerable time for the ideas of this group to have 'any marked effect on public opinion. After some twenty years, they were only being translated into policy in a limited form against the still vigorous opposition of adherents of the "old political economy"' (Black 1960: 245).

The most celebrated confrontation of the 'old' and 'new' political economy took place in the House of Commons, and the topic of debate was, significantly, Irish land. In the discussion of Maguire's Motion (10 March 1868) Mill, then a member of the House, clashed with Robert Lowe a staunch defender of traditional political economy. Lowe saw the principle of political economy as an oasis in the desert of politics. He entertained a 'prejudice' that a man was at liberty to do what he liked with his property, and that having land, it was 'not unreasonable that he should be free to let his land to a person of full age upon the terms upon which they shall mutually agree. That I believe to be reason and good political economy' (*Hansard* 16 March 1868c). In his reply Mill remarked that

> In my right hon. Friend's mind political economy appears to stand for a set of political maxims [...] my right hon. Friend thinks that a maxim of polit-ical economy if good in England must be good in Ireland [...] I am sure that no one is at all capable of determining what is the right political economy for any country until he knows the circumstances.
>
> (*Hansard* 1868d)

In the same debate, Charles Neate, MP for Oxford City and a former professor of political economy at Oxford, denounced Mill's views and asked that nothing be done in Ireland that was 'at variance with those principles of political economy and political wisdom under which England had grown great and pros-perous' (*Hansard* 1868a, quoted in Kinzer 2001: 195). Some years previously Mill had sought from Cairnes the 'circumstances' of Ireland before he started to write about it in the sixth edition of his *Principles of Political Economy* (see Boylan and Foley 1985). The way of traditional political economy was not the road to solving the problems of Irish land. As The O'Donoghue remarked in the House of Commons in the same debate, in almost every instance in Ireland the occupiers had 'ancient prescriptive titles to their farms, and although this might count for little in the arithmetic of the political economist, it should be con-sidered by those who wished to approach the difficulty in a true spirit' (*Hansard* 1868b). James Stansfeld, Liberal MP, and in 1869 Financial Secretary to the Treasury, said in a speech at Bristol, that political economy (of the 'new' kind obviously) might lay down that property in land was qualified but he admitted that what should be the 'nature of [...] interference and the degree of [...] restric-tion is a problem of very considerable complexity and difficulty' (quoted in Steele 1974: 266).[2] Even Lowe himself had to capitulate in his absolutism and it was the question of Irish land which forced him to relent. According to E.D. Steele, in 1869 Lowe produced 'a sketch of legislation involving a complete break with his notorious attachment to doctrinaire *laissez-faire*'. His aim was to legislate effectively for Ireland, 'without, or with the least possible, risk to prop-erty in Britain – and it was the second that mattered' (Steele 1974: 159). Lowe now insisted that abstract principles had to be put aside when dealing with Ireland. In Lowe's memorandum, according to Steele, the 'unsuitability of free contract to Irish conditions had [...] been the reason advanced for interfering drastically with property. Lowe had made a "temporary appeal to the principles of equity".' When Lowe was getting cold feet later in the year, Gladstone quoted this passage to him from his own memorandum and Lowe informed Cardwell that 'Gladstone's *argumentum ad hominem* has rather shaken me [...] the ground of property is gone' (quoted in Steele 1974: 288). In his one major contribution, made in committee, to the House's division of the 1870 Bill, Lowe, the great defender of economic orthodoxy, exclaimed: 'The principles of political economy! Why, we violate them everyday!' (quoted in Steele 1974: 306).

The reluctant acceptance of the limited nature of private property in land was the main ideological cost of the pacification of Ireland. As Steele has remarked, 'Parliament sacrificed on the altar of Anglo-Irish union the notion that the individual's rights of property were indefeasible, and with that cherished notion the concomitant freedom of contract' (Steele 1974: 315). It is scarcely possible to over-emphasise the importance of the 1870 Irish Land Act in the whole controversy about Ireland and the rights of landed proprietors. Land was then for Gladstone the chief Irish question and Ireland transcended all other questions. The state of Ireland presented 'the only real danger of the noble Empire of the Queen' and the 'stability of the Empire' depended on the 1870 Bill. As John Bright said to Gladstone, 'I know nothing more dangerous than the Irish land question' (quoted in Steele 1974: 290). In the debate preceding and during the Bill, in the cabinet and in the public arena, there was widespread anxiety about the limitation of private property and fears that principles accepted for the tranquilizing of Ireland might cross the Irish Sea. An editorial in *The Times* (13 September 1869) called a speech by Sir John Gray 'irreconcilable with all theory, of proprietary rights over land'. 'Nothing can be more preposterous', said the *Manchester Guardian,*

> than to imagine that grave interests [...] directly connected with all our ideas of property and private right, and rooted in the very foundations of the social fabric, can be dealt with according to one set of principles in Ireland, and on diametrically opposite principles in England and Scotland [...] It should be clearly understood that whatever is done [...] in regard to that right in Ireland will supply a precedent for the adjoining island which we may be sure no time will be lost in transplanting thither!
>
> (*Manchester Guardian* 31 August 1869)

Lord Clarendon clearly saw that the treatment of landed property could not 'be limited to Ireland' (quoted in Steele 1974: 120). Lord Hartington feared the 'enormous damage that might ensue to the interests of property of all kinds, not only in Ireland, but throughout this country'. Land and trade, he felt, should make common cause in defending property (quoted in Steele 1974: 127). The Tory C.N. Newdegate warned businessmen in Birmingham and Coventry that principles subversive of land ownership in Ireland would undermine the security of property in England (Steele 1974: 170). G.S. Noel, the Conservative Chief Whip, said that 'if we once broke through the rights of property we should find ourselves on the verge of revolution [...]. The same law [...] applied to Ireland must be applied to England, and to every sort of property' (quoted in Steele 1974: 268). And, finally, Lord Kimberly commented that Clause 4 of the Bill that stopped a landlord from preventing a tenant's improvements was 'obviously a principle that might easily cross the Channel' (quoted in Steele 1974: 293). 'It was acknowledged', according to Steele, who has made a close and extremely valuable study of the evolution of the 1870 Irish Land Act, 'by all in the cabinet that the right and duty of the state to intervene positively must acquire new dimensions' (Steele 1974: 288). It seems no exaggeration to claim that Irish land offered a major systematic challenge to the universality of the laws of political economy. On this question it is worth quoting at some length a review by J.S. Mill of Cliffe Leslie's book on land tenure systems written, significantly, in 1870:

> The Irish land difficulty having shown, by painful experience, that there is at least one nation closely connected with our own, which cannot and will not bear to have its agricultural economy ruled by the universal maxims which some of our political economists challenge all mankind to disobey at their peril; it has begun to dawn upon an increasing number of understandings, that some of these universal maxims are perhaps not universal at all, but merely English customs; and a few have begun to doubt whether, even as such, they have any claim to the transcendent excellence ascribed to them. The question has been raised whether the administration of the land of a country is a subject to which our current maxims of free trade, free contract, the exclusive power of every one over his own property, and so forth, are really applicable or applicable without very serious limitations; whether private individuals ought to have the same absolute control, the same *jus utendi et abutendi*, over landed property, which is it just and expedient they should be permitted to exercise over moveable wealth.
>
> (Mill 1870: 642)

To achieve these historicising purposes, and to counteract the more radical Land and Labour League, Mill founded, in 1870, the Land Tenure Reform Association, whose members included the Irish economists Cairnes and Cliffe Leslie.

Mill is usually regarded as a pioneer in his advocacy of increased state intervention in economic affairs and it is significant that his most unambiguous and provocative statements in the matter are to be found in a work on Irish land, *England and Ireland* (1868) easily his most controversial publication. In an earlier publication we, somewhat rashly, made the exaggerated claim that Cairnes's series of articles in *The Economist*, 'Ireland in Transition' (nine articles in all, published between 9 September and 4 November 1865), anticipated by a number of years, more systematically and with more cogent argumentation, the most controversial aspects of Mill's pamphlet (Boylan and Foley 1983, 1984a: 109).[3] So in this part of the paper we will sketch the evolution of Cairnes's thought on private property in land and the intimately connected question of the role of the state. We will demonstrate that his well-known papers of 1870 and 1871 on land and *laissez-faire* were not isolated contributions to these debates; they formed part of a searching inquiry sustained over several years.

In his *Inaugural Lecture* in Queen's College, Galway, in 1859, Cairnes vigorously defended the role of the state in education. It was common, he wrote, 'to hear political economy appealed to against the practice of endowing education by the State' (Boylan and Foley 2003: IV, 395). The principle of *laissez-faire*, while defensible in the realm of 'sense' had no justification in the area of 'intellect': 'An ignorant man is not sensible of his intellectual wants, and will give nothing in exchange for their satisfaction.' In the 'economy of our *mental* acquisitions, therefore, the machinery of individual enterprise and free competition breaks down', and this is the 'justification of the interference of the State in support of education' (Boylan and Foley 2003: IV, 397). On the question of state involvement in education there are some fascinating documents in the Cairnes papers. There is a letter from John Chapman, editor of the *Westminster Review*, to Cairnes (23 May 1860) concerning an article on Irish education which Cairnes's intimate friend Professor William Nesbitt of Galway had submitted to the *Review*. Here again the difference between Ireland and England with regard to state intervention was highlighted. Chapman stated that a condition of the acceptance of the article was:

> That state interference with education shall not be advocated as right in principle and shall only be justified in practice with reference to Ireland as an exceptional instance, the duty in this instance being alleged to rise out of the conditions resulting from the peculiar and exceptional relations of the Conquerors and Conquered.
>
> (Cairnes Collection 1860: MS 8944(6))

Chapman added that he would not occupy Cairnes's time by arguing the question as to the sphere and duty of government, though he thought 'Mill less sound on this point than either William Humbolt or Herbert Spencer' (Cairnes Collection 1860: MS 8944(6)). In another letter to Cairnes, Chapman wrote that he would be glad if Nesbitt reconsidered 'whether he cannot so far meet my views as to suppress his assertion of the principle against which I protest, viz., that the State ought to assume the duty of National Education' (Cairnes Collection 1860: MS 8944(6)).

It is interesting to note that Cairnes himself ran into some censorship trouble some years later, again on the question of the proper role of the state – this time in connection with land in Ireland. Henry Reeves, the editor of the *Edinburgh Review*, had sent Cairnes some books of Irish interest to review. In the article Cairnes's proposals were modest; he called for either a regime of 'status' or one of 'contract', rather than an attempt at wedding incompatibles. Soon he was to come out strongly in favour of a regime of status. In the review he felt that 'an enlightened public opinion' would be an adequate remedy against insecurity of tenure.[4] But when the review was published the last five pages had been suppressed (Cairnes 1864: 303). Writing to his friend Leonard Courtney,[5] Cairnes said his article had been 'massively mutilated', for reasons he was told 'purely mechanical' but, he added, 'I suggest because the doctrine was unpalatable' (Courtney Collection 1864: MS, Item 24). In a letter to Nesbitt on 23 December, Cairnes said that Reeves 'takes no objection to my doctrine (which astonishes me) although I specially called his attention to the position which I thought might be considered exceptionable' (Cairnes Collection 1863: MS 8941(8)). However, Reeves had been satisfied with the review 'so far as he has read it'. The article was, according to Reeves too long and Cairnes wanted the 'expository' parts to be shortened, rather than the 'controversial' (Cairnes Collection 1863: MS 8941(8)). But Reeves wanted to omit the end of the article which contained the controversial material: 'To say the truth', wrote Reeves to Cairnes (28 December 1863),

> there is not any portion of the earlier pages of the article which I should willingly sacrifice to retain the last passage. To you in Ireland that passage has a controversial interest which gives it peculiar value, but out of Ireland & among the readers of this review generally, there is, I suspect, no division of opinion on the matter. I cannot conceive any Englishman deliberately advocating legal interference in the adjustment of contracts with reference to land.
>
> (Cairnes Collection 1863: MS 8963)

When the review appeared, lacking the controversial matter, Cairnes wrote to Nesbitt saying he hoped to be able 'to get some separate copies printed with the deleted matter restored' (Cairnes Collection 1864: MS 8941(9)). This, apparently, he did and was rebuked by Reeves for so doing. Writing to Cairnes, on 1 February 1864, Reeves stated that it appeared to him 'entirely contrary to the principle of anonymous writing on which the Review has always been conducted, for a contributor to circulate copies of an article containing passages which are not published in the Review itself' (Cairnes Collection 1864: MS 8963).

Reeves, however, had set up the complete article in proof, most of which, including the censored material, is in the Cairnes papers in the National Library of Ireland. Here Cairnes distinguished between 'dealings respecting land tenures and ordinary transactions'. Land, unlike other commodities, was not the 'creation' of human industry, it was absolutely indispensable to human needs, was absolutely limited in supply, and it could be 'improved or deteriorated in value' according to the treatment it received. Owing to these causes 'there entered into dealings concerning land considerations of a more complex character, and consequently that there spring from them duties of a more varied kind, than any which connect themselves with the transactions of ordinary exchange'. An ordinary investor can change an investment, having only contractual engagements. 'Now, will it be contended', Cairnes asked rhetorically, 'that in the relations arising out of land tenure the case is equally simple?' There was more in the relationship of landlord and tenant 'than any mere doctrines of contract can solve' (Cairnes Collection 1863: MS 8983). At this stage Cairnes felt that informed public opinion would suffice, without having recourse to legislation. He saw no long-term conflict between landlord and tenant.

The 'Notes on Ireland' which Cairnes sent to Mill in December of the same year (1864) for the sixth edition of Mill's *Principles of Political Economy*, did not differ materially from the position which he took up in his *Edinburgh Review*

article (Mill 1965: 1075–86). However, in 1865, a change of the greatest significance took place in Cairnes's thinking about Ireland, land, and the role of the
state in the economy, involving a fundamental critique of the doctrines of contract and private property in land. This was in the series of provocative articles
which he contributed to *The Economist* in October and November of 1865. The
articles deserve close scrutiny both by students of Irish history and of the history
of economic thought. We have time but to glance briefly at some of the more
salient points relating to private property in land. Cairnes said the 'approved
doctrine' in England on landlord–tenant relations was 'in principle precisely the
same as all others arising out of contract, involving no other issues, and consequently amenable to precisely the same rules of legislation'. Let landlords and
tenants make their bargains 'like other vendors and purchasers', continued
Cairnes, 'and let the State see that that what is agreed upon is performed – such
is the simple panacea provided by the existing political pharmacopœia of Great
Britain for all disorders arising out of tenure of land' (Cairnes 2004: VI, 230).
There was, noted Cairnes a 'general sentiment' for which the 'received theory'
made no provision. Even in England, Cairnes believed, enactments on landlord–
tenant matters all proceeded 'upon the assumption that the obligations arising
out of this relation stand upon a different footing from those created by ordinary
contracts, and one which demands from the State a larger supervision and
control' (Cairnes 2004: VI, 231). The contradiction between 'fact' and 'theory'
was still more striking if other countries were considered:

> Indeed here the discrepancy is no longer between theory and fact, but
> between English theory and the theory and practice of the rest of the world.
> English writers are in the habit of speaking of the 'peculiar notion' of the
> Irish respecting property in land [...] but whether true or false, the Irish
> notion is certainly not 'peculiar'.
>
> (Cairnes 2004: VI, 231–2)

If anything, the 'Irish notion', which rejected contractualism and the commodifi-
cation of, and private property in, land, was more universal than the 'English' or
'British' notion:

> It is thus not the Irish, but the English, or rather the British, notion that is
> 'peculiar'. The doctrine of open competition and contract as the remedy for
> all social disorders arising from land tenure may be sound as its admirers
> believe, but it has certainly failed hitherto to recommend itself to the con-
> victions of any large proportion of mankind.
>
> (Cairnes 2004: VI, 232)

There might, after all, 'be a solid foundation in fact – a foundation of which
accepted theory takes no account'. Cairnes went on to explain, in the same terms
as he used in the censored section of his article for the *Edinburgh Review* (and
indeed his 'Notes on Ireland' for Mill) how landed property differed from other

forms of wealth (Cairnes 2004: VI, 232). These facts sufficed, concluded Cairnes, 'as it seems to us, not merely to explain the popular sentiment with reference to land tenure, but in a great degree to justify it'. He was convinced that 'a fair appreciation of the facts of Ireland's condition is not possible so long as Englishmen persist in looking at Irish facts through the medium of the prepossessions respecting land tenure current in this country [England]'. The laws regarding landlord and tenant were more-or-less the same in Great Britain and in Ireland, so why then did agriculture flourish in England and Scotland and not in Ireland? 'The reasoning', commented Cairnes, 'is doubtless irresistible, if we assume that a law which works well in England is of necessity framed in conformity with the universal requirements of mankind' (Cairnes 2004: VI, 233). Then Cairnes asked, what, consistent with free-trade principles, 'can the State do in this matter than simply allow things to take their course? We reply, it may modify its definition of property in conformity with the requirements of a new industrial epoch'. 'The right to property in land', added Cairnes,

> as distinguished from the value added to land by outlay and exertion – is not traceable to that act which forms in the last resort the natural title deed to almost all other wealth – human labour. Now, one consequence of this is, that this right, if pushed beyond a certain point, conflicts with the more fundamental principles on which property in other forms rests, in such a way that the claims of the owner of land can only be maintained by setting aside those of the producer. There may thus arise in the development of the conception of property a conflict of principles; and in fact this conflict of principles has actually occurred in Ireland. Interpreted in the landlord sense, which is also at present mainly the sense of England law, the right to property in land means the right to the land *and all that it contains*, albeit the contents owe their existence to the labour of another man. Regarded from the point of view of the cultivator, the right should be confined to the land taken strictly – the land *minus* the value that may have been added to it by others than its owner. Whether a tenant-compensation scheme involves a violation or not of the principle of property will entirely depend upon whether we adopt one or the other of those views – upon whether we regard the claim of the landowner to whatever has become attached to the soil, or that of the labourer to whatever his labour has produced as the more sacred title.
>
> (Cairnes 2004: VI, 238)

For his part, Cairnes had 'no hesitation' in saying that he regarded the latter as the 'paramount claim, paramount as being more directly implicated with the elementary ideas of justice, and as lying nearer the root of those grand and universal motives which constitute the main propelling force of human progress' (Cairnes 2004: VI, 238). At the level of policy, *The Economist* articles modestly set forth a scheme of tenant-compensation, compatible with the principles of free-trade, to promote peasant proprietorship. But this scheme was justified on the basis of a searching critique of the accepted theory of private property in land.

In a later article in *The Economist*, Cairnes argued that Fortescue's Irish Land Bill embodied 'a new principle in English legislation', the 'assertion in a general form of the subordination of the landlord's right in his property to the public welfare'. This principle was, in Cairnes's view, 'an entirely sound one, and one of which the recognition is absolutely indispensable to an effective dealing with the pressing requirements of Ireland' (Cairnes 2004: VI, 251). In a letter to Mill, in May 1867, Cairnes expressed the hope that the Bill would be passed 'as affording a recognition of the principles of the limited character of the landlord's property in the soil' (Mill–Taylor Collection 1867: MS vol. LV1(i), A, item 43). Cairnes was by now getting much bolder in his statements. In his article on Fortescue's Bill he asserted that 'confiscation' was not for him the 'horror' which it was for most Englishmen. 'We can well believe', he went on,

> that a well-devised scheme of confiscation might easily be made productive of solid benefits to Ireland; nor should we shrink from this expedient were it necessary for the regeneration of the country. But our objection to Mr Fortescue's measure is that while paying the cost of confiscation, it secures none of its gains.
>
> (Cairnes 2004: VI, 254–5)

This was in 1866. In the same year, in a letter to Leonard Courtney, he stated: 'I am delighted to find that your opinions on the land question are "revolutionary" and "socialistic".' In the same letter he spoke of the 'sacredness of landed property as at present recognized as a first principle in political reasoning' (Courtney Collection 1866: MS, item 41), a principle which, of course, he rejected. In 1869 he informed Courtney that with regard to land 'my ideas on the subject are becoming every day more and more revolutionary' (Courtney Collection 1869: MS, item 56). By 'revolutionary' he meant, according to another letter of his to Courtney (2 September 1869), 'upsetting radically existing notions respecting landed property' (Courtney Collection 1869: MS, item 58).

Cairnes had intended writing a book on Ireland but he never managed to complete it. He did, however, publish 'Fragments on Ireland', mostly dating from the 1860s, in his *Political Essays* which came out in 1873. Here Cairnes noted that the Encumbered Estates Court 'proceeded according to rules unknown to our existing system of jurisprudence; it set aside solemn contracts; it disregarded the cherished traditions of real property law'.[6] Isaac Butt, he remarked, did not overstate the case when he wrote that English history recorded 'no more violent legal interference with vested interests' than the 'provisions by which this statute forced the sale of a large proportion of the landed property of Ireland, at a time when no prudent man would have set up an acre to be sold by public competition'. It would not be easy, continued Cairnes, 'to disturb these statements of Mr Butt, or to prove that the measure, tried by the received maxims of English jurisprudence, was not a measure of confiscation'. The effects of the Court were, in Cairnes's opinion, accepted as being very beneficial, a fact which may perhaps be usefully borne in mind just now, when it is thought a sufficient condemnation of moderate proposals to describe them as 'revolutionary'. With our experience of the working of the Encumbered Estates Court, we may be permitted to think that to be 'revolutionary' is, after all, not so very violent a presumption against a measure of Irish land reform.

(Cairnes 2004: III, 174)

In 1869, John Morley, editor of the *Fortnightly Review*, asked Cairnes for a paper on the land question, the purpose of which was clearly to influence the debate on the 1870 Irish Land Bill. 'Political Economy and Land' was published in January 1870. Cairnes again examined the basis of property in land and reiterated his doctrine of the qualified rights of ownership, along with his arguments for state intervention in dealing with land. He stressed that only a political economy that was committed to *laissez-faire* could oppose such state intervention. He held that

the land of a country presents conditions which separate it economically from the great mass of the other objects of wealth, – conditions which, if they do not absolutely and under all circumstances impose upon the State the obligation of controlling private enterprise in dealing with land, at least explain why this control is in certain stages of social progress indispensable, and why in fact it has been constantly put in force wherever public opinion or custom has not been strong enough to do without it.

(Cairnes 2004: IV, 189)

Cairnes went on to ask if the

principle of *laissez-faire* – that play of interests developed by competition which in manufacturing and trading operations maintains the harmony of individual with general interests – does this suffice to secure, under ordinary circumstances, the same harmony in the transactions of which land is the subject? If it shall appear that it does not, then, I think, a case will have been made out for the interposition of some other agency – public opinion, custom, or, failing these, direct State action – to supply that which the principle of unrestricted competition has failed to supply.

(Cairnes 2004: IV, 198)

In respect to Ireland one thing was clear: 'no settlement of Irish land can be effectual which still leaves with landlords the power of indefinitely raising rent' (Cairnes 2004: IV, 202). So the obligation of deciding on a 'fair rent' had to be imposed on the state. 'The regulation of rent is thus of the very essence of the case', and, Cairnes added,

it is felt to be so by all who have really grasped the problem; and yet it will be found that this topic has in general been kept rather carefully in the background. The reason for this hesitancy is not difficult to guess. Few Englishmen can hear without something of a cold tremor a proposal to fix rent by law.

(Cairnes 2004: IV, 203)

Political economy furnished 'no presumption against the propriety of this course' (Cairnes 2004: IV, 204). Custom rather than contract, and 'Irish ideas' were the best guide to a solution of the problems of Irish land. As Black has pointed out, in this article Cairnes 'argued that the cultivator of the soil should not have to pay more for its use than the economic rent in the strict Ricardian sense' (Black 1960: 54). Henry Maine wrote a critical review of this paper in the *Pall Mall Gazette* (6 January 1870) in which he declared that investigations into the 'true foundations of property' were 'speculatively idle' and 'practically dangerous'. Writing to Mill, Cairnes wondered why such speculations were 'idle' when 'proprietary rights in a large portion of the Kingdom must receive modification' (Mill–Taylor Collection 1870: MS, item 55). As Black also mentioned, Cairnes's proposals to introduce fixed rents 'alarmed' Bright 'a good deal' (Black 1960: 58). According to E.D. Steele,

> Bright, still in the eyes of many the scourge of the landed class recoiled at a particular manifestation of the new British radicalism: an article in the *Fortnightly Review* for January by the economist J.E. Cairnes, vindicating the theory of state intervention to determine fair rent, and containing the statement that no reform of Irish land would succeed that did not directly control rent.
>
> (Steele 1974: 293)

Irish land was again the theme when Cairnes addressed the Political Economy Club on 1 April 1870. He spoke on the question: 'Assuming that the State undertake to settle by legislation the relation of Landlord and Tenant, can any criterion be suggested for determining Agricultural Rent in conformity with the moral basis of property, and consistently with public policy?' (Cairnes Collection 1870: MS 8940(17)). At the Radical Club (of which he was a member) Cairnes brought forward Longfield's tenant-right plan for discussion. The result was 'very satisfactory', he wrote to Eliza, his wife, the 'Scheme was generally and strongly approved of; and a resolution was taken by the M.P.s present to take it up at once' (Cairnes Collection 1870: MS 8940(17)). Incidentally, half the members of the Radical Club were MPs. The amendment was, as Black put it, 'too radical to secure acceptance at that stage of events' (Black 1947: 53).

Finally, let us consider briefly one of Cairnes's most celebrated essays, his 'Political Economy and *Laissez-Faire*', delivered at University College London, in late 1870 and published in the *Fortnightly Review* in July 1871. Cairnes began the essay with a meditation on why, as it seemed, political economy was widely regarded as having outlived its usefulness. The reason for this decline in the prestige was, he felt, because political economy was seen merely as a 'sort of scientific rendering' of the 'maxim' of *laissez-faire* (Cairnes 2004: IV, 241). But, there are those whose faith in *laissez-faire* is not quite so absolute as that of the majority; who hold that there are ends to be compassed in social and industrial life which can only be reached through the action of society as an organised whole; and that, while the mere negative and destructive part of industrial reform has been well-nigh completed, a work of positive and reconstructive reform still lies before us.

(Cairnes 2004: IV, 243)

Cairnes, in a much-quoted passage, endeavoured to show that the 'maxim of *laissez-faire*' had 'no scientific basis whatever', but was 'at best a mere handy rule of practice, useful, perhaps, as a reminder to statesmen on which side the presumption lies in questions of industrial legislation, but totally destitute of all scientific authority' (Cairnes 2004: IV, 244). The policy 'expressed by *laissez-faire*, has been steadily progressive for nearly half a century', wrote Cairnes, 'and yet we have no sign of mitigation in the harshest features of our social state' (Cairnes 2004: IV, 249). Human beings

know and follow their interests according to their lights and dispositions; but not necessarily, nor in practice always, in that sense in which the interest of the individual is coincident with that of others and of the whole. It follows that there is no security that the economic phenomena of society, as at present constituted, will always arrange themselves spontaneously in the way which is most for the common good. In other words, *laissez-faire* falls to the ground as a scientific doctrine.

(Cairnes 2004: IV, 250–1)

But Cairnes also rejected 'the opposite principle of State control, the doctrines of paternal government', and as a 'practical rule' he accepted *laissez-faire* as 'incomparably the safer guide' but only as a '*practical rule*, and not a doctrine of science', and 'above all a rule which must never for a moment be allowed to stand in the way of the candid consideration of any promising proposal of social or industrial reform'. Recently, remarked Cairnes, phrases like *laissez-faire* and freedom of contract had become bugbears:

It is enough to mention them, to discredit by anticipation the most useful practical scheme. What did we hear during the discussions on the Irish Land Bill? Political Economy again and again appealed to as having pronounced against that measure. Now, what did this mean? Simply that the Bill interfered with freedom of contract, violated the rule of *laissez-faire* – charges perfectly true, and which would have been decisive against the Bill had these phrases really possessed the scientific authority which members of Parliament supposed them to possess.

(Cairnes 2004: IV, 251–2)

It was, continued Cairnes, 'against this understanding of the doctrine that my argument is directed. So understood, I hold it to be a pretentious sophism, destitute of foundation in nature and fact, and rapidly becoming an obstruction and nuisance in public affairs' (Cairnes 2004: IV, 252). Political economy 'stands apart from all political systems of social or industrial existence', having nothing to do with '*laissez-faire* any more than with communism; with freedom of contract any more than with paternal government, or with systems of *status*. It stands apart from all particular systems, and is moreover absolutely neutral as between all' (Cairnes 2004: IV, 255–6).

This is the essay referred to by Keynes when he called Cairnes 'perhaps the first orthodox economist to deliver a frontal attack upon *laissez-faire* in general' (Keynes 1926: 26). William D. Grampp, in 'What Became of *Laissez-Faire*?', remarked that when classical economics passed to Cairnes 'the decline of the market continued and at a faster pace. He 'did not trouble to argue at length against *laissez-faire*, as Mill did, but simply denounced it' (Grampp 1982: 9). Clearly Grampp is not acquainted with Cairnes's long and intense engagement with, and his penetrating analysis of, the doctrine of *laissez-faire*. In his book, *The Great Economists: A History of Economic Thought*, H.D. Marshall has written that 'if Mill can be described as one who, despite his sympathy for social reform, still clung to the concept of individualism and *laissez-faire*', Cairnes might best be described as 'one who never had any doubts about the undesirability of opposing any proposal for interfering with the free operation of the market' (Marshall 1967: 126). And finally, P.T. Homan claimed that Cairnes undermined the adequacy of the classical system 'as a basis for the political precept of *laissez-faire*' by 'divorcing the system from a beneficent order of nature and by emphasizing the 'hypothetical nature of its laws' (quoted in Marshall 1967: 102).

A political economy based on English ideas and experience was in several respects inappropriate to Irish circumstances. Mutations of the essentially English discourse of political economy had to be generated in Ireland to explain specific Irish economic phenomena. Perhaps here we might begin to look for the reasons why what Professor Black has called the Dublin School produced a subjective theory of value almost forty years before Jevons; why Ireland produced two early and influential advocates of the historical method, Cliffe Leslie and John Kells Ingram; why Isaac Butt was almost alone among economists in these islands in defending a version of protectionism; and why, inexplicably, Cairnes made a last-ditch effort to defend the wages-fund theory when even Mill himself had recanted. It is worth reiterating that Cairnes's critique of *laissez-faire* came out of his protracted studies of the Irish land tenure systems. It was a doctrine that he felt to have been particularly inappropriate to a solution of that seemingly intractable problem. It was a doctrine rejected alike by Irish experience and Irish ideas. England forced on Ireland 'her own idea of absolute property in land', wrote Mill in his controversial pamphlet *England and Ireland* (Mill 1982: VI, 513). This was also the notion of landed property defended by traditional political economy. We have suggested that the Irish peasant exacted a measure of revenge on English ideas about property and on political economy itself. Irish experience and ideas offered a searching challenge to some of the settled orthodoxies of economic thinking. Irish ideas crossed the Channel; what was once 'peripheral' and 'eccentric' had now become central. Irish ideas, strange to relate, had become conventional wisdom. The doctrine of the limited nature of landed property became widely accepted as did that of the role of the state in the domain of land. We have suggested that from 1865 onwards a leading part in this process was played by John Elliot Cairnes, both in his strenuous and indeed passionate advocacy of these ideas and in the theoretical foundations with which he provided them. Both the 1870 and especially the 1881 Irish Land Acts were centrally informed by these principles.

There was a widespread debate in the British press, especially in the 'quality' periodicals of the day, surrounding the 1881 Irish Land Act, crucially concerning the principles on which it was seen to be based. The title of an article published by J.A. Farrer in the *Contemporary Review* in February 1881, 'The Failure of Free Contract in Ireland', set the tone of the debate. Farrar's central thesis was that freedom of contract between the owners and cultivators of the land in Ireland had been 'least interfered with by law' and the consequence had been 'the two chief evils of Ireland, rack-renting and evictions' (Farrer 1881: 250). The situation was exacerbated by the fact that there were in Ireland no other sources of livelihood to turn to. He argued that the free contract system 'may answer well in England, or sufficiently well in England not to justify disturbance, and yet fail in a country like Ireland (Farrar 1881: 257). He opposed free trade in land and the application of 'pure commercial principles to the tenure of land' (Farrar 1881: 263). But if freedom of contract remained sacrosanct he ingeniously argued for a solution on the Land League principle of collective bargaining by tenants.

In an article in the same review the previous month, Lord Monteagle disagreed with the view that interference with freedom of contract was a 'retrograde step' despite Sir Henry Maine's definition of progressive societies as moving from status to contract (Monteagle 1881: 165). The Irish, Monteagle wrote, 'have constantly been the victims of English theories, the legitimate outcome of English progress and experience being imposed on us before we were ready for them' (Monteagle 1881: 166). The Landlord and Tenant Act of 1860 abolished all status tenancies and assumed implicit contract but the 'sad truth' was that the Irish were 'not yet fit for contract pure and simple' (Monteagle 1881: 166).

George Campbell, the Indian official who visited Ireland in 1869 and wrote a book on Irish land which significantly influenced the 1870 Irish Land Act, again visited Ireland before the 1881 legislation. He wrote that the more he had seen of the 'primitive and aboriginal' parts of Ireland

> the more I am convinced that there is foundation for the view I formerly put forth, viz., that down to quite modern days the Irish tenants had not completely emerged from status tenure and old customary law or ideas founded on that law, nor really entered on the stage of social relations which is wholly regulated by contract.
>
> (Campbell 1881a: 18)

In his article of May 1881 he welcomed the Bill as, in effect, conceding the 'three Fs' (Campbell 1881b).

Alexander George Richey, a professor of law at Trinity College Dublin, an editor of some of the volumes of translations of the Brehon laws and the author of influential introductions to them, as well as historical writings on Ireland, gave an account of his reactions to the 1881 Land Bill in the May issue of the *Fortnightly Review*. He saw the legislation as embodying a 'new legal principle' which arose 'naturally' from the 'exceptional existing relations of landlords and tenants in Ireland' (Richey 1881: 543). It was, Richey argued,

> obvious that the actual relation of landlord and tenant in Ireland cannot be made to square with the legal theory of the hiring of land, and that the logical and necessary consequences of the doctrine of contract are precisely the causes of the present agitation, and constitute the evils which it is now proposed to remedy.
>
> (Richey 1881: 543)

He wrote that the 'great majority of Irish tenants from year to year' were customary, not contractual tenants and that, in consequence of the 1870 Irish Land Act, 'actually, although not technically, the tenants are themselves owners of an indefinite portion of the value of the holdings which they occupy' (Richey 1881: 544). Both of these 'facts' were, he claimed, 'foreign to English ideas' (Richey 1881: 543). The theory of contract was simply inapplicable to Irish circumstances. Since the 1870 Act the legal relationship between landlords and tenants was not so much a contract of hiring as a quasi-partnership.

Samuel Laing, railway administrator, Liberal politician, and author, writing sympathetically about the Plan of Campaign, believed that because of the gross inequality between a poor cottier and his landlord, the relationship between them could not be characterized as a contract. He saw a conflict between law and morality, especially in the 'confiscation of tenants' improvements' which he said was legal under English law until the 1881 Act (Laing 1887: 578). Describing the doctrine of free trade as 'only one application' of *laissez-faire*, Sidney Low, author and journalist, claimed, a half a century after the enactment of the Corn Laws, that 'the larger part of our recent legislation has been shaped in direct antagonism to the principle of *laissez-faire*' (Low 1896: 185).

Bernard Holland, a civil servant, complemented Lecky for his speech, in the House of Commons in March 1897, calling attention to 'the incapacity of the Cobden School of English Reformers to perceive that their *laissez-faire* doctrine, well as it might suit the circumstances of England for the time, was, of all others, the least suitable to Ireland' (Holland 1897: 631). Holland claimed that from the Select Committee of 1830 to the Recess Committee of 1896, 'every competent observer of Ireland' had been 'driven to the conclusion that the State in that Island should not merely keep the peace but should actively promote the social and industrial welfare of the people' (Holland 1897: 643–4). According to Holland, one might almost sum up the history of English dealings with Ireland by describing them as a series of unsuccessful attempts to introduce into Ireland a form of religion, a land tenure, a poor law, an educational system, a railway system, a fiscal system, in harmony with the circumstances of England, but in discord with those of Ireland.

(Holland 1897: 631)

This mode of analysis, generated by Cairnes, mainly in the context of Irish land, and beginning in the late 1850s, was powerfully and systematically argued and influentially promulgated by him until his untimely death in 1875. Writing in 1926, and referring to Cairnes's 1870 lecture, 'Political Economy and *Laissez-Faire*', Keynes stated that Cairnes's position 'for fifty years past' had been the view of 'all leading economists' (Keynes 1926: 26–7).

Notes

1 We are extremely grateful to the late Professor R.D. Collison Black for his valuable comments on an earlier version of this paper.
2 We wish to record our indebtedness to Dr Steele for his outstanding research on which we have drawn extensively in this section of the paper.
3 We were justly taken to task for our excessive zeal by Bruce L. Kinzer in his *England's Disgrace?: J.S. Mill and the Irish Question*, chapter V, and especially pp. 6, 181–2.
4 By 'public opinion' Cairnes meant, as did Bentham and Austin, the opinion of the 'civilized' world which he saw as a form of moral suasion which superseded violence or indeed legislation and which had, in Cairnes's view, made much progress in Great Britain by the 1860s.
5 Leonard Henry Courtney (1832–1918), 1st Baron Courtney of Penwit, Professor of Political Economy, University College London (1872–75), and Liberal MP (1875–1900).
6 The Encumbered Estates Court was established in 1849 to facilitate the sale of landed estates bankrupted by the Great Famine.

Bibliography

Manuscripts

Cairnes Collection, National Library of Ireland, MSS 8940(17), 8941(8), 8941(9), 8944(6), 8963, 8983.
Courtney Collection, London School of Economics, MSS items 24, 41, 56, 58.
Mill–Taylor Collection, London School of Economics, MSS vol. LVI(i) A, items 43, 55.

Secondary sources

Black, R.D.C. (1947) *The Statistical and Social Inquiry Society of Ireland: Centenary Volume 1847–1947*, Dublin: Eason.
—— (1960) *Economic Thought and the Irish Question, 1817–1870*, Cambridge: Cambridge University Press.
Boylan, T. and Foley, T. (1983) 'John Elliot Cairnes, John Stuart Mill and Ireland: Some Problems for Political Economy', *Hermathena* CXXXV: 96–119.

—— (1984a) 'John Elliot Cairnes, John Stuart Mill and Ireland: Some Problems for Political Economy', in A.E. Murphy (ed.) *Economists and the Irish Economy from the Eighteenth Century to the Present Day*, Dublin: Irish Academic Press.

—— (1984b) 'Cairnes, Hearn, and Bastable: The Contribution of Queen's College Galway to Economic Thought', in Diarmuid Ó Cearbhaill (ed.) *Galway Town and Gown 1484–1984*, Dublin: Gill and Macmillan.

—— (eds) (1985) 'Notes on Ireland for John Stuart Mill: The Cairnes–Longfield Manuscript', *Hermathena* CXXXVIII: 28–39.

—— (eds) (2003) *Irish Political Economy*, 4 vols, London and New York: Routledge.

—— (2004) 'Introduction', *Cairnes, Collected Works*, London and New York: Routledge, I: 1–40.

Burn, W.L. (1949) 'Free Trade in Land: An Aspect of the Irish Question', *Transactions of the Royal Historical Society*, 4th series, XXI: 61–74.

Cairnes, J. E. (1864) 'Ireland', *Edinburgh Review'* 119: 279–304.

—— (2003) *Political Economy as a Branch of General Education*, in T. Boylan and T. Foley (eds) *Irish Political Economy*, IV: 384–402.

—— (2004) *Collected Works*, 6 vols, T. Boylan and T. Foley (eds), London and New York: Routledge.

Campbell, G. (1881a) 'The Land Legislation for Ireland', *Fortnightly Review*, n.s 29: 18–34.

—— (1881b) 'Impressions of the Irish Land Bill—11', *Fortnightly Review*, n.s. 29: 552–9.

Daily News (1866) 12 July.

Farrer, J.A. (1881) 'The Failure of Free Contract in Ireland', *Contemporary Review* 39: 249–64.

Finlason, W.F. (1870) *The History of Law of Tenures of Land in England and Ireland: With Particular Reference to Inheritable Tenancy; Leasehold Tenure; Tenancy at Will; And Tenant Right*, London: Stevens & Haynes.

Grampp, W.D. (1982) 'What Became of *Laissez-Faire*?', *History of Economics Society Bulletin* 2: 5–10.

Hands, D.W. (2001) *Reflection without Rules: Economic Methodology and Contemporary Science Theory*, Cambridge: Cambridge University Press.

Hansard (1868a) 3rd ser., vol. CXC, cols 1316–17 (10 March).

—— (1868b) 3rd ser. vol. CXC, cols 1617–18 (13 March).

—— (1868c) 3rd ser. vol. CXC, col. 1493 (16 March).

—— (1868d) 3rd ser. vol. CXC, col. 1525 (16 March).

Holland, B. (1897) '*Laissez-Faire* in Ireland', *New Review* 16: 631–44.

Keynes, J.M. (1926) *The End of* Laissez-Faire, London: The Hogarth Press.

Kinzer, B.L. (2001) *England's Disgrace?: J.S. Mill and the Irish Question*, Toronto: University of Toronto Press.

Laing, S. (1887) 'The Plan of Campaign', *Contemporary Review* 51: 577–85.

Low, S. (1896) 'The Decline of Cobdenism', *Nineteenth Century* 40: 173–86.

MacDonagh, O. (1983) *States of Mind: A Study of Anglo-Irish Conflict 1780–1980*, London: George Allen & Unwin.

Manchester Guardian (1869) 31 August.

Marshall, H.D. (1967) *The Great Economists: A History of Economic Thought*, New York: Pitman.

Mill, J.S. (1862) *Westminster Review*, n.s. 22: 489–90.

—— (1870) *Fortnightly Review*, n.s. 7: 642.

—— (1963–91) *Collected Works*, 32 vols, J.M. Robson (ed.), London: Routledge.

—— (1965) *Principles of Political Economy*, in *Collected Works*, III, J.M. Robson (ed.) London: Routledge, Appendix H, pp. 1075–86.

—— (1982) *England and Ireland*, in *Collected Works* VI, pp. 507–32. Quotation is from p. 513.

Mineka, F.E. and Lindley, D.N. (eds) (1972) *The Later Letters of John Stuart Mill*, in *Collected Works*, XIV, London: Routledge.

Monteagle [Lord] (1881) 'The Three F's', *Contemporary Review* 39: 161–72.

Myrdal, G. (1953) *The Political Element in the Development of Economic Theory*, London: Routledge & Kegan Paul.

Nicholson, J.S. (1909) *Elements of Political Economy*, 2nd edn, London: A. & C. Black.

Northern Whig (1866) 5 January.

Pall Mall Gazette (1867) 19 June.

—— (1870) 6 January.

Richey, A.G. (1881) 'Impressions of the Irish Land Bill – 1', *Fortnightly Review*, n.s. 29: 543–51.

Schumpeter, J.A. (1954) *History of Economic Analysis*, London: Allen & Unwin.

Solow, B.L. (1981) 'A New Look at the Irish Land Question', *The Economic and Social Review* 12: 301–14.

Steele, E.D. (1974) *Irish Land and British Politics: Tenant-Right and Nationality 1865–1870*, Cambridge: Cambridge University Press.

The Times (1866) 2 November.

—— (1869) 13 September.

Thompson, R.E. (1874) 'Prof. Cairnes on Political Economy', *Penn Monthly*, September: 637–58.

8 Charles Francis Bastable on trade and public finance

Tom Boylan and John Maloney

Charles Francis Bastable was born in Charleville, County Cork in 1855, the only son of the Revd Robert Bastable, Rector of Knocktemple and Kilbolane. His early education was at Fermoy College, Fermoy, County Cork, from where he proceeded in 1873 to Trinity College Dublin. There he studied history and political science, a course which then included political economy. Graduating in 1878 with a Senior Moderatorship (first-class honours) in history and political science, he switched his attention to law and was called to the Irish Bar in 1881. He completed his MA degree in 1882 and was awarded a LL D in 1890 (Black 1947).

Unquestionably the Irish Bar would have provided Bastable with a distinguished legal career. But in 1882, after only a year at the Bar, the Whately Professorship of Political Economy in Trinity College Dublin, then a five-year fixed-term appointment, became vacant. Bastable applied, and, under the chairmanship of John Kells Ingram, the board of examiners appointed him from a field which included a future Lord Chief Justice of Ireland. On completion of his statutory five-year term the rules were changed to allow indefinite holding of the position. Bastable was re-elected and held the chair until his retirement in 1932 at the age of seventy-seven. By then the Whately Professorship was a 100 years old and Bastable had occupied it for fifty of them, a record which, his successor Professor G.A. Duncan commented, was 'memorable not so much for its mere duration as for its persistent civilizing influence upon successive generations of students' (Duncan 1945: 242). Bastable died at the age of eighty-nine, on 3 January 1945 at his home in Rathgar in Dublin.

The Whately Professorship was modestly paid, reflecting the less than onerous obligations demanded of its holder, and Bastable sought to supplement his income with other academic posts. He was appointed Professor of Jurisprudence and Political Economy in Queen's College, Galway (now the National University of Ireland, Galway) in 1883, a position he held until 1903. He further added to his portfolio of positions in 1902 when he was appointed Professor of Jurisprudence and International Law, and again in 1908 when he became Regius Professor of Laws, both in Trinity College Dublin. These two appointments, which he held until his retirement in 1932, meant that the largest proportion of his time and efforts was devoted to teaching and administration in the School of Law in Trinity College, though his real interest lay in political economy (Smith

1945). Bastable was also appointed George Rae Lecturer at the University College of North Wales and during the academic year 1909–10 he held the War-burton Lectureship at the University of Manchester (Black 2004).

Bastable also made an active contribution to the principal learned societies related to political economy in both Ireland and England. He acted as Honorary Secretary to the Statistical and Social Inquiry Society of Ireland from 1886–95 and was one of the Vice-Presidents from 1896 to 1915 (Black 1947; Daly 1997). From 1881 to 1895 he was an examiner for the appointment of suitable candid-ates to deliver the Barrington Trust Lectures, a series of lectures in political economy for the general public, which had been endowed in 1834 by John Bar-rington, and had since 1849 been administered by what was originally the Dublin Statistical Society but was later to become the Statistical and Social Inquiry Society of Ireland (Boylan and Foley 1992).

Between 1882 and 1893, Bastable delivered nine papers to the Society, ranging from contemporary monetary questions to issues in Irish trade and development. He was a founder member of the Royal Economic Society and served on its first council. From its foundation in 1891 and up to the early 1920s Bastable was an active contributor to the *Economic Journal*, contributing twenty-seven articles as well as being one of its most active book reviewers. He was president of Section F, Economics and Statistics, of the British Association in 1894, and 1921 he was elected a Fellow of the British Academy.

Bastable had wide interests across economic theory and policy, although his reputation rests on his contributions to international trade and public finance. From a doctrinal and methodological perspective, he kept faith with the classical tradition and defended the use of the historical method in economics as expounded by his compatriots T.E. Cliffe Leslie and John Kells Ingram. Bristow (1987) notes that, 'Bastable never appeared to recognize the significance of neo-classical innovations,' and that while Marshall's *Principles* was cited in various works, this was never 'in a context which suggests that anything of analytical significance is contained therein' (Bristow 1987: 203). Yet Bastable's students at Trinity College were not precluded from exposure to Marshall's work. While Bastable kept his commitments to the classical tradition, particularly the work of John Stuart Mill, along with his interest in the historical method, his syllabuses also came to incorporate the work of new authors including neoclassicists. All the same, his basic doctrinal and methodological antipathy to the neoclassical approach is not in doubt. At the methodological level, this shows up in his rather limited writings on the 'scope and method' of the discipline. These consist of his Introductory Lecture, delivered in 1884 shortly after he became Whately Profes-sor, entitled 'An Examination of Some Current Objections to the Study of Polit-ical Economy' and his presidential address to Section F, Economics and Statistics, at the 1894 meeting of the British Association in Oxford, with the title 'A Comparison between the Position of Economic Science in 1860 and 1894.'

The most interesting parts of the Introductory Lecture are his comments at the end, when he warns his students that there are many competing methods in Eco-nomics. These include the deductive, inductive, historical, mathematical, and experimental methods (Bastable 1884: 24). But on more careful examination these difficulties of different methods greatly diminish, arising as they do for Bastable 'from the different standpoints their advocates take up,' and their 'unfortunate tendency to exaggerate minor differences' (ibid.: 24). And, so far as the differences are genuine, many of them are differences of logic 'and should be credited to that science.' This included the whole deduction versus induction issue (which, to Bastable, was encapsulated by the dispute between J.S. Mill, Whewell and Whately as to the limits of induction), just as the 'proper place of experiment is also a matter for logicians' (ibid.: 25), And, when 'we commence the practical study of Economics, we find help and assistance from advocates of all these methods' (ibid.: 25). This Bastable illustrated with the writings of Cairnes, Jevons, Leslie and Newmarch on the Californian and Australian gold supplies and their economic effects, where the historical and analytical methods complemented each other. This tolerant, inclusive approach recurs in his 1894 presidential address to Section F, 'A Comparison Between the Position of Economic Science in 1860 and 1894.' Here Bastable identified the major causes that had contributed to a 'changed position of our science' over this period (Bastable 1894: 128): (i) the influence of foreign writers, mainly those from the German Historical School; (ii) the increasing power of the working classes, and in particular the rise of the trade unions; (iii) the influence of evolutionary thinking, arising from Darwin's work, which Bastable considered to have been more influential in its impact 'on the social than even on the biological sciences' (ibid.: 128). His concern was to adopt a more holistic approach to economics by grounding it in a larger nexus of cognate and relevant subjects. He chided British writers such as Senior and McCulloch for their neglect of foreign economists: this 'insularity of tone' was retarding progress in all departments of economics. Its 'evil effect' he argued, was to prevent 'any thorough consideration of the social and political groundwork on which all systems of economy rest' and to which 'all economic theories must, if they are to be enduring, pay adequate attention' (ibid.: 128). This methodological principle he felt was the 'great and saving merit' of the German contribution to political economy, just as it was the issue on which 'our English predecessors most signally failed' (ibid.: 128).

As for the emergence of the trade unions and evolutionary thinking, Bastable used both to call for a political economy which reflected the changing social and economic environment. The mere substitution of 'working class' for 'middle class dogma,' he argued, does not represent any scientific advance. For Bastable, no interpretation of industrial or other economic phenomena 'can claim to be adequate unless it takes into account the particular forms of social structure and the special political conditions which have helped to produce them' (ibid.: 129).

Of all the forces for change, it was the evolutionary thinking arising from Darwin's work which Bastable felt was most profound and far-reaching both in its actual effects and its implications for the future. As a lawyer he was particularly impressed by the way legal studies such as Henry Maine's *Ancient Law* had taken on board evolutionary ideas. In contrast he argued that the economists were rather slow in identifying the potential of evolutionary thinking for their subject, though he does correctly acknowledge both Cairnes and J.S. Mill for recognising the impact of Maine's work, at least as he puts it 'in some special points' of their work (ibid.: 130, fn. 1). But Bastable's central methodological point was the impact of the new evolutionary framework 'in bringing out the general similarity of the various sciences dealing with man,' which 'again made examination of the bonds joining economics to the related subjects a more prominent object' (ibid.: 130).

Bastable's training in jurisprudence and political science provided the framework for much of his thinking and he often refers to it. Other likely influences on his methodological thinking were his acquaintance with the continental writers, particularly the members of the German Historical School, the impact of his compatriot Cliffe Leslie and the influence of Ingram in Trinity College Dublin during Bastable's education and early career. Nor, it may be reasonably surmised, were the vibrant debates on the specifics of Irish conditions and the problems they posed for economic policy during the nineteenth century totally lost on Bastable given his commitment to specificity and historicity, and his insistence 'that it is the social basis rather than the slighter edifice of half-developed theory that gives life and power to our present work' (ibid.: 133).

But the shift from classical (real cost) to necolassical (subjective) value theory, it has been argued, bypassed international trade, where the idea of 'real' costs determining production 'was retained ... well into the 1930s' (Gomes 2003: 92). This argument must be viewed as part of a more extended argument that the 'classical trade model survived the "marginal revolution" of the 1870s,' and for three reasons: (i) the fact that Mill had identified and incorporated the role of demand in his analysis of international value; (ii) the transformation of Ricardo's labour theory of value into Marshall's 'real cost' theory; and (iii) the fact that trade theory was already emphasising the efficient allocation of a given stock of resources and its attendant corollary of rationality as informing the international exchange of commodities, so that it sat comfortably with the new paradigm of exchange which underlay the 'marginal revolution' (ibid.: 92).

If this was the theoretical background that Bastable encountered as he began to study international trade, there were equally significant shifts occurring in the area of trade policy. When Queen Victoria in 1852 told her uncle, the King of the Belgians, that 'protection is quite gone,' she was unquestionably echoing the spirit of the times (Clapham 1967). The British economy had entered a period of sustained growth and prosperity that was to last for twenty years, and which was largely attributed to a free trade policy which facilitated a very favourable international division of labour, certainly when viewed from Britain's perspective. The essential trade relationship was quite straightforward: Britain's prosperity was established on the success of its export of manufactured goods based on its superior technology, scale of production and expertise. These exports were in turn paid for in the form of raw materials and food imports from within the empire and outside it. The leading economists of the period were of one voice in acknowledging the contribution of free trade to the mid-Victorian boom (Gomes 2003). The free trade, or 'low-tariff', era of the mid-nineteenth century came in two stages marked by two major iconic developments: the repeal of the Corn Laws in 1846, and the signing of the Anglo-French (Cobden–Chevalier) commercial treaty in 1860.

For a quarter of a century following the repeal of the Corn Laws, the commitment to free trade remained the presiding idea in British economic and political discussion. Advocates of repeal had argued that it would provide the stimulus and example for other countries to reconsider their trade policies in favour of a low-tariff regime. In the short run these sentiments were validated. The Dutch and Belgians repealed their Corn Laws in 1847 and 1850 respectively. But it was the Anglo-French treaty of 1860, together with the tariff reductions implemented by Holland, the Scandinavian countries and the *Zollverein* that signalled the arrival of a free trade regime in continental Europe.

The Cobden–Chevalier treaty represented the high point of British free trade diplomatic achievements in the nineteenth century. By the 1870s, internal and external developments would conspire to undermine this triumph, and usher in a return to protectionism during the 1880s and 90s. The trigger was the onset of the depression in agriculture in 1874 and the more general slowdown which would beset the British economy over the next twenty years. These developments coincided with the emergence of Germany and the United States and the resultant relative decline of Britain's status within the international economy. This convergence of events led to a crisis of confidence and launched a fundamental debate on the state of the British economy, including a reaction against free trade. Meanwhile protection was on the rise in Europe, beginning with the introduction in 1879 by Germany of a series of levies on iron and steel and a range of agricultural imports. This was quickly followed by the French National Assembly, which in 1881 introduced a number of tariffs, to be followed by others. The era of free trade was over.

The debates that followed split both the political establishment and the economists. They came at a time when the economic community was itself in the throes of self-interrogation as to the purpose and nature of economics. The debates between the members of the English Historical School and the economic theorists were in full flight, with Marshall striving to achieve a compromise between the older classical tradition and the newly emergent marginalist mode of analysis with a view to establishing the academic and professional credentials of the discipline. The debate on free trade and the reform of commercial policy established policy battle-lines which largely followed the methodological ones. While the majority of the mainstream economic theorists defended the principles and policy of free trade, the case for protection was very actively presented by another group of academic economists, mostly but not exclusively economic historians. It was the interaction between these two groups that led to the development and refinement of international trade theory and policy from the 1880s, to which Bastable would be an important contributor, particularly in the context of the tariff reform debate of 1903, in which he sided with free trade.

Bastable's status in international trade theory and policy rested on his major work, *The Theory of International Trade*, first published in 1887, which went through four editions. This was followed in 1892 by his *The Commerce of Nations*, which went through eight editions, and a number of articles published in *The Economic Journal, The Quarterly Journal of Economics, Hermathena*, along with entries in various editions of *Palgrave's Dictionary of Political Economy* and the *Encyclopaedia Britannica* (Black 1945). In one of the many surveys of international trade theory and policy, Angell commented that Ricardo, following his original exposition of international trade theory, had the privilege, 'rarely enjoyed by the originators of new systems, of marking out virtually all of the main lines in the subsequent development of his own ideas.' Consequently 'the task of the later classical and post-classical writers has ... been, at bottom, one of refinement and elaboration alone' (Angell 1926: 80). The most significant refinements and elaborations included:

 i Mill's attempt to establish a more exact *a priori* determination of the ratios of international exchange, by the use of the 'Equation of International Demand';

 ii Cairnes's further refinement and extension of international demand through application of the concept of non-competing groups, a concept he had developed in the context of wage determination;

 iii The efforts, partly pursued by Mill but principally by Bastable, to analyze the variability in supply and demand schedules;

 iv Taussig's analysis of the determination of the level of prices and money incomes as between countries; and

 v Analysis of the effects of tariffs on international trade and prices, especially by Bastable and Marshall.

(Angell 1926: 80)

From this we get some insight into Bastable's contribution to post-Ricardian trade theory and policy.

Bastable is among those Angell sees as providing no more than 'an elaboration and a refinement of Mill' (Angell 1926: 99), but, as R.D.C. Black has commented, 'the extent of the refinement was considerable' (Black 1948: 56). Bastable began his analysis with an examination of international values along with the principle of comparative advantage. In the simplest cases of international trade, he demonstrated that the terms of exchange depended on comparative intensity of demand. He then introduced diminishing and increasing returns, which provided a more general formulation of the theoretical possibilities. He also gave a more extensive analysis of the obstacles to competition, and other hindrances to the free exchange of goods, than Mill had provided. Finally, he analysed in some detail the conditions influencing the distribution of the gains and the costs of trade through an application of varying elasticities of demand and variable returns in production. All this established Bastable as a significant contributor to this field of endeavour.

Nonetheless, *The Theory of International Trade* makes it clear that to Bastable Mill, for the most part, still represents the state of the art where trade theory is concerned – superior to Cournot (who ended up in far too ambivalent a position on free trade by taking diminishing returns as the only possibility and neglecting the fact that imports usually lead to more exports) and to Sidgwick (who went backwards from Mill by ignoring the role of comparative intensity of demand in determining the ratio of exchange). One of Bastable's criticisms of Mill, however, is that he devalues his own demonstration that a large country can in theory gain from protection by improving the terms of trade for itself. By using the example of two countries each with a global monopoly of a particular good, says Bastable, Mill manages to give the impression that this is the *only* case where the large-country argument works (Bastable 1903a: 117n.).

But for the most part Bastable is less interested in protecting protection than in demolishing it. He anticipates the counter-attack on the infant industry argument that he would develop more fully in *The Commerce of Nations* (see below). As for the 'national security' case for protection, the 'best known instance' is the Navigation Laws. Here Bastable finds Adam Smith's statement that these laws are 'perhaps the wisest of all the commercial regulations of England' distinctly ambiguous: what if they were the wisest only because he thought all the others 'supremely foolish'? (Bastable 1903a: 145n.). Protection as a means to a secure food supply is an exploded doctrine: England has never had a securer food supply than in the current age of free trade (ibid.: 146). As for protection to promote industry, Bastable finds no virtue in industrial society as such: on the contrary, 'there is surely no ground for [the State] seeking to increase the mass of those urban populations, which in all countries present so grave a problem to the statesman and the philanthropist' (ibid.: 148).

So *International Trade* is a good, readable exposition of trade theory as Mill left it, with a number of refinements and extensions. For true originality in Bastable, however, we have to look elsewhere – to his 1889 article in the *Quarterly Journal of Economics* and his clash with his compatriot Edgeworth in the pages of the *Economic Journal*. In the former, Bastable can be seen as a prefigurer of Keynes; in the latter, as the perpetrator of a startling logical error.

'Some applications of the theory of international trade' (Bastable 1889) takes up Mill's proposition that a creditor country benefits twice from debt repayment: first from the actual money and second from the shift of the terms of trade in its favour (the repayment is a specie flow which raises its price level relative to that of the debtor). Not so, says Bastable, because as soon as the money begins to flow in, the creditor will spend it on imports, some of them from the debtor country. Equilibrium will be reached by quantity, not price, changes.

As Angell (1926) was to point out, Bastable could have easily applied all this to international trade in general, not just the special case that arose from debt repayment. Had he done so, the classical picture of adjustment via price changes would have dissolved into a proto-Keynesian macroeconomics where adjustment came through aggregate demand acting on quantities. In the long run, of course, the world would still have been classical; Bastable shows no signs of wanting to abandon either Say's law or the classical faith that unemployment must eventually cure itself by bringing down the wage. And, in his later work, even his special-case analysis disappeared, thus remaining incomplete. The fact remains that he had arrived at a conclusion more significant than he himself, or indeed his contemporaries, appeared to realise.

The exchange with Edgeworth involved a number of other leading economists of the time. It was prompted by Henry Sidgwick's hypothesis that the removal of protection on manufactures would cause some workers to emigrate or remain permanently unemployed (Sidgwick 1883). This hypothesis was predicated on the existence of diminishing returns and increasing costs in agriculture. Given these hypothetical conditions, it was argued that agriculture would be unable to absorb the unemployed workers from industry arising from the cheaper imports of manufactured goods, and consequently adopting free trade was undesirable. Edgeworth agreed with this conclusion, as did J.S. Nicholson in his *Principles of Political Economy* of 1897. The implications of Sidgwick's analysis represented a direct challenge to the classical position which posited that a freely mobile factor, which labour was deemed to be, could not be adversely affected by the removal of a tariff. Nicholson observed that Sidgwick's position was indeed at variance with 'the popular view of English political economy,' but that it was correct to argue that the removal of tariff restrictions could 'force manufacturing workers into agriculture with disastrous results' (Nicholson 1897: 317–18).

Bastable took all this up in the second (1897) edition of *International Trade*. The entire analysis, he said, rests on diminishing agricultural returns. But in such a case, agriculture would still take on displaced industrial workers until increasing costs had eliminated its comparative advantage. And at that point, comparative advantage would be inherited by the secondary sector, which would take its workless labourers back again. Even more to the point, agriculture's loss of comparative advantage meant all its exports would now cease (Bastable 1897: 164–6).

This bizarre statement implies that the whole economy will be forever taking a ride on a particularly vengeful version of the cobweb theory. As soon as farm exports cease, agricultural costs will drop back again and comparative advantage in farming will be restored. Farm exports will start up again and factory workers will lose their jobs again, until every farm export is once again swept away by the consequences of diminishing returns. Reviewing Bastable, Edgeworth made the point, obvious to anyone used to thinking in neoclassical terms, that it would be agricultural exports at the margin that diminishing returns would choke off; the rise in agricultural costs *at the margin* would stop any *further* exports of farm products, not destroy the existing ones (Edgeworth 1897: 402). Remarkably, the third edition of *International Trade* ignores Edgeworth's point and restates the critique of Sidgwick (Bastable 1900b: 192) in words little different from the previous time round (except that Edgeworth himself has now been added to the charge sheet). Edgeworth, in an impeccably polite review, refrains from pointing out that he has already demolished the proposition that Bastable is now repeating, and repeats the demolition (Edgeworth 1900: 391). Bastable now changes the rhetoric but not the substance. Trying to impale Edgeworth on a cleft stick, he asks him if he thinks returns in agriculture are diminishing or not. If not, there can be no problem re-employing the displaced industrial workers; if so, then (for the third time – fourth if you count a supporting contribution from Achille Loria (1901)) all trade will come to an end (Bastable 1901: 227). Even with Bastable's disinclination to think about trade in marginalist terms, it is surprising that the man who had worked out the effects of diminishing returns on trade, so much more fully than Mill, should fail, and keep failing, to understand Edgeworth's elementary point.

If *The Theory of International Trade* (1887) was Bastable's major contribution to trade theory, *The Commerce of Nations* (1892) could be regarded as his 'policy-book,' though its third chapter provides a succinct summary of his theory of trade. *The Commerce of Nations* presented a careful and schematic treatment of the arguments for and against protection, a presentation that was delivered in Bastable's considered, reflective and even-handed manner. While Bastable sided with the 'free-traders,' who included Marshall, Giffen and Pigou, in the Tariff Reform Debate, and indeed was deeply committed to the merits of free trade, his balanced approach and intellectual fair-mindedness is evident in all his work, and is certainly reflected in *The Commerce of Nations*. A notable contribution contained in *The Commerce of Nations* was Bastable's articulation of the conditions that should be met to justify a form of protection, albeit for a limited period of time, in the early stages of industrial development. This was picking up on, and in fact complemented, John Stuart Mill's 'infant-industry' argument contained in his *Principles of Political Economy*. Mill's advocacy of an 'infant-industry' type argument was essentially to overcome the historical advantage enjoyed by the industrial leaders relative to the developing 'late-comers.' A protective tariff was justified for the latter, but should have a very finite life-span to facilitate a learning period after which the tariff should be removed. Bastable suggested that legitimising such protection to overcome a historical disadvantage was not in itself an adequate argument. He argued that the community should be compensated for the costs of protection afforded to the 'infant industry' during its initial period of development, and in addition, that when an appropriate discount was applied to both the period of excess cost, due to the protection, and to the eventually achieved cost savings, the commodity should still be able to justify its production. Kemp (1960) distinguished between the 'Mill test' and the 'Bastable test' for the infant-industry argument and combined them into what he termed the 'Mill–Bastable Infant-Industry Dogma.' Though intellectually and ideologically committed to free trade, at the end of *The Commerce of Nations* Bastable arrived at a perceptive and pragmatic conclusion which is worth noting:

> Though we cannot expect any speedy abandonment of the protective system, which will doubtless continue for a long time, we may look for breaches in it and at intervals steady and sustained reforms, leading finally, though by slow degrees, to the adoption of complete free trade.

> (Bastable 1904a: 211)

To this perhaps the attribute of prescience could also be added.

With these two important books, along with his journal papers related to trade theory, Bastable had established his position as a significant contributor to the development of international trade theory during the course of the 1880s and 1890s, a period of intense refinement and elaboration of the classical inheritance under the shadow of the emerging neoclassical paradigm (Gomes 1990). Allied to this were his contributions to policy issues, in particular his contributions to the Tariff Reform Debates in and after 1903. By the end of the first decade of the twentieth century, Bastable had made all his serious contributions to international trade theory and policy and one must look to his many reviews in the *Economic Journal*, to which he was a prolific contributor, for insights into his later thinking on developments in both trade theory and policy. That his work was highly regarded was not in question. In his review of the second edition of *The Theory of International Trade* in 1897 for the *Economic Journal*, Edgeworth, arguably the leading theorist of his generation, described it as 'the best manual on the most difficult part of economics' (Edgeworth 1897: 397), an assessment he extended to later editions of the work in which he described Bastable as the 'author of the best text book on the subject' (Edgeworth 1900: 389). Similarly, Bastable's *The Commerce of Nations* was described by L.L. Price, a former pupil and protégé of Marshall who sided with the tariff reformers in the Tariff Reform Debate, as 'the most scientific volume which has yet come under our notice in the series to which it belongs' (Price 1892: 324).

If international trade theory and policy represented one of the major areas of scholarship in Bastable's academic life, the other was unquestionably public finance. Public finance, said Bastable, had to recognise that the state was expanding everywhere. Retrenchment was theory; 'the older doctrines of economy and frugality have disappeared, and in nearly every direction proposals for new exertions on the part of the State are put forward' (Bastable 1903b: 261). How had this happened? There was the fashion for nationalisation, rising military spending across Europe and, 'many would add,' democracy (ibid.: 143). Here Bastable agreed that 'democratic finance is remarkable for its disregard of principles and its utter incapacity to measure financial forces' (ibid.: 143). But undemocratic Russia was no better: 'the real enemy of sound finance is ignorance on the part both of rulers and rules, and this is unfortunately too common under all forms of government' (ibid.: 144).

So what size was the ideal state? Various experts had applied upper limits but, said Bastable, this must depend both on the nature of the outlay and on the size of the economy. Taxing away 10 per cent of India's income would be more burdensome than taking 30 per cent of England's.

After noting Adam Smith's three permitted areas for the state (defence, justice, public works), *Public Finance* takes us through Bastable's own agenda. Defence leads to a discussion of how 'an outbreak of war' would damage the economy (ibid.: 170); the 1903 edition, despite the intervention of the Boer War, says in the conditional tense. He rehearses the arguments for and against poor relief by the state, before stating his own view that all relief should be given in the workhouse. Only in this way can the state stay on the knife-edge of treating the unemployed pauper better than the criminal but worse than the poorest wage-earner (ibid.: 89). Old age pensions from the vantage point of 1892, would cost an amount which 'would involve a grave disturbance in financial equilibrium, which could only be restored by a series of retrograde measures in respect to taxation (ibid.: 90).[1] On public works Bastable held firmly to the Treasury view: they created no more jobs than they destroyed by taxing or borrowing private savings.

Whatever the level of public spending, taxes should match it – but not in wartime. To those who said a prudent state would have piled up a war chest in advance, Bastable replied that it was impossible to know how much you would need, while the withdrawal of money into the chest would deflate the economy and damage trade. War, or any other 'abnormal pressure that cannot easily be met' must be financed 'by borrowing which is practically a distribution of the burden over a longer period' (Bastable 1926: 63).

Thus Bastable took a lenient view of the wartime budget of 1900. Resisting pressure to impose corn duties, the government had instead ceased debt repayment, borrowed a 'moderate amount' and raised income tax (Bastable 1900a). Unfortunately by the end of the war they had progressed from getting it exactly right to getting it exactly wrong. Salisbury's government had not just borrowed more than a year's income in the space of two years – and servicing it would mean a permanent 2d. on income tax – but had given in on the corn duty. Balfour had pleaded that this did not count as protection because it was too light to increase cultivation in Britain or reduce it abroad; this merely showed his 'ignorance or forgetfulness of the marginal principle universally accepted by economists' (Bastable 1902: 261).

Bastable was now giving the *Economic Journal* an annual commentary on the budget. In 1903 he praised the Chancellor for taking the obnoxious corn duty off again. 'It is both honest and courageous to confess a mistake, and this is what has been done' (Bastable 1903c: 245). It was his last good word for the Conservatives. The 1904 budget exhibited a fatal confusion between borrowing in wartime and borrowing to fund defence in peacetime. 'It ought to be clear that borrowing in order to build barracks, ships or public offices is as little justifiable as borrowing for the refitting of a Royal palace...' (Bastable 1904b: 305). By 1905 the Tories were not only running a deficit in peacetime, but trying to cover it up. Their alleged 'surplus' of £1.414 million for 1904–05 'was obtained only by neglecting the outlay of borrowed funds, these amounting to £9,796,000' (Bastable 1905: 246). Balfour's government was by now at its last gasp, and the following year Bastable was lauding the incoming Liberals for at any rate trying to balance the budget. By 1908 he was able to congratulate Asquith (the outgoing chancellor and incoming prime minister) on achieving a surplus of £4.726 million while paying off £15 million of the national debt. Thanks to this healthy position, old age pensions were affordable after all, although Bastable immediately and characteristically eliminated the issue as a question of public finance, handing it over to 'social policy.'

Bastable's annual commentaries ceased with Lloyd George's historic budget of 1909, which will be discussed later. On the financing of the First World War he was almost silent, though he did sign a memorial calling for higher taxes, economy in official and municipal expenditure and encouragement of 'organised thrift in all classes' (*The Times*, 15 February 1916, p. 6). Other signatories included Hobson, the Webbs, H.G. Wells, John Galsworthy, the Archbishop of Canterbury and Dr Spooner of mixed-syllable fame. Reviewing in 1920 Hartley Withers' book *War-Time Financial Problems* he agreed that taxes should have gone up more, but demurred when Withers excluded a capital levy as a way to help pay off the debt. No doubt there were political objections, but they might be slighter than the danger of returning to the gold standard (as was desirable) while leaving the nominal debt unchanged. The resulting amount of debt deflation 'would be a certain cause of discontent and even lead to the promulgation of extreme plans for getting rid of the public creditors' claims' (Bastable 1920: 94).

Bastable consistently held the view that an inconvertible currency was 'an expensive, dangerous and unjust form of forced loan' (Bastable 1903b: 697). This left bonds and taxes as ways of financing war. We have seen what Bastable thought about the Boer War budget of 1900, but in *Public Finance* he tackled the subject more generally.

Bastable's main thrust is against specious arguments against borrowing. Heading the blacklist is Mill, who had claimed that loans, unlike taxes, 'must come entirely from that portion of the country's capital that pays workers' (Bastable 1903b: 667), an unsubstantiated theory with the 'absurd' implication that where wages were already 'at a minimum' workers would now starve (ibid.: 667–8). Thomas Chalmers' contrast between loans, which came from 'the fund that assists production,' and taxes, which merely 'curtail immediate enjoyment' has some truth, but omits the counterweight that loans stimulate, while taxes check, saving (ibid.: 673). Bastable adds the points that a loan is voluntary, a tax not; that taxation, unlike borrowing, will press heaviest on people with temporary incomes; and that foreign loans will raise interest rates by less than domestic ones. Greater capital mobility was admittedly closing this gap but this issue '[does] not belong to public finance' (ibid.: 680).

None of this led Bastable into complacency about the debt itself. Echoing the Treasury view, he rebutted the idea that 'a debt may be the cause of wealth creation' (ibid.: 662), and agreed with Adam Smith that excessive debts could as well lead to bankruptcy at a national as at an individual level. Whether to redeem the debt or cut taxes (when the choice arose) must depend on the 'tax versus loan' arguments put into reverse gear. In particular Bastable warned against the delusion that the debt–income ratio would shrink of its own accord, in the sum of growth and rising prices. There was 'no sure ground for concluding that economic progress will continue indefinitely' (ibid.: 709). Still less could you trust to rising prices which, it might have been noticed, had fallen for most of the nineteenth century. Even if prices did rise, debtholders would want higher nominal interest rates to compensate. Anyway, 'to count on this change is really to speculate on a defect on the standard of value' (ibid.: 710).

As for countercyclical budgeting, provided the books balanced across the cycle Bastable did not reject it in principle. Reviewing David Kinley's history of the US Treasury, he agreed that some countercyclical variation – he meant automatic stabilisers, a term not yet invented – could smooth the economy's path. In practice, however, the timing of automatic stabilisers would do as much harm as good, cutting off booms too early and persisting too late during a slump. Modern economists would probably agree at least with the second point (Bastable 1893).

Bastable opposed, and blamed 'mainstream' economics for, the reduction of public finance to the economics of taxation. Nevertheless, the sections on taxation are the longest, most important and most interesting part of *Public Finance*. They certainly monopolised the attention of reviewers and fellow economists when the book first appeared.

Tax was a necessary evil but how could this evil press as lightly as possible? Did taxpayers as a whole get more relief from a limited number of taxes, or from a lot of taxes at low rates? At one extreme was the idea of a single tax. This could be rejected straight away, if only because it could not raise revenue 'without much irritation ... To disguise the burden is, so far as sacrifice is concerned, to reduce it...' – an interesting humanitarian argument for what would now be called stealth taxes (Bastable 1903b: 343). But Bastable also rejected Arthur Young's system of taxation 'bearing lightly on an infinite number of points, heavily on none.' This would be 'extremely prejudicial to the development of industry, irksome and inconvenient to the payers, and very costly in collection' (ibid.: 344–5).

As for the distribution of the tax burden between individuals, one basis would be in proportion to public services received. The trouble with this, argued Bastable, was that some services were immeasurable in both sense of the word: 'the most important of the benefits rendered by the state, security against aggression, is, literally speaking, an incalculable good.' More generally, activities found their way into the public sector precisely because they could not be bought and sold by individuals at a market price. 'Wherever the benefit to the individual can be even approximately estimated there is a strong presumption in favour of levying the cost incurred from him and converting the tax into a "fee"' (ibid.: 267).

Moving on to the incidence of taxation, Bastable begins with a double-barrelled blast against the extremes, as he sees them: the classical economists who (he alleges) thought that any one tax falls entirely on one class, and M. Canard, the aptly named French economist who thought that all taxes, whatever their ostensible form, fell equally on everyone. In what follows, a conventional analytical skeleton is forever poking through: the more elastic the demand relative to supply, the more the incidence falls on the seller. Bastable's ostensible purpose is to expose the limitations of this doctrine, the need to examine the tax system minutely, tax by tax and country by country, and the fact that, on the way to any neoclassical equilibrium, very different interim outcomes may crop up. It has to be concluded, however, that, after a thoroughly 'historicist' style of exposition, Bastable falls back into the orthodox neoclassical line without deviation. In the end he holds incidence in every case to turn on the factor's ability to reduce its own supply. Can rentiers take land out of cultivation? Can hard-pressed small businessmen shut down and become wage-earners themselves? Can workers reduce the aggregate supply of labour? Here Bastable adopts a human capital approach; 'a great deal of wages is really the return on capital invested in the education of the workers' (ibid.: 386–7). So far as tax disincentives reduce this investment, incidence will be shifted away from labour.

Bastable then compares indirect with direct taxation which, at this stage, he identifies entirely with income tax. This he praises for its 'greater facility and lower cost of collection, and the power of knowing the exact amount paid by each person liable' (ibid.: 350). Its other advantage is the underwhelming one that 'as income is the ultimate source of taxation, its immediate imposition is the most obvious and rational way of claiming a share on the produce for the state' (ibid.: 350). Against this, income tax is awkwardly obtrusive – 'the demand for payment ... brings home the existence of the charge without any possibility of escaping notice' (ibid.: 350). Bastable is still hankering for taxes that are stealthy.

The advantages claimed for indirect tax are simply a mirror-image of the disadvantages of direct, but the drawbacks are numerous. The fact that it is voluntary – if you do not want to pay tax on wine, do not drink it – is anything but a point in its favour, as Mill rightly realised: the only upshot is that the government loses its revenue, the vintner his profit and you do not enjoy the wine. Indirect taxes also deter innovation, and should therefore be confined to 'those industries in which intervention is not very active, or in which interference in it will not be seriously felt' (ibid.: 511).

Bastable then takes a leisurely look at an array of specific taxes. In each case a brief economic analysis is followed by a long cross-country history. No modern state could levy a poll tax: 'its inequality and directness combine to make it unpopular' (ibid.: 465). Property taxes score over income tax so far as they tax permanent, not temporary, income. Nonetheless, the difficulties of assessment and collection are so great that Bastable ends up agreeing with Seligman that property tax is 'beyond all doubt one of the worst taxes known in the civilised world' (ibid.: 474). Despite his unenthusiastic attitude to succession duties in general – they are easy to evade and, when not evaded, may fall on capital and retard progress – Bastable does not rule out a progressive succession duty (ibid.: 591). He does, however, rule it out of public finance, warning that 'the result of mixing up social and financial aims is not beneficial' (ibid.: 595).

Bastable nowhere condemns the existing distribution of wealth as unjust. Indeed he comes close to realising the imaginary vice, attributed by generations of radicals to neoclassical economists, of equating justice with distribution by marginal product. And Bastable's attitude towards taxation for the purpose of redistribution, enduring through all three editions of *Public Finance*, is a hostile one:

> The taxing power has often been employed to encourage industry, to improve taste, to benefit health, or to elevate morals, but in none of these applications

has the desired success been obtained. There is therefore, a strong presumption against its use as an agent for remedying the inequalities of wealth. Its definite and universally recognised function is the supply of adequate funds for the public services. To mix up with one every important objective another different and incompatible one is to run the risk of failing in both.

(Bastable 1903b: 335)

He does however go on to say that public goods should be financed without unfair pressure on any class, effectively on admission that all public finance has inescapable distributive implications, and follows this up with an attack on those who care nothing for social justice. The idea that taxation could be boiled down to 'placing the burden where it will give the least trouble and friction in collection' was based on illusion:

> Injustice in distribution is certain sooner or later to show itself in the very difficulties that the practical financier wishes to avoid. All the conditions of a good system of taxation are interdependent and the breach of one reacts on the others.
>
> (Bastable 1903b: 336–7)

And when Lloyd George introduced his budget of 1909, Bastable continued his policy of giving the Liberals a fair wind. He exerted himself to show Lloyd George's continuity with his predecessors, first in terms of prudence: 'Mr Lloyd George adheres to the Peel–Gladstone principle, viz. "To estimate expenditure liberally, to estimate revenue carefully, to make each year pay its own expenses."' (Bastable 1909: 290) but also in its redistributive aims:

> On the whole, it may be said that the new Budget carries on the line of policy marked out since 1906, perhaps since 1894, as essentially that of liberal finance. To increase the contribution from direct, in order to moderate the weight of indirect, taxation, is the aim which has in the main been followed.
>
> (Bastable 1909: 292)

Taxation solely for revenue purposes, Bastable's own previous principle, was now dubbed 'the stricter view,' and even those who held it now recognised:

> the political necessity of employing the resources of the community in the interest of the weaker classes of society. The fact that this involves greater pressure on the holders of property ... is, obviously not a reason for refraining from this course: it may even act as an inducement.
>
> (Bastable 1909: 288)

Presumably Bastable meant that squeezing the rich in public would help buy off demands for truly damaging redistribution.

That was the defence. Bastable now put the case for the prosecution. Surtax on incomes over £5,000 was 'open to the objection that it singles out a small class for particularly rigorous treatment' (Bastable 1909: 290). Worse still was the surcharge on 'unearned incomes' including quite small ones, while Bastable doubted if any of the changes would bring in much extra revenue. The budget chiefly failed in 'its excessive complication and want of proportion' (ibid.: 293). Again, this represented continuity so far as Gladstone had gone in for vastly complicated budgets, but 'Finance Ministers of the calibre of Gladstone are not easy to find' (ibid.: 293).

Despite the ultimate verdict (and the lofty concluding dismissal of Lloyd George himself), what most stands out here is Bastable's willingness to tolerate progressive taxation even if it were only going to bring in a meagre revenue. Had he shifted his position because of developments in economic theory? What role might have been played by the concepts of equal, proportional and minimum sacrifice?

Bastable's discussion of these issues in *Public Finance* had been unhelpful. Although he had stated precisely what minimum, or equimarginal, sacrifice would mean, he dismissed equal and proportional sacrifice as too ambiguous, and too liable to be confused with one another, to be of any use. In the end he could recommend nothing better than the 'ability to pay' principle, which he had already condemned as too vague to afford much practical advice: proportional tax, proportional tax with exemptions, and progressive tax were all avowedly based on the criterion of ability to pay.

Despite these difficulties, utilitarian considerations intrude constantly into Bastable's discussion of progressive taxation. The assumption that the last 10 per cent of a rich and of a poor man's income yield them equal utility is put forward without criticism as the reason for Sax's and Wieser's espousal of progression. Here Bastable is leaning too far in favour of progressive taxation. He is still discussing the implications of *equal* sacrifice of utility – and equal sacrifice, plus the logarithmic utility function his example implies, add up to proportional, not progressive, taxation.

But in the end the need to maintain production rules progression out for Bastable without any Benthamite refinements being needed. In addition, progressive taxes are arbitrary ('the possible scales are infinite in number') (Bastable 1903b: 308), an engine of evasion, and unlikely to bring in much revenue. Bastable even backtracks on the logarithmic utility function: what if '£10 from A's income may mean the loss of a certain amount of alcoholic drink' while 'B is having to give up £10,000 may lose the chance of purchasing an estate?' (ibid.: 314). In the end neither utility theory nor international evidence on progression – largely limited to Swiss cantons or smaller German states – can justify it as a policy for Britain.

Bastable never moved beyond this interested but sceptical approach to marginal utility as a basis for fiscal policy. A better clue to his relatively sympathetic reception of the 1909 budget comes in his comments on that of 1907. There he claimed that growth in indirect taxation had had regressive results which needed to be counteracted. He had always supported substantial exemptions from income tax for the poor (not counting this as 'progressive'). The ability-to-pay criterion might be vague and ambiguous most of the time, but it fully endorsed exemption of that income that bought the necessaries of life. And this led him on to the taxable capacity of England's poorer neighbour, Ireland.

Bastable's consistent position was that it was well-nigh impossible to measure Ireland's 'taxable capacity,' but that only made it all the more imperative to point out areas where it was over-taxed. Measurement was difficult because of evasion. In addition, as Alfred Milner had told the Royal Commission on the Agricultural Depression, the assessment and payment of income tax on farmers' profits was 'a complete farce, a complete and absolute farce' (Bastable 1896a: 192). 'Working class income' was altogether exempt 'and this, it is probable, carries with it a good deal of small dealers' profits' (ibid.: 192). Bastable then tried an aggregate approach, asking what one would expect the total tax burden of a country like Ireland to be. Portugal had almost the same area and population, with very similar conditions in other respects. It paid a lot more tax, but as an independent country you would expect it to. An independent Ireland, Bastable adds without a trace of irony, would incur 'all the extra expenditure of defending themselves against England' (ibid.: 195). But this was the point. To determine Ireland's present taxable capacity, you should at any rate attempt to distinguish between expenditure that was 'Irish' and that which was 'Imperial.' Bastable seemed to be approaching the 'tax as payment for services rendered,' a position he had so decisively rejected, but at the last minute swerved and came back to the necessity, and impossibility, of calculating Ireland's income over and above necessaries. He ended up exactly where he started.

Listing areas where Ireland was over- or under-taxed relative to England was easier. Ireland suffered from heavy duties on tea, tobacco and spirits, 'all objects of comparatively large consumption in Ireland' (ibid.: 200). But in the same issue of the *Economic Journal* that he wrote this, Bastable contributed a book review shooting down the more extreme claims on Ireland's behalf. *England's Wealth Ireland's Poverty* was full of howlers, such as the statement that the Irish consumed three tablespoonfuls of spirits per head per day, which 'comes to ten gallons a year.' A year later Bastable is back on the Irish whiskey, opposing the idea that it be seen as a 'merit good' and thus be relieved from some of its duty. 'A good deal has been said as to the necessary use of alcohol in countries like Ireland, but … many Irishmen in the wettest part of the country are total abstainers and in no wise suffer thereby' (Bastable 1896b: 237).

In the end, Bastable comes back to generalisation: if Ireland pays one-twentieth of the UK's direct taxes – and there is no reason to think this is anything other than fair – her contribution of one-ninth of total excise revenue must be excessive. This seems to rest on just such an estimate of taxable capacity that he has supposed impossible (Bastable 1896a: 200).

Bastable's first publication, back in 1883, had been on the causes of Ireland's poverty (Bastable 1883–84). They did not include laissez-faire: indeed there had been much intervention that had made things worse (the poor law had damaged mobility of labour). As for the claim that free trade had harmed Irish industry, Bastable did not rebut it, arguing rather that agriculture had 'suffered equally from English legislation' (ibid.: 471). Shortage of capital was no root cause of backwardness but a symptom of the true causes: poor natural resources, absence of the 'industrial spirit' and Ireland's 'unhappy past.'

How far the unhappy past dictated the options for the present, Bastable did not say: but in his inaugural lecture at Trinity College Dublin, he identified the system of land tenure as the link. Unlike Cliffe Leslie, who had blamed orthodox political economy for impeding land reform, Bastable cited refusal to listen to political economy as the trouble:

> Recent events have, I believe, forced on us the conviction that it would have been well for all classes if the teachings of Economic Science had been effective in securing a reconstruction of our land laws, in order that ownership in land might be more widely protected from what was morally robbery. If successful prediction be the test of true science, then in these particulars Economic Science has stood it successfully.
>
> (Bastable 1884: 10)

After this, Bastable's intervention in Irish affairs was for many years confined to his inconclusive remarks about its taxable capacity. But in 1908 he supported the idea of an Irish co-operative credit bank, and in 1913 joined the mediation committee which tried to settle Dublin's general strike. In the meantime his public finance credentials had drawn him into the Home Rule debate.

It started when *The Times* (2 April 1913, p. 6) put Bastable among those 'Home Rulers' who were calling for amendments to the government's current home rule scheme. Two days later Bastable wrote in *The Times* (4 April 1913, p. 8) denying that he was a Home Ruler, or a Unionist, or a Nationalist. But attempts to enlist him for Home Rule continued. In December, John Redmond published a pamphlet in which he ridiculed the idea that the Home Rule bill was 'financially impossible' and called up Bastable in his support (*Irish Independent* 13 December 1913, p. 5). However, there is no trace of Bastable ever saying anything remotely enthusiastic about Home Rule, let alone about Irish independence, and this may explain why he played so small a role in the counsels of the Irish Free State in the 1920s. A committee 'to advise the government of financial matters arising out of the settlement between Ireland and Great Britain' in 1922 was going to include Bastable but never got off the ground (Fanning 1978: 134). He did, however, joint the Fiscal Inquiry Committee which reported in December 1923. This was to look at the case for unfree trade. Bastable, as we have consistently seen, was better at ruling things out of his remit than ruling them in: it is not fanciful to see his fingerprints on the committee's decision that it was unentitled to deal with actual or potential customs duties 'for purely revenue purposes.' Nor did it feel at liberty to make proposals which 'would involve any considerable increase in the existing revenue receipts' (Fiscal Inquiry Committee, Final Report, 1923: 10). This more or less committed the inquiry either to remove a tariff for each one they imposed, or to recommend doing nothing.

They chose the latter. In their report they said that most of the witnesses they had heard from industry did not want protection (ibid.: 34); that many of industry's disadvantages were temporary and did not require alleviation (ibid.: 35–42); that there were no cases where the infant industry argument applied (ibid.: 47); that tariffs would push up prices and wages would respond, with great damage to exports (ibid.: 48); and that protection on national security grounds was, once again, beyond their scope (ibid.: 61). In the end they left things exactly as they were save for a few very minor proposals in a free-trading, not a protectionist, direction. *The Times* (18 December 1923, p. 4) reported disquiet about the number of academics on the committee, but the Irish government was more worried by attributions of 'sinister and malignant' motives to the commissioners. The Department of Industry and Commerce told the Dáil that 'the Government … has no preconceived opinions in favour of one economic dogma against another. It regards the problem as one entirely of expediency.'[2] In the end, expediency of one kind or another prompted the government to replace the Commission's imperceptible nudges towards still freer trade by almost equally minor gestures towards protection.

Bastable's only other engagement with Irish independence was his contribution to a symposium on whether Ireland should adopt a separate currency. As with Home Rule, he knocked down some of the flimsier arguments against change (some contributors, no doubt looking at postwar Germany, tried to argue that a new currency would equate to hyperinflation). But, uncommitted to the last, he concluded that 'a decision taken hurriedly might spell calamity in our financial system.' The *Irish Independent* (15 June 1923, p. 5) was 'disposed to agree with Professor Bastable that the utmost care and sobriety of judgement will be called for if disaster if to be avoided.'

At the end of his uniquely long academic career in 1932, Bastable must have been disappointed to witness the western world mired in the trauma of the Great Depression and the attendant collapse of free trade between nations. More specifically, and with perhaps some irony, the same year as Bastable retired saw the arrival of Mr De Valera's administration and the rapid implementation of one of the most extensive experiments in protectionist trade policy in the twentieth century. He did not live long enough to witness its abandonment in the late 1950s and the eventual triumph of trade liberalisation as the presiding regime of trade policy in Ireland, Europe and throughout the world. With postwar public finance he would have been less happy.

Notes

1 This comment appears in all three editions of *Public Finance*.
2 Notes filed with the *Final Report of the Fiscal Inquiry Committee*, p. 11.

References

Angell, J.W. (1926) *The Theory of International Prices: History, Criticism and Restatement*, Cambridge, MA: Harvard University Press.

Bastable, C.F. (1883–84) 'On some economic conditions of industrial development with special reference to the case of Ireland,' *Journal of the Statistical and Social Inquiry of Ireland* 8: 461–73.

—— (1884) *An Examination of Some Current Objections to the Study of Political Economy: Being an Introductory Lecture Delivered in Trinity College, During Trinity Term, 1884*, Dublin: Hodges Figgis & Co.

—— (1887) *The Theory of International Trade with Some of its Applications to Economic Policy*, 1st edn, London: Macmillan & Co.

—— (1889) 'Some applications of the theory of international trade,' *Quarterly Journal of Economics* (October) 4.1: 1–17.

—— (1892) *The Commerce of Nations*, 1st edn, London: Methuen.

—— (1893) 'Review of David Kinley, *The History, Organisation, and Influence of the Independent Treasury of the United States*,' *Economic Journal* 11: 502–4.

—— (1894) 'A comparison between the position of economic science in 1860 and 1894,' in R.L. Smyth (1962).

—— (1896a) 'Ireland's place in the financial system of the United Kingdom,' *Economic Journal* 22: 185–203.

—— (1896b) 'Review of Thomas Lough, *England's Wealth Ireland's Poverty*,' *Economic Journal* 6: 237–8.

—— (1897) *The Theory of International Trade with Some of its Applications to Economic Policy*, 2nd edn, London: Macmillan & Co.

—— (1900a) 'Note on the Budget of 1900,' *Economic Journal* 10: 208–10.

—— (1900b) *The Theory of International Trade with Some of its Applications to Economic Policy*, 3rd edn, London: Macmillan & Co.

—— (1901) 'On some disputed points in the theory of international trade,' *Economic Journal* 11: 226–9.

—— (1902) 'The Budget of 1902,' *Economic Journal* 12: 261–3.

—— (1903a) *The Theory of International Trade with Some of its Applications to Economic Policy*, 4th edn, London: Macmillan & Co.

—— (1903b) *Public Finance*, 3rd edn, London: Macmillan & Co.

—— (1903c) 'The Budget of 1903,' *Economic Journal* 13: 244–6.

—— (1904a) *The Commerce of Nations*, 3rd edn, London: Methuen.

—— (1904b) 'The Budget of 1904,' *Economic Journal* 14: 305–7.

—— (1905) 'The Budget of 1905,' *Economic Journal* 15: 246–8.

—— (1909) 'The Budget of 1909,' *Economic Journal* 19: 288–93.

—— (1920) 'Review of Hartley Withers, *War-Time Financial Problems*,' *Economic Journal* 30: 92–5.

—— (1926) 'General principles of finance,' in H.Higgs (ed.) *Palgrave Dictionary of Political Economy*, 2nd edn, Vol. 2, London: Macmillan.

Black, R.D.C. (1945) 'A select bibliography of economic writings by members of Trinity College, Dublin,' *Hermathena* 66: 55–68.

—— (1947) *The Statistical and Social Inquiry Society of Ireland Centenary Volume 1847–1947*, Dublin: Eason & Son.

—— (1948) 'Economic studies at Trinity College, Dublin. Part II,' *Hermathena* 71: 52–63.

—— (2004) 'Bastable, Charles Francis,' *Oxford Dictionary of National Biography*, Oxford: Oxford University Press, Vol. 4: 279–80.

Boylan, T.A. and Foley, T.P. (1992) *Political Economy and Colonial Ireland: the Propagation and Ideological Function of Economic Discourse in the Nineteenth Century*, London: Routledge.

Bristow, J.A. (1987) 'Bastable, Charles Francis (1855–1945),' in J. Eatwell, M. Milgate and P. Newman (eds) *The New Palgrave: A Dictionary of Economics*, Vol. 1, London: Macmillan Press.

Clapham, J.H. (1967) *An Economic History of Modern Britain*, Vol. 1, Cambridge: Cambridge University Press.

Daly, M.E. (1997) *The Spirit of Earnest Inquiry: the Statistical and Social Inquiry Society of Ireland 1847–1997*, Dublin: Statistical and Social Inquiry Society of Ireland.

Duncan, G.A. (1945) 'Charles Francis Bastable,' *Proceedings of the British Academy* 31: 241–44.

Edgeworth, F.Y. (1897) 'The theory of international trade,' *Economic Journal* 7: 397–403.

—— (1900) 'The theory of international trade,' *Economic Journal* 10: 389–93.

Fanning, R. (1978) *The Irish Department of Finance 1922–58*, Dublin: Institute of Public Administration.

Fiscal Inquiry Committee (1923) *Final Report*, National Archive, Dublin, T/D S.3107.

Gomes, L. (1990) *Neoclassical International Economics*, London: Macmillan.

—— (2003) *The Economics and Ideology of Free Trade: A Historical Review*, Cheltenham: Edward Elgar.

Kemp, M.C. (1960) 'The Mill-Bastable infant-industry dogma,' *Journal of Political Economy* 68: 65–7.

Loria, A. (1901) 'Notes on the theory of international trade,' *Economic Journal* 11: 85–9.

Nicholson, J.S. (1897) *Principles of Political Economy*, Vol. II, London: Macmillan.

Price, L.L. (1892) 'The Commerce of Nations,' *Economic Journal* 2: 324–5.

Sidgwick, H. (1883) *Principles of Political Economy*, London: Macmillan.

Smith, J.G. (1945) 'Obituary: C.F. Bastable,' *The Economic Journal* 55: 127–30.

Smyth, R.L. (1962) *Essays in Economic Method: Selected Papers Read to Section F of the British Association for the Advancement of Science, 1860–1913*, London: Duckworth.

9   The peculiarities of place

The Irish historical economists

Roger E. Backhouse[1]

Introduction

In the 1860s, two Irish economists, Thomas Edward Cliffe Leslie (1825–1882) and John Kells Ingram (1823–1907), became leading members of what later came to be called the English Historical School of economics, which mounted what, by the late 1860s, was the most threatening challenge to English classical political economy. In terms of age, Ingram was the senior figure, but it was Leslie who first turned to historical economics and who was the movement's leading representative. Their work is important as representing one of the ways in which Irish economics turned in the mid-nineteenth century.

By the 1840s, the Whately professors at Trinity College Dublin had established a distinctive approach to economics (see Chapter 5), but their most important students chose to turn in other directions. Leslie's contemporary, John Elliot Cairnes (1823–1875) turned to the Ricardian doctrines of English classical political economy, albeit modifying them in distinctive ways (see Chapter 7). In contrast, Leslie turned to the historical method, mounting a radical critique of abstract economic theories in general. However, despite their differences over economic theory, Cairnes and Leslie were both responding to the peculiarities of the Irish situation, brought into stark relief by the Great Famine of the late 1840s (see Chapter 6). Even Cairnes had to acknowledge that Ricardian ideas needed to be modified to take account of the Irish system of land tenure and the implications this had for the way markets worked. Leslie, together with Ingram, took this a stage (or perhaps several stages) further, incorporating the specificity of Irish experience into more wide-ranging historical critique of Ricardian doctrines.

However, although these economists were Irish, and influenced by Irish conditions, they lived and worked as important members of a broader, British, economic community, centred on London, in which John Stuart Mill was the leading figure. It was a period when British economics was in transition. In the age of Malthus and Ricardo, few British economists had been full-time academics, but by the second half of the century this was changing. However, though the subject was beginning to become professionalized, this process was far from complete. Economists might be academics, with a division emerging between their work and the writings of, say, political figures, but they still published in journals whose editors were literary figures and politicians (such as John Morley, the historian and prominent Liberal politician), not in specialized journals edited by their economist peers. The audience for their work remained broad one, though it was narrowing.

If economics was institutionally in a period of transition, it was also in a period of transition as regards doctrine, confidence in English classical political economy having weakened considerably (cf. Hutchison 1953, chapter 1). Cairnes's modifications to Ricardian theory were symptomatic of this, as were the moves away from strict Ricardianism found in Mill's work. However, both Cairnes and Mill chose to remain within the classical mould, as did many of the generation of Liberals who came after Mill, such as Herbert Somerton Foxwell and Henry Sidgwick. Even Alfred Marshall did not free himself completely from the older way of thinking, though his departures from it were more radical than he was prepared to admit. Leslie, and to a lesser extent Ingram, played an important role in this transition. As Hutchison (1953) has pointed out, the first theoretical challenge to the classical system came not from marginalism, but from Leslie and other historical economists. Their critiques of the prevailing orthodoxy chimed with those of John Ruskin and those who argued that economics had become too much associated with dogmatic laissez-faire. It is important to remember that even though their historical successors ended up creating economic history, a discipline independent of economics (see Backhouse 2004), this was not what Leslie and his contemporaries were seeking to create: their goal was a historical *economics*. It would be going too far to claim that they came close to succeeding (this involves is a historical counter-factual that is impossible to assess) but it can certainly be argued that the Irish historical economists were far from being peripheral to this transition in British economics, either institutionally or intellectually.

T.E. Cliffe Leslie

Leslie graduated from TCD in 1847, took an LL B in 1851, and was called to the bar in Ireland in 1850 and in England in 1857.[2] He then held the post of Professor of Jurisprudence and Political Economy at Queen's University, Belfast from 1853 until his death in 1882. His duties in Belfast allowed him to spend most of his year in London. It was in London that, while studying law, he attended, in 1857, the lectures of Henry Maine, a fellow member of Lincoln's Inn. Maine analysed law not as something static, but as evolving: the product of particular times and places. In the article in which he laid out his challenge to orthodox economics, 'The political economy of Adam Smith' (Leslie 1879a, chapter 10 [1870]),[3] Leslie argued that it was Maine who had 'explained the fallacies lurking in the terms Nature and Natural Law', for such terms had been understood differently at different times (ibid.: 152). As a result it was necessary to look at positive law, seeing how this had evolved 'as a more or less imperfect attempt towards a system of natural jurisprudence' (ibid.: 153). He applied

Maine's arguments to economics. Economists were no more able to know natural laws than were lawyers, which placed severe limits on what the possibilities for 'speculating a priori about "Nature," and seeking to develop from a particular hypothesis the "Natural" order of things' (ibid.: 150). A historical method was required.

This, however, was not Leslie's first major work, by a long way. By that time he had a substantial reputation as what, using modern terminology, is perhaps best described as an applied social scientist. This anachronistic term is used to denote the inter-disciplinarity character of his work, in which it is hard to draw any clear dividing line between philosophy, politics, international relations, political economy (in its modern sense) and technical problems of applied monetary economics. Black (2002: 19)[4] classifies his applied economics into five categories: the political economy of military systems; fiscal reform; price levels and the supply of gold; wage determination; and land tenure in Europe with special reference to Ireland. He makes the point that, though Leslie wrote of the influence of Maine, there did not spring from that exposure a fully developed programme for historical economics. Rather, Leslie began, after some early work in the 1950s that was innocent of the historical method, gradually to apply the historical method to a series of applied problems. The impossibility of demarcating any clear disciplinary boundaries is shown by his early work on war, peace and the political map of Europe (Leslie 1879a: chapters 6 and 7 [1860]). His problem, of whether the nations of Europe were passing beyond war, was clearly one of politics or international relations. He approached it historically, with a long table (Leslie 1879a: 63–72) that listed the wars in which Britain and Continental powers had been involved since 1816: not a single entry in either column was blank. The economic relevance of this was that the case for free trade argued by John Bright and others was that it would reduce the likelihood of war. Though a free trader, Leslie was sceptical about this claim, providing reasons why nations would find reasons for war, despite the costs they might incur.

Paradoxically, his work on the military systems of Europe (Leslie 1856, 1879: chapter 9 [1867]) came closer to being purely economic analysis, for his concern was with the cost of recruiting the necessary personnel. Though he argued that honour rather than simply money would serve to induce suitable men to apply, and though his argument required historical and institutional knowledge of how European armed forces were recruited, his focus on incentives can be seen as involving characteristically economic reasoning. However, this work involved reasoning about economic incentives with discussions of the motivations of political actors: of political economy in the modern sense. Black (2002: 23) has argued that the influence of Maine's historical method was the key factor in accounting for the transformation from the 'ponderous style, pedestrian argument and restricted scope' of his early writing on military systems to the 'confident clarity and passionate vision' of his articles on international relations only four years later.[5]

Much of Leslie's work, including that reviewed in the preceding paragraphs, shows clearly his background in jurisprudence. In the early 1860s and early

1870s, he turned to the more conventionally economic topic of the money supply and the price level (1879a: chapters 20–4 [1864, 1865, 1872, 1873, 1874]). Much of this work involved analysing statistics and using patterns to address questions of causation. This work was a direct response to issues of prices and the cycle to which his contemporaries, Cairnes and William Stanley Jevons were also responding. Furthermore, though Leslie may not have exhibited the originality of Jevons in his statistical analysis there was no methodological gulf between them: they were contributing to the same discourse. Black (2002: 24–6) has seen Leslie's emphasis on the influence of gold supplies on prices as varying from place to place and from one time to another as illustrating his historical sensibility. This was certainly the case, though it is worth noting that this is a theme that goes back at least to a much earlier Irish economist, Richard Cantillon (see chapter 1).

The area in which Leslie's applied work related most closely to his Irish background was land tenure. The response of the classical economists to Ireland's long-term problems involved a direct application of Ricardian theory: the problem was that population growth had outstripped the accumulation of capital, accounting for low wages and competition for land. This could be solved, they argued, by extending capitalist agriculture on the English model to Ireland, consolidating small farms, and increasing investment. The surplus population could either be employed as agricultural wage-labourers or could leave the land, either to work in industry or to emigrate (Black 1960, 1995: chapter 1). The Great Famine tested the prevailing economic theory still further, for whilst the British government's initial response was to provide aid in the form of food, buying maize to distribute to the poor should food prices rise too high, attempts were made to employ the poor on relief projects, but these were soon overwhelmed. Similarly, the attempt to move away from distributing food to providing poor relief through the workhouses, following the English Poor Law, overwhelmed them too. Throughout, they sought to place the burden of poor relief on Irish taxpayers.[6]

The Irish land question was more than simply a conflict between large absentee English landowners and poor Irish tenant farmers, for the social structure was much more complex. The poor, including many small tenants who were forced to leave their land, suffered greatly but above that was a class of tenant farmers that prospered, being able to acquire land very cheaply. The details do not matter here, simply the general point, which is that Irish land tenure was very different from the English model. As a result, policies modelled on English conditions appeared, to many in Ireland, to ignore the realities of the Irish situation. In the 1850s and 1860s, Leslie came to be seen as an authority on land tenure, thought by many to lie at the heart of Ireland's economic problems (see, for example Leslie 1870). His denial, quoted above, that economics comprised universal laws, and his claim that it had to be considered historically, could be seen as arising directly from the Irish situation.

Thus when Leslie wrote his celebrated article on Adam Smith, he was already an accomplished applied economist, whose applied work had apparently been transformed by his exposure to the historical method. This may account for the confidence with which he launched his attack on Robert Lowe's claim that '[p]olitical economy belongs to no nation ... It is founded on the attributes of the human mind, and no power can change it':

> Political economy is not a body of natural laws in the true sense, or of universal and immutable truths, but an assemblage of speculations and doctrines which are the result of a particular history, coloured even by the history and character of its chief writers; that, so far from being of no country, and unchangeable from age to age, it has varied much in different ages and countries.
>
> (Leslie1879a: 148)

He went on to argue that political economy had focused on the deductive method, ignoring the inductive. Though Smith's authority was cited by the followers of Ricardo, his work, Leslie contended, combined both methods. Writing before Maine's work, Smith had failed to see the problematic nature of natural law, and he had failed to escape from the influence of theological ways of thinking; however, he also thought inductively and historically. His use of induction had saved him from the errors into which subsequent generations of economists, seeing economics as a deductive science, had fallen (Leslie 1879a: 163). Thus Smith argued that the circumstances under which wages tended to equality were narrowly circumscribed. Furthermore, though Smith had based his system on 'the obvious and simple system of natural liberty', and though he considered it a law of nature, Smith applied it 'only to one-half of mankind, excepting women. His allegedly universal laws were far from applying universally.

This assault on deductive theory was developed in 'On the philosophical method of political economy' (Leslie 1879a: chapter 14 [1876]). His claim there was that the deductive method could shed 'hardly any light on the nature of wealth' (Leslie 1879a: 217). Wealth was heterogeneous. So too were human motivations. The production and distribution of wealth had to be considered against the background of legal systems, which varied historically. To understand it, therefore, historical analysis was necessary. Leslie concluded,

> The amount of wealth has been proved to depend on all the conditions determining the direction and employments of human energies, as well as on the state of the arts of production, and the means of supply. And the distribution of wealth has been shown to be the result, not of exchange alone, but also of moral, religious, and family ideas and sentiments, and the whole history of the nation.... Every successive stage ... has an economy which is indissolubly connected with the physical, intellectual, moral, and civil development.
>
> (Leslie 1879a: 241–2)

As in the applied work discussed earlier, heterogeneity was the key. Deductive theory failed through imposing an artificial homogeneity.

In Britain, much of Europe and the United States, the business cycle was particularly severe in the 1870s, the boom of 1873 being followed by an acute depression which continued for the rest of the decade. One of the few economists to attach a percentage, F.A. Walker, claimed that as much as a quarter of US productive capacity lay idle during this period (Backhouse 1994: 165) and that it was possible that the correct figure might be as high as a third.[7] Leslie (1879b: 934) argued that the main characteristic of this depression was not so much its depth or extent, but 'the sense of being in the dark, and surrounded as it were by the unknown'. He went on from there to mount a critique of the full knowledge assumption found in deductive theory.

> It is thus a fundamental error of the *a priori* or deductive political economy that it takes no cognizance of the cardinal fact that the movement of the economic world has been one from simplicity to complexity, from uniformity to diversity, from unbroken custom to change, and therefore from the known to the unknown.
>
> (Leslie 1979b: 936)

He thus linked the absence of full knowledge, brought to the fore by recent experience of the cycle, to the themes of heterogeneity and historical evolution that pervade his other work. Once again, he defended Smith as better than his followers in attaching supreme importance to industrial liberty and the division of labour, which 'produce an economic world, the vastness, complexity, and incessant changes of which are absolutely incompatible with the main postulates of Ricardian theory' (Leslie 1879b: 941).

John Kells Ingram

Ingram was born in Donegal, educated in Newry and was an undergraduate at Trinity College from 1837 to 1843. In 1846, the year before Leslie and Cairnes graduated, he was appointed to a fellowship, receiving a dispensation from the normal requirement to take holy orders. He subsequently held a succession of positions, including Erasmus Smith Professor of Oratory, where he gave the first formal instruction in English literature, and Regius Professor of Greek. He was a polymath, his work spanning mathematics, literature and etymology, as well as being a member of the Irish bar. He was, in 1847, one of the founders of the Statistical Society of Ireland. He also achieved fame as a poet, for a poem he published in 1843. Entitled 'The memory of the dead', this commemorated the uprising of 1798 and became an anthem of Irish nationalism for much of the nineteenth century. Though he did not defend his beliefs publicly until after his retirement, believing this inconsistent with his academic position, he was converted to Auguste Comte's religion of humanity, corresponding with Comte and his British disciple, Frederic Harrison, and was an active supporter of the Positivist Church from the 1950s until his death, not simply subscribing financially but becoming actively involved in its pastoral and other activities.[8]

Leslie and Ingram kept in close contact, even when Leslie moved away from Dublin to London. Their most tangible cooperation was when Ingram was involved in the publication of Leslie's *Essays in Political and Moral Philosophy* (1879a). Their correspondence[9] reveals them discussing reviews of each other's work, the problems involved in getting papers published in different periodicals, complaining about how journal editors had forced them to change material, offering advice on presenting ideas, sharing views on other economists, exchanging anecdotes,[10] sharing ideas and lending each other books and periodicals. They appear to have met frequently, though as Leslie became ill, there were several occasions when he expresses his disappointment at not being able to travel to Ireland, and not to meet Ingram.[11]

In view of the immense range of his other activities, it is hardly surprising that Ingram had nothing to compare with Leslie's range of applied economic work. His first intervention on behalf of the historical method came in his Presidential address to the British Association in August 1878, for which Leslie appears to have suggested the title for the published version.[12] Though he lambasted the Ricardian school, praising Leslie and the German historical school, he differed from Leslie in arguing for a general sociology, on lines laid out by Comte. Economics could not legitimately be studied in isolation from other social phenomena. Like Leslie, he praised Smith, though focusing on his bringing together of politics, jurisprudence and political economy, and his plan, revealed by his literary executors, for 'a connected history of the liberal sciences and elegant arts which would have supplied ... a view of the intellectual progress of society' (Ingram 1962 [1878]: 51).

Aside from seeking to analyse economic phenomena in isolation from the rest of society, the other main faults of political economists subsequent to Smith were that they adopted 'a viciously abstract' view of the conceptions with which they dealt and that they 'exaggerated immensely' the role of deduction (Ingram 1962: 55, 59). They were also excessively dogmatic in the practical conclusions they drew from their deductions. Interestingly, in view of the later importance of evolution, Ingram cited not simply Maine but also Herbert Spencer in support of his claim that to understand phenomena, it was necessary to understand where they had come from: to understand their history.

Whereas all Leslie's books comprised collections of articles, Ingram's major work in economics was written as a book, his *History of Political Economy* (1967 [1888]). This traced historically 'the course of speculation regarding economic phenomena, and contemplating the successive forms of opinion concerning them in relation to the periods at which they were respectively involved' (Ingram 1967: 1). He was not the first to write a history of economics in relation to historical context – a relativist account – but his was the most systematic such account, at least in English (see Backhouse 2004). He distinguished three main periods, the ancient, the medieval and the modern worlds, but dispensed with the first two very quickly, outlining only their general features. Scientific sociology required theorems taken from physics and biology, so could not be established until those sciences had developed. However, even within the modern world, his main concern was not with the first two phases (the break-down of the medieval system and mercantilism) but with the third, the 'system of natural liberty'.

For a British economist, Ingram's book is characterized by its cosmopolitanism. The age of liberal thought covers economic thought in France, starting with Pierre de Boisguilbert, before going on to cover Italy, Spain, Germany and the Netherlands. There then follows the heart of the chapter (at almost eighty pages), a discussion of Smith, 'with his immediate predecessors and his followers'. Under this heading he covers the whole of English economics up to his contemporary, Cairnes. That is followed by discussions of France, America, Italy, Spain and Germany, the focus being mostly on Smith's influence, but also on those who questioned free-trade ideas, notably the Germans, Adam Müller and Friedrich List. This set the stage for what for Ingram was the culminating chapter (apart from a short conclusion), on the Historical School.[13]

In this book, Ingram was obviously presenting the history of economics in a manner that was sufficiently balanced that it could be used for teaching. However, it mounted a clear case for historical economics. This message starts with the chapter headings: the progression is from advocates of natural liberty to a school based on the historical method. The latter begins with Comte's sociological method, emphasizing the scientific credentials of historical economics. German historical economics was a second manifestation of this new movement. He defends it against critics and concludes that what German historical work has shown is the need 'not merely [for] a reform of political economy, but [for] its fusion in a complete science of society' (Ingram 1967: 206). After brief sections on Italy and France, Ingram then turned to England, where his emphasis was on the inroads made by historical methods, even amongst economists associated with other approaches. Thus he argued that Mill and Sidgwick turned to the inductive method in their treatment of production, and that Sidgwick saw the a priori method as having a very subordinate place in studying wealth from the dynamic point of view. Similarly, with Jevons, Ingram emphasizes the statistical and empirical inquiries on coal, commercial crises, and money, as well as his criticisms of laissez-faire. His writing on utility is critically discussed in some detail, leading to Ingram's conclusion that, 'His name will survive in connection, not with new theoretical constructions, but with his treatment of practical problems,... and ... his energetic tendency to a renovation of economic method' (Ingram 1967: 229). Thus Ingram's accounts of those who explicitly supported historical methods (Richard Jones, Cliffe Leslie, J.E. Thorold Rogers and Arnold Toynbee) were presented as part of a deeper, more wide-ranging move towards a historical approach.

Thus Ingram's strategy is to argue that Comte's work had been highly successful and was coming to be the dominant, scientific, approach to economics. This comes out early on when Ingram opines that Mill would never have remarked that Comte's treatment of economics could be superficial 'if he could have foreseen the subsequent march of European thought, and the large degree in which the main points of Comte's criticism have been accepted or independently reproduced' (Ingram 1967: 195). At the end of the book, he bemoaned the fact that economics had previously been undertaken not by a scientific class, but 'had fallen for the most part into the hands of lawyers and men of letters' (Ingram 1967: 294). This explained why economic theory had been based, unscientifically, on assumptions that were far less universal in their scope than economists had claimed. To be scientific, economics had to be subordinated to sociology – as well as dynamic and historical. Moreover, it needed to be more than an academic discipline, but, 'part of an applied art of life, modifying out whole environment, affecting our whole culture, and regulating our whole conduct – in a word, directing all our resources to the one great end of the conservation and development of Humanity' (Ingram 1967: 300).

The Irish historical economists and British economics

Leslie and Ingram were both Irish and their approach to the subject can be related to specific Irish circumstances.[14] Yet they were also part of a broader historical school centred in England.[15] Leslie's debt to Henry Maine as the source of his historical thinking has already been mentioned, though it was Leslie, not Maine who applied historical ideas to economics. There were also historical economists at Oxford, with whom Leslie came to be associated. Reference here is not so much Thorold Rogers, but to the younger generation. In September 1880, Leslie was contacted by Arnold Toynbee, who stated that he had 'long been a student and admirer' of Leslie's writings, that he had read almost everything he had written, and that at Oxford as well as at Cambridge there were some 'who teach Political Economy not according to the method and in the spirit of the school of Ricardo but according to the method and in the spirit of the school with which your name is so conspicuously associated' (*IP* 55/1). Leslie responded by sharing the letter with Ingram. In a letter a week later Toybee defended Marshall's book (presumably Marshall and Marshall 1879) on the grounds that he recommended it as very much the best available. The wording suggests that Leslie had criticized Marshall for blurring the differences between historical and deductive economics (*IP* 55/1). Thorold Rogers had been advocating history at Oxford, but he stood apart from those like Toynbee, who came to economics out of the Oxford history school. He had not provided the philosophical foundation for a new approach to the subject that Toybee took from Leslie.

Leslie was also closely involved with those who are seen as representatives of the English classical school, notably Mill and Cairnes, even though his relations with the latter were, perhaps not surprisingly, strained for reasons that went beyond their professional differences (see Foley and Boylan 2000). He emphasized the need for a new method, as when, in response to Herbert Foxwell's claim that further controversy was unnecessary once the wage fund had been abandoned, he responded that this failed to address the differences in their methods. Leslie was confident that the new approach was gradually displacing the old, but he felt that Foxwell and Cairnes were deliberately obstructing its progress.

However, it is important not to underestimate the extent to which there was agreement in applied work. In his work on slavery and on money, Cairnes combined deductive theorizing with extensive historical analysis. Mill went a considerable distance towards historical methods and even towards Comte (though, unlike Ingram, he never accepted the religion of humanity). He even criticized in Parliament the idea that one type of political economy could be applied to all countries (Boylan and Foley 1992: 138). Whatever their differences (and Cairnes was closer to Mill than was Leslie), Mill clearly considered Leslie a valued colleague. He recommended him very warmly to others as a writer and editor (*MLL* 702–3, 726–7, 1222, 1810); he offered Leslie considerable, detailed advice on his work (*MLL* 733, 756–8, 897–8, 1557–8, 1857–9); he took his side when Leslie was criticized unfairly in a review (*MLL* 857); he sought to reassure Leslie when he was concerned about the way he had been treated by an editor; and he kept him informed about work other people were doing (*MLL* 881–2).

Leslie had similar interactions with other English economists. Leslie borrowed things from Jevons, and discussed journal editorial policies with him (*JPC* IV: 273); he appears to have brought Jevons into contact with Ingram when he was undertaking research into Cantillon (*JPC* V: 124–6). When Leslie became seriously ill, just before his death, Fawcett, Sidgwick and Foxwell organized a petition to Gladstone to get him a government pension (*JPC* V: 169, n.1), and Jevons wrote an appreciative obituary in the *Economist* (*JPC* V: 171). But more than that, despite their disagreements, there was genuine intellectual engagement: though Leslie was critical of Jevons's use of mathematics, he recognized that they shared a belief in the importance of inductive work and, critically, though he criticized the mathematics of Jevons's *Theory of Political Economy* (1879), he offered a carefully reasoned scepticism, questioning the extent to which relevant economic quantities were actually measurable: he did not dismiss Jevons's economic theory in the same way that he dismissed Ricardo's.[16]

These interactions provide a picture of the involvement of Leslie and Ingram in the life of the British economics community that is far from complete, but they are enough to provide a clear picture of a community that was in transition from the world of Malthus, James Mill and Ricardo to the professionalized academic economics that emerged in the twentieth century. They were academic economists, performing many of the tasks familiar to modern academics (lecturing, examining, applying for posts, writing references, submitting articles to journals, dealing with unsympathetic editors, and advertising their ideas). But they engaged on equal terms with non-academic economists such as Mill and Lowe. When they complained to each other about journal editors, these were not fellow economists, but generalists, whose receptivity to their articles depended as much on their ability to understand economics and on their interest in economic issues in general, as on the merits of the work in question. This was a British community into which Leslie and Ingram were fully integrated.[17]

Nationality and identity

In this chapter, Leslie and Ingram have been described as Irish historical economists. This is justifiable in that they were both Irish and they were both historical
economists. However, that raises the question of whether it is legitimate to go
further and talk of either 'Irish historical economics' or an 'Irish historical
school'. Though their work can be related closely to Irish conditions, such a designation is problematic for at least three reasons. The first is that, as has already
been explained, not only were Leslie and Ingram thoroughly integrated into the
British economic community. They were not part of any separate Irish economics community distinguishable from English economics. The second is that
they were part of a broader movement, commonly labelled the 'English' Historical School, comprising Rogers, Toynbee, Ashley and others as well as Leslie
and Ingram. Given that Leslie acquired historical ideas in London, listening to
Maine, it is not even possible to argue that the historical approach originated in
Ireland. Furthermore, though his historical economics was linked to a concern
with specifically Irish problems related to land tenure, Mill too was involved in
such issues: concern with Irish problems did not stop at the Irish Sea. The third
arises because to describe their economics as Irish rather than English raises the
question of how these terms were understood at the time, for the labels did not
simply refer to two distinct nations or geographical areas, but had identifiable
ideological implications.[18]

In 1801, Ireland had become part of the United Kingdom of Great Britain and
Ireland. Following on from the Act of Union with Scotland, in 1707, the idea of
Britishness had developed to describe the inhabitants of the new, enlarged nation
and its culture. As Colley (2005) has shown, this identity was tied up with the
Empire, in which Scots played a vital role. It was always the British Empire,
never the English Empire, over which Victoria ruled. After 1801, Ireland became
part of the British nation, and the Irish could consider themselves British.
However, this raised problems, for, even more than with Scotland, Ireland's relation with the rest of the United Kingdom was a colonial one, the memory of
Elizabeth I, Cromwell and protestant settlements in Ireland remaining strong.
Ingram's poem on the uprising of 1798 was commemorating a rebellion against
this Empire.

Had the word 'English' been reserved to refer to one part of the larger political unit, things would be simple, but that was not the case: the word was used to
refer to the culture of the nation as a whole, where one might think 'British'
would have been more appropriate. It was possible to use the words 'English'
and 'British' interchangeably. However, to do so carried an ideological message,
even if this was sometimes only implicit, especially in relation to Ireland. This
became particularly true during the period when Leslie and Ingram were writing.
Catholic emancipation in 1829 threatened an English identity associated, *inter
alia*, with protestantism. The essence of Englishness therefore came to be associated more with the institutions of representative government and the national
character but the religious dimension never disappeared. Matthew Arnold, in his

influential *Culture and Anarchy* (1869) argued that belonging to the national life involved affiliation with certain English institutions – the Church of England, or the Universities of Oxford and Cambridge – defining it as English, Protestant and as excluding the working class. The use of 'English' rather than 'British' was highly significant, for the so-called 'Celtic' cultures were seen as inferior, their peoples having different characteristics. Notions of culture were inextricable from racial stereotyping. Assimilation within the English system and culture was thus the route though with the Irish race could progress. Levy and Peart (2005) have used cartoon representations of the Irish to show how those who asserted their independence from English rule were portrayed as sub-human – almost apelike – in their appearance.

Thus it is clear why Leslie and Ingram would never have described themselves as an Irish historical school: to do so would have been to condemn it in the eyes of many of their readers.[19] However, despite being Irish, and despite Ingram's being associated, at least in his youth, with Irish nationalism, they appeared to share, at least to a certain extent, the ideology of Englishness. Ingram, in his history, has no problem describing Irish and Scottish economists as English. Leslie clearly accepted the evolutionary view of progress that underlay much of the racial stereotyping underlying the notion of Englishness (see Leslie 1879a: 228, 407). The point where he comes closest to addressing the issue explicitly is in 'The political economy of Adam Smith' where he chooses as one of his main targets, Henry Buckle's *History of Civilization in England* (1857–1861), of whom he says:

> Mr. Buckle, who in his excellent chapters on the Intellectual History of France justly traces to England the origination of the spirit of liberty which in the eighteenth century took possession of French philosophy, nevertheless does injustice at once to France and to Great Britain in overlooking the influence of Montesquieu over Scotch philosophy in Adam Smith's age. And the same oversight, coupled with a view of political economy which Mr. Buckle himself adopted from Ricardo and his school, leads him to describe Adam Smith's method as entirely deductive. The philosophy of Great Britain, Mr. Buckle affirms, owes nothing to France; and he represents the intellect of Scotland as having, under clerical guidance, become wholly deductive.
>
> (Leslie 1879a [1870]: 157–8)

Here, as nowhere else, Leslie appears to draw back from equating Great Britain with England, thereby questioning Buckle's historical narrative, but he appears to miss the much larger narrative of Englishness that might be called into question by his undermining of Buckle's treatment of Scotland.

Conclusions

Leslie, aided and abetted by Ingram, was the leading figure in the historicist challenge to the English classical school of political economy in the 1870s. His opposition to deductive economics owed much to his awareness of the specific circumstances of Ireland in the 1840s, to which the abstractions of Ricardian economics seemed inappropriate. Though his historical method derived from Maine's work on English Law, Leslie's economics could be seen as development from the preceding Irish tradition in political economy. However, Leslie was thoroughly integrated into British economics, in which he was a much more significant figure than would appear given the way economics has subsequently developed. Many of his concerns relating to Ireland were shared within that wider community (notably by Mill) and his most important follower in relation to the historical method was arguably Toynbee, an inspirational figure for his generation. Ingram's historicism was thoroughly tied up with his Comtism, a religion that clearly had limited appeal. In Ireland, with the peculiarities of its land tenure system, and the complex relationships between economics, class and religion, political economy was even more intertwined with ideology than in England but, despite their concern with the Irish situation, neither Leslie nor Ingram appear to have escaped from the prevailing ideology of Englishness.

Notes

1 A few paragraphs of this chapter are drawn, with modifications, from an earlier paper, Backhouse (2006).
2 The biographical material in this and the following paragraph are taken from *ODNB*.
3 The convention is adopted in this chapter of giving the date of the edition used and, on the first citation, providing the date of original publication in square brackets.
4 The discussion of Leslie's applied economics draws extensively on this article.
5 Citing Moore (1995), Black also draws attention to Leslie's reading of Francis Bacon and writings on the methods of political reasoning.
6 See, for example, Hoppen (1998: 572–8).
7 Backhouse (1994) cites some more recent estimates of industrial production which suggest Walker's figures may not have been far out. However, it would also appear that the production did not fall so sharply in Britain.
8 See *IP*, which contain substantial files documenting his involvement.
9 These remarks are based on the collection of Leslie's letters to Ingram (*IP*). One problem with drawing detailed inferences from these is that many of them are not dated.
10 Leslie's account of his encounters with Sidgwick provide a nice illustration of the way they corresponded:

> The little I have seen of Sidgwick I did not admire. Some time ago I was in a railway carriage with him, but not remembering his face did not speak to him. He dragged a huge German book out of a bag, saying aloud to a friend, that he 'rather despised the man who could not read German', and then fell asleep over it. Coming back a few days afterwards, he was again in the same carriage, and again lugged out this big German book, spoke contemptuously of the men who don't read German, and went asleep. On this second occasion he spoke to me, asking if I did not remember him – and I believe the German performance was to attract my admiration.
>
> (*IP* 43/26)

11 For example, 'I had looked forward for months with pleasure to seeing you in October.... I feel it as a disappointment and a loss to miss you.' (15 September, *IP* 43/30).

12 A letter from Leslie to Ingram dated 9 August says, 'I suggest a title such as "The present state and prospects of political economy" to "a plea for a new method"' (*IP* 43/29). He also suggested that if Ingram revised it, this could be indicated on the title page.

13 The editor of the third edition, William A. Scott, added a seventh chapter, on 'The Austrian School and recent developments', but this should clearly be ignored here.

14 For a detailed account of these circumstances, see Black (1960) and Boylan and Foley (1992).

15 The question of national identity is explored in Section 5.

16 See his review of the *Theory of Political Economy*, reprinted in *JPC* VII: 157–62.

17 Thus when Alfred Marshall and others sought to found a British Economic Association (significantly, in view of what follows, not English) it was natural for him to invite Ingram to participate (Whitaker 1996 I: 349). (Leslie had died by this time.)

18 This argument is developed in more detail in Backhouse (2006). It complements the more wide-ranging discusion of ideology in Boylan and Foley (1992: chapter 6).

19 As the first person to lecture on English Literature in Trinity College, it is hard to believe that he would not have been aware of the cultural implications of the term.

References

IP   Ingram Papers, PRONI.

JPC   *Papers and Correspondence of William Stanley Jevons* (7 volumes), R.D.C. Black (ed.), London: Macmillan, 1972–1981.

MLL   *The Later Letters of John Stuart Mill, 1849–1873*, (4 volumes) in Francis E. Mineka and Dwight N. Lindley (eds) *Collected Works of John Stuart Mill*, volumes 14–17, London: Routledge and Kegan Paul, 1972.

ODNB   *Oxford Dictionary of National Biography* (online).

Arnold, M. (1869) *Culture and Anarchy,* London: Smith, Elder and Co.

Backhouse, R.E. (1994) *Economists and the Economy*, New Brunswick, NJ: Transaction.

—— (2004) 'History of economics, economics and economic history in Britain, 1824–2000' *European Journal of the History of Economic Thought* 11(1): 107–27.

—— (2006) 'Nationality, place and identity: locating the English (Irish?) historical school', Paper given to ECHE Conference on economics and place, Nanterre.

Black, R.D.C. (1960) *Economic Thought and the Irish Question, 1817–1870*, Cambridge: Cambridge University Press.

—— (1995) *Economic Theory and Policy in Context: The Selected Essays of R.D. Collison Black*, Cheltenham: Edward Elgar.

—— (2002) 'The political economy of Thomas Edward Cliffe Leslie (1826–82): A reassessment', *European Journal of the History of Economic Thought* 9(1): 17–41.

Boylan, T.A. and Foley, T.P. (1992) *Political Economy and Colonial Ireland: the Propagation and Ideological Function of Economic Discourse in the Nineteenth Century*, London: Routledge.

Buckle, H. (1857–1861) *The History of Civilization in England*, 3 vols, London: Longmans Green.

Colley, L. (2005) *Britons: Forging the Nation, 1707–1837*, New Haven, CT: Yale University Press.

Foley, T. and Boylan, T. (2000) 'Brotherhood at arms: the Cairnes–Leslie controversy', in A.E. Murphy and R. Prendergast (eds) *Contributions to the History of Economic Thought: Essays in Honour of R.D.C. Black*, London: Routledge, pp. 201–26.

Hoppen, K.T. (1998) *The Mid-Victorian Generation, 1846–1886*, Oxford: Oxford University Press.

Hutchison, T.W. (1953) *A Review of Economic Doctrines, 1870–1929*, Oxford: Oxford University Press.

Ingram, J.K. (1962) 'The present position and prospects of political economy', in R.L. Smyth (ed.) *Essays in Economic Method: Selected Papers Read to Section F of the British Association for the Advancement of Science, 1860–1913*, London: Duckworth, pp. 41–72.

—— (1967) *A History of Political Economy* [1888] with supplementary chapter by William A. Scott and Introduction by R.T. Ely, 1915 edn, New York: Augustus Kelley.

Jevons, W.S. (1979) *Theory of Political Economy*, 2nd edn, London: Macmillan.

Leslie, T.E.C. (1856) *The Military Systems of Europe Economically Considered*, Belfast: Shepherd and Aitchison.

—— (1870) *Land Systems and Industrial Economy of Ireland, England and Continental Countries*, London: Longmans Green.

—— (1879a) *Essays in Political and Moral Philosophy*, Dublin: Hodges, Foster and Figgis.

—— (1879b) 'The known and the unknown in the economic world', *Fortnightly Review*, 1 June.

—— (1879) [1867] 'The military systems of Europe in 1867', *North British Review*, December.

Levy, D. and Peart, S. (2005) *The 'Vanity of the Philosopher': From Equality to Hierarchy in Post-Classical Economics*, Ann Arbor, MI: University of Michigan Press.

Marshall, A. and Marshall, M.P. (1879) *Economics of Industry*, London: Macmillan.

Moore, G.C.G. (1995) 'T. E. Cliffe Leslie and the English Methodenstreit', *Journal of the History of Economic Thought* 17(1): 57–77.

Whitaker, J.K. (1996) *The Correspondence of Alfred Marshall, Economist*, 3 vols, Cambridge: Cambridge University Press.

10 Irish contributions to nineteenth-century monetary and banking debates

John D. Turner

Introduction

In the first half of the nineteenth century, Britain faced several major issues regarding the appropriate structure and organisation of its banking and monetary systems in a rapidly industrialising era. Although the famous debates surrounding these issues have long passed into the annals of political economy, they are still relevant today as much of modern monetary and banking theory has its genesis in these controversies.

The first major monetary controversy arose at the beginning of the nineteenth century, following the suspension of convertibility of Bank of England and Bank of Ireland notes into gold. The key issue in this debate was – what was the ultimate cause of rising prices and the fall in the value of the pound. Once this controversy had subsided, two further debates arose in the second quarter of the nineteenth century. First, there was a controversy over the establishment of joint-stock banks and their appropriate regulation. Second, there was a debate about how monetary policy should be conducted and the appropriate design of monetary institutions.

Irish contributions to these three debates came in two forms. First, Irish monetary and banking experiences informed English parliamentarians and political economists. Second, Irish economists, bankers and parliamentarians made their own contributions to these debates. The aim of the first part of this essay is to explore the substantial contributions which Irish experiences and commentators made to the first of these three controversies – the bullionist debate. The aim of the second part of this essay is to examine the contribution to the three debates by Henry Parnell, an Irish MP, who is regarded as a major contributor to the monetary and banking controversies which took place in the first half of the nineteenth century (Arnon 1999).

Ireland and the bullionist controversy

The bullionist and anti-bullionist positions

Prior to the Napleonic Wars, England had been on a de facto gold standard, with the circulation mainly consisting of metallic currency as well as Bank of England

and private (or country) bank notes, both of which were convertible into specie on demand. In early 1797 rumours of a French invasion resulted in a 'general clamour for gold' (Viner 1937: 122), and on 26 February 1797, convertibility of Bank of England notes into specie was suspended by an Order in Council, which was repeatedly confirmed and reinforced by subsequent Parliamentary Acts. This suspension of convertibility was to last until 1821.

Although the restriction of specie only applied to the Bank of England, it was implicitly accepted that Scottish banks and English country banks could redeem their currency with Bank of England notes rather than specie (Fetter 1950). Such a policy was necessary because of the pyramiding of specie reserves unto the Bank of England. In other words, the Bank of England, as Bagehot (1873) was later to highlight, held a large proportion of Britain's specie reserves (Laidler 1989: 61).

Despite the reservations of many commentators, the suspension of convertibility appeared to have little initial impact, but by the beginning of the nineteenth century, there were indications that all was not well with the economy. As well as rising prices, the value of Bank of England paper in terms of bullion had fallen, as had the sterling exchange rate in Hamburg. This resulted in a flurry of pamphlet publishing which tried to explain (and allocate blame for) the inflation and posed questions as to how to determine the optimal quantity of money (Viner 1937: 125). The inflationary pressures had subsided by 1803, but their re-emergence in early 1809 resulted in the renewal of the controversy, and the eventual Parliamentary appointment in February 1810 of the *Select Committee on the High Price of Bullion*.

The parties involved in the debate surrounding the high price of bullion fell into two distinct camps. The bullionists were opposed to the government's restriction on the convertibility of the currency. Notable amongst the bullionist contributions were those of Boyd (1800), Ricardo (1810) and Thornton (1802). Indeed, Thornton's contribution is now viewed as a classic amongst modern monetary economists and central bankers. The opposition party were given the appellation 'anti-bullionist' as they defended the government and the Bank of England against the accusations of the bullionists. The most notable contributions from this party were made in Parliamentary speeches and in several tracts (Viner 1937: 121).

Bullionists, although disagreeing on the minutiae of the controversy, were in accord that the suspension of convertibility had removed a check on the Bank of England's note-issuing powers, with the result that there was an excess of notes. For the bullionists, this explained the increase in the price of gold bullion and fall in the exchanges. Most bullionists conceded that in the short run this was not evidence of an excess issue, but the fact that it was substantial and prevailed for a considerable period of time was, for them, proof positive of an excess issue by the Bank of England (Viner 1937: 127). The solution for the bullionists was simple – end the Restriction.

Anti-bullionists, on the other hand, argued that the exchange-rate depreciation and premium on bullion was due to large war-time foreign remittances, and not to the Bank of England's note-issuing policy. Although moderate bullionists such as Thornton (1802) agreed that extraordinary remittances could cause these phenomena, this would only be the case in the short run. Some anti-bullionists also claimed that the real bills doctrine prevented the Bank of England over-issuing notes. The main tenet of this doctrine is 'that bank notes which are lent in exchange for "real bills" ... cannot be issued in excess; and that, since the requirements of the non-bank public are given and finite, any superfluous notes would return automatically to the issuer' (Green 1989: 310). Thornton (1802) and the 1810 Bullion Report clearly reject the notion that the Bank of England could maintain price level stability with an inconvertible currency by simply discounting only good short-term bills.

Defenders of the Bank of England also argued that the increase in the price level was due to an expansion in the country banks' note issue. However, bullionists denied the possibility of a relative over-issue of country bank notes because they were convertible, upon demand, into Bank of England notes (Viner 1975: 235).

The bullionists may have won the intellectual debate, but Parliament did not accept the policy proposals of the 1810 Bullion Report – to end the suspension of convertibility within two years. However, convertibility was restored at the pre-suspension rate in 1821, and in the interim, the inflationary fears of the bullionists were not realised.

Thompson and Hickson (2001) view a gold standard with an inbuilt suspension option as vital to the survival of early democracies such as Britain. They suggest that such suspensions of convertibility were necessary for emergency war finance, and that they need not necessarily result in inflation. In Britain, the independent common-law judiciary would have ensured that the government (and by extension, Bank of England) could credibly commit to redeem notes at the same rate after the emergency situation was over. Notably, this may explain the absence of inflation once the threat began to subside following the Russian defeat of Napoleon in 1812.

The depreciation of the Irish paper pound

The restriction on convertibility did not apply to the Bank of Ireland, but within a week of the English suspension of convertibility, the Lord Lieutenant and Privy Council instructed the Bank of Ireland to suspend the convertibility of its notes. This suspension was subsequently given legislative backing by the Irish Parliament (Hall 1949: 80–3). Following the Act of Union, the restriction on the Bank of Ireland was subsumed under the English Restriction legislation, with no expectation that the Bank of Ireland had to redeem its notes into Bank of England notes; this effectively meant that the Bank was permitted to follow its own monetary policy (Fetter 1955: 15).

As can be seen from Table 10.1, the Irish currency depreciated slightly after the restriction on convertibility, but by 1803, the depreciation was particularly large. Of particular note, as can also be seen from Table 10.1, was that the London–Belfast exchange rate was close to par, probably because specie was the medium of exchange in the north of Ireland, and very few bank notes circulated.[1] This state of affairs resulted in a series of pamphlets being published. Three parliamentarians, King (1803), Foster (1804) and Parnell (1804), adopted a bullionist stance, by suggesting that the exchange depreciation was mainly attributable to an over-issue of Bank of Ireland paper. Although, as can be seen from Table 10.1, the Bank of Ireland note issue expanded relatively more than that of the Bank of England after the Restriction, this is not evidence of over-issue. It may simply be reflecting the fact that Ireland relied more on specie as a circulating medium prior to the suspension (Ó Gráda 1994: 47). These three commentators all agreed that, similar to English and Scottish banks, the Bank of Ireland should be made to redeem its notes into Bank of England paper. Furthermore, King (1803) advocated restricting the Bank's note issue to some maximum, and Parnell (1804) suggested that the two currencies be amalgamated.

Supporters of the Bank of Ireland, such as Henry Boase (1804) and several anonymous commentators (see Hall 1949: 86), suggested, in a similar vein to later anti-bullionist defenders of the Bank of England, that remittances to England created an adverse balance of payments, resulting in an increased demand for bank notes. As one anonymous Dublin merchant (1804: 5) stated:

> Neither the high exchange in Ireland, not the high premium paid there for guineas arise from any depreciation of the value of bank paper, but solely from the balance of demands being greatly against Ireland, calling for remittances to England far beyond the value that the exports of Ireland amount to, and in consequence, any paper or value, through the medium of which a payment can be made in England, must bear a premium in proportion to the extent of the inability of Ireland to pay in full the demands on her.

According to this Dublin merchant (1804: 8), the adverse balance of payments was a culmination of the great importation of British manufactured goods in 1799, the scarcity and subsequent importation of Irish corn in 1800 and 1801, and the increasing number of absentee landlords which followed the 1798 Rebellion and the Act of Union. Unsurprisingly, the remedy of this school of thought centred on ways to rectify the adverse balance of payments. For the Dublin merchant (1804: 14), absentees had to return, exports had to increase, and a larger proportion of the British navy and military should be based in Ireland.

The 1804 Irish currency report

At the beginning of March 1804, Parliament appointed a committee to inquire into whether there was, and to what extent there was, an unfavourable exchange rate, as well as the causes and remedies of the depreciated currency. The report of this committee has been described by Ó Gráda (1994: 47) as a 'landmark in the history of monetary theory'. This committee, chaired by John Foster, had forty-nine members, including the leading statesmen of the day and Henry Thornton, the banker and economist.

Table 10.1 Bank of Ireland note issue and exchange rates, 1798–1804

	Bank of Ireland note issue (Jan.) (£'000s)	Bank of England note issue (Feb.) (£'000s)	Premium on English currency in terms of Irish currency on Dublin–London exchange (%)		Premium on English currency in terms of Irish currency on Belfast–London exchange (%)	
			Highest	Lowest	Highest	Lowest
1798	1,214	12,200	9.25	7.75	8	6
1799	1,452	13,400	14	8.375	10.5	6.5
1800	2,193	15,000	13	9	10	7
1801	2,259	14,600	15	9	10	5.5
1802	2,473	17,100	12.75	10	8	6.5
1803	2,624	16,000	19	10.25	8.75	5.25
1804 (Jan.–Mar.)	2,937	17,200	18	14	7.75	6

Sources: Cannan (1925: xliv); Hall (1949: 84–5).

Note
As 13 units of Irish currency were equal to 12 units of English currency, the exchanges were at par when the premium was $8^{1}/_{3}$ per cent.

Puget, a Bank of England director, and two of the Bank of Ireland's original directors (Colville and D'Olier) were witnesses before the committee who took a very strong anti-bullionist position. For these witnesses, the Bank of Ireland's monetary policy had not caused the depreciation; rather the depreciation was attributable to the adverse balance of payments between the two countries. Indeed, for these witnesses over-issue by the Bank was improbable because of the real bills doctrine.

Unsurprisingly, pro-bullionist witnesses suggested that the Bank of Ireland's lax monetary policy was the chief cause of the depreciation, and not the balance of trade between England and Ireland. One of the main witnesses to give such evidence was Robert Marshall, who as Inspector General of Imports and Exports of Ireland was well placed to comment on the balance of trade between Ireland and England (Hall 1949: 93). However, as well as stating that the depreciation was partly due to an excessive issue of bank notes, he also argued that it was also due to Ireland's internal political difficulties as well as the external threat of invasion. Marshall was implicitly recognising that the convertibility suspension and the subsequent inflation was a source of emergency war finance. Surprisingly, apart from Siblerling (1924) and Thompson and Hickson (2001: 189–93), subsequent scholars have had little to say about this observation. Siblerling, in criticising the bullionist position, argues that the availability of credit to finance emergency national-defence situations

> requires a flexibility in the financial institutions which cannot exist if their lending power is restricted by cash reserves that are constantly subject to depletion by the unusual commercial difficulties interposed by naval warfare, by alarms and hoarding among the masses of the people, and by tactical machinations of an enemy cognizant (as Napoleon was) of the power of credit as a military weapon.
>
> (Siberling 1924: 418)

Silberling (1924) was particularly critical of the extreme bullionists for their naivety and short-sightedness in not perceiving the emergency-war-finance benefits of the Restriction. More recently, Thompson and Hickson (2001: 190–11) laud the flexibility of the British gold standard, which permitted the Bank of England to expand the currency during military emergencies by suspending convertibility, without creating proportionate increases in the price level.

After several months of interviews and deliberations, the final report of the 1804 committee stated the following:

> That this depreciation in Ireland arises almost entirely, if not solely, from an excess of Paper, appears highly probable: and Your Committee, in adverting to the Issues of the Bank of Ireland, do not mean to decide whether the Directors of it might not have had strong reasons for their conduct; but they conceive it their duty to call the attention of the House to a matter of so much importance.
>
> (Fetter 1955: 72)

Although this is a bullionist statement, it acknowledges that the Bank may have had very good reason for issuing excess notes. The Report is not uncritical of the role of private banks in augmenting the circulation of paper money as it highlights the increase in note-issuing banks from eleven in 1801 to forty by 1804, and the increase in small-denomination notes as a result (Fetter 1955: 73–4). However, it was acknowledged that

> the Restriction has made it necessary for every private Bank to keep a stock of Bank of Ireland paper, equal, or nearly so, to what it would have otherwise deemed prudent to keep in Specie for paying its Notes, the facility of procuring that stock is increased by the increase of its quantity in the market; and although such part of that Paper as is employed in forming that stock may be said for the time to be locked up from circulation, yet it must be remembered, that all such stock gives room to and necessarily implies an issue of the private Banks Paper equal not only to it but to such further amount as Bankers in general may in prudence suffer their outstanding Notes to exceed their stock of Specie lying in their coffers.
>
> (Fetter 1955: 72)

The Report of Irish Currency Committee did not recommend, like the Bullion Report, its more famous descendant, that the Restriction be ended, but it did suggest that the Bank of Ireland redeem its notes in Bank of England notes. The report of the committee, published in May, was practically ignored by Parliament, probably because the depreciation of the Irish currency on the exchanges improved greatly from May 1804 onwards (Fetter 1959: 103).

Although it was ignored by Parliament at the time, the Irish Currency Report had a significant impact on the Bullion Report of 1810. First, six of the twenty-two members of the Bullion Committee had served on the Irish Currency Committee. Second, the findings and evidence presented before the Irish Currency Committee are referred to at length in the Bullion Report (Cannan 1925: 39–43). In particular, the Bullion Report makes an argument from the lesser to the greater by contrasting the relationship the Bank of Ireland had with private banks and that which the Bank of England had with country banks: even though 'the Bank of Ireland does not possess the same exclusive power of supplying any part of that country with a paper currency, which the Bank of England enjoys in respect of the metropolis of the Empire', it was still able to control (although not precisely) the volume of private bank note issues (Cannan 1925: 42).

The Bullion Report was further along the bullionist 'spectrum' than that of the Irish Currency Report in that it made no allowance for non-monetary disturbances (Fetter 1959: 104). Furthermore, the Bullion Report recommended in a dogmatic and doctrinaire fashion that the Restriction be ended so as to stem the over-issue of Bank of England notes. The Irish Currency Report, on the other hand, was much more judicious and it made no such recommendation; it even explicitly recognised, as mentioned above, that the Bank of Ireland may have had good reason for its excess note issue.

The Irish Currency Committee may have played a significant role in the thought formation of Henry Thornton. According to Hayek (1939: 53) and Fetter (1955: 31), both the testimony of Francis Horner (a fellow committee member) and the nature of the questions put to witnesses are suggestive of Thornton having a major responsibility for the work of the Irish Currency Committee. Thornton had previously observed in Parliament in 1802 that no danger could result from the Restriction on the Bank of England because that institution was well managed, and 'were sufficiently disposed to restrain the circulation of their own paper', whereas this was not the case in Ireland (Hayek 1939: 52). However, several weeks into the Irish Committee's investigations, it appears that Thornton had changed his mind about the Bank of England, and he suggested that the Report of the Committee on the Irish Currency should be used to drop a large hint to the Bank of England to curtail its currency issue (Hayek 1939: 53).

A polemic against the Bank of Ireland

Although the Report of the Irish Currency Committee was judicious, the Earl of Lauderdale, possibly in response to this Report, published a pamphlet in 1805 which is best described as a polemic against the Bank of Ireland. He argued that the Restriction had given the directors of the Bank of Ireland the freedom to do as they wanted, and 'besides giving extended discounts and other accommodations to all their friends', they had rewarded shareholders royally (Lauderdale 1805: 106). To support his case, the Earl of Lauderdale presented monthly stock prices for the Bank over a seven-year period. As such, he was a precursor of the modern efficient-financial-market economist in that he believed that the stock market is one of the best revealers of information. His data, presented in Figure 10.1, reveals that in the early years of the suspension, Bank stockholders enjoyed significant capital appreciation, but it is noticeable that the share price fell in 1803 when the depreciation of the Irish pound was at its height. Bank shareholders also enjoyed substantial returns via dividends. The dividend increased by 0.5 per cent to 7 per cent in 1800. It then increased to 7.5 per cent in 1801. In addition, a 5 per cent bonus was paid to shareholders in December 1803.

A recent cliometric study appears to partially absolve the Bank of Ireland by suggesting that the Bank's monetary policy was not the cause of the depreciation of the Irish pound (Ó Gráda 1993). According to Ó Gráda (1994: 47, 49–50), the increase in the circulation was more due to the Bank accommodating, somewhat reluctantly, Treasury requests for funds rather than the Bank taking advantage of the Restriction. Although this ties in with the emergency-war-finance explanation for the suspension and subsequent inflation mentioned above, it does not appear to coalesce well with Lauderdale's evidence. However, although the Bank of Ireland may have over-issued following pressure from the Lords of Treasury, arising from the internal and external threats to Ireland's security, it appears that the Bank profited from and may even have taken advantage of this state of affairs.

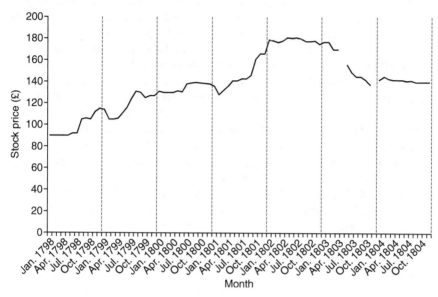

Figure 10.1 Bank of Ireland stock price, 1798–1804 (source: Lauderdale (1805: 115–17)).

Note
Stock prices are the lowest reported price of the month.

The views and contributions of Henry Parnell

Henry Parnell (1776–1842), raised to the peerage as 1st Baron of Congleton, was born into a financial and political family, his father, Sir John Parnell, being Chancellor of the Irish Exchequer. On the death of his father in 1801, he inherited the family estate in Queen's County (modern-day County Laois). After a brief time in Parliament in 1802, he was MP for Queen's County from 1806 to 1832, and MP for Dundee from 1833 to 1841. From 1835 to 1841 he was Paymaster-General. Parnell was a prominent liberal Whig and wrote several famous tracts on penal and financial reform, the most notable of which is his treatise on public finance (see Parnell 1830).

Parnell and the bullionist debate

Parnell was probably the most notable Irishman to make a contribution to the Irish Currency debate. He published a pamphlet in 1804, which argued 'that it may be safely assumed, that the cause of the depreciation of Bank of Ireland paper, is the excessive issue which has been made of it under the authority of the Bank Directors' (Parnell 1804: 4).

For Parnell (1804: 3–4), the increased supply of notes above what is required to conduct trade 'necessarily contributes to diminish the value of the whole circulation'. Similar to the views of Lauderdale, Parnell (1804: 29) believed that the Bank of Ireland was simply augmenting its profits by an unwarrantable system of discounting. The evidence that the Bank was acting in this way was irrefutable for Parnell. As well as the discount on the Bank's paper, Parnell highlighted that the northern exchange was at par with London (Parnell 1804: 5).

Parnell (1804: 15), similar to moderate bullionists such as Thornton, was prepared to acknowledge that an adverse balance of trade could cause a small depreciation of the currency, but not of the order of 10 per cent. Parnell (1804: 37) suggested that the payment of interest on loans borrowed by Ireland in London and the remittances to absentee landlords was a very small sum compared to Ireland's total export trade 'that the effect produced on the exchange is inconsiderable'. Indeed, Parnell (1804: 15) even suggested, although without presenting evidence, that the balance of trade was actually in Ireland's favour.

Parnell (1804: 41–50) also addressed the question as to what extent the depreciation of the Irish currency was due to the private banks. He did not deny the existence of large issues by private banks, but for him they were simply 'the consequence not the cause of the depreciation of the currency' because private bank notes are convertible into Bank of Ireland notes (Parnell 1804: 49–50). Notably, he quotes from Malthus's *Essay on Population* that the law of reflux will check excessive issue by private banks. As we shall see later, the law of reflux was to become an important pillar in Parnell's monetary theory.

With regards to policy prescriptions, Parnell's (1804: 29) first preference was a monetary union, and if that was unachievable, he suggested that Bank of Ireland notes should be convertible into Bank of England paper. He also advocated that some control should be exercised by Parliament over the conduct of the Bank of Ireland's directors. Interestingly, when viewed in the context of his later writings, Parnell (1804: 28) highlights that the Bank of England showed admirable restraint in not over-issuing their notes, and he suggests that this was because they were subject to Parliamentary scrutiny in that they had to give sessional reports to Parliament on the amount of their notes in circulation. Concomitantly, Parnell (1804: 28) argues that if the Bank of Ireland had been subject to such oversight, 'they never could have overloaded the market, as they have, with their paper'. However, what Parnell failed to see was that even the Bank of England could over-issue during the suspension of convertibility if their Parliamentary overseers requested it. Notably, in his 1804 pamphlet, Parnell demonstrates none of his later anti-central-banking or free-banking sentiments. Indeed, if anything, he commends the Bank of England for their restraint, and his policy prescription that the Bank of Ireland's notes should be convertible into Bank of England paper would have further cemented and established the Bank of England's central position in the British monetary system.

Parnell's 1804 pamphlet is also interesting in that he identifies the winners and losers of the depreciation of the currency. He suggests that although merchants, manufacturers and farmers may have benefited from the inflation, 'that improvement arises from causes which have been productive of the most injurious effects of the landed and other interests' (Parnell 1804: 7). By other interests he meant individuals who derived incomes under contracts made prior to the restriction of payments on specie. According to Parnell (1804: 11) the landlord class suffered a 10 per cent loss in their income because their rental contracts were long term and they were unable to increase rents to take account of the depreciation of the currency. Consequently, the demands of northern gentry that their rents be paid in specie (Parnell 1804: 7) may not have been due to the backward state of the northern economy (see Ó Gráda 1994: 61–2); rather it may have been due to their shrewd financial acumen.

Parnell, a landlord himself, argued that 'the great evil attending a depreciated currency is an actual violation of all contracts', and the landlord in particular is the chief loser. Notably, Silberling (1924: 413) suggests that many bullionists were landowners 'to whom the fall in the purchasing power of money rents seemed a far greater calamity than any change in the fortunes of England or France'. In other words, Silberling suggests that bullionists were blinded by the narrow economic interests of the landed classes rather than victory over the Napoleonic forces. Parnell's emphasis on the cost of the depreciation to the landlord in his 1804 pamphlet adds some weight to Siblerling's thesis.

Parnell on paper money and banking

In his 1804 pamphlet Parnell wrote approvingly of the restraint manifested by the Bank of England in not over-issuing its notes, and, as discussed above, he believed that this was because of Parliamentary oversight (Parnell 1804: 28). However, his views on the Bank of England had changed dramatically by the time of the publication of a pamphlet in 1827 (with a second edition in 1828) entitled *Observations on Paper Money, Banking and Overtrading*. The lessons of experience had taught Parnell that:

> [e]very one agrees in respect to the injury that has arisen from the conduct of the Directors of the Bank of England, in suddenly and extensively enlarging their issues at one time, and in as suddenly and extensively contracting them at another; and no one can doubt, who has paid attention to their proceedings, as described in these pages, of the mischievous effects, in many other ways, of the uncontrolled power, which they possess and exercise over the currency.
>
> (Parnell 1828: 3)

An explanation for this volte-face was that Parnell had not only witnessed the depreciation of the English currency during the Napoleonic Wars, but the monetary and banking crisis of the mid-1820s, which had some of its origins in the re-introduction of convertibility at pre-war rates.

Although the Bank of England was the main focus of his pamphlet, he reserved his most polemical words for the Irish situation. He began the section on Ireland by stating that 'in no country, perhaps, has the issuing of paper money been carried to such an injurious success as in Ireland' (Parnell 1828: 37). Scathingly, he suggests that the improvement in the Irish exchange after 1804 was not due to the Bank of Ireland becoming more circumspect in its note issuing, but simply due to the Bank of England depreciating its currency to the same extent as that of the Irish currency (Parnell 1828: 38).

Commenting on the Bank of England's abuse of its position and the havoc it had caused, Parnell (1828: 3) stated that 'the obvious remedy for these evils is to diminish this power, and to place it under the control of continual and efficient competition'. Parnell advocated that the Bank of England should be split into several smaller banks and that note-issuing banks should be allowed to establish freely in London.[2] He suggested the same remedy for Ireland:

> As the main source of the evil consists in the interference of the law in creating a national bank with exclusive privileges, the first step that ought to be taken for introducing a good system into Ireland is the getting rid of such a bank, and opening the trade of banking in Dublin.
>
> (Parnell 1828: 42)

White (1995: 72) argues that Parnell's 1827 pamphlet should be considered the first major contribution to the Free Banking School; a school of thought which believed that the Bank of England was the only English bank which could over-issue, and therefore advocated the end of the Bank's semi-monopoly, and the principle of free trade being applied to note issue. In a somewhat similar vein, Vera Smith (1936: 72) describes Parnell as the chief advocate of applying the principles of free trade to banking. However, for reasons which will be outlined below, Arnon (1999) has recently questioned the validity of describing Parnell as an advocate of free banking.

In order to support his case to end the Bank of England's monopoly of note issue in London and its environs, Parnell appealed to the example of the Scottish banking system:

> The case of the Scotch banking is perhaps the most perfect and satisfactory illustration of the principles of a science that has ever existed. It leaves nothing to be desired in order to establish, beyond the possibility of dispute, the conclusion, that, if bankers are restrained from issuing notes for less than twenty shillings, and are subjected to the obligation of an immediate and unconditional payment of their notes, as soon as presented, the trade of banking may, with safety to the public, be rendered in all other respects free.
>
> (Parnell 1828: 15)

According to Parnell (1828: 19) this system free of restraint was not prone to over-issue of notes because of the practice of Scottish banks, where they exchanged notes twice a week, and balances on the exchanges were paid with short-term bills on London. This is the famous law of reflux, which, according to modern free bankers, forces errant banks, operating under a commodity-exchange monetary regime, to internalise the cost of over-issuing notes (White 1995: 12–17). However, as recognised by Hickson and Turner (2004: 907), the law of reflux, although it may prevent over-issue per se, 'is not sufficient to ensure the stability of free banking, because bankers can opportunistically increase the riskiness of their assets'.[3] Parnell (1828: 10, 42) may have been aware of this weakness with the law of reflux because in his policy prescriptions for England and Ireland, he suggests that every bank should be required to give security to the full amount of the notes which it issues. He believed that this would assure note-holders as to the value of their notes, and would consequently 'establish the most perfect confidence, in the mind of the public, in paper money' (Parnell 1828: 6). It would also prevent the bank runs and failures which he had witnessed over the previous decades. Parnell (1828: 7) quotes with approbation from the *Edinburgh Review* the concept that security for notes should consist of government funds, which are deposited with the government. Parnell was correct in identifying the need for banks to provide some sort of security for their note issues. However, he overlooked an important feature of bank ownership, whereby bank owners had joint and several unlimited liability, which meant that the wealth of every owner right down to their last acre and sixpence provided security for the note issue. Hickson and Turner (2004) have argued that unlimited shareholder liability resolves the time inconsistency problem as it discourages bankers from opportunistically increasing the risk of their assets. The security provided by unlimited shareholder liability had been greatly augmented by the liberalisation of banking in the mid-1820s which permitted banks to form as joint-stock companies with diffuse ownership.

Parnell's advocacy of a forfeitable hostage bond posted with the government for each bank's note issue raises the question as to whether White (1995) and Vera Smith (1936) have correctly identified Parnell as a classical forerunner of the pure free banking position. Arnon (1999) has also voiced such concerns, except he bases his argument on Parnell's support of the Scottish system, which he, as well as several others, suggests was not a pure example of a free banking system (Cowen and Kroszner 1989; Dow and Smithin 1992; Sechrest 1991).

Parnell clearly believed that the best monetary system was one with competing banks issuing notes and no special monopoly privileges being afforded to one individual bank. However, in his 1827 pamphlet and in an 1832 pamphlet, he makes it clear that he prefers several large (and by implication strong) banks dominating a monetary system rather than many small (and by implication weak) banks (Parnell 1828: 5, 1832: 76). Parnell's advocacy of the Scottish system has led Arnon (1999: 96–7) to interpret Parnell as advocating a few big banks managing the currency in a collaborative, if not cartel-like, fashion. By 1832, Scotland had seven major banks issuing notes, as well as several large provincial banking companies. Although these banks cooperated through the note exchange clearing mechanism and may have provided mutual insurance, they were free from government control of their note issue. Indeed, free bankers would argue the fact that these Scottish banks did cooperate and set standards for new entrants is what one might expect from a free banking system – it was in the self-interest of banks to establish these private arrangements. Indeed, the subsequent establishment and rapid growth of several large joint-stock banks after Parnell had written his pamphlets demonstrates that this system was unable to erect large barriers to entry for well-capitalised new entrants.

Parnell's admiration for the Scottish banking system with its large well-capitalised banks can be partially explained by his antipathy towards small banks, an antipathy which was shared by Adam Smith (1776: 422). Parnell had witnessed at first hand the misery caused by the failure of many small English and Irish banks during the first half of the 1820s (Parnell 1828: 11). For Parnell the weakness and smallness of these English and Irish banks was due to the trade of banking *not* being free from government interference. For example, Parnell argues:

> Had the trade of banking been left as free in Ireland as it is in Scotland, the want of paper money that would have arisen with the progress of trade, would, in all probability, have been supplied by joint stock companies, supported with large capitals, and governed by wise and effectual rules.
>
> (Parnell 1828: 37)

This also explains why Parnell advocated that banks post forfeitable hostage bonds for their notes. He argues that this would make it impossible for weak banks to exist, and hence contribute to the severity of panics when they arise (Parnell 1828: 10). However, such a policy would have been unnecessary with the subsequent rapid growth and development of well-capitalised unlimited liability joint-stock banks.

As is discussed elsewhere in this volume, Ireland's contribution to this debate did not end with Parnell. S. Mountifort Longfield, the first holder of the Whately Chair in Political Economy at Trinity College, in a series of articles in 1840, opposed the free banking views espoused by Parnell. Longfield (1840a, 1840b, 1840c, 1840d) took the side of the Currency School, defending the exclusive and monopolistic privileges of the Bank of Ireland.

Conclusion

This essay has reviewed Ireland's contribution to the classical nineteenth-century monetary debates. Ireland's main contribution to the bullionist debate was the impact of the Irish Currency Report on bullionist opinion in Parliament. The bullionist controversy also resulted in the publication of one of Henry Parnell's first pamphlets. Although Parnell was scathing in this pamphlet about the behaviour of the Bank of Ireland's directors, he was not hostile to the Bank of England, and, if anything, was complimentary of its restraint during the first seven years of the Restriction. However, the bitter experience of the following two decades appears to have changed Parnell into an advocate of free trade in banking. The free banking school, of which Parnell was a leading light, lost the policy debate as the policy recommendations of the Currency School were implemented in the mid-1840s by Peel, and as a result the influence of this school of thought waned until its revival in the 1980s. Notably, the modern free banking school views this Irish politician as one of their major classical forerunners.

Notes

1 Hall (1949: 85), adopting a bullionist tone, notes that 'in view of the fact that the Bel-fast–London exchange was actually favourable to Belfast, it was possible to infer that English paper currency had depreciated in terms of gold'.
2 The Banking Copartnership Act (1826) allowed note-issuing banks to constitute freely on a joint-stock basis for the first time, provided they were located outside a sixty-five mile radius of London.
3 White (1995: 7) notes that the law of reflux is only effective if banks are solvent.

References

Anonymous Dublin Merchant (1804) *Observations on the Exchange Between London and Dublin*, Dublin: M.N. Mahon.

Arnon, A. (1999) 'Free and not so free banking theories among the classicals; or, classical forerunners of free banking and why they have been neglected', *History of Political Economy* 31: 79–107.

Bagehot, W. (1873; Reprint 1999) *Lombard Street: A Description of the Money Market*, London: John Wiley and Sons.

Boase, H. (1804) *A Letter to the Right Honourable Lord King in Defence of the Conduct of the Directors of the Bank of Ireland*, London.

Boyd, W. (1800) *Letter to the Right Honourable William Pitt on the Influence of the Stoppage of Issue in Specie at the Bank of England; on the Prices of Provisions, and other Commodities*, London.

Cannan, E. (1925; Reprint 1969) *The Paper Pound of 1797–1821: The Bullion Report 8th June 1810*, New York: Augustus M. Kelley.

Cowen, T. and Kroszner, R. (1989) 'Scottish banking before 1845: a model for laissez-faire?', *Journal of Money, Credit and Banking* 21: 221–31.

Dow, S.C. and Smithin, J. (1992) 'Free banking in Scotland, 1695–1845', *Scottish Journal of Political Economy* 39: 374–90.

Fetter, F.W. (1950) 'Legal tender during the British and Irish bank restrictions', *Journal of Political Economy* 58: 241–53.

Fetter, F.W. (1955) *The Irish Paper Pound 1797–1826: A Reprint of the Report of the Committee of 1804 of the British House of Commons on the Condition of the Irish Currency*, London: George Allen and Unwin.

Fetter, F.W. (1959) 'The politics of the bullion report', *Economica* 26: 99–120.

Foster, J.L. (1804) *An Essay on the Principle of Commercial Exchanges, and More Particularly of the Exchange Between Great Britain and Ireland*, London.

Green, R. (1989) 'Real bills doctrine', in J. Eatwell, M. Milgate and P. Newman (eds) *The New Palgrave: Money*, London: Norton.

Hall, F.G. (1949) *The Bank of Ireland 1783–1946*, Dublin: Hodges, Figgis & Co.

Hayek, F.A. (1939; Reprint 1978) *An Introduction to Henry Thornton's An Inquiry into the Nature and Effects of the Paper Credit of Great Britain*, New York: Augustus Kelley.

Hickson, C.R. and Turner, J.D. (2004) 'Free banking and stability of early joint-stock banking', *Cambridge Journal of Economics* 28: 903–19.

King, Lord (1803) *Thoughts on the Restriction of Payments in Specie at the Banks of England and Ireland*, London: Cadell and Davies.

Laidler, D. (1989) 'The bullionist controversy', in J. Eatwell, M. Milgate and P. Newman (eds) *The New Palgrave: Money*, London: Norton.

Lauderdale, Earl of (1805) *Thoughts on the Alarming State of the Circulation, and on the Means of Redressing the Pecuniary Grievances in Ireland*, Edinburgh: James Ballentyne.

Longfield, S.M. (1840a) 'Banking and Currency I', *Dublin University Magazine* 15: 3–15.

Longfield, S.M. (1840b) 'Banking and Currency II', *Dublin University Magazine* 15: 218–33.

Longfield, S.M. (1840c) 'Banking and Currency parts III and IV', *Dublin University Magazine* 16: 371–89.

Longfield, S.M. (1840d) 'Banking and Currency parts III and IV', *Dublin University Magazine* 16: 611–20.

Ó Gráda, C. (1993) 'The Irish paper pound of 1797–1820: some cliometrics of the bullionist debate', *Oxford Economic Papers* 45: 148–56.

Ó Gráda, C. (1994) *Ireland: A New Economic History*, Oxford: Clarendon Press.

Parliamentary Papers (1810) *Report from the Select Committee on the High Price of Bullion*.

Parnell, H. (1804) *Observations Upon the State of Currency in Ireland, and Upon the Course of Exchange Between London and Dublin*, Dublin: M.N. Mahon.

Parnell, H. (1828; Reprint 1993) 'Observations on paper money, banking, and overtrading', in F. Capie (ed.) *History of Banking* vol. 5, London: William Pickering.

Parnell, H. (1830) *On Financial Reform*, London: John Murray.

Parnell, H. (1832) *A Plain Statement of the Power of the Bank of England*, London: James Ridgeway.

Ricardo, D. (1810; Reprint 1951) 'The high price of bullion, a proof of the depreciation of bank notes', in P. Sraffa (ed.) *Works and Correspondence of David Ricardo*, Cambridge: Cambridge University Press.

Sechrest, L.J. (1991) 'Free banking in Scotland: a dissenting view', *Cato Journal* 10: 799–808.

Silberling, N.J. (1924) 'Financial and Monetary Policy of Great Britain During the Napoleonic Wars', *Quarterly Journal of Economics* 38: 397–439.

Smith, A. (1776; Reprint 1986) *The Wealth of Nations Books I–III*, London: Penguin.

Smith, V.C. (1936; Reprint 1990) *The Rationale of Central Banking and the Free Banking Alternative*, Indianapolis: Liberty Fund.

Thompson, E.A. and Hickson, C.R. (2001) *Ideology and the Evolution of Vital Economic Institutions: Guilds, the Gold Standard, and Modern International Cooperation*, Boston: Kluwer.

Thornton, H. (1802; Reprint 1978) *An Inquiry into the Nature and Effects of the Paper Credit of Great Britain*, New York: Augustus Kelley.

Viner, J. (1937; Reprint 1975) *Studies in the Theory of International Trade*, Clifton, NJ: Augustus M. Kelley.

White, L.H. (1995) *Free Banking in Britain: Theory, Experience, and Debate 1800–1845*, London: Institute of Economic Affairs, 2nd edition.

Part III

Into the twentieth century – Irish contributions to economic theory

11 Francis Ysidro Edgeworth on the regularity of law and the impartiality of chance

Alberto Baccini

A man of science may write one great work which adequately expresses his contribution to human knowledge; another may prefer to publish the results of his labours as they are achieved and let the world reap the immediate benefit. There is much to be said for and against each method; but work published in small discrete *quanta* is liable to be become so absorbed in the common stock of knowledge that its sources are forgotten.

(Sanger 1925: 601)

In 1925 Charles Percy Sanger did not hesitate in depicting his friend Francis Ysidro Edgeworth as a scientist who does not write treatises, but who could nevertheless influence the work of other scholars. In Edgeworth's obituary in the *Economic Journal*, John Maynard Keynes (1926: 149) took a different view and suggested that the failure to venture on treatises was a contributory motive in the failure of *Mathematical Psychics* to fulfil its early promise.

After eighty years, it is now clear that Keynes was wrong and Sanger was right in their estimate of Edgeworth's contribution. In fact, it is even difficult to list all the scholars who credit Edgeworth of some path-breaking contributions in economics and statistics. As foreshadowed by Sanger, Edgeworth's contributions have been absorbed in the common stock of knowledge as devices for modern microeconomics, contributing to the development of neoclassical economics. With the appearance of modern game theory, Edgeworth's conjecture has acquired a new relevance as for example in Shubik (1959) and Scarf (1962). Ronald Coase (1988), in his 'Note to the problem of social cost', attributed to the unconscious reminiscences of Edgeworth's *Mathematical Psychics* a substantial part in his famous theorem, as the basis of the modern economic analysis of law. Edgeworth's contributions to the probabilistic foundation of statistics are now considered a substantial part of the 'statistical revolution' in the social sciences at the end of nineteenth century (Stigler 1978, 1986, 1999); and he is considered the precursor of many modern statistical devices, such as two-way analysis of variance, correlation coefficients, tests of significance and Edgeworth expansion.

The fate invariably encountered by his contribution is to be rediscovered years later. This may be due to his idiosyncratic style and pattern of research and to the fact that his works appear fragmented and without a clear discernible path.

This fragmentation is evident from his bibliography which includes at least four books, 198 journal articles, 204 reviews and 139 entries for *Palgrave* (Baccini 2003). In fact a comprehensive reconstruction of Edgeworth's works is still lacking in the literature; and the interested reader must refer to the partial stories offered by Creedy (1986), Newman (1987) and Mirowski (1994) for economics, Bowley (1928) and Stigler (1978, 1986, 1999) for statistics, Baccini for probability (1997, 2001, 2004) and ethics (2007).

Nearly all scholars studying Edgeworth papers are puzzled by his pattern of research, especially in the years between 1878 and 1890, when he switched abruptly from ethics, to economics, to probability theory and finally to statistics. On one interpretation, these changes are attributable to external causes such as favourable or critical reviews or his personal search for a hero. On another interpretation, the changing pattern of interests can be explained as facets of his pursuit of a general scientific approach. This chapter takes the latter view and argues that the unitary approach of Edgeworth's analysis can be grasped if attention is focused on the foundations of the various disciplines to which Edgeworth contributed and on the role played by probability theory. This procedure was also adopted by Mirowski (1994) but despite some common points, his reconstruction differs radically from the one presented here.

A biographical sketch

Edgeworth was born on 8 February 1845 at Edgeworthstown, County Longford, Ireland. His Irish family was an extraordinary one (Butler and Butler 1927); his grandfather Richard Lovell Edgeworth was an eccentric inventor of mechanical devices and member of circle of savants which included the luminaries of the industrial revolution. Francis Ysidro's father, Francis Beaufort was born in 1809. At the age of twenty-two, he met and married, Rosa Florentina Eroles, a beautiful Catalan refugee aged sixteen, whom he encountered in London. Edgeworth was the seventh child and sixth son (Barbé 2004: 303). After the deaths of his father (1846) and his aunt, the novelist Maria Edgeworth (1849), Rosa completed the education of the children by teaching them Spanish and Italian, and providing private tutors in classics and mathematics.

Edgeworth entered Trinity College Dublin in the academic year 1861–1862, obtaining the first place at the July entrance examination as well as prizes for Greek verse and Greek prose compositions. In the term examinations of 1862 and in the following two years he confirmed his proficiency in the classics; in 1862 he was third in the ranking of the junior freshmen in mathematics. John P. Mahaffy was for several years his college tutor; in 1873 he wrote a testimonial remembering that during the years in the college 'he was considered the ablest [sic] man in his class, and made himself deservedly popular by his genius as well as kindliness'. R.Y. Tyrrel, his professor of Latin, remembered that

> in Trinity College there are two verdicts pronounced on every student of eminence; one that of Lecturers and Examiners, the other that of the elite of

the students. The latter verdict was pronounced in favour of Mr. Edgeworth with an enthusiasm to which I remember no parallel.

The brilliant Francis Ysidro arrived in Oxford in 1867. As student of Balliol College he took a First Class at the Final Examination in *Literae Humaniores* in 1869. He left Oxford in 1869, and for twelve years, as he wrote in 1881, he was 'engaged in studying and teaching the science which I desire to profess'. Biographical details of this period are lacking. Probably he lived in two small rented rooms at 6, Mount Vernon, Hampstead. He studied commercial law, and was admitted as a member of the Inner Temple 31 January 1874. Although called to the Bar in 13 June 1877, Edgeworth never practised as barrister. In 1875 he was candidate for a professorship of Greek at Bedford College. For two years, he lectured on Logic and Mental and Moral Science to candidates for the India Civil Service at Walter Wren's Institution.

Edgeworth's first publication, a two-page paper on an argument of ethics appeared in the journal *Mind* in 1876. A year later, his first book was privately published with the title *New and Old Methods of Ethics* (hereinafter *NOME*). In the years between 1879 and 1881 Edgeworth applied himself to the study of economics. In 1881, this culminated in the (private) publication of his second and best-known book *Mathematical Psychics. An Essay on the Application of Mathematics to the Moral Science* (from now on referred to as *MP*). It was reviewed by Alfred Marshall and William Stanley Jevons, and warmly welcomed by Francis Galton in a private letter.

From 1880, Edgeworth was for eight years on the staff of King's College, London, lecturing on Logic, and on Political Economy at the Ladies's Class in Kensington. In 1887 he was elected to the office of examiner in Political Economy at the University of London. In 1888 he was appointed to the vacant professorship of the Principles and Practice of Commerce at King's and, in 1890, to the Tooke Chair of Economics and Statistics. In 1890, Edgeworth became the first editor of the *Economic Journal*. Although, this was a role which Edgeworth was to fill with great distinction over the next thirty-five years, it is clear from Marshall's correspondence that Neville Keynes and not Edgeworth was Marshall's first choice for the role (Whitaker 1996, I: 287, n. 260). In 1891, Edgeworth was appointed to the Drummond Professorship of Political Economy at Oxford, which Marshall welcomed writing to him a 'Hurrah, Hurrah, Hurrah!' (Whitaker 1996, II: 7–8, n. 340). He became a fellow of All Souls College where he lived for the rest of his life in his 'palatial room'. He received several academic honours: twice President of section F of the British Association (1889, 1922), President of the Royal Statistical Society (1912) and Fellow of the British Academy.

Pleasure machines

As we have seen Edgeworth's first substantial known work was *NOME*. It is a strange book for modern readers as it must have been for Edgeworth's contemporaries. For the former, it is the discussion of utilitarian ethics with particular reference to the works of Henry Sidgwick and Alfred Barrat that sounds strange. For Edgeworth's contemporaries, the second part of the book must have presented problems. Edgeworth had imported arguments drawn from the frontiers of the psycho-physics research tradition and applied differential calculus in solving the problem of the maximization of social welfare in utilitarian ethics. Newman (1987) has provided a complete synthesis of Edgeworth's arguments in modern notation. Others have focused on specific aspects of the work e.g. Howey (1960) on context and Creedy (1986) on methodology. Rather than repeat aspects of these investigations, the present work focuses on some points of interest which are important for our reconstruction.

In *NOME*, the general objective of utilitarian ethics is the maximization of social welfare: 'the utilitarian end is the greatest quantity of happiness of sentients, exclusive of number and distribution' (Edgeworth 1877: 35). The problem to solve is how to distribute 'among a given set of sentients' a given amount of 'stimulus (…), corresponding to a given amount of material means' in view of the 'production of the greatest quantity of happiness' (Edgeworth 1877: 40). Every sentient is represented as a *pleasure machine* whose pleasure function is an increasing concave function f of the stimulus. Edgeworth formalized the law of pleasure as $\pi = k|f(y) - f(\beta)|$ where y is the quantity of the stimulus, β denotes the sensibility to the stimulus of the sentient, i.e. the 'threshold', or the minimum value of the stimulus for which the sentient has any pleasure, and k the capacity for pleasure (Newman 1987: 90). Edgeworth then discussed the problem of the distribution of a given quantity of stimulus in the case in which β and k are the same for all the sentients, and in the four cases in which β and k vary. Edgeworth demonstrated that in the first case the solution is an equal distribution of the material means; and that in the other cases an unequal distribution is required 'such that most means are assigned to those who have most felicific power' (Edgeworth 1877: iii). This rough summary does not do justice to the subtleties of Edgeworth's reasoning; but our emphasis is not on the results but on the foundations. It is therefore useful to briefly consider the question of the nature of agents.

The problem at hand related to the foundations of ethics, or more precisely the representation of human actions in ethics (Baccini 2007): can these be reduced to simple 'contractions' (searching for pleasure) and 'irritations' (fleeing from pain) of our nervous system, or are they instead relative to the sphere of consciousness? Edgeworth was fascinated by Alfred Barrat's reductionist view that all human actions have their origin in physical pleasure, and was favourably disposed to accept that a physical origin of human actions exists. However individuals experience a difference between reflex actions and volitive actions, and between hedonistic preferences and non-hedonistic preferences. Consequently it is as difficult to sustain Barrat's view that *all* actions derive directly from pleasure, as Sidgwick's one that human actions have their origin only in the 'idea' of pleasantness.

Edgeworth's proposal was to blend Barrat's perspective with Sidgwick's one: body and mind are interdependent; every movement in the *material substrate* of the mind is associated with a mental phenomenon. The search for pleasure and the flight from pain can be explained by the fact that, in the nervous system, certain inter-relations are constituted that associate pleasure and pain with previous experiences of pleasure and pain more or less remote in time. These experiences are of two kinds: some already had by the individual during previous periods of his life; and some handed down to the individual by the species to which he belongs, through the physical connections internal to the structures of the nervous system, which he inherits from the species.

Recognition of that second kind of experience originates from Herbert Spencer's psychology (1870). According to Spencer, human beings are born with a nervous system inside of which connections handed down from the species are defined. These connections, inherited by the species, determine for the individual a 'preparedness to cognize'. The nervous system is something organic, subject to evolution, which incorporates a priori knowledge within its structure. The individual experience not only furnishes the concrete material at the basis of all thoughts, but without it the organized structures of the nervous system would not, on their own, give rise to knowledge.

According to Edgeworth, the physical structure of the human brain, in which the past experience of the species and the actual experience of the individual are stored, is the framework which justifies the statement that, ultimately, 'definite physical phenomena (which Mr. Barratt (...) calls *pleasure*) are the cause of all human action' (*NOME*: 10). This is the *physical* foundation of ethics: every action can be attributed either to individual experiences of pleasure/pain, or to the experiences handed down to the individual by the species. In this way, it is possible to justify also apparently non-hedonistic actions as referring to an ancestral experience of pleasure and pain. The key concept for this foundation of ethics was the extension of the domain of the *experience of pleasure*, including the one carried out by the species and handed down genetically to successive generations. The *ancestral experience* served to legitimately represent, in a utilitarian context, many forms of real behaviour.

All that we have seen above is the nature of the *pleasure machine* studied in *NOME*. It is useful to note that not all machines are equal; they differ in respect to their capacity for happiness and to their threshold of sensitivity to pleasure. The solutions of the utilitarian problems of maximizing social welfare depend therefore on the distribution of sentients in a population in relation to their different characteristics. However, Edgeworth concluded that

> [w]ith regard to the theory of distribution, there is no indication that, at any rate between classes so nearly in the same order of evolution as the modern Aryan races, a law of distribution other than equality is to be wished.
>
> (Edgeworth 1877: 78)

The justification for this last statement is obscure: how is it possible to represent synthetically the plurality of agents as a unique pleasure machine with the same β and k? Or more generally, what is the status of the notion of man as a pleasure machine?

Edgeworth developed this point in a paper published in 1879 and entitled 'The hedonical calculus'. The problem tackled in this paper is a generalization of the utilitarian one posed in *NOME*, where the maximization of social welfare is developed in relation not only to the distribution of given 'means', but also to labour and the conditions of its reproduction. The egalitarian solution proposed in *NOME*, is abandoned for an anti-egalitarian one, based on the different capacity for pleasure and work of different individuals in society, offering a poisonous brew of utilitarianism and eugenics (Newman 1987: 92–93).

From our perspective, the paper is very important because of its suggestions with regard to the relevance of probability theory to the question of the measurability of pleasure. Edgeworth introduced the following axiom: 'Pleasure is measurable, and all pleasures are commensurable; so much of one sort of pleasure felt by one sentient being equateable to so much of other sorts of pleasure felt by other sentients' (Edgeworth 1879: 396). The idea behind this is that all pleasure machines can be considered as having the same sensibility to the stimulus β. This idea was drawn from the notion of *Ebenmerklich* or 'just noticeable (or perceivable) difference', utilized in psycophysics by Gustav Fechner and William Wundt (Newman 2003: 157–158). Obviously, the relevance of this last point is related to the question of the cardinality of the utility function. In fact, if there is a unit of pleasure perceived by every sentient, it is possible to sum up not only all the units of pleasure perceived by the same individual to measure his total pleasure, but it is also possible to sum up the pleasure of different individuals of a group or society, and finally it is possible to compare the pleasures of two or more individuals or groups of individuals. The cardinality of the pleasure function was therefore based in Edgeworth's view, on empirical results drawn from the frontiers of psychology of his time.

But here we are more interested in justifying the cogency of the axiom above. In 1879 this justification was based on the analogy between the methods of measuring pleasure and the methods of measuring probability; the axiom at the basis of the utilitarian calculus cannot be rejected precisely as

> one cannot reject the practical conclusion of Probabilities, though one may object, with Mr. Venn, to speaking of belief being numerically measurable. Indeed these principles of μετρητική [metretikè: science of measuring] are put forward not as proof against metaphysical subtleties, but as practical; self evident *a priori*, or by whatever επαγωγή [epagoghé: argument from induction] or εθισμός [ethismos: habituation] is the method of practical axioms.
>
> (Edgeworth 1879: 395–396)

In this citation, we can see the reference to the already encountered a priori knowledge, but in relation to probability and to John Venn who will have a fundamental importance in the subsequent work of Edgeworth. This passage, in reality, is far from clear. To have a precise statement of the same concept, but not its explication, it is necessary to wait until 1881 when Edgeworth published his *Mathematical Psychics*, in which he explicitly introduced the idea of a common method of measurement of pleasure and probabilities.

The law of one price and the law of error

Mathematical Psychics (*MP*), in particular the first subdivision of the second part (15–56) and its appendix, contained the origin of many of the basic concepts of modern microeconomic theory: a generalized utility function – which substituted the Fechnerian law of pleasure of *NOME*; indifference curves; the structure which is now called Edgeworth's box; and the marginal rate of substitution.

The main novel element of Edgeworth's thought was the subdivision of the 'calculus of pleasure' in two parts: the 'Economical calculus', which 'investigates the equilibrium of a system of hedonic forces each tending to maximum individual utility', flanked the already developed Utilitarian calculus, dedicated to 'the equilibrium of a system in which each and all tend to maximum universal utility' (Edgeworth 1881: 15–16). The switch from utilitarian ethics to economics is universally attributed to the influence of Jevons who was Edgeworth's neighbour in Hampstead.

The main theme of the economical calculus was the statement of this new theorem on contract and competition: '(α) Contract without competition is indeterminate, (β) Contract with *perfect* competition is perfectly determinate, (γ) Contract with more or less perfect competition is less or more indeterminate' (Edgeworth 1881: 20).

Its logical primitives are *agents*, who may be individuals or combinations of individuals; *articles* of the contract may be economic goods, but also property rights; *actions* are what agents do. All actions can be classified as *war* or *contract* 'according as the agent acts *without*, or *with*, the consent of others affected by his actions'. The action of *recontracting* without the consent of others is war (Edgeworth 1881: 15–16). 'The *field of competition* with reference to a contract, or contracts, under consideration consists of all the individuals who are willing and able to recontract about the articles under consideration'. A *'perfect* field of competition' is a field with perfect communication between individuals in which: (i) any individual is free to recontract with any out of an indefinite number of other agents; (ii) any individual is free to contract with an indefinite number, so each article of contract is perfectly divisible and (iii) any individual is free to recontract with another without the consent of any third party.

Edgeworth proposes two solution concepts for the problem of competition. The first one reads: 'A *settlement* is a contract which cannot be varied with the consent of all the parties to it'. Or in modern jargon: a contract is a Pareto optimal allocation for the parties to the contract. The second one reads: 'A *final settlement* is a settlement which cannot be varied by recontract within the field of competition', i.e. with renegotiation with any or all of the parties outside the contract, but inside the field. This signifies, in modern jargon, that a final settlement lies in the *core*. Therefore, and finally, a contract is indeterminate when there are an infinite number of final settlements.

Edgeworth's central interest was the indeterminateness of contracts and not, as suggested by his modern interpreters other than Newman (1987, 1994), the conditions of its perfect determination. According to him, contract is indeterminate when the market is not perfect, i.e. when the number of competitors is limited, or the articles of contract are not perfectly divisible, or in case of the existence of *combination* of agents, as trade unions in the labour market. Almost every species of social and political contract is affected by indeterminateness:

> throughout the whole region of in a wide sense *contract*, in the general absence of a mechanism like perfect competition, the same essential indeterminateness prevails; in international, in domestic politics; between nations, classes, sexes. The whole creation groans and yearns, desiderating a principle of arbitration, an end of strifes.
>
> (Edgeworth 1881: 51)

The principle of arbitration is the utilitarian maximization contained in the 'hedonical calculus' (Edgeworth 1879) which Edgeworth reprinted with the addition of some notes, as the second subdivision of the second part of *MP*. (On the logical weakness of this point the interested reader can see Newman (1994)).

If this, in a nutshell, is the content of *MP*, it is necessary for us to underline the use of probability in it. *MP* starts with the analogy between the calculus of probability and the calculus of pleasure. In the first part of the book, dedicated to the discussion of the applicability of mathematical methods to social sciences, Edgeworth introduced the argument with which we have closed the preceding paragraph. The loose quantitative estimate available for measurements of pleasure are based on the notion of just perceivable increment of pleasure or of utility, which 'implied equatability of time-intensity unit'. This is 'a first principle incapable of proof' (Edgeworth 1881: 7). This principle 'may be compared, perhaps, to the first principles of probabilities, according to which cases about which we are equally undecided, between which we perceive no material difference, count as equal' (Edgeworth 1881: 99); and it 'is doubtless a principle acquired in the course of evolution' (Edgeworth 1881: 7). As the conception of man as a pleasure machine is based on the possibility of roughly measuring utility, the calculus of probability too is based on the possibility of roughly measuring probability. These two measurement processes depend on the same inherited a priori experience which allows the definition as axioms of two equivalences: the one between atoms of pleasures experienced by different sentients, and the one between probabilities of indistinguishable events. The justification of the second one needed the analysis of the foundations of probability.

In *MP*, probability appears also in two other contexts. The second one, the less interesting for our narrative, is related to the equiprobability of the points of a final settlement: under imperfect competition the solution is indeterminate, comprehending all the points on a tract of the contract curve. According to Edgeworth every point of this tract has the same a priori probability to be selected by 'objectable arts of higgling' (Edgeworth 1881: 30).

The first one instead opens a new perspective. In writing about a market without competition, he affirmed:

> if competition is found wanting, not only the regularity of law, but even the impartiality of chance – the throw of a die loaded with villainy – economics would be indeed a 'dismal science', and the reverence for competition would be no more.
>
> (Edgeworth 1881: 50)

The explication of this puzzling phrase needs a reference to a two-page paper published in *Philosophical Magazine* December 1883, entitled 'The physical basis of probability'. It illustrates two analogies between the equilibrium of a particle in a system with a plurality of attractive centres, and the expression of a mean of several observations calculated with the method of least squares; and between those and the 'mathematical theory of exchange'. The process of exchange is described as one in which

> the forces at work, the taste of buyers and sellers, are of inconceivable complexity. Yet the position of equilibrium is characterized by a feature of geometrical simplicity, uniformity of rate-of-exchange [in modern terms: the same marginal rate of substitution].

The possibility of

> mathematically representing maximum advantage is due to the same cause in the market as in the observatory: what may be called the law of great numbers. The sum of squares (...) makes its appearance in virtue of the exponential law of error or probability-curve incidental to the method of least squares; and this simple form arises when the observations are independent of each other and indefinitely numerous. Similarly the law of unity of price holds good where the competitors are independent and indefinitely numerous. In both cases uniformity is due to plurality; definite order to infinite numbers.
>
> (Edgeworth 1883: 434).

In a companion two-page paper, published on the *Journal of the Royal Statistical Society* March 1884 and entitled 'The rationale of exchange', Edgeworth again presented this argument and stated clearly 'the *rationale* why the complex play of competition tends to a simple uniform result is to be sought in (...) law of great numbers' (Edgeworth 1884: 261). It rests, for us, that in the bulk of the construction of perfect market competition and market clearing mechanism, Edgeworth posed his 'beloved law of error'. The existence of the equilibrium price depends on the great numbers of buyers and sellers, and on the irreducible differentiation of their tastes.

This point is not well covered in the vast mass of literature on Edgeworth's theory of exchange. It is true that this is not an analytical demonstration of the unity of price; and Edgeworth himself wrote, probably with his characteristic 'chuckle and smile', that the derivation of this principle is 'far-fetched' (Edgeworth 1884: 165). But Edgeworth's rationale for equilibrium in the market is very different from the Smithian invisible hand, or the Walrasian auctioneer. This rationale probably sounds *dated* to modern readers; but it is absolutely original and based on the frontier of knowledge of his time. The application of probability theory and statistical inference to the social sciences had not yet arrived; and consequently Edgeworth's proposal can be seen as a step in this direction.

Foundations of probabilities

At this point, it is simple to understand why Edgeworth turned his attention to probability and statistics. From a very general point of view probability furnished a solution to the two big foundational problems of his *MP*: the possibility of depicting man as a pleasure machine is based on the same knowledge as is necessary to define a priori probability, and the existence of a market price is dependent on the law of error. Probability and the law of error became his new research topics, so that from October 1883 to December 1885 he published an impressive series of thirteen papers dedicated to the foundations of probability and statistics.

The landscape of those works is characterized by the epistemological fog of the nineteenth century debate on the nature of probability. *The Logic of Chance* by Venn (1888), which canonically systematized the frequentist theory of probability (Chatterjee 2003; Galavotti 2005; Gillies 2000), had a fundamental relevance in this debate, and was Edgeworth's principal reference text. In the frequentist tradition, probability can be defined only in the context of a random experiment or trial, whose outcome is unpredictable beforehand and which is capable of indefinite repetition under identical conditions, at least conceptually. The totality of possible outcomes is the domain, and probabilities are assigned to various sets – the events – in this domain. Primitive probabilities – the simplest kind of probability – are empirically measurable as the relative frequency of events. In the frequentist tradition, probability is not a property attributable to a single event; so all probability statements refer to sets of events, and not to the individual event (Chatterjee 2003: 40; Jonathan Cohen 1989: 48–49; Galavotti 2005: 83).

Venn named the sets of events, series; the existence of the series and the numerical proportion of their characteristic properties can be ascertained only by resorting to experience which 'is our sole guide' (Venn 1888: 74–75). So in Venn's theory the body of evidence utilizable in fixing probabilities is very small, based as it is only on experienced statistical evidence. As a consequence, he denied that it is possible to define a priori probabilities, i.e. values of probabilities not determined by statistics, as for example, the probability of six in tossing a die never tossed before. In his approach, a priori probability can be defined only as an epistemic or subjective measure, depending on the status of the non-experiential knowledge of the observer. But if it is impossible to define cogently a measure of a priori probability, it is also impossible to construct Bayes's theorem: the posterior probability calculated by Bayes's theorem looses its objective characterization because it is based on subjective prior probability. On this basis Venn had excluded from theory Bayes's theorem and inverse probability, that is, crudely speaking, the art of inferring from observed events the probability of their causes. This exclusion blocked the development of a complete theory of statistical inference in the frequentist framework (Dale 1991: 324–326).

Edgeworth's aim was to escape this dead-end theoretical result. The first step in this direction was to admit that probability must be referred to two different spheres, one *objective*, relative to the frequencies observed in a certain phenomenon, and one *subjective*, relative to the mental condition associated with those frequencies: 'Probability may be described, agreeably to general usage, as importing partial incomplete belief (...) as differing somehow in degree from perfect belief or rather credibility. (...) Thus the object of the calculus is probability as estimated by statistical uniformity' (Edgeworth 1884a: 223). As Venn, he considered as primitives the notions of event and series of events. Starting from events and series he defined primitive probabilities 'as measured by the number of times that the event is found by experience to occur, in proportion to the number of times that it might possibly to occur' (Edgeworth 1911: 376, but see also 1884a: 223, 1899: 208). But the body of evidence available to construct primitive probabilities is larger than the one used by Venn:

> I only contend that Mr. Venn (...) has not made the foundation wide enough, and that therefore he is unable to carry up the structure to the full height of generality. He is unable to rise an axiom of equal distribution of quantity in general, above the view that, in the absence of any such (specific) information, we are entirely in the dark.
>
> (Edgeworth 1884b: 160–161)

So, beside statistical probabilities, Edgeworth introduced primitive a priori probability, that is probabilities 'not determined by statistics' (Edgeworth 1884c: 204), or probabilities measured 'when probability, founded upon statistical fact (...) has reached the utmost degree of tenuity' (Edgeworth 1884a: 229). A priori probability emerges when we have probability defined in reference to the antenatal experiential knowledge which belongs to humans and is inherited through the physical structure of their brain. This kind of experiential knowledge is the basis on which is founded the Laplacean principle of indifference, according to which, for example, the same probability value is attributed to the faces of a dice which is known to be unloaded.

The strategy of this enlargement of the notion of experience is clearly the same which Edgeworth had applied to the foundation of ethics and economics. The analogy which was proposed in *MP* was completely developed in the context epistemological foundations of probability: the inherited experiential knowledge at the basis of Edgeworth's theory of probability, has the same nature as the inherited memory of past experience of pleasure at the basis of the *pleasure machine* of *NOME* and *MP* (Baccini 2007). As for ethics and economics, also for theory of probability this point is topical.

Complex probabilities are the result of the application of the calculus to primitive probabilities. The enlarged notion of experience allowed Edgeworth to define an experientially primitive a priori probability and then to accept Bayes's theorem and inverse probability, 'the most perfect type of probability' (Edgeworth 1911: 377), in a frequentist framework. In fact, according to Edgeworth, the derivation of the posterior distribution is simply an exercise in inductive inference; the prior distribution being objective, the posterior probability has the same objective interpretation. It is possible, therefore, contrary to Venn's speculation, to develop a complete theory of statistical inference in a frequentist framework.

In 1887 Edgeworth published a booklet *Metretike* completely dedicated to a deep discussion about probabilities involved in Bayes's theorem. It has at first sight a strange construction, based as it is on variations on the analogy between the measurement of probability in probability theory and of utility in economics. But, in our pattern of reconstruction of his ideas, it does not sound so off-key. Edgeworth was searching for a common foundation of social sciences, the role of probability is central for this scope and *Metretike* represented the non-technical synthesis of his works in this direction.

The theory of statistics

With his work on the foundations of probability theory, Edgeworth paved the way for his passage to the theory of statistics. In 1885 he read a series of four papers to the Cambridge Philosophical Society, to the international gathering to celebrate the jubilee of the Royal Statistical Society, and to two meetings of the British Association. The first one entitled 'Observation and statistics' (Edgeworth 1885) summarized the papers of the previous years on the probabilistic foundation of statistics. The second one on 'Methods of statistics' (Edgeworth 1885a) was methodological, presenting an exposition, an application and an interpretation of significance tests for the comparison of means. These two papers became the basic reference – in England and on the continent – for the theory and application of statistical techniques to social and economic data (Stigler 1999: 104) until the appearance of Arthur L. Bowley's *Elements of Statistics* (1901). The third paper 'On the methods of ascertaining variations in the rate of births, deaths and marriages' (Edgeworth 1885b) worked on two-way classifications and contained many ideas that anticipated modern analysis of variance. The fourth one on 'Progressive means' (Edgeworth 1886) contained a discussion on the use of linear least squares for detrending time series, and comparing different series.

In this firework exhibition of theoretical ideas, probability theory still occupied the central place. And this is not an unimportant detail. According to Stigler (1978), all those papers contributed to change the intellectual climate at the end of nineteenth century by opening the way to the application of probability-based statistical methods in the social sciences.

To illustrate synthetically the point in reference to economics, it is useful to linger on the jubilee meeting of the Royal Statistical Society in 1885 where Alfred Marshall also presented a paper on 'The graphic methods of statistics'. The distance between the methodological approach in Marshall's paper and Edgeworth's one is sideral (Baccini 2006). Marshall's paper contained a detailed description of the usefulness of systematically collecting time series data for the social scientist. The implicit model of data systematization was his 'red book', in which he collected lifelong facts and data with the only aim being to suggest causal connection between phenomena. Broadly speaking Marshall took the view that the usefulness of statistics was primarily heuristic: his red book could suggest new ideas and new connections between facts. Marshall was not interested in statistical inference or estimation; on at least two occasions he referred to the method of least squares as vitiated by an assumption of symmetry that led him to regard them 'as mathematical toys' (Whitaker 1996, II: 301, n. 634; III: 264–265, n. 977).

Edgeworth's approach was exclusively theoretical, with probability theory and the law of error playing the central role. In a nutshell he conceived two different uses of the law of error: (i) the direct one, according to which, under assigned conditions, we can infer the theoretical probability of given means and standard deviations; and (ii) the inverse use, according to which we can infer the existence of a 'cause other than chance' by comparing the actual distribution with the counterfactual one represented by the normal law of error. According to Edgeworth, the task of the statistician is to study the techniques which permit a systematic comparison of means, and to evaluate whether differences in *figures* are also differences in *facts*. The statistician does not assume that the law of error is always fulfilled, because it is necessary to prove that 'what is true of games of chance is true' also for social and economic data. He develops tests of significance and of appropriate assumptions, and develops a mathematical methodology for analysing variance and evaluating deviations in complex situations.

Marshall's major influence on the discipline of economics contributed to prevent the diffusion of Edgeworth's methods in the application of statistics to economic data, probably retarding the development of econometrics. Edgeworth's influence was greater in statistics, where he 'oversaw the final break with the past in what has been called the modern revolution in statistics and played (with Karl Pearson and Galton) a vital role in producing that revolution' (Stigler 1999: 127).

Concluding remarks

Edgeworth's studies did not stop with his academic success in 1890, but it is impossible to summarize the hundreds of contributions of the following years on various specific topics in economics, statistics and methodology, flanked by hundreds of reviews of the major books on economics. In collecting his thirty years work in economics alone for the *Papers Relating to Political Economy*,

Edgeworth himself underlined the difficulty of 'palliating' the 'deficiency' of 'unity of design' in 'a collection of papers written at different times and for various destinations' (Edgeworth 1925: viii). To this end he classified his papers in seven groups: value and distribution, monopoly, money, international trade, taxation, mathematical economics and reviews. As we have already said, a complete reconstruction is still lacking in the literature, but it is not our scope to fill the gap of this dimension. Our aim is to suggest a general interpretation of Edgeworth's research path, and at this point, this is possible.

The interpretation proposed in this paper is that the shifting of attention from ethics to economics, to probability and finally to statistics, is the result of a unitary philosophical project: the search for a common foundation for the social sciences. This common foundation consisted of the identification of a unitary epistemological basis, which involved the possibility of utilizing cognitive material of the same species, although of a different *genus*. This epistemological foundation permits the coexistence in Edgworthian scientific programme of the 'regularity of law' with the 'impartiality of chance'.

The impartiality of chance is the device which allowed Edgeworth to reduce complexity of human motives for action to the simplicity of the pleasure machine hypothesis. This hypothesis does not give any indication regarding the real behaviour of concrete persons in the individual cases (like frequentist probability for single case), but make it possible to grasp an average trend that is characteristic of the human species (like frequentist probability for the series). The representation of humans as pleasure machines facilitates abstraction from the complexity of human nature and the use of mathematics to solve problems of economic and utilitarian calculus, i.e. to treat the human behaviour as if it was governed by the regularity of the law of mathematics.

The impartiality of chance incorporated in the law of error determines the emergence of the price equilibrium in a 'field of competition' in which there are many different agents with different real behaviours. And again, the impartiality of chance is the device which permits the construction of the hypotheses on which are based the practical and theoretical instruments of the statistical inference. Under these hypotheses, statistical inference is governed by the regularity of the law of the calculus.

The interpretation here proposed challenges the traditional stereotypes according to which Edgeworth was a crass utilitarian, and an ingenuous advocate of a rather primitive neoclassical economics. His plea for the use of mathematics, and his choice of deterministic models for the description of the economic behaviour, appear more innovative when the role of chance is considered.

Bibliography

Baccini, A. (1997) 'Edgeworth on the fundamentals of choice under uncertainty', *History of Economic Ideas* 2: 7–31.

Baccini, A. (2001) 'Frequentist probability and choice under uncertainty', *History of Political Economy* 33.4: 743–772.

Baccini, A. (2003) 'Bibliography of Edgeworth's writings', in P. Newman (ed.) *F.Y. Edgeworth's* Mathematical Psychics *and Further Papers on Political Economy*, Oxford, Oxford University Press, pp. 621–647.

Baccini, A. (2004) 'High pressure and black clouds: Keynes and the frequentist theory of probability', *Cambridge Journal of Economics* 28.5: 653–666.

Baccini, A. (2006) 'Francis Ysidro Edgeworth', in T. Raffaelli, G. Becattini and M. Dardi (eds) *The Elgar Companion to Alfred Marshall*, Cheltenham: Edward Elgar.

Baccini, A. (2007) 'Edgeworth on the foundations of ethics and probability', *European Journal for the History of Economic Thought* 14.1: 79–96.

Barbé, L. (2004) 'Francis Ysidro's Edgeworth's Catalan grandfather', *European Journal of the History of Economic Thought* 11.2: 295–307.

Bonar, J. (1926) 'Memories of F.Y. Edgworth', *Economic Journal* 36.144: 647–653.

Bowley, A.L. (1901) *Elements of Statistics*, London: P.S. King.

Bowley, A.L. (1928) *F.Y. Edgeworth's Contributions to Mathematical Statistics*, London: Royal Statistical Society (Clifton, NJ: A.M. Kelley, 1972).

Bowley, A.L. (1934) 'Francis Ysidro Edgeworth', *Econometrica* II: 113–124.

Butler, H.V. and Butler, H.E. (1927) *The Black Book of Edgeworthstown and Other Edgeworth Memories 1585–1817*, London: Faber & Gwyer.

Chatterjee, S.K. (2003) *Statistical Thought: a Perspective and History*, Oxford: Oxford University Press.

Coase, R.H. (1988) *The Firm, the Market and the Law*, Chicago: University of Chicago Press.

Creedy, J. (1986) *Edgeworth and the Development of Neoclassical Economics*, London: Basil Blackwell.

Dale, A.I. (1991) *A History of Inverse Probability*, New York: Springer Verlag.

Edgeworth, F.Y. (1876) 'Mr. Matthew Arnold on Butler's doctrine of self-love', *Mind* I: 570–571.

Edgeworth, F.Y. (1877) *New and Old Methods of Ethics, or Physical Ethics and Methods of Ethics*, Oxford and London: James Parker and Co.

Edgeworth, F.Y. (1879) 'The hedonical calculus', *Mind* IV: 394–408.

Edgeworth, F.Y. (1881) *Mathematical Psychics. An Essay on the Application of Mathematics to the Moral Sciences*, London: Kegan Paul & Co.

Edgeworth, F.Y. (1883) 'The physical basis of probability', *Philosophical Magazine* XVI: 433–435.

Edgeworth, F.Y. (1884) 'The rationale of exchange', *Journal of the Royal Statistical Society* XLVII: 164–166.

Edgeworth, F.Y. (1884a) 'The philosophy of chance', *Mind*: 223–235.

Edgeworth, F.Y. (1884b) 'Chance and law', *Hermathena*: 154–163.

Edgeworth, F.Y. (1884c) '*A priori* probabilities', *Philosophical Magazine*: 204–210.

Edgeworth, F.Y. (1885) 'Observations and statistics: an essay on the theory of errors of observation and the first principles of statistics (read May 25th, 1885)', *Transactions of the Cambridge Philosophical Society*, 1887, XIV (II): 138–169.

Edgeworth, F.Y. (1885a) 'Methods of statistics', *Journal of the Royal Statistical Society*, Jubilee volume: 181–217.

Edgeworth, F.Y. (1885b) 'On the methods of ascertaining variations in the rate of births, deaths and marriages', *Journal of the Royal Statistical Society*, XLVIII: 628–652.

Edgeworth, F.Y. (1886) 'Progressive means', *Journal of the Royal Statistical Society*, XLIX: 469–475.

Edgeworth, F.Y. (1887) *Metretike or the Method of Measuring Probabilities and Utilities*, London: Temple Company.

Edgeworth, F.Y. (1899) 'Probability', in R.H.I. Palgrave (ed.) *Dictionary of Political Economy*, London: Macmillan and Co., vol. III: 208.

Edgeworth, F.Y. (1911) 'Probability' in *Encyclopaedia Britannica*, XIth edn, pp. 376–403.

Edgeworth, F.Y. (1925) *Papers Relating to Political Economy*, London: MacMillan and Co.

Galavotti, M.C. (2005) *Philosophical Introduction to Probability*, Stanford: CSLI.

Gillies, D. (2000) *Philosophical Theories of Probability*, London: Routledge.

Howey, R.S. (1960) *The Rise of the Marginal Utility School 1870–1889*, New York: Columbia University Press.

Jonathan Cohen, L. (1989) *An Introduction to the Philosophy of Induction and Probability*, Oxford: Clarendon Press.

Keynes, J.M. (1926) 'Obituary: Francis Ysidro Edgeworth, 1845–1926', *Economic Journal* 36: 140–153. (*Essays in Biography*, vol X. dei *Collected Writings*, London: Macmillan, 1972: 251–266).

Mirowski, P. (1994) *Edgeworth on Chance, Economic Hazard and Statistics*, Lanham, MD: Rowman & Littlefield Publishers.

Newman, P. (1987) 'Edgeworth, Francis Ysidro', in J. Eatwell, M. Milgate and P. Newman (eds) *The New Palgrave: A Dictionary of Economics*, London: Macmillan, Vol. II: 84–98.

Newman, P. (1990) 'Reviews by Edgeworth', in J.D. Hey and D. Winch (eds) *A Century of Economics*, London: Basil Blackwell, pp. 109–141.

Newman, P. (1994) 'Edgeworth's economical calculus', *Metroeconomica* 45.2: 99–126.

Newman, P. (ed.) (2003) *F.Y. Edgeworth's* Mathematical Psychics *and Further Papers on Political Economy*, Oxford: Oxford University Press.

Sanger, C.P. (1925) 'Review of F.Y.Edgworth's *Paper Relating to Political Economy*', *Economic Journal* 88.4: 601–603.

Scarf, H.E. (1962) 'An analysis of markets with a large number of participants', *Recent Advances in Game Theory*, Philadelphia, PA: The Ivy Curtis Press.

Shubik, M. (1959) 'Edgeworth market games', in A.W. Tucker and R.D. Luce (eds) *Contributions to the Theory of Games, volume IV*, Princeton, NJ: Princeton University Press, pp. 267–278.

Spencer, H. (1870) *The Principles of Psychology*, second edition, London: William & Norgate.

Stigler, S.M. (1978) 'Francis Ysidro Edgeworth, statistician', *Journal of the Royal Society of Statistics* (A), 141: 287–322.

Stigler, S.M. (1986) *The History of Statistics*, Cambridge, MA and London: Belknap Press.

Stigler, S.M. (1987) 'Edgeworth as a statistician', in J. Eatwell, M. Milgate and P. Newman (eds) *The New Palgrave: A Dictionary of Economics*, London: Macmillan, vol. II: 98–99.

Stigler, S. (1999) *Statistics on the Table. The History of Statistical Concepts and Methods*, Cambridge, MA and London: Harvard University Press.

Venn, J. (1888) The *Logic of Chance*, London: Macmillan (first edition 1866; second 1876; citations from the third).

Whitaker, J.K. (1996), *The Correspondence of Alfred Marshall, Economist*, vols I–III, Cambridge: Cambridge University Press.

12 Roy Geary

John E. Spencer[1]

Introduction

Roy Geary was born in Dublin on 11 April 1896, where he died on 8 February 1983. His career in Irish official statistics began in 1923 and culminated in his appointment in 1947 as Director of Statistics and in 1949 as Director of the newly established Central Statistics Office (CSO). Apart from an academic year at Cambridge 1946–47 and secondments as consultant, notably to UNO, Lake Success in 1950 and FAO, Rome in 1953, he remained in Dublin until his retirement from the CSO in 1957, when he moved to New York for three years to head the National Accounts Branch of the United Nations Statistical Office. In 1960 he returned to Dublin to lead the newly established Economic and Research Institute, where he was to spend the rest of his life, as Director until 1966, as Consultant thereafter. Many honours came his way, including Honorary Doctorates from NUI, QUB and TCD and Honorary Fellowships of the Royal Statistical Society and American Statistical Association. He was a Council Member of the International Association for Research in Income and Wealth (IARIW) from 1951, Chairman, 1965–67 and in 1951 was elected Fellow of the Econometric Society in 1951, serving as a Council Member 1952–54.

He studied mathematics in UCD, receiving his BSc and MSc, both with First Class Honours, and, after further specialist courses in the Complex Variable, Integrals and Integral Equations, won in 1918 a two-year Travelling Studentship in Mathematics, to finance his studies at the Sorbonne, 1919–21. Arthur Conway, mathematical physicist, later to become President of the College, was among his teachers in UCD. In June 1922, he described Roy as a 'brilliant student indeed' and pointed to Roy's research capacity by stating that he had already obtained 'some very interesting results on Associated Legendre Functions' while studying under Conway himself.

Among his teachers in Paris were several famous mathematicians, including Borel, Goursat, Cartan, Lebesgue and Hadamard. On completing his studies, he returned to Dublin, probably in summer 1921, and in December 1922 was offered a job in the Department of Statistics in the Ministry of Industry and Commerce at £41.34 per month. He accepted, eager to play his part in the new state, and began work as Junior Administrative Officer on 1 January 1923.

Early days as official statistician

In a paper to the Statistical and Social Inquiry Society of Ireland (SSISI), Stanley Lyon, Roy's boss from 1930, described pre-1900 statistics as meagre and dispersed with the exceptions of agriculture and vital statistics (Lyon 1933). In 1899 a Statistics and Intelligence Branch had been set up as part of the organisation of the newly created Department of Agriculture and Technical Instruction. That Branch compiled data on various items including agriculture and agricultural prices, banking, exports and imports. In 1919 an Irish Department of the Ministry of Labour was created, it too with a Statistics and Intelligence Branch. This Branch collected wage and employment data and data on retail prices, and reported these to London. When the Free State was set up, the two Branches amalgamated and formed in 1923 the Statistics Branch of the Department of Industry and Commerce, under John Hooper as Director. Hooper (1878–1930), an excellent first Director (Black 1947), was succeeded by Lyon in 1930, and by Roy himself in 1947.

Shortly after the merger, a Committee was set up (with Bastable of TCD, in the Chair and with Busteed of UCC and Hooper as members) to advise on policy for economic statistics. Its report in 1925 led to the Statistics Act of 1926 giving powers to the Minister of Industry and Commerce for the collection, compilation and publication of statistics relating to any matter affecting the general activities of Saorstat Eireann, including population, employment and unemployment, emigration and immigration, agriculture, industry, commerce and banking. (In 1949 the office was transferred to the Department of the Taoiseach, renamed the CSO, and given improved status, with Roy appointed Director and Donal McCarthy recruited from UCC as Deputy Director. Other new staff then included the future Director Tom Linehan, one of four junior statisticians appointed in 1949. Much of the history is available in Linehan's 1998 address to SSISI, and available through the CSO website.)

In 1924 two papers were read to SSISI by C.H. Oldham, George O'Brien's predecessor in the Chair of National Economics in UCD. Oldham (1859–1926), home ruler, supporter of women's rights and founder in 1885 of the *Dublin University Review*, was the author of various economics books and papers on Ireland (O'Brien 1926; Black 1947). In 1883 he graduated from TCD in mathematics and sciences. He was called to the Bar in 1890 and practised for five years. In 1909 he was appointed Professor of Commerce in UCD, succeeding Kettle to the Chair of National Economics in 1917. In these papers, Oldham passionately spoke of the national need for more measurement and more statistics. There was currently a great opportunity for civil servants to make personal reputations and render great national service in this field. Irish statistics, once superior to British, were now in a chaotic state. The statistics needed to be produced and interpreted to inform the legislators and in a way that could be understood by ordinary people. The following year, on 3 December 1925, Oldham, now President, repeated the plea, this time stressing the need for Irish data to be analysed through comparisons with elsewhere.

Sadly, this was to be his swan song, for he died on 20 February 1926. Roy probably attended these meetings and through his life he took great interest in the society. He himself read a paper to it in February 1925 (Geary 1925) and in 1926 was elected Honorary Secretary, a post he held until 1946 when he became President (1946–50). These views of Oldham, like Roy mathematically well trained, might have seemed new and attractive to the young Geary – in any case, they are strikingly similar to what Roy came to believe.

Thus, in 1924, Roy was joining a newly reorganised Statistics Branch in a new government and at a time of great national need. Statistics had not emerged as an academic subject in Ireland and economics in the universities was weak and under-resourced (Fanning 1983).

Linehan (1997) has outlined much of the work that Roy undertook in the Branch in those first few years, using an account in the CSO files written by Roy in 1931. In this account Roy wrote that he was 'intimately associated' with Hooper in the preparation of most of the analytical reports which had been issued. These included reports on trade, agricultural output and population. Old series had to be maintained and new ones initiated. His first publication dealt with agricultural statistics and he presented a method of sampling of ratios which he showed mathematically would work reliably (Geary 1925). His second published paper (Geary 1927) again dealt with sampling and was applied to data on agriculture, trade and population. His other two papers prior to 1931 were a life table for the new state and a study of correlations between various factors and the incidence of tuberculosis in the country.

Thus, from the beginning, his theoretical work was motivated by practical considerations. During the first ten years of the new state, economic policy was to encourage agriculture and maximise farmers' incomes. Government favoured free trade and a small public sector. Emigration was high and the population was falling. In 1932, Fianna Fáil came to power, under de Valera, with a protectionist policy. It was also the time of the Great Depression and complications with Britain led to an economic war, 1932–38. Through these years Roy continued in his official duties, though now producing regular papers in mathematical statistics and building up his reputation internationally as a theoretical as well as an official statistician.

Population

In November 1935 he read a paper (Geary 1935a) to SSISI on 'The future population of Saorstat Eireann', describing 'experiments in forecasting population' in Ireland for 1936, 1946,... 2016. He set out assumptions on birth rates and emigration (that emigration and immigration were nil), defending the simplicity of the assumptions on the ground that he did not wish to give any misleading impression of accuracy in the forecasts, but did wish to show a corrective to some other current estimates, pointing out – characteristically, as we can now see – that 'bad statistics are often better than no statistics when they help to clarify thought by giving it a quantitative basis'. There was a common belief at the time that with low emigration, the Irish population could rise to pre-Famine levels, perhaps even to twelve or sixteen million. Roy's paper was valuable in debunking this. Although his estimates up to the 1970s have turned out mainly to be too high, owing to emigration, his estimates for 1986 and 1996 were rather close to the outcomes – his two figures for 1996 were 3.334 million and 3.608 million, compared to the current CSO figure for 1996 of 3.626 million – and his 2006 estimates are low. After discussing his calculations, he turned to emigration, pointing out that US immigration restrictions, then current, were assisting the Irish drive towards industrialisation at home. He reckoned from the evidence that emigration was more induced by good prospects abroad than by poor conditions at home, and thought that emigration to US would likely pick up again when the US immigration restrictions were lifted. He suggested that some rethinking of the Irish negative attitude towards emigration might be in order, though he took it as axiomatic that the Government would not accept a permanent decline in the population at home. The remittances from abroad, recently calculated, were now realised to be a great help in meeting the visible trade deficit. He was, however, given his view of the importance of quantification, more concerned to offer his computations than to propound theories.

The Preliminary Report of the 1936 Census, soon to appear, showed that the 1936 population at 2.966 million was less than Roy's estimate for 1936 by about 85,000, owing to his underestimation of emigration to Britain. Actually this meant that the population had fallen by 1936 compared with 1926, thus continuing a trend since 1841. By 1941, Roy had recalculated his forecasts, as more details were then available from the 1936 Census (Geary 1941), this time allowing for net emigration at a positive, though declining rate. He saw his forecasts, not as prophecies, but as merely the implications of different sets of assumptions, emigration being inherently unpredictable. New sets of forecasts for the years 1946, 1956,... 2036 were shown, with 1936 now known. The calculations showed there was no real danger of a declining population unless emigration was to be higher than his assumed pattern. Despite this possibility, Roy opposed recent views that emigration was necessarily bad. The views of the parents of emigrants and emigrants themselves were important, not just the view of the state. People who provided essential services to the State should not be allowed to leave, but most emigrants benefited themselves and the general standard of living at home by leaving. The principal objection to emigration, assuming it did not lead to further depopulation at home, was that many emigrants have been unfavourably circumstanced abroad. He thought it very difficult, however, to decide on the correct attitude towards emigration and felt that the State perhaps could set out the relevant axioms from which the issue could be logically determined – though it seems that the post-independence politicians were not then paying much attention to the topic (O'Brien 1936). O'Brien regarded the issue as most important and Roy agreed, remarking at a SSISI meeting in January 1945 that 'the country is badly in need of a lead in demographic policy'. He saw it as an advantage that it was not a politically controversial issue, the government being apathetic. While, in 1936, he had stated in *Ireland Today* that the forces controlling population were mysterious and attempts to interfere with them would require very careful consideration, by 1945 he seemed more optimistic about the efficacy of emigration controls, should control be thought desirable. If the right policy on emigration could be established, all the other Irish demographic problems, including education and juvenile unemployment, and many of the economic problems, would automatically tend to adjust.

No doubt influenced by those such as Geary and O'Brien, a Commission to investigate demographic issues and to advise on policy, was established in April 1948. The two dozen members included Geary, Lyon and McCarthy. In all, the Commission held 115 meetings and the Report did not appear until 1954. There were also many sub-committee meetings and specific research undertaken by individuals and Roy was closely involved throughout.

The Commission (1954) saw Irish demographic history over the previous hundred years as unique. The population had halved, owing to high emigration and low marriage rates and this had led to the current unbalanced sex-distribution and the high and increasing proportion of elderly dependent people. A rising population was seen as desirable and government should aim for this by creating conditions for the greatest possible population increase. Emigration was still large and the main cause was deemed to be economic, though a psychological acceptance of emigration as inevitable was also seen as a factor. It was hoped that improved domestic economic conditions, brought about partly through increased and well-directed investment spending, would give people less desire to emigrate, and the Commission recommended that economic policy should widen to include demographic criteria.

Eleven projections for population for 1986 were prepared, presumably by Roy, on different assumptions on fertility and emigration, with one assumption on mortality maintained throughout. The results varied from 2.5616 million to 5.6395 million but an expectation of a population increase to between 3.5 million and 4 million by 1986 was deemed highly optimistic. (The actual figure turned out to be 3.541 million.)

In an Addendum to the Report, Roy and Donal McCarthy expanded a little. The low density of population was prejudicial to economic development, but they thought it unlikely that the population would change much in the next few decades (the 1951 figure was 2.961 million). They pointed to the significant decline in the non-Catholic part of the population, noting that if the 1926 non-Catholic population had stayed static, the total population would have been increasing at each of the Census dates since then and the 'lamentable' trend of the eighty years prior to 1926 would have been reversed. Regarding emigration, they pointed out that emigration was neither good nor bad ethically. It had effects, of course, on the individual and on the country. These effects could be undesirable for the country if emigration was to cause the population to fall, or if it was to result in a distorted age-distribution or social disintegration. But the individual must be allowed to act in his own perceived self-interest. Economic development was a necessary, not sufficient, condition for population increase and economic development required improved productivity, increased investment (to come, in the main, from the private sector) and increased exports. The national outlook needed to be changed, with a great improvement in 'practical patriotism', as they put it.

On 9 May 1954 a symposium on 'The Irish Population Problem' was held in the Gresham Hotel, and Roy's contribution (Geary 1954a) was widely reported in the press. He regarded it as extremely difficult to establish any relation between emigration and the economic level and trend at home. Emigration could certainly have bad effects but it was an ingrained national instinct. It was the inalienable right of the individual to sell his labour where he chose and, anyhow, curbs on emigration were impossible to administer. He suggested the Irish should re-examine their attitude to it. In present circumstances the survival of the nation was not endangered and while it was reasonable to want less emigration, it was not reasonable to regard all emigration as bad. On available data, the natural increase in the population was about 28,000 per annum so there was plenty of scope for emigration and a rising population, which was to be desired and indeed was a test of the success of national economic policy.

The good sense of Roy's views on population is now evident. He was important in effectively challenging the longstanding, popular view that emigration was evil. He consistently pointed to the realistic middle ground between a view, widely held until the mid-thirties, that high, perhaps pre-Famine, population levels could again be achieved and a common view in the early fifties that Ireland's population was 'vanishing'. He greatly clarified the factors on which the future population would depend and was consistently and courageously opposed to a moral or ethical stance on emigration. While he did not wish to see the population declining and was very sensitive to the negative aspects of emigration, he stressed the individual's freedom to choose. He also saw emigration as contributing to an increase in the standard of living at home, and possibly for the emigrant, and, by 1954 certainly, he was stressing the potential costs and practical difficulties of curbing emigration (Geary 1954a).

He was not dogmatic in his population economics, but he tended to see recent emigration as a result of pull factors, given his inability to establish any major link between emigration and lack of economic development at home. The major factor was the pull of former emigrants, whose forefathers were 'pushed' out by the Great Famine. This pull was augmented by economic conditions and high living standards abroad (and the pull of fares sent home to relatives by former emigrants). He realised the importance of remittances to the home economy and was clear on the important idea that economic activity, emigration and population characteristics were interdependent and needed to be analysed together. He also was good on the age structure of the population and its implication for the economy. In his 1935 and 1941 forecasts, he forecast not just the population and its sex-distribution, but also its division into various age groups.

National income and accounts

Ireland's first official estimates appeared in a White Paper in March 1946. Roy later related, at a meeting of SSISI on 12 November 1981, that it had all started during the war when McElligott, then Secretary of the Department of Finance, exhorted Lyon and himself to 'have a try', national income being 'in the fashion'. It is likely that Roy, with Lyon's support, was the key figure in the production of these first official estimates (see Linehan 1997). The primary responsibility was with the Statistics Branch of Industry and Commerce though the Department of Finance helped with the Public Sector accounts and T.K. Whitaker, then Assistant Principal in Finance, had the key responsibility for the public sector figures. The outcome included a set of estimates for national income for the years 1938 to 1944, with a novel four-point grading of the figures A (firm) to D (conjectures). Separate figures were given for public income and expenditure and there was a separate section on prices, including wholesale price indices, a topic which Roy had been working on with publications (Geary 1944c, 1944d). Overall, many hands were involved, but the style and content of the report point to Roy as pre-eminent – indeed Paddy Lynch recalled that McElligott referred to the figures as 'Geary's guesses' (Kennedy 2002–03). Certainly it is typical Geary in page 6 where, after pointing out that pains had been taken to ensure the substantial reliability of the data, he continues 'it is felt, however, that meticulous accuracy is not necessary in statistics compiled for the consideration, formulation and criticism of public policy; even approximate statistics may be conducive to clarity of thought'.

In 1945 the League of Nations had convened a group to develop national accounting guidelines and the resulting Report (UN 1947) with an Appendix by Richard Stone recommended that national income estimation be set within a social accounting, sectoral approach and it set out the framework for internationally comparable systems – pointing out that official estimates along the lines of the Stone Appendix had already been compiled in six countries including Eire.

When Stone invited Geary to Cambridge in 1946 they had never met, though Stone knew and admired Roy's work in mathematical statistics and national accounting. Seemingly, most of their conversations were in the former, as was Roy's work there. Following his year at Cambridge, Roy's interest in national accounting resumed and he was involved in the Paris meetings finalising the OEEC Standardised System of National Accounts published in 1952. His standing in the field was by this time high as is clear from his high profile with the IARIW and from his 1957 invitation to head the National Accounts Branch in the Statistical Office of the UN, New York.

The IARIW was founded in 1947 by individuals who were actively engaged in national income accounting research and development. Roy was, of course, one such individual and he attended the Association's first meeting in 1949 in Cambridge. He was to prove influential in this organisation as a Council member, 1951–69, and as Chairman, 1965–67. In fact, one of Roy's most important conceptual innovations in national accounting arose in work presented to IARIW. This issue concerned the setting out a fully articulated set of national accounts in constant prices. Stone had argued (Stone 1956) that it was impossible to find a unique set of deflated values of the non-commodity transactions such that the accounts balance in real terms. Burge and Geary argued that a balancing set of real accounts *could* be produced that preserved the meaning of the various components *provided an extra variable*, the real trading gain (T'), put to zero in the base year, be added to the set. This paper, presented to the fifth conference of the IARIW in 1957, appeared, with marginal changes and additions, though without named authors, as chapter 2 of UN (1957), where it is described as a 'tentative' UN technical report on a system of price and quality indexes for national accounts circulated for comment. The IARIW, seeing the issue as important, decided to make 'Deflation of National Accounts' a major topic at the next meeting, to be held in Portoroz in 1959, when Roy organised the relevant session.

Geary (1961) provides a summary. Real income measures the purchasing power of the incomes generated from domestic production, so that when the terms of trade change, given production, welfare can change. Real gross domestic income equals real gross domestic product plus this trading gain or, in Roy's 1961 notation, $Y' = P' + T'$, where primes denote real (deflated) values. Since $P' = C' + I' + X' - M'$, in standard notation, T' is accommodated in the real balance of payments account through the equation $B' = X' - M' + T'$, where the current values surplus $B = X - M$. T' thus is $B/P_B - (X' - M')$, where P_B is the price deflator for B. The commodity flows X, M can each be deflated as $X' = X/P_X$, $M' = M/P_M$, P_X and P_M being conceptually readily definable. But how should B be deflated? Geary and Burge suggested using P_X as deflator if B were positive, otherwise P_M, an approach which leads to the real trading gain $T' = \text{Min}(X, M).(1/P_M - 1/P_X)$. They also mentioned as reasonable a weighted average of the two price indices. Later, Roy suggested that P_B be defined as the specific average $(P_X + P_M)/2$ (Geary 1961) for this would guarantee that certain desirable criteria, discussed at Portoroz, for the trading gain would be satisfied. Though the different choices for P_B have different implications for the estimate of the trading gain, Roy hoped that there would be little practical difference (Geary and Pratschke 1968).

The trading gain can be large, though it is now accepted that choice of deflator, P_B, can matter in practice. Paragraphs 16.155–6 of the 1993 UN System of National Accounts, recommended that T' should indeed be treated as an integral part of the system, though choice of P_B should be left to the statistical authorities in the country, taking account of their particular circumstances. If the statistical authorities are uncertain, they should use the 'Geary method', an arithmetic average of P_X and P_M and, in any case, some measure of the trading gain should always be calculated. All of this remains in the updated version available on the web, UN (1993), a document described there as a 'framework that sets the international statistical standard for the measurement of the market economy'.

Neary (1997) also addresses the issue and discusses Roy's work in multilateral international comparisons, the 'Geary–Khamis' method (Geary 1958). This paper dealt with the problem of using official exchange rates in international comparisons of flows expressed in different currencies. The paper was motivated by the problem of computing a world index of agricultural output which is consistent with indices of the individual countries. This problem presumably arose in Roy's work for FAO in Rome in 1953, for that was when he first produced the solution (Khamis 1984). Given n countries and k traded commodities, Roy defined a set of linear, homogeneous equations which determined international prices and exchange rates. In the case of two countries, it turned out elegantly that the ratio of the two exchange rates was the ratio of weighted price indices, where the weights were the harmonic means of the quantities. The approach is widely used in international comparisons of income and is described in Paragraph 16.93 of the web-based UN System of Accounts (op. cit.) as the most commonly used approach which involves examining the countries together as a block, rather than via pair-wise comparisons. Khamis (1984) looks back over some of the history, applications and his own contributions.

In assessing Roy's work on official statistics, he can certainly be seen as the outstanding figure within Ireland. Lyon, his Director from 1931 to 1947 should also, of course, receive some of the credit for the successful developments achieved during the years of his Directorship. Linehan (1997), Director of CSO, 1957–91, points to Lyon's importance in the administrative side and it is surely appropriate to credit Lyon, and perhaps Hooper, with allowing Geary to develop as he did, though there is little real evidence on this.

While much of his contribution in the area of official statistics must have been in unpublished government papers and memoranda, one can gain a useful picture of his philosophy on national income accounting and related matters from his published papers, e.g. Geary (1944c, 1944d, 1947b, 1953, 1961, 1973) and Geary and Pratschke (1968). He saw national income and social accounting as of enormously wide scope. Even starting with modest objectives he found that the requirements kept expanding until they included 'nearly the whole corpus of economic statistics' (Geary 1947b) and he argued that ultimately 'all statistics for which the official statistician asks are "behind" national accounts' (Geary 1973). The accounts, as for all official statistics, are not an end in themselves but 'a means towards the end of better control and understanding of the economic and social system' (ibid., and throughout his writing). The underlying variables were what mattered, not the accounts. He also stressed the interdependencies within the accounts and maintained that in national income accounts, each economic statistic appeared in its proper relation to other statistics (Geary 1947b). He emphasised real national income rather than national income at current prices, mainly to facilitate comparisons over time. He was much less enthusiastic about trying to make comparisons over space and, accordingly, put particular effort into the index number problem (e.g. Geary 1944c, 1944d, 1973).

Notwithstanding the high regard in which he and his work were held in national income circles, he made no claims to be methodologically pioneering in the field, except in his work on price deflation. On this, there were a number of related contributions. His work on the trading gain and on international measurement of prices stands out, but he also contributed importantly to the measurement of real GDP. In Ireland, during the war, gross output in agriculture remained fairly high but inputs fell sharply. Accordingly, to measure quantity of work done (value added at constant prices), gross output and input were each measured at constant prices and subtracted (Geary 1944c). Later it was discovered that Fabricant (US) and Wilson (Australia) had also independently suggested this double deflation method (Geary and Pratschke 1968). The approach was less successful in application to Irish industry (Geary 1944d; Geary and Forecast 1955), principally because of data limitations rather than problems in principle (Geary and Pratschke 1968; Geary 1973).

He also clarified the concept of overall GDP deflation. Thus, writing, in textbook notation, $Y = C + I + G + X - M$ (all in nominal terms), real GDP (Y') is defined as the sum of the five variables each separately deflated by its own price index i.e. $Y' = C' + I' + G' + X' - M'$. The GDP price index is then defined as Y/Y'. This approach, contrasting with the view that the same price index should be used for all the flows, is now standard and is known as 'the Geary method' (e.g. Stuvel 1956; Gutman 1981), presumably on account of Geary (1944c).

One can summarise his conceptual contributions in official statistics with a quotation from Roy himself. Roy is credited in Kendrick and Carson (1972) as the pioneer in the statistical implementation of the value added approach. Roy, in a review of the book in *Economic and Social Review* 1973: 279–81, is revealing on this.

> I must be honest and demur. I was, indeed, very conscious of the current value-added approach in the early 1930s, but this was due mainly to the work of those eminent pioneers of the English school, Flux, Stamp and Bowley, none mentioned here. Where Ireland pioneered was in value-added at *constant prices...*

Statistical theory

Roy's contributions to statistical theory were immense, and almost entirely produced when at work as an official statistician or as Director of ERI. Predominantly, they were a result of thinking about practical problems. His first paper (Geary 1925) is an example. Owing to political upheavals, full enumeration of certain agricultural populations was not then feasible. It was possible, however, to enumerate data on geographic units in which garda barracks were situated. Base date enumerations were known for all the units, current enumerations were known only for the garda collected data. He presented two estimates for population totals, the usual estimator, using current data, and a ratio estimator, using information from the base period. He showed that the latter would be more efficient, if the correlation between outputs on the units over the two periods was greater than 0.5. The theory was then applied to the pig population 1852–72. Later he clarified and extended his ratio estimator (Geary 1949b).

This result led to his famous 1930 *Journal of the Royal Statistical Society* paper (Geary 1930), on the distribution of the ratio X_2/X_1, where X_1, X_2 are jointly normal with zero means, variances σ_1^2, σ_2^2 and correlation ρ. Writing $z = (X_2 + b)/(X_1 + a)$, Roy showed that a transformation of z with a, b constant was distributed $N(0, 1)$, provided $X_1 + a$ was unlikely to be negative. He found, through transformations and integration, that $t = (az - b)/(\sigma_1^2 z^2 - 2\rho\,\sigma_1\sigma_2\,z + \sigma_2^2)^{1/2}$ is distributed very closely $N(0, 1)$, provided $P(X_1 + a > 0)$ is near unity. Hinkley (1969) revisits the issue. As usual, an application was included – on the statistical significance of an increase in TB mortality in a town between 1905 and 1925 of 5 per cent, i.e. $X_2/X_1 = 1.05$, when the national figure fell by 40 per cent. It might have been this early paper that brought Roy's name to the academic world. R.A. Fisher in writing a reference for Roy in 1940 must surely have had this work in mind with his remark that Geary was one of the rather few mathematicians capable of making original contributions to knowledge of exact frequency distributions. This issue was, for Fisher, the central one in statistics at that time, since he felt that other key problems had only become tractable by reason of a number of these distributions.

Two other important papers on stochastic ratios are his 1933 *Biometrika* paper and his 1944b *JRSS* paper, in which he generalised a 1937 theorem of Cramer on the distribution of the ratio of independent variates where the denominator is non-negative with finite mean to the case of dependence.

The main result in the 1933 paper, clarifying a result of Fisher, is $E(m_p^r/m_2^{rp/2}) = E(m_p^r)/E(m_2^{rp/2})$ under normality, where $m_p = \Sigma(x - m)^p/n$ and m is the sample mean. This result, that the expectation of the ratio is the ratio of the expectations, follows from the fact that the ratio is independent of the denominator. Roy proved this by taking an orthogonal transformation of the x's, where $x \sim N(O,I)$, namely, $v = Cx$ where C is orthogonal and $v_n = m\sqrt{n}$. He then transformed $v_1 \ldots v_{n-1}$ into generalised polar (spherical) coordinates $\rho, \varphi_1, \ldots, \varphi_{n-2}$ and pointed out that ρ is independent of the angles φ. Since $\rho^2 = n.m_2$ and since $m_p/m_2^{p/2}$ is an explicit function of the φ's only, the result follows. This argument is in essence identical to that of von Neumann (1941). In fact, this independence was crucial to the determination of the approximate distribution of d_L and d_U in the later Durbin and Watson theory, though the credit for the result in the Durbin–Watson literature seems to go invariably to von Neumann and to Pitman (1937), where it was shown that the sum of independent gamma variables and a homogeneous degree zero function of them are independent. Denis Conniffe discusses this issue further in Conniffe (1997b), and Conniffe and Spencer (2001) consider Geary (1933) in a more general context.

Roy gave great importance to testing for normality and robustness, in order to justify t and F tests and the like. By 1930, large sample approximations to the densities of $\sqrt{b_1}$ ($= m_3/m_2^{3/2}$) and b_2 ($= m_4/m_2^2$), the sample analogues of $\sqrt{\beta_1}$ and β_2, the classical measures of skewness and kurtosis, had been established. These statistics are the basis for traditional tests of normality of K. Pearson. Under normality, $\sqrt{\beta_1}$ and β_2 are 0 and 3, respectively, and normality is judged by how far the sample values are from these values, 0 and 3. By 1935, several of the lower order moments of normal $\sqrt{b_1}$ and b_2 had been derived by various authors including Wishart, Craig and Fisher, moments useful in approximating the distributions of normal $\sqrt{b_1}$ and b_2. Roy contributed to these issues in a number of important papers, including Geary (1935b, 1935c, 1936a, 1936b, 1947c).

In *Biometrika* papers 1935b, 1935c and 1936b Roy pointed out that $\sqrt{b_1}$ was really only a test of symmetry, not normality, and that testing with b_2 was not necessarily reliable for small or moderate sample sizes. He suggested instead the ratio of mean deviation to standard deviation, i.e. w, and he gave its mean and variance, using his 1933 result, and probability points for normal samples, sizes between 11 and 1001. (w is asymptotically normal and E(w) approaches its limiting value $\sqrt{(2/\pi)}$ = .79788 quickly, under normality. For n = 10, E(w) = .8203, for n = 20, it is .8084.) His 1938 brochure, with E S. Pearson, on Tests of Normality (Geary and Pearson, 1938), gave tables and diagrams of probability points of w, $\sqrt{b_1}$ and b_2. High values of w indicate platykurtosis, low values leptokurtosis. In 1947a, he developed small sample close approximations to the null distribution of $\sqrt{b_1}$, work undertaken not just on account of the importance of the matter, but also to gain experience which might help in analysing the b_2 problem. His method was an elaboration of that used earlier in his work on w, involving known moments and the relation between the frequency for n and n-1, for small n, taking account of singularities in the distribution. For $n \geq 8$, Gram–Charlier expansions were shown to be adequate. In his 1947c *Biometrika* paper he suggested a more general class of absolute moment tests w and developed results on their power. He showed that $\sqrt{b_1}$ and b_2 were, for large samples, the most efficient tests of symmetry and kurtosis, but that other tests, including his own, were important supplements. In particular, other tests would be important when sample sizes were not large and perhaps depending on the type of non-normality.

His w test is simple to compute, applies to all sample sizes and has good sensitivity to departures from normality, especially those arising from kurtosis, or those arising in cases combining skewness with low kurtosis (D'Agostino and Rosman 1974; Gastwirth and Owens 1977). Thus, it has been traditionally suggested as a small sample kurtosis test (e.g. Pearson and Hartley 1966) and it has an asymptotic optimality property for a class of alternatives (Uthoff 1973). Nowadays, perhaps tests such as the Shapiro–Wilk W test, the D'Agostino–Pearson K^2 test or, particularly in econometrics, the Jarque–Bera test are used more, as omnibus tests for non-normality from either skewness or kurtosis. Recently, however, a transformation of the Geary w has been suggested, namely ω = 13.29 (ln (1/w)), where 13.29 is chosen so that when w is at the theoretical value $\sqrt{(2/\pi)}$, the statistic ω will equal 3 (Bonnett and Seier 2002). High kurtosis now goes with high ω, and increases without bound with increasing leptokurtosis. The authors propose a test based on ω, which they show is a powerful test of leptokurtosis in symmetric distributions. They also propose a joint test involving ω and b_2, which seems to be uniformly powerful across a wide range of symmetric non-normal distributions. They conclude by suggesting that the population ω be referred to as Geary-kurtosis in honour of Geary and to distinguish it from Pearson's measure.

These Geary papers are still widely cited, especially 1947c which surveyed normality tests fairly generally and discussed the implications of parent non-normality for Fisher's two-variance Z-test (Z = ½ log F) and one and two sample t-tests. In his 1936 *JRSS* paper (1936a), Roy had found expansions to terms in n^{-2} of the first four moments of t, valid for any population, and had shown that a false assumption of parent normality would not seriously invalidate the distribution, even with small samples, if the underlying distribution was symmetrical. In his 1947c paper he found similar expansions for the first six cumulants of t and he used these to generate an approximation to the distribution of non-normal t and showed, if population skewness were positive, i.e. $\sqrt{\beta_1} > 0$, then E(t) and $\sqrt{\beta_1}$ (t) will be negative, so the probability of falling below –2.262 (say) will be greater than the theoretical 0.025. The error could be substantial, though, since t is asymptotically normal in any case, the effect will diminish as n increases. Results for the two sample t test of differences of means suggest that what really matters is whether the two populations are the same. If they differ, the probability of a low value of 't' is again too high, sometimes substantially so, when the true means are in fact the same.

Similar analysis for the z-test on equality of variances showed that departures from normal kurtosis are the main problem, even with large samples. When the parent populations are the same, he showed that the variance of z depends positively on β_2, the parent kurtosis. This effect does not vanish with large samples, and, if kurtosis is high, the null will tend to be rejected too often. With a population β_2 of 4.0, the large sample probability of rejection is shown to be about 0.11, instead of the normal 0.05.

These results have stood up remarkably well over time — see e.g. Pearson and Please (1975), Bowman *et al.* (1977), Thode (2002) — and the field remains active, often involving Monte Carlo studies. In 1947c Roy recommended further work, especially on the experimental side. Interestingly, he tells us that he is disappointed to find that normality matters so much, as it limits the relevance of standard methods – 'we so wanted to find the theory as good as it was beautiful'. Of course, other kinds of violations of assumptions matter too, e.g. errors in measurement of data, and indeed allowing for such errors was perhaps his greatest concern in dealing with time series and the estimation of relationships.

His early papers (1942b, 1943) on estimation are little noticed, though described in Spencer (1976), but the 1949 *Econometrica* paper (Geary 1949a) is a classic and pioneering in its early advocacy and analysis of instrumental variables (IVs). Aldrich (1993) has shown how this and some of his earlier papers in the 1940s fit into the historical development of econometric procedures and has concluded that his 1949 paper, which was the only one which he devoted wholly to the method, marks the real arrival of the method and was the definitive paper on IV estimation for the errors in variables model.

Roy contributed many other important and attractive results. Thus, for example, he showed that maximum likelihood minimises the generalised variance for large samples (Geary 1942a), and he reversed the well-known theorem that normality implies independence of sample mean and variance by showing the deeper converse that independence implies normality (Geary 1936a). He also clarified the relation between Pitman's closeness and efficiency (Geary 1944a) – see Keating and Mason (1997).

One of his most cited papers, across many fields including geography, ecology, medicine and economics, is Geary (1954b) on the contiguity coefficient. This coefficient measures the extent of contiguity of some variable between physical areas, such as Irish counties. Its two-dimensional character was seen by Roy as readily generalisable. If the data for contiguous counties were closer than those for counties not adjoining, the coefficient would be less than one. Random ordering would give a mean value of unity. He worked out the statistical theory in two ways – assuming normality, and using randomisation techniques. This permitted the researcher to calculate a standard error and apply significance tests for contiguity. The theory was also extended to regression problems and examples given. The paper was ahead of its time as the importance of spatial autocorrelation was not then appreciated (Taylor and Goddard 1974). It has, however, proved influential. The paper was brought to the attention of US social scientists by Beshers (1960) and to geographers by Duncan *et al.* (1961) (Unwin and Hepple 1974) and was given prominence in the well-known work of Cliff and Ord, e.g. Cliff and Ord (1973). It was outlined in a *JASA* survey of quantitative methods in geography (Berry 1971) and Jeffers laid out a computer sub-routine and provided an interesting historical note (Jeffers 1973).

Conclusion

Almost all Roy's work, theory and applied, was grounded in practical needs, both in statistical inferential procedures and national statistics. He consistently and strongly believed that official statistics were vital in safeguarding democratic principles, in settling disputes between interested parties, and in guiding policy makers. He stressed timeliness and reliability of the data, and the importance of public confidence in the figures. If policy makers thought that the available statistics were inadequate, they should come to the CSO and ask for the right kind of data and he hoped that the national data would increasingly come to have an Irish dimension, to reflect that they were designed for Irish purposes (Geary 1953).

He saw little value in academic economics unless it was accompanied by real understanding of the underlying economic variables. Certainly, he thought it of little value when it came to matters of policy. See Spencer (1997a) for an account of his antipathy to economic theory. He did, however, value descriptive, historical and statistical economics and his main criticism of the economists was for not doing the right kind of economics, for not stressing the quantification of relations and policy effects. He did, after all, contribute to economics himself, notably in deducing the ('Stone–Geary') utility function underlying a well-known demand system (Geary 1950), his work on international purchasing power and exchange rate comparisons (Geary 1958) and his work on the trading gain — each, certainly the latter two, having statistical and econometric implications. And he wrote economics pieces on economic development in Ireland, though largely statistically based, e.g. Geary (1949c, 1951).

When he returned from UN in 1960, he assumed the Directorship of the newly established Economic Research Institute (ERI). Details are in Kennedy (1993). The ERI, set up in June 1960 with funds from the Ford Foundation and help from the Government, was primarily to be a source of research on economic and social issues in Ireland. In August 1960, the ERI issued a statement that its work would to a considerable extent be based on the statistical material available from the CSO. Roy was the obvious choice as Director and his availability helped Whitaker and colleagues persuade the Ford Foundation to provide the funding.

In February 1962, the Department of Finance asked the ERI to examine the economic implications of various assumptions on growth rates for the period 1962 to 1970. The request led to Roy's work on an Input–Output decision model for Ireland, available in November 1962 and presented to SSISI in January 1964 (Geary 1964). In this paper he developed an inter-industry model using a CSO IO table, examined the implications of changing coefficients and estimated the optimal export pattern for the country. He was a firm believer in the value of IO for planning and, while emphasising the experimental nature of the work, he stated his intention that the figures would help 'guide prudent policy in the light of information known now and as it becomes available'.

In the period of greatest work, 1930 to 1957, however, Roy as a civil servant was not free to advise directly on policy. He took this constraint seriously and was on the whole content to work within it. In Geary (1953) we find a useful summary of his position when he says that the CSO should have no direct concern with policy making and should not even venture policy advice in confidential memoranda. But he adds that 'we would not hesitate' to give views, as individuals, informally at conferences. And such views would at least be consistent with the data, even though they might well not be rigorously demonstrated. He was, of course aware of difficulties in showing causal connections in economics. In a private manuscript, written late in his life, he adds a little. He tells us that he has attempted only work that he felt was manageable, and that he always chose his own research problems. He sought information needed for the solution of the problem but, while chary of propounding policy, he usually had a policy end in view, to guide his fact finding. While a civil servant, he was always a researcher, and while reared to think of policy as politics, did sometimes find the right policy forcing itself on him and on occasion did sail close to the policy wind. He does not elaborate but, as an example of this, his work on population springs to mind, especially his work in the heated climate of the early 1950s, when there was widespread fear that high emigration was a national disaster (Spencer 1997a). And it is surely right to suggest that much of his work would have helped prevent bad policy. He believed fervently that to aspire to suggesting improvements required first an understanding of why things were as they were. This in turn required detailed knowledge of what they actually were, and in this his official statistical work was surely of supreme importance. Later, from the time of ERI onwards, he would presumably have felt free to recommend policy. He had a lifelong desire to be useful (Spencer 1997a) and his later work on economics, broadly summarised in Walsh (1997) reflects this.

There were two main strands in his career. There was his mathematical statistics, mainly 1930 to 1957, perhaps his greatest accomplishment. But there was also his enormous contribution particularly, though not exclusively, to Ireland, through his work and leadership in official statistics and leadership in the ERI. That he managed to combine the two, along with many other interests (Spencer, 1983a, 1983b, 1993, 1997a), is an extraordinary achievement.

Notes

1 Much of the material is drawn from Spencer (1997a, 1997b), which can be consulted for many more details and references.
2 Details of all of R.C. Geary's 117 publications are available in Spencer (1997b).

References[2]

Aldrich, J. (1993) 'Reiersol, Geary and the idea of instrumental variables', *Economic and Social Review* 24: 247–73.

Berry, B.J.L. (1971) 'Problems of data organisation and analytical methods in geography', *Journal of the American Statistical Association* 66: 510–23.

Beshers, J.M. (1960) 'Statistical inferences from small area data', *Social Forces* 38: 341–8.

Black, R.D.C. (1947) *The Statistical and Social Inquiry Society of Ireland Centenary Volume 1847–1947 with a History of the Society*, Dublin: Eason & Son.

Bonnett, D.G. and Seier, E. (2002) 'A test of normality with high uniform power', *Communicational Statistics & Data Analysis* 40: 435–45.

Bowman, K.D., Beauchamp, J.J. and Shenton, L.R. (1977) 'The distribution of the t-statistic under normality', *International Statistical Review* 45: 233–42.

Cliff, A.D. and Ord, K. (1973) *Spatial Autocorrelation*, London: Pion.

Commission on Emigration and other Population Problems (1954) *1948–1954 Reports*, Pr. 2541, Dublin: Stationery Office.

Conniffe, D. (ed.) (1997a) *Roy Geary 1896–1983: Irish Statistician. Centenary Lecture by John E. Spencer and Associated Papers*, Dublin: Oak Tree Press.

Conniffe, D. (1997b) 'Geary's use of the von Neumann ratio for testing regression specifications', in D. Conniffe (ed.) (1997a).

Conniffe, D. and Spencer, J.E. (2001) 'When moments of ratios are ratios of moments', *The Statistician* 50: 161–8.

D'Agostino, R.B. and Rosman, B. (1974) 'The power of Geary's test of normality', *Biometrika* 61: 181–4.

Duncan, O.D., Cuzzort, R.P. and Duncan, B. (1961) *Statistical Geography: Problems in Studying Areal Data*, Glencoe, IL: Free Press of Glencoe.

Fanning, R. (1983) 'Economists and governments: Ireland 1922–52', *Hermathena* 135: 138–56.

Gastwirth, J.L. and Owens, M.E.B. (1977) 'On classical tests of normality', *Biometrika* 64: 135–9.

Geary, R.C. (1925) 'Methods of sampling applied to Irish statistics', *Journal of the Statistical and Social Inquiry Society of Ireland*, Sessions 77 and 78, XV: 61–81.

Geary, R.C. (1927) 'Some properties of correlation and regression in a limited universe', *Metron* VII: 83–119.

Geary, R.C. (1930) 'The frequency distribution of the quotient of two normal variates', *Journal of the Royal Statistical Society* XCIII: 442–6.

Geary, R.C. (1933) 'A general expression for the moments of certain symmetrical functions of normal samples', *Biometrika* XXV: 184–6.

Geary, R.C. (1935a) 'The future population of Saorstat Eireann and some observations on population statistics', *Journal of the Statistical and Social Inquiry Society of Ireland*, Session 89, 1935–36: 15–32. Discussion 33–5.

Geary, R.C. (1935b) 'The ratio of the mean deviation to the standard deviation as a test of normality', *Biometrika* XXVII: 310–32.

Geary, R.C. (1935c) 'Note on the correlation between β_2 and w'', *Biometrika* XXVII: 353–5.

Geary, R.C. (1936a) 'The distribution of 'Student's' Ratio for non-normal samples', *Supplement to Journal of the Royal Statistical Society* III, 2: 178–84.

Geary, R.C. (1936b) 'Moments of the ratio of the mean deviation to the standard deviation for normal samples', *Biometrika* XXIII: 295–305.

Geary, R.C. (1941) 'Irish population prospects considered from the viewpoint of reproduction rates', *Journal of the Statistical and Social Inquiry Society of Ireland*, Session 94, XVI, 1940–41: 91–118. Discussion 118–22.

Geary, R.C. (1942a) 'The estimation of many parameters', *Journal of the Royal Statistical Society* CV: 213–7.

Geary, R.C. (1942b) 'Inherent relations between random variables', *Proceedings of the Royal Irish Academy* XLVII, Section A: 63–76.

Geary, R.C. (1943) 'Relations between statistics: the general and the sampling problem when the samples are large', *Proceedings of the Royal Irish Academy* XLIX, Section A: 177–96.

Geary, R.C. (1944a) 'Comparison of the concepts of efficiency and closeness of estimate for consistent estimates of a parameter', *Biometrika* XXXIII: 123–8.

Geary, R.C. (1944b) 'Extension of a theorem by Harald Cramer on the frequency distribution of the quotient of two variables', *Journal of the Royal Statistical Society* CVII: 56–7.

Geary, R.C. (1944c) 'Some thoughts on the making of Irish index numbers', *Journal of the Statistical and Social Inquiry Society of Ireland*, Session 98, XVII: 345–70. Discussion 370–80.

Geary, R.C. (1944d) 'The concept of net volume of production with special reference to Irish data', *Journal of the Royal Statistical Society* CVII, III–IV: 251–9, 290–2.

Geary, R.C. (1947a) 'The frequency distribution of $\sqrt{b1}$ for samples of all sizes, drawn at random from a normal population', *Biometrika* XXXIV: 68–97.

Geary, R.C. (1947b) 'Presidential Address: some reflections on tendencies in the theory and practice of statistics in Ireland and elsewhere', *Proceedings of the Statistical and Social Inquiry Society of Ireland: Centenary* 1847–1947: 5–24. Discussion 24–30.

Geary, R.C. (1947c) 'Testing for normality', *Biometrika* XXXIV: 209–42.

Geary, R.C. (1949a) 'Determination of linear relations between systematic parts of variables with errors of observation, the variances of which are unknown', *Econometrica* 17: 30–58.

Geary, R.C. (1949b) 'Most efficient sample sizes for the two-stage sampling process in the case of the limited universe', *International Statistical Institute*, 26th Session: 228–39.

Geary, R.C. (1949c) *Industrial Development in Ireland: A Statistical Review*, Manchester: Manchester Statistical Society, pp. 1–46.

Geary, R.C. (1950) 'A note on a constant utility index of the cost of living', *Review of Economic Studies* XVIII(I), 1950–51: 65–6.

Geary, R.C. (1951) 'Irish economic development since the treaty', *Studies* XL: 399–418.

Geary, R.C. (1953) 'Statistics in the Irish public service', *Administration* 1: 13–26.

Geary, R.C. (1954a) 'Some reflections on Irish population questions', *Studies* XLIII: 168–77.

Geary, R.C. (1954b) 'The contiguity ratio and statistical mapping', *The Incorporated Statistician* 5: 115–41.

Geary, R.C. (1958) 'A note on the comparison of exchange rates and purchasing power between countries', *Journal of the Royal Statistical Society*, Series A (General), 121: 97–9.

Geary, R.C. (1961) 'Chapter 1: Introduction', and 'Chapter 3: Productivity aspects of accounts deflation: Data for Ireland', in Phyllis Deane (ed.) *Studies in Social and Financial Accounting*, Income and Wealth Series IX: 3–8, 31–45.

Geary, R.C. (1964) 'Towards an input–output decision model for Ireland', *Journal of the Statistical and Social Inquiry Society of Ireland*, 1963–64, Session 117, XXI (2): 67–119.

Geary, R.C. (1973) 'Reflections on national accounting', *Review of Income and Wealth*, Series 19: 221–51.

Geary, R.C. and Forecast K.G. (1955) 'The use of census of industrial production material for the estimation of productivity', *Review of the International Statistical Institute* 23: 6–19.

Geary, R.C. and Pearson, E.S. (1938) *Tests of Normality, London*: Biometrika Office, University College, London. 15pp.

Geary, R.C. and Pratschke, J.L. (1968) *Some Aspects of Price Inflation in Ireland*, Dublin: The Economic and Social Research Institute, Paper No. 40.

Gutman, P. (1981) 'Measurement of terms of trade effects', *Review of Income and Wealth*, Series 27: 433–53.

Hinkley, D.V. (1969) 'On the ratio of two correlated normal random variables', *Biometrika* 56: 635–9.

Jeffers, J.N.R. (1973) 'A basic sub-routine for Geary's contiguity ratio', *The Statistician* 22: 299–302.

Keating, J.P. and Mason, R.L. (1997) 'Roy Geary's contribution to Pitman closeness', in D. Conniffe (ed.) (1997a).

Kendrick, J.W. and Carson, C. (1972) *Economic Accounts and their Uses*, London: McGraw-Hill.

Kennedy, F. (2002–03) 'Patrick Lynch 1917–2001', *Administration* 50: 3–8.

Kennedy, K.A. (1993) 'R.C. Geary and the ESRI', *Economic and Social Review* 24: 225–45.

Khamis, S. (1984) 'On aggregation methods for international comparisons', *Review of Income and Wealth* Series 30: 185–205.

Linehan, T. (1997) 'Geary and official statistics', in D. Conniffe (ed.) (1997a).

Lyon, S. (1933) 'The organisation of official statistics in Saorstat Eireann and in some other countries', *Journal of Statistical and Social Inquiry Society of Ireland*, Session 86, 1932–33: 29–61.

Neary, J.P. (1997) 'R C Geary's contributions to economic theory', in D. Conniffe (ed.) (1997a).

O'Brien, G. (1926) 'Charles Hubert Oldham', *Economic Journal* 36: 320–1.

O'Brien, G. (1936) 'The coming crisis of population. The future population of Ireland', *Studies* 25: 567–80.

Pearson, E.S. and Hartley, H.O. (1966) *Biometrika Tables for Statisticians*, Vol. 1, 3rd edn, Cambridge: Cambridge University Press.

Pearson, E.S. and Please, N.W. (1975) 'Relation between the shape of population distribution and the robustness of four simple test statistics', *Biometrika* 62: 223–41.

Pitman, E.J.G. (1937) 'The "closest" estimates of statistical parameters', *Proceedings of the Cambridge Philosophical Society* 33: 212–22.

Spencer, J.E. (1976) 'The scientific work of Robert Charles Geary', *Economic and Social Review* 7: 233–41.

Spencer, J.E. (1983a) 'Robert Charles Geary — An appreciation', *Economic and Social Review* 14: 161–4.

Spencer, J.E. (1983b) 'Robert Charles Geary 1896–1983', *Econometrica* 51: 1599–601.

Spencer, J.E. (1993) 'Aspects of the life and personality of R.C. Geary', *Economic and Social Review* 24: 215–24.

Spencer, J.E. (1997a) 'R.C. Geary: his life and work', in D.Conniffe (ed.) (1997a).

Spencer, J.E. (1997b) 'Geary's curriculum vitae and publication list', in D. Conniffe (ed.) (1997a).

Stone, J.R.N. (1956) *Quantity and Price Indexes of National Accounts*, Paris: OEEC.

Stuvel, G. (1956) 'A new approach to the measurement of terms of trade effects', *Review of Economics and Statistics* 38: 294–307.

Taylor, P.J. and Goddard, J. (1974) 'Geography and statistics: an introduction', *The Statistician* 23: 149–55.

Thode, H.C. (2002) *Testing for Normality*, New York: Dekker.

UN (1947) *Measurement of National Income and the Construction of Social Accounts. Studies and Reports on Statistical Methods No 7*, Geneva: United Nations. (The greater part of the report was Stone's Appendix: Definition and measurement of the national income and related totals.)

UN (1957) *A System of Price and Quality Indexes for National Accounts*, Economic and Social Council, E/CN.3/L.46, 27 December 1957.

UN (1993) System of National Accounts Document Symbol ST/ESA/STAT/SER.F/2/ Rev.4 Online. Available at http://unstats.un.org/unsd/sna1993/introduction.asp (accessed 1 June 2007).

Unwin, D.J. and Hepple, L.W. (1974) 'The statistical analysis of spatial series', *The Statistician* 23: 211–27.

Uthoff, V.A. (1973) 'The most powerful scale and location invariant test of the normal versus the double exponential', *Annals of Statistics* 1: 170–4.

von Neumann, J. (1941) 'Distribution of the ratio of the mean square successive difference to the variance', *Annals of Mathematical Statistics* 12: 367–95.

Walsh, B. (1997) 'The later applied work of R.C. Geary', in D. Conniffe (ed.) (1997a).

13 W.M. Gorman

Patrick Honohan and J. Peter Neary[1]

Introduction

William Moore Gorman, known to all as Terence, died in Oxford on 12 January 2003. The greatest Irish economist since Edgeworth, he was, like Edgeworth, totally unknown to the general public, both in his native country and in Britain where he made his career. He was the purest of pure theorists, whose life was devoted to scholarship and teaching, and whose work of forbidding technical difficulty was incomprehensible to most of his contemporaries. Yet, paradoxically, he was always concerned with applied issues, and the tools and theorems he developed have had a lasting influence on empirical work.

The life

Gorman was born in Kesh, County Fermanagh, on 17 June 1923. His father, a veterinary surgeon, having died when he was young, he was raised by his mother and spent part of his childhood in what was then Rhodesia. He liked to recount that it was his African nanny who rejected William as a not very Irish name and rechristened him Terence, by which he was thereafter universally known. Back in Ireland he attended Mount Temple College in Dublin and Foyle College in Derry before going up to Trinity College Dublin in 1941. He served as a Rating and then Petty Officer in the Royal Navy from 1943 to 1946, and then returned to Trinity where he graduated in Economics in 1948 and in Mathematics in 1949.[2]

After Trinity, Gorman moved to Britain where he held a succession of posts at some of the leading economics departments. From 1949 to 1962 he taught in the University of Birmingham, which was a leading centre for theoretical research in the 1950s, with Frank Hahn and Maurice McManus among his colleagues. In 1962 he was appointed to a chair in Economics at Oxford and in 1967 he moved to a chair at the London School of Economics. He returned to Oxford in 1979 as an Official Fellow of Nuffield College, becoming Senior Research Fellow in 1984 and Emeritus Fellow in 1990. He also spent periods as Visiting Professor at several US universities, including Iowa, Johns Hopkins, North Carolina and Stanford. Meanwhile honours and awards were piling up, most notably Presidency of the Econometric Society in 1972, as well as Fellowship of the British Academy, membership of Academia Europaea, honorary foreign membership of the American Academy of Arts and Sciences and of the American Economic Association, and honorary doctorates from the Universities of Birmingham and Southampton. Even in Ireland his achievements were recognised, with an honorary doctorate from the National University of Ireland in 1986 and an honorary fellowship from Trinity College Dublin some years later. After retirement, he continued to live in Oxford, also spending summers in County Cork with his wife Dorinda, whom he had met in Trinity, until in his last year's illness impaired his mobility.

The work

It was sometimes said that Gorman published relatively little, and it is true that many of his papers circulated for years in mimeo form, some of them to be rescued by the editors of his *Collected Works* (Blackorby and Shorrocks 1995). However, his published output was still formidable, and, at least in the 1950s and 1960s, would have satisfied the most demanding research assessment exercise.

Gorman's own summary of his principal contributions is worth quoting in full:

> James Davidson at Foyle College, Derry, and George Duncan at Trinity College Dublin, taught me to think of mathematics and economics as styles of thought, not collections of theorems, and Birmingham taught me to think of the social sciences as a unity with history as one way of holding them together. My research has accordingly been devoted to the end of flexible modelling, that is, to allow economists to immerse themselves in their data and in the opinions of other social scientists, and then to choose forms which seem capable of handling this information. This has been even more true of my teaching, largely through workshops for students beginning research.
>
> (Blaug 1986: 328)

A reader unfamiliar with Gorman's works might interpret this as the manifesto of a woolly inter-disciplinarian. But the key phrase is "flexible modelling". Gorman was younger than Hicks, who in *Value and Capital* relegated his mathematics to appendices, and Samuelson, who in his *Foundations* proselytised for the value of a mathematical approach to economics. To Gorman, technical difficulty was taken for granted, though not as an end in itself. Most of his research pursued the goal of using whatever tools were appropriate (and frequently developing new ones) in order to throw light on a central issue in economic theory: the links between individual preferences and market behaviour. Here we comment on some of the main topics which he illuminated.

Aggregation

In his first published paper, Gorman (1953) provided the definitive answer to a key question in economics: when does a society of utility-maximising individuals behave as if it was a single individual? In other words, when does a community indifference map exist? He showed that a necessary and sufficient condition is that, assuming all individuals face the same prices, their income–consumption or Engel curves should be parallel straight lines. Thus for individual (or household) h, the Hicksian demand function for good i should take the following form:[3]

$$x_i^h(p, u) = f_i^h(p) + u^h g_i(p)$$ 13.1

The location of the h superscripts on the right-hand side is crucial. Individuals can differ greatly in their responses to price changes as far as the f_i^h functions are concerned. However, their differences must be independent of income (or utility): all individuals must have the same g_i function, so that at the margin they have identical responses to changes in u. Hence aggregate demands have the same form as 13.1:

$$X_i(p, u) = F_i(p) + U g_i(p)$$ 13.2

where X_i, F_i and U are the sums over all individuals of the corresponding micro terms.

In his 1961 *Metroeconomica* paper, Gorman returned to this question, now using the much more powerful tools of duality which he and others had developed in the interim (Gorman 1961). This short paper is bed-time reading by contrast with the 1953 paper, yet it contains what is probably his best-known contribution. Here Gorman derived an explicit expression for the form of preferences which give rise to linear Engel curves. He showed that individual h's expenditure function must take the simple form:

$$e^h(p, u^h) = f^h(p) + u^h g(p)$$ 13.3

where the functions $f^h(p)$ and $g(p)$ are homogeneous of degree one in prices (so ensuring that this property is exhibited by the expenditure function itself), and their derivatives equal the coefficients in 13.1. They have nice interpretations: $f^h(p)$ is the expenditure needed to reach a reference utility level of zero, while $g(p)$ is the price index which deflates the excess money income $e^h(p, u^h) - f^h(p)$ needed to attain a level of utility or real income u^h. Inverting 13.3 gives utility as a function of prices and expenditure:

$$v^h(p, I^h) = \frac{I^h - f^h(p)}{g(p)}$$ 13.4

which Gorman called "the polar form of the underlying utility function". With this unconventional term Gorman was drawing attention to the fact that using what we would now call the indirect utility function amounts to switching from Cartesian to a form of polar coordinates in describing the indifference surface. Specifically, I may be taken as analogous to the radius and the vector of prices p

to the angle in solid geometry. In any case, the term "Gorman polar form" has come to be universally applied to the functional form in 13.4.[4]

By construction the Gorman polar form plays a central role in consumer theory, and it has also been hugely important in empirical work. On the one hand, special cases with various functional forms for $f^h(p)$ and $g(p)$ proved amenable to estimation, even before the advent of high-speed computers. Gorman himself showed that, if the marginal propensities to consume (which equal $p_i g_i/g$) are constant, then the function $g(p)$ can be written as a geometric mean of prices:

$$g(p) = \Pi \, p_i^{\rho_i}, \qquad \rho_i = p_i g_i /g, \qquad \Sigma \rho_i = 1 \qquad\qquad 13.5$$

The linear expenditure system, developed by R.C. Geary among others, is a further special case, corresponding to the combination of 13.5 with a linear form for $f(p)$.[5] On the other hand, Gorman's results did not prove a barrier to extending the theory to more general demand systems which avoid the implausible restrictions on income effects of 13.3. Muellbauer (1975) showed that a richer family of demand systems could be generated if the traditional requirement, used by Gorman, that aggregate demands behave like the sum of individual demands, was replaced by the weaker requirement that they generate only the same budget *shares*. This in turn has spawned a huge empirical literature applying members of Muellbauer's family and its extensions, such as the "Almost Ideal" demand system of Deaton and Muellbauer (1980).

Gorman also explored the conditions that must be satisfied for the existence of an aggregate stock of a fixed factor such as capital (Gorman 1968a). The necessary and sufficient condition turns out to be formally very similar to that for aggregation of demands over individual consumers. Each firm must have a restricted profit function similar in form to 13.3, where utility is replaced by a function of the amount of capital used by the firm. In his own words, this result "certainly does not help justify the practice of fitting aggregate production functions". Gorman's contribution to the capital theory controversies of the 1960s lacked the fireworks of those that emanated from the two Cambridges (England and Massachusetts), but it is probably of more lasting importance.

Separability

"Suppose you were interested in the demand for tomatoes in Ireland." Thus begins Gorman's (1987) article on separability in the *Palgrave Dictionary of Economics*, recalling his own early applied work, characterised by his widow Dorinda as involving "careering around Dublin on a bike, looking in greengrocers' windows" (private communication). For him, separability assumptions were what allowed the researcher to abstract from the mass of institutional detail accumulated on such trips: detail that could conceivably be relevant, but was certainly going to make analysis impossibly complex. "Separability", he wrote, "is about the structure we are to impose on our model: what to investigate in detail, what can be sketched in with broad strokes without violence to the facts."

As for the researcher, so also for the household or the enterprise. Practical decision-making often calls for short cuts relative to full intertemporal optimisation of a preference function. Gorman was confident that in reality most households engage in two-stage budgeting, in which the family budget is first allocated between broad classes of spending (clothing, food, etc.) and then choices are made within each class.

But just how good is this as a way of making decisions? Each of the two stages is problematic. Can the first-stage allocation safely be made just on the basis of some price aggregates for each class of goods, and without looking at the relative prices of all goods? Even if the first-stage allocations are correct, can the choice of goods within each class safely be made without reference to the prices on offer or quantities chosen of goods in other classes? It turns out that the validity of such a procedure for achieving the optimum requires that the household's utility function satisfy some fairly drastic separability restrictions – more stringent than had been recognised in the literature.

In particular, Strotz (1957) had argued that a sufficient condition for two-stage budgeting is that the household's utility function be separable, i.e. expressible in the form:

$$u \;=\; F\Big[\, v_1(x_1), v_2(x_2), \; \ldots \;, v_n(x_n)\,\Big] \tag{13.6}$$

where x_r denotes the vector of consumptions in class r. Gorman showed that, while necessary, separability is not sufficient.[6] In addition, it is required that the sub-utility functions, which Gorman called "specific satisfaction functions", v_r enter utility either additively or through an intermediate function which is homogeneous of degree one in its components.[7]

That these constraints were severe was for Gorman "in a sense a good thing"; since (he knew) households did adopt two-stage budgeting, it must be that their preferences were so restricted. Knowledge of this fact would ease the task of applied researchers wishing to estimate the relevant parameters.

What motivated Gorman here was the tension between two goals of economic modelling. On the one hand, the conceptual need for a coherent and psychologically or organisationally credible theoretical representation of decision-making; on the other hand, the operational need to have a workable algebraic representation of this behaviour. The basic assumptions of utility theory are too weak to yield specific functional forms or to make many predictions about individual or aggregate behaviour. Further assumptions are needed if real progress is to be made in applied economics, but these assumptions must be more-or-less reasonable. Looking from the other side, it is evident that simple algebraic representations of behaviour are needed for applied econometrics. Simplicity is also needed if the theory is to be mathematically manipulated to yield secondary predictions. But all such uses are empty if the algebraic specification implies incoherent decision-making. In practice, most of the algebraic representations with which demand and production theory deal are linear functions of prices or quantities, or are simple transformations of linear functions. Here questions of separability become central.

An interesting example of how specific separability assumptions could help in underpinning a linear representation of behaviour is provided by Gorman's paper "Facing an uncertain future" (Gorman 1982). In this paper, Gorman's goal is to show that the assumptions required to justify a linear representation of the intertemporal objective function are much weaker and more credible than had hitherto been recognised in the literature.

For a static environment, Allais, Samuelson, Von Neumann and Morgenstern and others had presented the conditions under which decision-making under conditions of uncertainty could be represented as the maximisation of a linear function – a weighted average – of the various alternative possibilities.[8] The key assumption in this expected utility hypothesis, Samuelson's weak independence axiom (or "sure thing principle"), is one of separability.

If we widen the focus to intertemporal decisions (still under uncertainty), can we get as simple an objective function with equally weak assumptions? The objective function that is commonly – indeed almost universally used – is a double sum:

$$\sum_s \sum_t f^{st}(y_{st})$$

13.7

where y_{st} is the vector of flows which occur in period t if state s occurs.[9] Can we derive such a simple form from assumptions that are as mild and acceptable as those underlying expected utility? If we are prepared to assume an extended version of the sure thing principle, so that it applies over time as well as between uncertain states of the world, we will get this double summation form of the objective function. But Gorman points out that extending weak independence in this way is logically problematic.

Before doing so, he notes that such an extension to a second dimension is permissible in the case of a social welfare function under uncertainty, where households rather than time are the extra dimension. Thus, if social welfare is increasing in every household's utility, if each household is "self-regarding",[10] and if Samuelson's weak independence axiom holds, then, drawing on a powerful theorem from an earlier paper of his on the structure of utility functions (Gorman 1968b), Gorman shows that the social welfare function can be expressed in the same double summation form as 13.7, except with y_{sh} as the consumption of household h in state of the world s instead of y_{st}. These simple and acceptable[11] assumptions are thus all that is needed to produce "Bentham and Bernoulli at a stroke".

But to assume that households or firms are not only able to calculate their utility over all possible future states of the world but assert independence of each set of states of the world and time periods is a step too far for Gorman. Such an argument "assumes from the outset that we are all very bright, and especially so at computation". Instead, he proposes the contrary idea, that "we are all pretty limited beings, only able to hold a few things in our minds at a time ... and that organizations are collectively quite as limited as their members". Specifically, he assumes that "we look ahead two periods in detail, summarizing the impact of our choices on more distant prospects in a single figure". He then proceeds to show that this, more realistic, vision of decision-making, embodying a very weak (undemanding) form of intertemporal separability – based on the idea of not looking ahead in detail for more than two periods – is enough to generate the double summation form of the objective function.

Here, Gorman has armed applied econometricians with a justification for doing what they had always intended — use a linear functional form. The behavioral assumptions are somewhat restrictive, but also characteristically down-home: the firm is planning for now and next year, and for a general sense of what it will bequeath later years. If that is not how firms and households behave exactly, yet it seems not too unrealistic.

Characteristics

Separability may be justified between goods that satisfy widely different needs; but for other goods it is their close similarities that attract attention. It is not on the basis of their essence that a consumer will choose between goods, but on the basis of the satisfaction they will produce. Even for closely related goods, this in turn may depend on more than one characteristic.

Switching from tomatoes to eggs in deference to his original audience for the topic – an agricultural economics seminar in the Iowa State College of Agriculture and the Mechanic Arts in 1956 – Gorman entitled his first paper on the topic of characteristics "A possible procedure for analysing quality differentials in the egg market". This paper finally appeared in 1980: see Gorman 1980. Ever concerned with the interests of the applied economist, he saw the paper as a response to the need of Iowan farmers to understand what drove price differentials for eggs of different qualities.

The basic idea is simple: consumers buy different varieties of eggs solely for certain measurable characteristics (for example, he suggests, their vitamin content). If only two characteristics are relevant, then, given arbitrary prices, we may expect that at most two varieties of eggs will be bought by any given consumer; if three characteristics are relevant, at most three varieties.[12] Only in the "degenerate case" where the relative prices happened to be just right would the consumer be indifferent between three or more varieties. But – and here is where things get interesting – as soon as we consider market equilibrium, the prices will not be arbitrary: the degenerate case will prove to be the normal one, as it is "*the only case in which every type of egg could find a sale*" (emphasis in the original). This degenerate case can be characterised by a shadow price q_j of characteristic j such that, if purchased variety i delivered quantity a_{ij} of characteristic j, the price p_{it} of each variety i at each time t should always equal the value of the sum of its characteristics measured at the shadow prices:

$$p_{it} = \sum_j a_{ij} q_{jt} \qquad\qquad 13.8$$

Building on this insight, essentially an argument from the assumption that market prices should not embody arbitrage opportunities, Gorman proposed an empirical research agenda. The specific quantity of each characteristic delivered by each variety, though measurable for the consumer, is unknown to the researcher, as are the shadow prices. But a sufficiently long time series on prices of different varieties could allow both to be identified, even if the prices were also somewhat influenced by other, less important, elements. If the number of varieties is I and the number of characteristics J, then price data for T time periods yields IT data points to estimate $I + J$ parameters. Statistical techniques such as factor analysis are available for such analysis. Gorman sensed that many of these ideas were already known,[13] but the arbitrage argument seems to be original to him.

For all his warmth towards the challenges faced by applied econometricians, Gorman had little real interest in pursuing applied empirical work. His attempts to operationalise the characteristics model on an ambitiously large scale using quarterly regional data on the consumption of over a hundred categories of food 1956–71 proved somewhat inconclusive (see Gorman 1976).

Yet the characteristics model has assumed an empirical life of its own:[14] far from egg or tomato markets, this insight now underpins the most widely used asset-pricing models in modern finance theory. After all, most financial assets are closely substitutable, and investors' choices between them are largely driven by their potential to deliver a relatively small number of yield characteristics. Whereas Markowitz (1959) asserted that investors were seeking to balance portfolio risk and return, measured by mean and variance, modern theories allow the goals of investors to be unmeasured characteristics of the stream of future returns. Market-clearing prices of the various assets must, in these theories, be adapted to the shadow prices of these characteristics in the market just as Gorman saw. Thus, such price processes are estimated by factor-analysis type methods (Campbell *et al.* 1997). Even the famous option pricing model of Black and Scholes (1972) and Merton (1973) appeals to precisely the same arbitrage logic so lucidly presented by Gorman more than fifteen years earlier.

Duality

Over and above his substantive contributions, a recurring them in Gorman's writings was the need to select the appropriate technical tools for the problem at hand. Typically, this meant using "dual" tools, functions defined over prices rather than quantities. Because households and firms typically take prices as given, it is much easier to understand their behaviour in terms of expenditure, cost and profit functions than in terms of the primal utility and production functions. The latter only take account of tastes and technology, the former add optimising behaviour. Gorman was not alone in advocating this approach, but he was one of its most ardent proponents. The great virtue of duality is that it avoids matrix inversion, which he called "the only technically difficult operation in general equilibrium theory". Even a cursory comparison between modern textbooks and Hicks's *Value and Capital* or Samuelson's *Foundations* shows how much more powerful are dual methods.

A nice example of the value of the dual approach was Gorman's contribution to the issue of household equivalence scales. Such scales, which attempt to correct consumption patterns for differences in household composition, had been used for years in applied budget studies, though without any theoretical foundation. Barten (1964) pioneered the exploration of such scales in the context of utility theory. But Barten used the primal approach, expressing utility as a function of consumption per "equivalent adult" where the scale which determines equivalence varies between commodities. Gorman (1976) argued that the insight of an "otherwise obtuse" schoolmaster he once had put it better: "When you have a wife and baby, a penny bun costs threepence." Leaving aside the banality (and, to a modern ear, the sexism) of the aphorism, Gorman noted that it gets to the heart of the issue: differences in household composition are better thought of as altering the effective prices which must be paid, rather than the effective number of consumers. This approach, implemented using the expenditure function, led to a substantial simplification and extension of Barten's results.[15]

Expenditure and profit functions are usually the appropriate tools. However, in some problems quantities may be the exogenous variables. In such cases the appropriate technical tool is the distance function, defined as the scalar by which an arbitrary consumption bundle must be multiplied to yield a target level of utility: $u[q/d(q,u^0)] = u^0$. This can be viewed as the natural inverse of the direct utility function. But it also turns out to bear a dual relationship to the expenditure function. Just as (by Shephard's Lemma) the price derivatives of the expenditure function equal the optimal quantities, so the quantity derivatives of the distance function equal the optimal shadow prices. Gorman developed this concept in full, independently of others. In Gorman (1965) he gave what appears to be the first statement of the duality between cost and distance functions, while in Gorman (1970) he examined the properties of the distance function in detail. These papers however remained unpublished, so modern treatments typically give precedence to Debreu (1951) and Malmquist (1953) and pass over Gorman's pioneering explorations.

Gorman's emphasis in all this was on the need for careful thought about which theoretical tools were appropriate for a particular problem. As he wrote in notes for a 1986 seminar in University College Dublin, doing economic theory "is like eating an apple pie. If you know there is one in the fridge, and where the light switches are, there is nothing to it. Look around when you next visit a strange house, in case you should feel hungry in the night."

Conclusion

Gorman (1953) wrote in his first paper: "In writing this article I have been torn between a desire for rigour and a desire for simplicity, and each has had to be sacrificed in part to the other." Even to today's technically trained economists, his writings seem characterised more by rigour than by simplicity. Yet his legacy, carried on in part by generations of students to whom he devoted so much of his time and attention, is a set of results and of tools which make it immeasurably easier for future economists "to tailor models for particular problems and particular data".

Notes

1 First published in the *Economic and Social Review*, Summer/Autumn, 2003, 34: 195–209.
2 Gorman always spoke fondly of the then Whately Professor in Trinity, George Duncan. In a late paper on the Le Chatelier Principle, which appeared in a *festschrift* for Ivor Pearce, Gorman wrote "I would like to praise George Duncan ... who introduced me to economics as an engine of thought, and who, in particular, taught me to expect the result that I will attempt to prove, and that in one of the first lectures of the first term of my first year in Trinity College Dublin." Gorman continued, with his characteristic bluntness, that Duncan was "[a] man in many ways like Ivor [Pearce] who might have become just as distinguished had he known more mathematics. He could not make head nor tail of the accelerator: but taught us about what have come to be known as Arrow–Debreu goods in one of his first lectures" (Gorman 1984: 1 and 16).
3 This result was independently obtained by Antonelli (1886) and Nataf (1953). However, taken together, Gorman (1953) and Gorman (1961), provide an explicit characterisation of the preferences which are consistent with exact aggregation.
4 Blackorby *et al.* (1978) appear to have been the first to refer to it as such.
5 See Neary (1997) for further discussion and references.
6 See Gorman (1959). Gorman had refereed Strotz's paper but (according to the account he gave to Blackorby and Shorrocks 1995: 31) his report, handwritten and covered with strawberry jam, was disregarded by the editor, Robert Solow!
7 More precisely, the condition is that the utility function must be expressible in one of the following three forms, where f is homogeneous of degree one:

   i $u = F(v1, v2)$ (the case where there are only two classes)
   ii $u = F[v1, f(v2,..., vn)]$ (all but one class can be grouped into a homogeneous function)
   iii $u = F[v1 + ... + vd + f(vd + 1, ..., vn)]$ (classes 1 to d and a homogeneous function grouping the remaining classes, all enter additively).

8 The weights are usually interpreted as subjective probabilities, an interpretation which Gorman found unhelpful: "Frequently they seem to me to obscure, rather than enlighten" (Gorman 1982: 215).
9 We often make the further simplification $f\,st(yst) = \delta s\,rt\,yst$, where δ is a probability and r a discount factor, but Gorman does not force such an interpretation.
10 That is, considers only its own consumption; this is what gives separability or independence in the additional dimension.
11 He was of course fully aware of the continuing controversy over the weak independence axiom for choice under uncertainty and the fact that it has been rejected by many empirical experiments.
12 Determined by the tangent of the consumer's indifference curve with the convex hull of the affordable combinations of the two characteristics.
13 The idea of hedonic indexes can indeed be traced back to Waugh (1928). Griliches (1961) advocated their use for the US CPI, and this suggestion was acted on from 1984. A recognition of more rapid and systematic quality change has led to increasingly widespread use of such price indices.
14 It has also been applied in a great variety of other fields, notably through the later work of Lancaster (1966).
15 Muellbauer (1974) independently rederived Barten's results using the dual approach.

References

Antonelli, G.B. (1886) *Sulla Teoria Matematica dell'Economia Politica*, Pisa; English translation in J.S. Chipman, L. Hurwicz, M.K. Richter and H.F. Sonnenschein (eds) (1971) *Preferences, Utility and Demand: A Minnesota Symposium*, New York: Harcourt Brace Jovanovich, pp. 333–360.

Barten, A.P. (1964) "Family composition, prices and expenditure patterns", in P.E. Hart, G. Mills and J.K. Whitaker (eds) *Econometric Analysis for National Economic Planning*, London: Butterworth.

Black, F. and Scholes, M. (1972) "The valuation of option contracts and a test of market efficiency", *Journal of Finance* 27: 399–418.

Blackorby, C.B. and Shorrocks, A.F. (1995) *Separability and Aggregation: Collected Works of W.M. Gorman, Volume 1*, Oxford: Clarendon Press.

Blackorby, C., Boyce, R. and Russell, R.R. (1978) "Estimation of demand systems generated by the Gorman polar form: a generalization of the S-branch utility tree", *Econometrica* 46: 345–363.

Blaug, M. (1986): *Who's Who in Economics: A Biographical Dictionary of Major Economists 1799–1986*, second edition, Sussex: Wheatsheaf Books.

Campbell, J.Y., Lo, A.W. and MacKinlay, A.C. (1997) *The Econometrics of Financial Markets*, Princeton, NJ: Princeton University Press.

Deaton, A.S. and Muellbauer, J. (1980): "An almost ideal demand system", *American Economic Review* 70: 312–326.

Debreu, G. (1951) "The coefficient of resource allocation", *Econometrica* 19: 273–292.

Gorman, W.M. (1953) "Community preference fields", *Econometrica* 21: 63–80.

Gorman, W.M. (1959) "Separable utility and aggregation", *Econometrica* 27: 469–481.

Gorman, W.M. (1961) "On a class of preference fields", *Metroeconomica* 13: 53–56.

Gorman, W.M. (1965) "Consumer budgets and price indices", unpublished typescript.

Gorman, W.M. (1968a) 'Measuring the quantities of fixed factors' in J.N. Wolfe (ed.) *Value, Capital and Growth: Papers in Honour of Sir John Hicks*, Edinburgh: Edinburgh University Press, pp. 141–172.

Gorman, W.M. (1968b) "The structure of utility functions", *Review of Economic Studies* 35: 367–390.

Gorman, W.M. (1970) "Quasi separable preferences, costs and technologies", paper read at Harvard University, November 1970.

Gorman, W.M. (1976) "Tricks with utility functions", in M.J. Artis and A.R. Nobay (eds) *Essays in Economic Analysis*, Cambridge: Cambridge University Press, pp. 211–243.

Gorman, W.M. (1980) "The demand for related goods: a possible procedure for analysing quality differentials in the egg market", *Review of Economic Studies* 47: 843–856.

Gorman, W.M. (1982) "Facing an uncertain future", Technical Report No. 359, Institute for Mathematical Studies in the Social Sciences, Stanford University.

Gorman, W.M. (1984) "Le Chatelier and general equilibrium", in A. Ingham and A. Ulph (eds) *Demand, Equilibrium and Trade: Essays in Honour of Ivor F. Pearce*, London: Macmillan, pp. 1–18.

Gorman, W.M. (1987) "Separability", in J. Eatwell, M. Milgate and P. Newman (eds) *The New Palgrave: A Dictionary of Economics*, Volume 4, London: Macmillan Press, pp. 305–311.

Griliches, Z. (1961) "Hedonic price indexes for automobiles: an econometric analysis of quality change", in *The Price Statistics of the Federal Government*, Report no. 3, General Series no. 73, New York: NBER, pp.173–96.

Lancaster, K. (1966) "A new approach to consumer theory", *Journal of Political Economy* 74.2: 132–157.

Malmquist, S. (1953) "Index numbers and indifference surfaces", *Trabajos de Estadistica* 4: 209–241.

Markowitz, H. (1959) *Portfolio Selection: Efficient Diversification of Investments*, New York: John Wiley.

Merton, R. (1973) "Rational theory of option pricing", *Bell Journal of Economics and Management Science* 4: 141–183.

Muellbauer, J. (1974) "Household composition, Engel curves and welfare comparisons between households: a duality approach", *European Economic Review* 5: 103–122.

Muellbauer, J. (1975) "Aggregation, income distribution and consumer demand", *Review of Economic Studies* 62: 525–543.

Nataf, A. (1953) "Sur des questions d'agrégation en économétrie", *Publications de l'Institut de Statistique de l'Université de Paris*, 2, Fasc. 4: 5–61.

Neary, J.P. (1997) "R.C. Geary's contributions to economic theory", in D. Conniffe (ed.) *Roy Geary, 1896–1983: Irish Statistician*, Dublin: Oak Tree Press and Economic and Social Research Institute, pp. 93–118.

Strotz, R.H. (1957) "The empirical implications of a utility tree", *Econometrica* 25: 269–280.

Waugh, F.W. (1928) "Quality factors influencing vegetable prices", *Journal of Farm Economics* 10: 185–196.

Part IV

Policy and economic development – shifting economic paradigms

14 Political economy – from nation building to stagnation

Graham Brownlow

Introduction

As part of his wider critique of long-run Irish economic performance, Joe Lee has claimed that Irish social scientists, including economists, have been much more proficient at theoretical and empirical imitation than innovation (Lee 1989; Conway 2006: 7). Lee's position has gained support amongst writers concerned with examining the history of sociology in Ireland. These authors have claimed that Irish sociology during the twentieth century was a theoretically derivative rather than innovative project (Conway 2006: 29). Likewise, Lee is not alone in his claim that Irish academic economists have lagged in terms of originality. Ronan Fanning went so far as to indeed claim that 'the winds of change in Irish economics blew vigorously in the corridors of the public service long before the faintest zephyr disturbed the tranquillity of the groves of academe' (Fanning 1984: 155). Ronan Fanning's narrative of a heroic and modernizing civil service triumphing over academic conservatism and ineptitude is inconsistent with more recent historical interpretation, however. Fourcade has demonstrated that internationally it was public or quasi-public agencies that often harboured the most mathematical forms of economic research before they became commonplace within academic economics (Fourcade 2009: 247). In the Irish case anyway Fanning exaggerated the civil service's receptivity to new economic ideas (Garvin 2004: 77). He also rather too conveniently ignored the fact that a 'hero' in his narrative, Roy Geary, had commented favourably on one of the 'villains' pioneering application of statistics to price theory (Duncan 1933–34).

Bryan Fanning's *The Quest for Modern Ireland* provides a detailed and balanced analysis of Irish intellectual life between 1912 and 1986 (Fanning 2008). This more recent research is an antidote to the oversimplifications of Joe Lee and Ronan Fanning. Bryan Fanning's book is concerned with a range of intellectual debates that it is claimed stimulated the transition to modern Ireland (Fanning 2008). While it is especially perceptive in terms of the interpretation of Irish sociology it provides, *The Quest for Modern Ireland* would have been even stronger if outlets such as the *Economic and Social Review*, *Irish Banking Review* and *Journal of the Statistical and Social Inquiry Society of Ireland* (*JSSISI*) had been considered in addition to the literary and socio-political outlets.[1]

Two contributions of Fanning's book to the study of Irish economics deserve special mention as they are topics returned to throughout this chapter. First, the intellectual portrait that Fanning paints of George O'Brien (1892–1973) is especially insightful. O'Brien's earlier nationalistic economic histories are not discussed by Fanning. It is clear however from the material presented within *The Quest for Modern Ireland* that O'Brien had by the 1940s a very different outlook on issues such as protection and unemployment than his earlier research implied. The importance of George O'Brien to key debates within the economics profession is a major feature of this chapter.

Fanning's second contribution derives from the respective chapters on *Christus Rex* and *Administration*. This material is especially valuable for the insights it provides on the relationship between the Church and academia and the rise of technocratic approaches to Irish social, political and economic development. In terms of academic economic debate within Ireland, until the first publication of the *Economic and Social Review* in 1969, the *JSSISI* and *Studies* were the main forums. There was an unmistakable focus in both major journals of providing case studies and discussing policy issues. However, each journal had a different emphasis. The *JSSISI* was the more statistically orientated of the two: *Studies*, which was launched in 1912, was in contrast the more comparative and it was also more closely associated with UCD. It was, and remains, published by the Jesuits and it was conceived as a review for UCD, which in 1909 had seen its control handed over from the Society of Jesus to the National University of Ireland (Fanning 2008: 67). Despite these religious origins, and in stark contrast to *Christus Rex*, *Studies* was not dominated by Catholic Church teaching when economic theory and policy came to be discussed.

The early national income calculations, as well as Duncan's work on the demand for wheat, can all be placed in the category of pioneering empirical work in the *JSSISI* (Duncan 1933–34, 1939–40, 1940–41).[2] My use of the word 'pioneering' is deliberate, as it is worth noting that Meade and Stone developed the first UK national income estimates while working from the Cabinet Office in 1941 (Fourcade 2009: 141). What is notable for understanding the policy impacts of academic economics is that it is quite common to find copies of papers in the *JSSISI*, or references to them, in the files of governmental departments (Daly 1997a: 42). Given such an influence, academics with free trade sympathies were rational not to publish articles on the folly of self-sufficiency. Potential patrons of academia would not have looked favourably on scholarly critiques of the then lynchpin of national economic strategy. In the case of the *JSSISI* the relative absence of discussion on protection may also have been influenced by law 16, the regulation which prohibited the Society from the discussion of topics connected with religion or party politics (Daly 1997b: 166). Within these constraints it was perhaps inevitable that Johnston's forceful critique of protectionism appeared in a book published in London rather than a journal published in Ireland (Johnston 1934b).

Intellectual traditions within Irish political economy, following R.D.C. Black's distinction, can be divided between the 'quantifiers' who have favoured mathematical and statistical methods and the more historically and philosophically inclined 'qualifiers' (Black 1985–86: 210). Black observed that during the twentieth century the Irish economics profession became ever more dominated by the quantifying style (Black 1985–86: 218). More recent research on the psychological, attitudinal and professional profile of economists in Ireland tends to confirm Black's observation (Lucey and Delaney 2007). It is clear that the trend identified by Black is a global one. By the early years of the new millennium the qualifying style, in Ireland as elsewhere, had been crowded out by 'scientific' quantifiers (Fourcade 2009).

Black elsewhere examined first, what the Irish had contributed to political economy in the period from 1800 to 1920; second, Black considered what political economy had contributed to Ireland during the same period (Black 1995: 3). In response to the first question, Black concluded that its economists were moving towards inductive and comparative methods at the same time as economists elsewhere were moving in the opposite direction (Black 1995: 12–13). Black's answer to the second question however was less clear and less simple. Economists attempted to improve Ireland, but whether they were well directed was not so clear (Black 1995: 14).

In this chapter I will provide answers to the same two questions for the period 1922 to 1992. Special attention is paid to the period 1922 to 1966 and the relationship between academic economics within Ireland and wider foreign and domestic social, political and intellectual developments that affected Irish economics. The focus in the first half of the chapter is on the development of academic economics in Ireland between 1922 and 1945. The chapter's second half is concerned with the impact of internationalization on Irish economics. Answers to Black's questions are provided in the chapter's conclusion. Fourcade's recent work on the history of economic thought in Britain, America and France between the 1890s and the 1990s suggests that 'Economics is always and everywhere a political endeavor' (Fourcade 2009: 125). Fourcade's thesis, that economic methods have political underpinnings and implications, will be shown in this chapter to find support in the Irish case. Furthermore, it will be argued that this assessment in turn has implications for answering Black's questions in the context of the twentieth century.

Nation building and economic thinking, 1922–45

Was Irish economics a pale replica?: The case of George O'Brien

We need not dwell too much on the relationship between macroeconomic policy and lacklustre performance in examining what political economy did for the Irish during the first three decades after independence. This topic has been covered well elsewhere (Ó Gráda 1997; Garvin 2004). Nation building in the first two decades after political independence was not associated with experimentation in policy or institutions. The second Banking Commission report for instance copied British financial practices rather than considering alternative blueprints (Coyne 1939: 22; Fanning 1984: 150). This propensity for imitation is all the more surprising when it is recalled that the ideology of revolution had urged the need for an autonomous banking system. The daily reality of governance, during the Great Depression, however encouraged institutional imitation. Examples of this 'pale replica' tendency have been recognized in other areas of Irish political and cultural life (Jacobsen 1994). Academic economists in Ireland, given the worldwide authority of British economics before the war, had good reasons to imitate. Irish academic economists during most of the twentieth century had close links with journalism, business and politics. In this regard Irish economics followed the practice identified in Britain in contrast to America or France (Fourcade 2009).

The direction of academic economic research in the British case was dominated by Cambridge, and to a lesser extent Oxford and London, for much of the twentieth century, but this domestic Oxbridge dominance waned as American economics came to dominate the global profession (Fourcade 2009). Within Irish economics, Dublin has consistently performed a similar intellectual function to Cambridge; unlike the British case it has retained its dominance. Within economics at TCD, an institution that has always consciously imitated Oxbridge, there were at least two economists during the inter-war period whose work was especially well regarded within elite British academic circles.

Joseph Johnston (1890–1972) had two papers published in the *Economic Journal* on the topic of Irish agriculture (Johnston 1934a, 1937).[3] Johnston's colleague George Duncan (1902–2005), who held the Whately Chair in Political Economy between 1934 and 1967, was the other figure especially respected within British academic circles.[4] Duncan was an economic advisor to the British Ministry of Production for two years during the Second World War. In addition to publication in Irish outlets, Duncan also published papers in the *Quarterly Journal of Economics* and the *Economic Journal* (Black 1995: xiii; Murphy 2006). A life-long supporter of the Austrian School and a member of the Mont Pelerin Society, Duncan promoted Mises and Hayek's work at a time when Keynesianism was becoming the dominant influence within academic economics (Murphy 2006).

However, Duncan's independence of thought, such as his rejection of protectionism and embracing of free markets, was partly responsible for reducing his own influence on policy formulation (Murphy 2006: 73). More generally the influence that TCD economists could have on the direction of Irish economic policy was reduced by the general stigma of Protestantism that surrounded the institution (Lee 1989: 163). In 1944, Archbishop McQuaid declared it a mortal sin for any Catholics in the Archdiocese of Dublin to attend TCD (Garvin 2004: 73). The effect of this decision was to herd the sons and daughters of the emergent Catholic upper middle class into UCD (Garvin 2004: 73).

Even if the organization of economic research consciously and unconsciously imitated the British model, the example of George O'Brien shows that Irish economists did not always slavishly follow trends in the UK. O'Brien was Professor of Political Economy and National Economics at UCD between 1926 and

1961.[5] His long, prominent and varied career in the academic and business life of the country as well as his role within UCD made him arguably Ireland's most influential economist of the first half of the twentieth century. O'Brien's wrote of Samuel Johnson that: 'In the course of his long life Dr. Johnson touched, at one time or another, on almost every topic, and, if his opinions are not always consistent, they are at least never uninteresting' (O'Brien 1925: 80).

The truth is that O'Brien's assessment of Dr Johnson could equally be applied to O'Brien's own academic career. Few economists in a two-year period (1940–41) could boast of being able to write equally erudite pieces in one journal (*Studies*) on topics as varied as a comparison between the Irish and New Zealand economies, Portuguese finances and the place of gold in the world economy.

O'Brien was a man of many parts. As in the case of eminent British economists, links with journalism and politics were part and parcel of O'Brien's distinguished career (Fourcade 2009). In addition to his academic responsibilities he was involved in politics via membership of the Irish Senate and he served on a range of government commissions as well as pursuing journalism and business ventures (Anonymous 1974; Meenan 1980). His first involvement in public affairs was in 1919, in the Irish Dominion League and forty-five years later he was still a representative of UCD in the Irish Senate (Meenan 1974: 17). O'Brien's influence was further increased by the fact that his circle of acquaintances and friends included most of the leading literary figures within the Ireland of his time (Black 1995: xv). It has been claimed that for many decades few people interested in Irish affairs visited Dublin without approaching him (Meenan 1974: 28). Thus, O'Brien rather than Johnston or Duncan was the pivotal figure in Irish economics during the first half of the twentieth century. His career demonstrates the relationship between Irish economics and wider intellectual, cultural and political developments.

O'Brien published four books on Irish economic history between 1918 and 1921. It is for these books, with their stridently nationalistic tone, that he is still best remembered (Johnson and Kennedy 1991: 13). O'Brien wrote little more on Irish economic history after the 1920s (Johnson and Kennedy 1991). In O'Brien's own words the books had 'served the purpose for which they were designed'. The books appear to have been designed to secure a chair at UCD rather than usher in a sustained research agenda (Meenan 1980: 187, 212; Johnson and Kennedy 1991: 12). Yet O'Brien was far from silent after the 1920s. The quantity and quality of his scholarly output was impressive by the publishing standards of the time.[6]

By the time O'Brien had obtained a UCD chair he had abandoned his earlier espousal of the ideas of Swift and Berkeley and had become an intimate of Patrick Hogan and a key economic advisor to Cumann na nGaedheal (Murphy 2005: 73). O'Brien's views were sometimes prone to change quickly. In 1923 as a member of the Fiscal Inquiry Commission (FIC) the previously great supporter of Irish protectionism transformed into a supporter of free trade (Johnson and Kennedy 1991: 13). W. Murphy claims that it was during deliberations of the

FIC that O'Brien underwent a 'conversion' to 'the economic truth of liberal economics' (Meenan 1980: 139–140; Murphy 2005: 73). O'Brien's partisan political association coloured contemporary attitudes towards his research and it arguably also influenced subsequent historical interpretation. His brand of liberal economics included at various times combinations of arguments associated with classical political economy, Marshall, Keynes and Hayek. It is therefore hard to categorize O'Brien's economic analysis beyond observing that it was consistently anti-socialist. As early as 1920, O'Brien already had expressed the view that socialist economic doctrines were 'essentially unhistorical' and subject to 'innumerable evils' (O'Brien 1920: 32).

O'Brien's hostility to socialist economic planning, and corresponding receptiveness to economic liberalism, however predated his public commitment to the virtues of free trade. Adopting a gymnastic rather than a religious metaphor, Johnson and Kennedy observed that O'Brien was not alone in performing such an 'intellectual somersault' on the issue of free trade. Government ministers such as Hogan and O'Higgins became free traders once in office having previously been advocates of protectionism (Johnson and Kennedy 1991: 14). O'Brien's opinions continued to evolve throughout his long and varied career. O'Brien's macroeconomic perspectives changed for instance in response to the Hayek–Robbins view of the business cycle being submerged in the Keynesian 'avalanche' (McCormick 1992). It is important to restate however that while O'Brien changed his mind on the merits of protectionism and the causes of unemployment, he consistently tended towards market solutions for contemporary economic problems albeit increasingly from an eclectic position.

Bryan Fanning has observed that O'Brien popularized the economics of both Keynes and Hayek (Fanning 2008: 150). In this sense, he formed a middle ground between Duncan's neo-Austrian economics and the emerging Keynesian outlook of younger Irish economists. O'Brien's ability to reconcile Hayek's and Keynes' shared liberalism in his critique of planning anticipates Skidelsky's recent attempt at such an intellectual reconciliation (Skidelsky 2006). It was O'Brien's liberalism inherited from Kettle, with its antipathy to state intervention, which explains in large part why he popularized both Hayek's and Keynes' alternatives to socialist economic planning.

O'Brien saw very little that was revolutionary in Keynesian economics. In his view, Keynes was a saviour of capitalism rather than a promoter of socialist alternatives (O'Brien 1946a: 193). O'Brien was not an advocate of permanent fine tuning. He equated demand management with the erection of temporary measures needed to 'stimulate and, if necessary, to supplement private consumption and private investment' rather than providing a justification for collectivist economics (O'Brien 1946a: 196). O'Brien opined that once unemployment was cured, by the expansion of demand, the benefits of the invisible hand would return and the temporary expedient of Keynesianism could be reversed. Hayek's intellectual appeal to O'Brien was that Hayek identified that the interventionism associated with Keynesian economics could involve potentially a sacrifice of liberty (Fanning 2008: 150).

Despite his undoubted propensity for intellectual somersaults, O'Brien was frequently a penetrating and original writer on a range of economic issues (Meenan 1980). For example, Venn praised the freshness of O'Brien's 1929 book on agricultural economics. Venn identified it as being different from contemporary British works on the subject because it balanced theoretical considerations with policy analysis (O'Brien 1929; Venn 1929: 421). While accepting Pigou's analysis of unemployment, O'Brien was not supportive of Pigou's style of presentation. O'Brien wrote that the Pigouvian 'bush is certainly teeming with good fruit, well worth picking, but painful to pick because the thorns are terrible' (O'Brien 1933a: 518). Similarly, it was the 'thorns' of abstraction in Joan Robinson's model of imperfect competition that drew O'Brien's attention rather than the 'fruit' of the analysis (O'Brien 1933b: 520). Mathematical formalism, but not statistics, was suspect in O'Brien's opinion because abstraction promoted a form of analysis devoid of realistic content (O'Brien 1933a, 1933b, 1942–43). O'Brien regarded the empirical evidence obtained from statistical techniques as contributing to better theories and he was ever eager for his students to be exposed to statistical techniques (O'Brien 1942–43: 6–11).[7] O'Brien stated that Marshallian theories, albeit refined with some continental touches, was the basis of 'orthodox' economics (O'Brien 1934, 1940–41: 2). His *Agricultural Economics*, with its emphasis on the scissors of supply and demand, certainly can be placed in this category (O'Brien 1929). Other academic economists tended to agree with this aspect of O'Brien's approach to economic methodology (O'Brien 1940–41: 26).

O'Brien's later views on the implications for economic analysis of historical specificity were however less influential methodologically. The significance of historical specificity was in O'Brien's opinion underestimated because of the desire of some economists to generate universally appropriate models. O'Brien contended in "Economic relativity" – his 1942 Presidential Address to the Statistical and Social Inquiry Society of Ireland (SSISI) – that the desired objective of universal applicability was not an achievable one and that every model was a product of the age in which it was conceived (O'Brien 1942–43). It may be argued that this line of reasoning reflects another aspect of his eclecticism.

He was confident enough to take some minority positions on theoretical as well as methodological issues. On the so-called 'calculation debate', for instance, O'Brien did not side with the widely held Lange–Lerner arguments on the feasibility of market socialism (O'Brien 1940–41: 11–21). O'Brien's main arguments against the feasibility of economic planning were not however based on the Austrian school's division of knowledge insight either. Instead, his argument focused on a more historical and institutional critique of socialist economics. He was particularly concerned that planning impaired the link between efforts and rewards and discouraged healthy rivalry (O'Brien 1948b: 251). O'Brien's eclecticism furthermore led him into some areas of economics that were novel by the standards of the time, but which had some connections with the teachings of classical economists. By way of illustration, a collective action rationale for government intervention in education can be discerned in the following comments from O'Brien:

...there is room for considerable investment in improving the quality of the populations of even the most developed countries ... investment in nurture and education tends to fall far short of the optimum, and there is a possibility of investing capital productively on these objects ... The fact that the nurture and education of children is one form of the investment of national savings has not been generally seen in the correct perspective, possibly because the investment takes the form mainly of the consumption of 'consumer's goods'.

(O'Brien 1940–41: 9)

These comments indicate that the private and social marginal benefits of educational provision were out of line. As in any collective action problem, the solution identified by O'Brien was to devise institutional arrangements that brought social and private benefits into alignment.

O'Brien's eclecticism and ability to anticipate later economic theories continued after 1945. The analysis contained in *The Phantom of Plenty*, O'Brien's last book, is a case in point (O'Brien 1948a). At the time of its publication it was dismissed as a 'résumé of the Neo-Malthusian point of view' (Peacock 1949: 175). This Malthusian element has shaped subsequent dismissive interpretations of the importance of *The Phantom of Plenty*. Meenan, while acknowledging the book's environmental themes, claimed that it anticipated only a little (Meenan 1980: 191). Yet with the benefit of hindsight, Meenan underestimated O'Brien's originality, however; the book is more eclectic than its reputation as a Malthusian manifesto implies. O'Brien for instance, provides a defence of inequality on the grounds that the luxuries of the rich will, as innovations permeate throughout society, eventually become the necessities of the poor (O'Brien 1948a: 66–70; Peacock 1949: 175). O'Brien here echoes Schumpeter's observation that the 'capitalist achievement' was to bring silk stockings 'within the reach of factory girls' (Schumpeter 1942: 67). Hayek later used a variant of this argument in his *Constitution of Liberty* (Hayek 1960: 44). Moreover, O'Brien also devoted a chapter to discussing how deindustrialization was associated with the failure of productivity growth in services to keep pace with the situation in manufacturing (O'Brien 1948a: 40–48). O'Brien attributed such structural imbalances to the lack of technical changes that could raise productivity in a range of service occupations (O'Brien 1948a: 44). O'Brien's recognition of the links between deindustrialization and productivity growth, and his discussion of the arts in this regard, anticipates by nearly two decades Baumol and Bowen's analysis of 'cost disease' (Baumol and Bowen 1966).

Irish economists on unemployment, money and cycles

Ronan Fanning stated that '... it is impossible to absolve university economists from Geary's charge of sulking in their tents clutching to the tenets of pre-Keynesian creeds' (Fanning 1984: 154). Fanning's assessment is not consistent with more recent research (Laidler 1999; Blaug 2003). This more recent research demonstrates that inter-war macroeconomics was diverse and that the line demarcating economics before and after the *General Theory* was a blurry rather than a clear one (Laidler 1999: 323). The IS–LM model rather than representing a fabled 'Keynesian Revolution', in which everything that had gone before was swept away, was actually fabricated from parts of what Ronan Fanning termed 'pre-Keynesian creeds' (Laidler 1999: 323–340).

Arguably Laidler's most important finding, for the purposes of this chapter, is his observation that, rather than derive unemployment impacts from models of the cycle, English economists often used Marshallian supply and demand analysis in their discussions of unemployment (Laidler 1999: 155). Irish economists in contrast held a wide range of opinions on the mechanics of the business cycle. While some Irish economists copied the approaches of Cambridge authors, others were more continental in their approach. At TCD, it was these Continental approaches to trade cycles that students were immersed in during their undergraduate studies (Black 1995: xii). Prior to the publication of the *General Theory*, O'Brien viewed the depression as the necessary corrective to the preceding boom (O'Brien 1933–34, 1934). John Colbert, who would later sit on the Banking Commission with O'Brien and Duncan, in contrast took a less overtly 'Hayekian' approach. He blamed cyclicality instead on the fluctuations in the stock exchange and his analysis also linked the cycle to technological progress (Colbert 1932–33). Colbert indicated that cyclical upswings generated technical improvements. Improvements in living standards hence were inextricably linked with the existence of the business cycle (Colbert 1932–33: 8). Such an innovation-based model of the cycle can arguably be traced back to the theories of Schumpeter, Wicksell and Robertson (Laidler 1999: 90–91).

In terms of studies of unemployment again a diversity of perspectives can be found. Johnston's investigation is the most original such paper. Johnston presented an informal model in which inefficient distribution, combined with excessive retail prices, tended to create unemployment as inadequate farm output resulted in a deficient demand for industrial goods (Johnston 1927). The paper is significant because Johnston can be interpreted as trying (albeit without recourse to a multiplier–accelerator type mechanism) to combine analysis of the cycle with that of unemployment.

The publication of the *General Theory* had the impact of diminishing the pluralism of Irish discussions of unemployment. Subsequent debates would focus on deficient demand as an explanation of unemployment. O'Brien's line of argument evolved along increasingly 'Keynesian' rather than 'Hayekian' lines. Writing in 1944, in support of the Beveridge report and the British White Paper on Employment Policy, he suggested that the two major theoretical contributions of the previous two decades were first, the demonstration that depression required expansionary fiscal policy and second, that full employment was not inevitable in an advanced economy (O'Brien 1944: 311). In his later writings he supported using demand management to secure full employment, but he was simultaneously critical of the effectiveness of more ambitious or activist forms of planning (O'Brien 1946a, 1948b). O'Brien argued that the advocates of interventionism failed to distinguish between what he regarded as the government's legitimate role in maintaining the volume of production and an overambitious and inappropriate desire to guide the direction of producers (O'Brien 1944: 312). His 'liberal' and characteristically eclectic interpretation of the *General Theory* was an interpretation not held by an emerging generation of economists. It was claimed by these younger economists that the Irish economy required extensive state planning as a policy response to the inadequate investment, which they held responsible for deficient aggregate demand (Lynch 1944–45: 439–440).[8] O'Brien in contrast saw a decline in Irish agricultural exports due to depression in the leading industrial countries as the primary mechanism linking Ireland with more developed economies. Accordingly he saw the success of demand management in Britain as the basis of maintaining low unemployment in Ireland (O'Brien 1944: 313). If capital expenditure was to be increased then O'Brien thought it should be spent on transforming the supply-side. Boosting agricultural productivity and tourism promotion were investments that O'Brien supported (O'Brien 1944: 314).

O'Brien's 'liberal' or eclectic Keynesianism, with its associated emphasis on the impact that a large degree of openness to international trade would have on reducing the feasibility of economic planning, would lose out to a more interventionist and optimistic interpretation of the potential that Keynesian fine tuning offered in Irish circumstances (Lynch 1944–45: 457). Returning to Black's questions from the start of the chapter, it should be clear that Irish economists made a greater contribution to economics than Ronan Fanning's comments indicate and that political nationalism rather than a well worked out economic strategy underpinned Irish protectionism.

From nation building to model building, 1945–66

Toolkits and formalism

The 'Keynesian revolution' in economic policymaking and the 'formalist revolution' were to have major implications for the direction that economics would take internationally in the post-war period (Weintraub 1999; Blaug 2003; Fourcade 2009). Morgan and Rutherford trace two stages in the evolution from interwar pluralism to post-war neoclassicism within American economics. In the first stage they note that objectivity came to be associated with the use of a scientific set of tools (Morgan and Rutherford 1998: 9). The second stage in the formalist revolution, as reflected in the 'measurement without theory' debate, involved a switch to greater abstraction (Morgan and Rutherford 1998: 10; Mirowski 2002).

The methods that can be placed in the early 'toolkit' category include cost–benefit analysis, agricultural economics and econometrics (Morgan and Rutherford 1998: 9). In the case of American economics, this toolkit approach was given a major spur by the experience of military and economic planning during the Second World War (Morgan and Rutherford 1998: 13; Mirowski 2002). During the Cold War a turn towards geometry, algebra and measurement (and the image of objectivity it presented) offered a defence to academics from political opposition to ideas that might have been regarded as radical if presented in the form of words (Morgan and Rutherford 1998: 15–17). In Ireland during the 1960s, similar outside pressures for political conformity existed and these tended to promote toolkit rather than literary forms of analysis. Yet even this toolkit form of economics would seem quaint by the 1990s.

In the inter-war period, as at the turn of the century, the proponents of mathematical economics and econometrics believed that successfully using mathematics meant hooking it onto the economic world (Morgan and Rutherford 1998; Weintraub 1999: 147; Mirowski 2002). As we shall see later, this was very much Roy Geary's methodological outlook; it was also an outlook similar to O'Brien's. Yet by mid-twentieth century, mathematical economics became a mechanism for expressing abstract general theories rather than a tool for investigating the economy. This later formalism was marked by 'an absolute preference for the form of an economic argument over its content' (Blaug 2003: 145). Hence at nearly the same time as economists found it opportune to favour the more widespread use of mathematical analysis, the scientific role of mathematics was itself loosening its links to the scientific (economic) world (Morgan and Rutherford 1998: 19; Weintraub 1999: 147).

Stagnation and Ireland in the formalist 'revolution'

The Second World War profoundly affected the economy because it closed off Ireland from international trade (Ó Gráda 1997: 47). The main consequence of the war on Irish economics was that it acted as a stimulus to official attempts at quantification (O'Brien 1946b). In contrast, to combatants, the Second World War did little to integrate economic research within formal policy making. It is notable that George Duncan acted as an economic advisor within the British rather than Irish civil service. The restoration of peace did little to end economic stagnation. Ireland grew by only 8 per cent between 1949 and 1956. The British figure for the same period was 21 per cent and the Western European figure was 40 per cent (Ó Nualláin 1958–59: 124). Net emigration reached levels unequalled since the 1880s as a consequence of this weak performance (Ó Gráda and O'Rourke 1996: 401). During the 1950s, in part due to the holiday visits of permanent emigrants, the public became much more aware than before of the substantial gap in living standards between Ireland and the UK (FitzGerald 1968: 11–12). Consequently in the 1950s concerns over living standards became the dominant theme within political debate (Fanning 1984: 138). Returning to Black's questions it may be posited that the main contribution of academic economics to Irish life between 1945 and 1966 was not primarily to the promotion of internationally recognized economic theory: the primary contribution of economists was instead to encourage the modernization of Irish society. This promotion of modernization had clear political implications and underpinnings.

Recent research indicates that within developed economies there was an extremely close relationship between the drive to planning and the drive to

measurement and formalization. The evidence suggests that the institutionaliza-
tion of economics within the state apparatus was the single greatest impetus to
formalization (Fourcade 2009: 247). Ireland was no exception to this relationship. The advocates of Irish government intervention indeed made much of the
fact that planning implied forecasting, and forecasting implied the existence of a
reliable econometric toolkit (Lynch 1953: 246, 1963). Roy Geary's contribution
to Irish economics needs to be understood as an example of the relationship
between formalization and planning. Geary, according to Spencer, held the
opinion that the 'only serious topic in economics' was concerned with supporting economic programming or planning (Spencer 1997: 38–39). He was furthermore one of the major supporters of Morgenstern's (ultimately unsuccessful)
attempt in 1953 to prevent the 'Bourbakist turn' in the Econometrics Society
(Mirowski 2002: 395).[9] It is notable that Geary's criticisms of the abstract drift
of *Econometrica* were so severe that around 1964 he was removed from the journal's council (Spencer 1997: 39).

The absence of academic discussants for the first econometric piece published
in the *JSSISI* is claimed by Ronan Fanning to demonstrate merely the intellectual
conservatism of academics relative to civil servants (Tintner 1948–49; Fanning
1984: 151–152). Yet in other countries it was civil servants rather than academic
economists that were vital in promoting planning and econometrics (Fourcade
2009).[10] Fanning conveniently ignores the fact that Duncan's empirical piece on
wheat predated Tintner's by a decade and a half (Duncan 1933–34). Moreover,
there is more to Tintner's paper and the identity of its discussants than Fanning
assumed. The paper's methodological content reflected Geary's desire to steer a
middle way between what Tintner described as the 'non-theoretical empiricism
of the statistical economists' and the 'non-empirical theorizing of some "pure"
economists' (Tintner 1948–49: 164; Geary 1962).[11] Geary's position was thus
certainly closer to the early toolkit rather than the later Cowles or Bourbaki
approach to mathematical economics. His hostility to excessive abstraction was
unarguably closer to O'Brien's methodological position than their very different
opinions on the merits of planning versus the market. Subsequent events would
indicate that although O'Brien 'lost' the methodological debate (as formalism
won the day), he posthumously 'won' the policy debate. Geary in contrast,
having initially prevailed on the issue of quantification, eventually lost both
debates as the Cowles–Bourbaki approach triumphed and planning was eventually abandoned. Applying Morgan and Rutherford's terminology, while Geary
successfully backed the first stage of the formalist revolution he unsuccessfully
opposed the second.

Morgan and Rutherford's explanations for the initial success, and subsequent transformation, of toolkit economics in America have a number of
other parallels in the Irish case. There has been some attempt to present the
creation of public enterprises and other elements of economic planning as
evidence that secularism and pragmatism were by the 1960s the order of the
day. As the then academic economist, and future prime minister, Garret
FitzGerald expressed it:

It is clear that in the 1950s and early 1960s the Irish people were instinctively pragmatic in their approach to problems, tending to reject ideological attitudes as divisive, and concerned to secure a consensus on important issues of policy ... This represented a very sharp change from earlier decades, when the country was deeply divided on matters of political ideology, if not social or economic ideology. It may well be that the depth of these earlier divisions, and their disruptive effect on Irish society for several decades, together with the fact that in retrospect many of the political issues that had divided people so deeply began to be seen as unreal, may have induced a positive reaction against the divisive effects of ideological commitments of any kind, encouraging instead a search for a consensus; in which the form of indicative economic planning adopted in Ireland could play an important role.

(FitzGerald 1968: 197–198)

However, FitzGerald's interpretation seems to be grounded more in wishful thinking than in the historical record. In the 1950s and 1960s public attitudes to partition, the Irish language, sexual behaviour, abortion and divorce were hardly 'instinctively pragmatic'.[12] Instead of a consensus there was a cultural 'fault line' running through Irish public opinion (Garvin 2004). A deeply dissatisfied educated minority had, even by the early 1960s, little influence on the direction of policy relative to a conservative majority (Garvin 2004: 256).

The existence of the cultural divide bred resentment within the universities and by the 1960s this resentment provided a fertile soil for a shift against conservative influences within Irish higher education and society. James Meenan had predicted this anti-clerical turn at the time of McQuaid's prohibition on Catholics attending TCD (Garvin 2004: 74). Garvin has claimed, with strong justification, that it was McQuaid's 'engineering of an intellectual takeover of the social sciences' at UCD that by the 1960s had 'handed over a young generation to liberal or socialist anti-clericals' (Garvin 2004: 259). Younger economists, especially those associated with UCD such as Alexis FitzGerald, Garret FitzGerald and Patrick Lynch, were unarguably part of this tendency. Irish economists were in this sense part of the liberal side of the cultural divide that increasingly characterized Irish intellectual life and political debate.

A contrast between the strong influences that the Roman Catholic Church exhibited over Irish sociology relative to the comparatively autonomous direction that academic economics took highlights issues of relevance to the study of Irish economics as well as the more general relationship that existed between religious and economic thought during the nineteenth and twentieth centuries.[13] Historians of economics have recently considered the rise and fall of Catholic economic thought within Europe. Catholic economics between the 1830s and the 1950s developed in response to church teaching (Almodovar and Teixeira 2008). Irish economics (outside of TCD), especially after political independence for the reasons discussed by Garvin, may have been expected to have been strongly influenced by this tendency (Garvin 2004). However, Catholic economic thought was to some extent marginalized within Ireland after independence. Following a literary metaphor, it was a case of the 'dog that did not bark'. There is no evidence of it being a significant force in the shaping of Irish economics between 1945 and 1966. Economic papers even within *Studies* were not merely exercises in the application of papal encyclicals to either economic theory or policy. *JSSISI* for its part kept Catholic economic thought out of its pages through the constitutional prohibition on discussion of political or religious topics within the journal.

The Banking Commission of the 1930s illustrates that Catholic economic thought, even if it had no support within academic economics, still was a political consideration for economic policy makers. The report contained an Appendix 15, co-authored by Bishop MacNeely and George O'Brien, on the impact of papal encyclicals on Irish monetary affairs; the existence of this appendix was political rather than scholarly in origin. O'Brien, who according to Meenan 'was not very interested in papal encyclicals', was probably only given the job in order to prevent Alfred O'Rahilly, who was at the time Professor of Mathematical Physics and Registrar of University College, Cork and who had left the Jesuits before ordination, writing the material on the relationship between papal encyclicals and banking (Meenan 1980: 138; Fanning 2008: 68). O'Rahilly –reflecting his far more hard-line religious views – wrote a minority report on the same topic as Bishop MacNeely and O'Brien. O'Rahilly's analysis was highly critical of what he regarded as an attempt to analyse Irish monetary conditions without sufficient reference to religious teaching. His somewhat alarming conclusion, which was in line with the virulent anti-socialist leanings of Catholic economic thought, was that 'if we silence Rome, Moscow will be heard' (Stationery Office 1938: 608).

Contemporaries between 1945 and 1966 were well aware of the place of economics in the wider cultural debate on Irish modernization. Black, writing in a symposium on *Economic Development*, was explicit in noting the tensions that existed between the need for economic modernization and what he termed 'the ideas of the past' that would block the social changes associated with such modernization (Ó Nualláin 1958–59: 123–124). In the same symposium, Lynch observed that it was the young that were most enthusiastic about what many of them interpreted as a focus on planning within the Whitaker's report (Ó Nualláin 1958–59: 146). It should be noted that Whitaker was himself far less convinced of the merits of economic planning and formal techniques than most of these younger economists (Brownlow 2009).

Hence the trend towards toolkit economics may have been consolidated in part by the cultural divide. Economic planning was an especially appealing option for younger economists wanting to secure and preserve the autonomy of economics from religious and political interference. It is notable that the presentation of the programmes in terms of technical material, such as input–output tables and linear programming, had the result of ensuring that the public debate on the purpose and function of planning was minimal (FitzGerald 1968: 198). Planning deliberately placed the allocation of resources in the hands of economists rather than political or religious leaders (Lynch 1963; FitzGerald 1968: 204).[14] In the next section of this chapter a more detailed focus is placed on the changing fortunes of economic planning.

The rise and fall of economic planning

Ó Gráda assessing the experiments in economic planning between the 1950s and the 1980s concludes that they had decidedly patchy results (Ó Gráda 1997: 78–79). Overall the lessons that he drew from these experiments were similar to the predictions made by O'Brien in the 1940s. Ó Gráda observed that the creation and implementation of comprehensive medium-term growth targets for a small open economy was at best a complicated exercise (Ó Gráda 1997: 78–79). The turning point in the post-war development of planning is usually taken to be the 1958 publication by the Department of Finance of the official 'grey' paper *Economic Development* and the (*First*) *Programme for Economic Expansion* the white paper, which covered the period 1958–63, that followed it (Lee 1989: 344; Ó Gráda 1997: 74). Lee, typical of most political historians, has described these documents as 'historic' (Lee 1989: 344).

I have elsewhere provided a more sceptical account of the place of *Economic Development* within Irish economic thinking (Brownlow 2002: 312–354, 2009). I have argued specifically that the 'big bang' accounts of political historians exaggerate the importance of the documents as well as misrepresenting the contents. In spite of the claims by some historians to the contrary, *Economic Development* is no Keynesian document either. Whitaker presented West Germany's social market policies rather than demand management as the preferred policy model (Brownlow 2002: 334). Whitaker's views on Keynesianism were in any case not the same as Patrick Lynch's. It is moreover notable that neither *Economic Development* nor the *First Programme* advocated a combination of demand management and supply-side interventionism (Brownlow 2009).[15]

The focus here will instead be on the academic debate on the links between Keynesianism and economic planning during the 1950s and 1960s. The outcome of this debate continued to have ramifications until the eventual transformation into a much milder form of planning in the 1980s and 1990s. The *First Programme* was succeeded by the more detailed *Second* (1964–70) and the *Third* (1969–72) *Programmes*. These two later *Programmes* both failed to meet their targets. With hindsight it is notable that the Central Bank was critical of the potential macroeconomic impacts of the *Second Programme*'s proposals for public sector growth (Ó Gráda 1997: 76–78).

Bryan Fanning's discussion of *Administration*, the journal established as the 'intellectual house journal of the Irish public sector' in 1953, identifies T.K. Whitaker and Patrick Lynch as two of the three pivotal figures in civil service discussion on technocratic approaches to economic planning (Fanning 2008: 192).[16] Moreover, to be more specific, it was within the pages of *Administration* that Whitaker's *Economic Development* came to be venerated as a classic of Irish economic writing (Fanning 2008: 194). Whitaker's thesis that cultural change was a precondition for improved economic performance mutated into a mantra that a cultural change had precipitated the economic boom of the 1960s and that 1958 was the key date in modern Irish history (Fanning 2008: 197). However, a more nuanced interpretation would be that *Economic Development* was not nearly as modernizing a document as some of its most fervent cheerleaders would have us believe (Brownlow 2009).

Indeed prior to 1958, Whitaker was highly sceptical of both the aim of full employment and the use of planning as a means of attaining unemployment reduction. Whitaker, like O'Brien, considered that the high degree of openness to international trade was a vital consideration in the formulation of macroeconomic policy because a high level of openness undermined the applicability of the multiplier concept (Whitaker 1955–56: 197). Whitaker's critique of the multiplier has a number of components to it. However, his most radical dissent from this aspect of what was fast becoming the textbook Keynesian framework was his contention that under Ireland's economic circumstances any pump-priming based on the multiplier framework could promote contraction rather than expansion:

> Much of the new incomes [generated by an expansion] would be spent on imports – initially perhaps the greater part – and the process of generating incomes might cause such a serious upset in the balance of external payments – with loss of external resources or reduction in the exchange value of the currency – as to impair public confidence and negative (sic) the initial boost given by the increase in home investment.
>
> (Whitaker 1955–56: 197)

Whitaker and O'Brien's approach to macroeconomic policy fell out of favour in the 1960s. Yet the failure of the *Second* and *Third Programmes* (and the related macroeconomic problems of the 1980s associated with the debt and stagnation caused by failed expansions) necessitated a shift away from these interventionist and planning-based interpretations of Keynesianism. Irish economic policy by 1992 was closer to that advocated by O'Brien and Whitaker than the policy model advocated by Lynch and FitzGerald in the 1960s. Economic forces in Ireland, as elsewhere in the developed world, forced its politicians to attempt a predominantly market-led escape bid from stagnation. Returning once again to R.D.C. Black's questions, perhaps it was this retreat from planning that was the major contribution of economics to late twentieth century Ireland.

Irish economics and internationalization, 1945–92

Internationalization as a concept

Historically national traditions have existed within the economics profession. A large element in determining the existence and durability of these traditions has been the institutional structures within which economics has been researched.

Since the 1940s these national traditions have tended to evaporate. Yet there is some evidence that as late as the 1990s economists in Europe and North America still differed in certain respects in their approaches to economic research. However, authors proposing an internationalization thesis have suggested that even these differences have receded over time as institutions have converged towards an 'Americanized' model of research and teaching (Fourcade 2006). Recent comparative studies of 'European' and 'American' economics have demonstrated clearly that the earlier divergence has narrowed as the respective European professions have tended to absorb American practices (Backhouse 2000: 20; Fourcade 2009). A popular interpretation of this finding is that the convergence has created an 'internationalized' economics profession (Baumol 1995; Fourcade 2006). Coats noted that after 1945 internationalization implied that distinctive national ways of doing economics disappeared as academic training around the world came to share a common set of theories, methods and concepts (Coats 2000a). The resulting harmonization of economic knowledge led to a common set of empirical measures being adopted (Coats 2000a: 8).[17]

Harry Johnson's (1973) division of the economics profession into three distinct groups provides further insights into the process of internationalization. Johnson divided the profession into an international elite group at the top. This group had graduate school training from the 'best' places and pursued an active research career. The two other groups consisted of those with a research degree but without a publication agenda, and those without any research-orientated training. The first group were responsible for the dominance of econometrics and formal theory in the profession and were the international (though American-dominated) elite. Johnson claimed that in contrast to the homogeneity of research produced by members of the first group, the work undertaken by the second and third groups would reflect differences in national culture, university systems and research funding. The economists in these two 'lower' groups would be disproportionately applied and concerned with national, or local, economic problems.

Placing Ireland within internationalization

Coats identified a number of general features and trends in the post-1945 development of economics in Western Europe (Coats 2000b: 247–248). First, Coats noted that the number of professional economists grew after 1945; second, the number of economics students grew, so that both the supply and demand for academic economics increased; third, there was a switch away from the study of politics, sociology, history and philosophy amongst students of economics; fourth, there was a corresponding increase in the study of mathematical techniques and econometrics; and fifth, there was a switch towards increased emphasis on professional credentials, publications and professional society memberships (Coats 2000b: 247–248). Irish economics has conformed to the process of internationalization that Coats described.

In interpreting the effects of the internationalization process on Irish economics it is interesting to note that British economics has been viewed as a

'Mid-Atlantic' research model (Backhouse 2000). As with British economics, and more than was the case in continental Europe, North American Ph.D.s have done much since the 1960s to transform research and teaching in Ireland.[18] Coats highlighted that one important mechanism for internationalization has been the general phenomenon of a series of graduate students from a given country studying abroad at a particular foreign university noted for its 'cutting-edge' research. Coats observed that often these students have returned to their native land and spread their newfound knowledge. He noted that the relationship that existed between Yale and Greek students followed this pattern (Coats 2000a: 9).[19] Since the 1960s similar diffusion mechanisms have affected Irish economics. Most academic economists within Ireland have studied outside Ireland and the research cultures of these foreign institutions have in turn shaped the subsequent research programmes within Irish economics.[20]

Internationalization, the ERI/ESRI and the Ford Foundation

The 1960s were a turning point for higher education. University numbers grew from around 3,000 to 10,000 (exclusive of extra-mural students) between 1924 and 1962 and the total number in all categories of third-level education grew from 18,000 to 93,000 between 1964–65 and 1993–94 (O'Brien 1962: 23; Garvin 2004: 202). Rising student numbers reflected, and in turn further stimulated, a structural shift towards managerial and financial employment. Whitaker and other policy makers were eager in the wake of *Economic Development* for the universities to play a greater research role in policy making. Yet as a number of academic figures argued, the universities were too overstretched with teaching commitments to fulfil this role adequately (Ó Nualláin 1958–59: 121; Kennedy 1993: 226). Ó Nualláin, in a symposium on the Whitaker report, suggested that an 'Economic and Social Research Centre' be established to fill this gap by conducting research on important social and economic matters (Ó Nualláin 1958–59: 121).

The Economic Research Institute (ERI), which was established in 1960, was hence created to fill the research gap identified by Ó Nualláin. However, as the name suggests, the ERI was initially only concerned with economic issues in its research agenda. The scope was only broadened to include sociological matters when the government took over the major financing in 1966. The ERI was at this point renamed the Economic and Social Research Institute (ESRI) (Meenan 1980: 206). The ERI was formed in 1960 on the basis of a grant obtained from the Ford Foundation of $280,000, equivalent at the time to £IR100,000 (Whitaker 1986: 10). The lack of an organized research capability explains why for their part, senior economists were so eager to secure funding for a research centre.[21]

The Ford Foundation favoured a research model that promoted 'basic theories', albeit only of certain intellectual hues, being subjected to 'the acid test of verification' (Brady 2006; Goodwin 1998: 77). It was along these lines that the Britain's National Institute for Economic and Social Research (NIESR) was supported by the Ford Foundation between 1957 and 1962 (Backhouse 2000: 34). The NIESR had an emphasis on applying formal techniques to issues affecting the UK economy. The ERI faithfully copied this research model. The ERI/ ESRI was instrumental in applying the toolkit approach through the 1960s.[22] Furthermore, the Institute also pioneered the application of mathematical methods, such as operational research, to policy making (Kennedy 1993: 238). The ERI therefore provides a crucial example of how an American donor's preferences in large part were responsible for moving Irish economics in the direction of an internationalized research programme.

In the early 1960s there was no hope of securing senior staff at home because of a shortage of suitable candidates (Kennedy 1993: 229). Hence the Institute from its very inception was international in staffing; in its first five years it had no Irish research staff (Kennedy 1993: 231). C.E.V. Leser, a German econometrician employed at the ERI, was for instance an important pioneer in the development of quantitative economics within Ireland (Daly 1997b: 177). Another significant organizational aspect of the ERI/ESRI's role in promoting internationalization was that it was instrumental in bringing major international conferences to Dublin (Kennedy 1993: 238). Such conferences promoted internationalization by providing Irish-based economists with examples of 'best practice' from which they could learn.

In line with the Ford Foundation's wishes, and even after the government took over funding, the research programme at the ERI/ESRI came to be equated with the production of econometric forecasts based on Keynesian models as well as quantitative studies of microeconomic topics. This was exactly the kind of toolkit and planning research programme Geary had been advocating since the 1940s. Yet it was only in the 1960s that initially foreign and then domestic government financial sources could be found to support Geary's outlook. Furthermore, the Institute influenced further generations of researchers even after the experiment in planning was abandoned. Academics often started their career at the ESRI before moving into academia (Kennedy 1993: 230). However, by 1992 this ESRI research programme could be contrasted with the more abstract theoretical work being conducted within academia (especially at UCD and TCD). Toolkit economics was eclipsed in Ireland, as elsewhere, by the more formalistic approaches to economic research identified by Morgan and Rutherford.

Internationalization and Ireland's publication culture

Barrett and Lucey's empirical study is concerned with the journal article output of Irish-based economists between 1970 and 2001 (Barrett and Lucey 2003). Using EconLit data they suggested that output levels increased during the 1990s. Barrett and Lucey noted surprise at the extent to which Irish economists remained reliant on domestic journal outlets even in the 1990s. They noted however that this reliance declined over time (Barrett and Lucey 2003: 115–117). Further empirical evidence can be found in a paper based on three different quality-based rankings of the journal publishing record of Irish

Republic-based economists in the period 1990–2000 and 1995–2000. As in the first half of the twentieth century, economic research was found to be centralized in Dublin. Academics from UCD and TCD dominated in all three rankings (Coupé and Walsh 2003). For example, in terms of a ranking based on impact factors for 1990–2000 the four most influential scholars (from rank four to one) were M. Kelly (UCD), P. Honohan (TCD), J.P. Neary (UCD) and K.H. O'Rourke (TCD). For the same exercise for the period 1995 to 2000 the most influential scholars were D. O'Neill (Maynooth), P.R. Lane (TCD), J.P. Neary (UCD) and M. Kelly (UCD) (Coupé and Walsh 2003: 148–149).[23]

Applying Harry Johnson's insights, outlined earlier in the chapter, Ireland between the 1960s and the 1990s increasingly had a segment of the international elite within its boundaries. This predominately Dublin-based group were often focused on theoretical research. The remaining academics and some policy economists filled the two lower rungs. The theorists increasingly became drawn from Ph.D. programmes that focused on constructing abstract models rather than applying tools to actual economic problems. Similarly, Ireland has also contributed to producing the elite found in other countries. Scholars as eminent as Canice Prendergast, John Sutton and Peter Neary can be placed in this category.[24] To summarize, the brand of 'quantifying' research that came to dominate Irish economics by 1992 was a very different research programme than that which existed at the time of independence. Economic research being conducted in Irish universities in 1992 was also profoundly different compared to that being conducted in 1945; it was even different from the toolkit economics of the 1960s. The transition away from the age of 'qualifiers' was complete.

Conclusion

Following the questions Black posed for the nineteenth century this chapter has sought answers to the same questions applied to the twentieth. During the first seven decades of political independence the short answer to the two questions is that political economy had more effect on the Irish than the other way around. With some notable exceptions, such as Geary and Gorman, during the first seven decades of political independence the original technical contributions of Irish economists to the global profession were modest. Joe Lee's criticisms outlined at the start of the chapter apply to this aspect of Irish economic research.

Ireland's academic and policy economics developed in ways recognizable to historians of other developed economies (Fourcade 2009). This acceptance of mainstream currents was in clear contrast to the nineteenth century reaction against the mainstream that R.D.C. Black described (Black 1995). This chapter has also shown that Irish economics, as elsewhere, moved from an inter-war pluralism, as evidenced by O'Brien's eclecticism being able to co-exist along with Duncan's Austrianism and Johnston's free trade position, to a post-war neoclassical synthesis in which interventionism and toolkit economics had by the 1960s come to the fore. Factors specific to Irish circumstance, such as nation building and the reactions against economic stagnation and religious control over higher learning all contributed to the intellectual transition from 'qualifiers' towards 'quantifiers'. In addition factors shared with the rest of the developed world transformed the last vestiges of Irish economics into an 'Irish' economics. Between 1945 and 1992 the extent of internationalization was dramatic. Yet the story does not end there: between 1922 and 1945, academics were not always as conservative or unoriginal as they have sometimes been portrayed. However, the answers provided in response to Black's questions here imply that internationalization eroded any remaining faint intellectual distinctiveness while reinforcing the centralization of research within Dublin.

Economists were, contrary to the preferred self-image of some amongst their number, enthusiastic participants in Ireland's transition towards intellectual and socio-political modernity. Irish economics did not develop in isolation from wider cultural considerations; in this regard it was not very different from the experience in America, Britain and France (Fourcade 2009). The ineffective opposition of Irish economists to protection between the 1930s and 1950s is explicable in political terms. A major political contribution of Irish economists during the 1950s and 1960s was to provide intellectual ammunition for those who favoured moving independent Ireland in a more liberal direction. Indeed future research may well conclude that their greatest academic achievement was to ensure that economics within universities did not become dominated by overtly religious or nationalistic teaching and research agendas. The preservation of this academic autonomy was no mean feat given the socio-political environment that higher education operated in during much of the twentieth century.

Notes

1 Bryan Fanning's book devotes three chapters to analysis of the contents of *Studies* as well as one chapter each to a similar review of *The Crane Bag*, *The Bell*, *Christus Rex* and *Administration*. It is Fanning's contention that the journals taken together 'give a broad sense of the intellectual politics that played out in Ireland after independence' (Fanning 2008: 1).

2 It should be noted that Kiernan's pioneering national income calculation for the Irish Free State was published in the *Economic Journal* rather than *Studies* or the *JSSISI* (Kiernan 1933). Papers within *Studies* likewise considered the lessons that could be drawn from other agricultural economies (Coyne 1939; O'Brien 1940).

3 Johnston's later *Irish Agriculture in Transition* was also reviewed favourably in the same outlet (Johnston 1951; Blagburn 1952).

4 As was common in British economics of the time, both Johnston and Duncan studied classics prior to becoming academic economists. Indeed Johnston studied ancient history and archaeology at Oxford. While Duncan as a TCD undergraduate took firsts in both his degrees in Classics and Legal and Political Science (Murphy 2006: 72).

5 O'Brien was appointed Professor of the National Economics of Ireland in 1926. With the retirement of Father Tom Finlay in 1931, the previous holder of the Professorship in Political Economy, it was decided to merge the chairs. So from 1931 until his retirement, O'Brien was Professor of Political Economy and National Economics (Anonymous 1974; Meenan 1980).

6 Within *Studies* he was easily the most regular contributor of articles and book reviews on economic topics. For instance (excluding book reviews) between 1938 and 1948 there were thirty-nine pieces published in *Studies* that can be broadly classified as being about economic and social issues. Of those articles no less than twenty-two were written by O'Brien!

7 O'Brien made a point of keeping abreast of and communicating the latest developments in economic theory (O'Brien 1940–41; Meenan 1980). Some important new research findings were incorporated quickly into O'Brien's teaching. For instance, the *General Theory* was integrated into lectures within months of its publication; later the same was done with the *Theory of Games and Economic Behaviour* (Meenan 1980: 191). In addition, O'Brien's course on National Economics utilized statistical material prepared by John Hooper and Roy Geary (Meenan 1980: 181). The contents of O'Brien's papers therefore indicate that he was not opposed to either empiricism or new theoretical developments. However, he was averse to the kind of formalism, which after 1945 was increasingly divorced from economic reality.

8 Multiplier type arguments were also referred to as a justification for an interventionist type of Keynesianism. It was predicted for instance that electrification would have 'subsidiary by-products' in terms of employment creation (Lynch 1944–45: 441). It is noteworthy that T.K. Whitaker, in the same discussion, suggested that Keynesian models faced 'great practical and political difficulties' in being applied in Irish conditions (Lynch 1944–45: 447).

9 Bourbakism was a trend within post-war mathematics, originating in France, which stressed the formal elements of analysis. Set theory and topology were favoured approaches to building an axiomatic rather than an applied approach to the study of mathematics. In Mirowski's estimation it tended to 'conflate mathematical rigor with the search for rationality and truth' (Mirowski 2002: 394). Bourbakism was introduced into American economics in large part via the Cowles Commission. Within Cowles, Bourbakism encouraged the view that Walrasian general equilibrium could serve as a foundation for rigorous economic research (Mirowski 2002: 394; Fourcade 2009: 88).

10 Ronan Fanning is ignorant of the fact that any Irish economists critical of econometrics were in exemplary company. Keynes was famously sceptical at the emergence of econometrics (Keynes 1939; Fourcade 2009: 150).

11 This methodological criticism of formalism was a consistent theme throughout Geary's career. As late as 1981, in his Boyle lecture, Geary dismissed, along lines similar to Leontief, Worswick and Phelps-Brown, what he regarded as the excessive regard within mainstream economics for mathematical rigour to the detriment of relevance. He went so far to state that 'most papers in the best-known social science journals are derivative, trivial and incomprehensible' (Geary quoted by Kennedy in Black 1985–86: 224).

12 Biever's survey evidence, based on questionnaires taken in 1962, demonstrates that attitudes to the Catholic Church varied little by class or region of birth (Biever 1976). Over two-thirds of the sample endorsed the view that one could not go wrong following a priest's advice (Biever 1976: 270; Garvin 2004: 253). Yet whereas 88 per cent of respondents endorsed the view that the Catholic Church was the nation's greatest force for good, 83 per cent of those educated beyond the age of seventeen or eighteen disagreed (Garvin 2004: 256). Thus by the 1960s students and academics (particularly at UCD and TCD) were often far more liberal on socio-economic issues, and politically to the left, than the society in which they lived (Garvin 2004: 260). It was for instance within Dublin universities that Irish Anti-Apartheid Movement found leadership (Quinn 2005).

13 Conway and Bryan Fanning have observed that the Roman Catholic Church was essential to the direction that sociology as a discipline within Ireland took during the twentieth century (Conway 2006; Fanning 2008). In Conway's view the church con-

trolled the discipline not merely via academic appointments and promotions but also through the contents of textbooks (Conway 2006: 13). As Fanning has put it censorship within Irish sociology continued 'long after literary censorship and other forms of cultural isolationism became unfeasible' (Fanning 2008: 133). Patrick Lynch's and Garret FitzGerald's critiques of Irish sociologists' opposition to state interventionism becomes more explicable when set in the context of this wider cultural divide (Lynch 1965; Conway 2006: 18).

14 Moreover, formal tools, such as input–output modelling or linear programming, were easy to present as facilitating a modern quantifiable and scientific alternative to the 'very powerful demagogic pressures' associated with political ideology, religious teachings and economic nationalism (Lynch 1963: 150–158; FitzGerald 1968: 197, 204).

15 Even one of its most enthusiastic advocates acknowledges that the *First Programme* was ultimately characterized by a 'conservative philosophy' (FitzGerald 1968: 79). Furthermore, the most sustained attempt at formalizing *Economic Development* characterizes it as being based on an export-led growth model in which policy and foreign direct investment expand capacity (Fanning and Bradley 1981–82: 108).

16 The third pivotal figure identified by Fanning was Tom Barrington, the first Director-General of the Institute of Public Administration (IPA).

17 While the internationalization (or Americanization) thesis has commanded wide ascent among historians of economics, support is not universal (Mirowski 2006: 347–348). There is not room here to consider Mirowski's objections in detail, but it is sufficient to note that his argument that three separate schools of thought based at the University of Chicago, the Cowles Commission and at MIT/Harvard came to create post-war 'mainstream' neoclassical economics. Mirowski argues that over time the distinctiveness of these three groups waned as they started to trade graduate students with each other and to entertain similar analytical concerns (Mirowski 2006: 355–356). The global economics profession has been, according to Mirowski, shaped by an 'elite' subset of American economics rather than universities from across the United States.

18 As just one indicator of the influence of North American Ph.D.s on Irish academic economics consider that by the 1995 edition of O'Hagan's *Economy of Ireland* eight of the contributing fifteen authors either had (or were about to receive) Ph.D.s from American universities at the time of publication. Whereas half of these scholars had (or where about to receive) Ph.D.s from Harvard only two authors had a Ph.D. from an Irish university (O'Hagan 1995).

19 It is relevant to note that one of the key factors that stimulated the internationalization of Irish sociology was the absence of a postgraduate programme at UCD. Aspiring academic sociologists tended to study in America or the United Kingdom before returning to teach and research in Ireland. It is reasonable to suppose that these experiences of American and British training altered the subsequent research path that Irish sociology followed (Conway 2006: 19).

20 Indeed a survey of economists conducted in 2004 indicated that the majority view (55.3 per cent) among respondents was that it was desirable for economists within Ireland to have been trained outside of Ireland. A further 17 per cent regarded this exposure to outside training as being essential (Lucey and Delaney 2007: 846).

21 The Ford Foundation was the most generous private patron between the 1930s and the 1960s. Between 1953 and 1968 the Foundation granted a total of $95 million to individuals and institutions associated with economic research (Goodwin 1998: 77). The Foundation, reflecting the concerns of American business during the Cold War era, was keen to support research that offered politically feasible alternatives to communism. In practice this meant that support would be granted for an empirically based neoclassical research programme (Goodwin 1998: 77–78). By way of illustration, in Belgium, Dréze's influential Centre for Operations Research and Econometrics (CORE) formed in 1966 was established with a Foundation grant. James Buchanan's

and Ronald Coase's Thomas Jefferson Center for Studies in Political Economy at the University of Virginia in contrast failed to secure funding on the grounds that it represented a definite 'point of view' unlike the (more Keynesian and formalistic) Economics departments at Harvard or Yale (Brady 2006).

22 The ESRI for instance provided advice for the development of an input–output analysis of the economy in 1970 as part of the *Second Programme* (FitzGerald 1968: 71; Kennedy 1993: 239). The contribution of the ESRI to economic planning was important because while Roy Geary and the ESRI's C.E.V. Leser had advocated an input–output model as a basis for planning, other major figures within Irish economics such as Whitaker and Garret FitzGerald had been more suspicious of such techniques (Daly 1997b: 173–176).

23 Coupé and Walsh use three different ranking systems (Bauwens index method, impact factor method and Laband–Piette index method). Yet regardless of which method is used, academics based at TCD and UCD were dominant.

24 Brian Arthur, hailing from north of the border, is ahead of these scholars in terms of Google Scholar citations.

References

Almodovar, A. and Teixeira, P. (2008) 'The ascent and decline of Catholic economic thought, 1830–1950s', in B. Bateman and H.S. Banzhaf (eds) *Keeping Faith, Losing Faith: Religious Belief and Political Economy*, Annual Supplement, *History of Political Economy* 40: 62–88.

Anonymous (1974) 'Professor George O'Brien', *The Irish Banking Review*, March: 1.

Backhouse, R.E. (2000) 'Economics in Mid-Atlantic, 1945–95', in A.W.B. Coats (ed.) *The Development of Economics in Western Europe since 1945*, London: Routledge.

Barrett, A. and Lucey, B. (2003) 'An analysis of the journal article output of Irish-based economists, 1970 to 2001', *Economic and Social Review* 34(2): 109–143.

Baumol, W.J. (1995) 'What's different about European Economics?', *Kyklos* 48(2): 187–193.

Baumol, W.J. and Bowen, W.G. (1966) *Performing Arts: The Economic Dilemma*, New York: Twentieth Century Fund.

Biever, B.F. (1976) *Religion, Culture and Values: A Cross-cultural Analysis of Motivational Factors in Native Irish and American Irish Catholicism*, New York: Arno Press.

Black, R.D.C. (1985–86) 'Of quantity and quality', *Journal of the Statistical and Social Inquiry Society of Ireland* 25(3): 209–221.

Black, R.D.C. (1995) *Economic Theory and Policy in Context: The Selected Essays of R.D. Collison Black*, Aldershot: Edward Elgar.

Blagburn, C.H. (1952) 'Review of *Irish Agriculture in Transition*', *Economic Journal*, 62(247): 647–649.

Blaug, M. (2003) 'The formalist revolution of the 1950s', *Journal of the History of Economic Thought* 25(3): 145–156.

Brady, G.L. (2006) 'James Buchanan's run-in with the Ford Foundation', Online. Available at www.gmu.edu/jbc/fest/files/brady.htm (accessed 9 October 2006).

Brownlow, G.A. (2002) 'Institutional change and the two Irelands 1945–1990: an application of North's institutional economics', unpublished thesis, the Queen's University of Belfast.

Brownlow, G.A. (2009) 'Fabricating *Economic Development*', Paper presented at the conference *Politics, Economy and Society: Irish Developmentalism, 1958–2008*, 12 March 2009.

Coats, A.W.B. (2000a) 'Introduction', in A.W.B. Coats (ed.) *The Development of Economics in Western Europe Since 1945*, London: Routledge.

Coats, A.W.B. (2000b) 'Concluding reflections', in A.W.B. Coats (ed.) *The Development of Economics in Western Europe Since 1945*, London: Routledge.

Colbert, J.P. (1932–33) 'Capitalism and crises', *Journal of the Statistical and Social Inquiry Society of Ireland* 17: 1–9.

Conway, B. (2006) 'Foreigners, faith and fatherland: the historical origins, development and present status of Irish sociology', *Sociological Origins* 5(1) (special supplement): 5–36.

Coupé, T. and Walsh, P. (2003) 'Quality based rankings of Irish economists', *Economic and Social Review* 34(2): 145–149.

Coyne, E.J. (1939) 'Contemporary New Zealand and its lessons for Ireland', *Studies* 28: 223–236.

Daly, M.E. (1997a) 'The society and its contribution to Ireland: past, present and future', *Journal of the Statistical and Social Inquiry Society of Ireland* 27(5): 33–45.

Daly, M.E. (1997b) *The Spirit of Earnest Inquiry: The Statistical and Social Inquiry Society of Ireland 1847–1997*, Dublin: Statistical and Social Inquiry Society of Ireland.

Duncan, G.A. (1933–34) 'The determination of demand curves in relation to wheat', *Journal of the Statistical Social Inquiry Society of Ireland* 15: 29–42.

Duncan, G.A. (1939–40) 'The social income of the Irish Free State', *Journal of the Statistical and Social Inquiry Society of Ireland* 16: 1–16.

Duncan, G.A. (1940–41) 'The social income of Eire 1938–40', *Journal of the Statistical and Social Inquiry Society of Ireland* 16: 140–41.

Fanning, B. (2008) *The Quest for Modern Ireland: the Battle of Ideas 1912–1986*, Dublin: Irish Academic Press.

Fanning, C. and Bradley, J. (1981–82) 'Twenty-five years of modelling the Irish economy – retrospect and prospect', *Journal of the Statistical and Social Inquiry Society of Ireland* 25(4): 107–131.

Fanning, R. (1984) 'Economists and governments: Ireland 1922–52', in A.E. Murphy (ed.) *Economists and the Irish Economy: from the Eighteenth Century to the Present Day*, Dublin: Irish Academic Press.

FitzGerald, G. (1968) *Planning in Ireland*, Dublin: Institute of Public Administration.

Fourcade, M. (2006) 'The construction of a global profession: the transnationalization of economics', *American Journal of Sociology* 112(1): 145–94.

Fourcade, M. (2009) *Economists and Societies: Discipline and Profession in the United States, Britain and France*, Princeton, NJ: Princeton University Press.

Garvin, T. (2004) *Preventing the Future: Why Was Ireland so Poor for so Long?*, Dublin: Gill and Macmillan.

Geary, R.C. (1962) 'Commentary: a personal statement', in R.C. Geary (ed.) *Europe's Future in Figures*, Amsterdam: North-Holland.

Goodwin, C.D. (1998) 'The patrons of economics in a time of transformation', *History of Political Economy* 30(4): 53–81.

Hayek, F.A. (1960) *The Constitution of Liberty*, Chicago: University of Chicago Press.

Jacobsen, J.K. (1994) *Chasing Progress in the Irish Republic: Ideology, Democracy and Dependent Development*, Cambridge: Cambridge University Press.

Johnson, D.S. and Kennedy, L. (1991) 'Nationalist historiography and the decline of the Irish economy: George O'Brien revisited', in S. Hutton and P. Stewart (eds) *Ireland's Histories: Aspects of State, Society and Ideology*, London: Routledge.

Johnson, H. (1973) 'National styles in economic research: the United States, the United Kingdom, Canada and various European countries', *Daedalus* 102(2): 65–74.

Johnston, J. (1927) 'Some causes and consequences of distributive waste', *Journal of the Statistical and Social Inquiry Society of Ireland* 15: 353–383.

Johnston, J. (1934a) 'The purchasing power of Irish Free State farmers in 1933', *Economic Journal* 44(175): 453–459.

Johnston, J. (1934b) *The Nemesis of Economic Nationalism*, London: King.

Johnston, J. (1937) 'Price ratios in recent agricultural experience', *Economic Journal* 47(188): 680–685.

Johnston, J. (1951) *Irish Agriculture in Transition*, Oxford: Basil Blackwell.

Kennedy, K.A. (1993) 'R.C. Geary and the ESRI', *The Economic and Social Review* 24(3): 225–245.

Keynes, J.M. (1939) 'Professor Tinbergen's method', *Economic Journal* 49(195): 558–577.

Kiernan, T.J. (1933) 'The national income of the population of the Irish Free State in 1926', *Economic Journal* 43: 74–87.

Laidler, D. (1999) *Fabricating the Keynesian Revolution: Studies of the Inter-war Literature on Money, the Cycle and Unemployment*, Cambridge: Cambridge University Press.

Lee, J. (1989) *Ireland 1912–1985: Politics and Society*, Cambridge: Cambridge University Press.

Lucey, B.M. and Delaney, L. (2007) 'A psychological, attitudinal and professional profile of Irish economists', *The Journal of Socio-Economics* 36: 841–855.

Lynch, P. (1953) 'The economist and public policy', *Studies* 42: 241–260.

Lynch, P. (1963) 'Escape from stagnation', *Studies* 52: 136–163.

Lynch, P. (1965) 'The sociologist in a planned economy', *Studies* 54: 31–40.

Lynch, P. with other discussants (1944–45) 'Discussion on the problem of full employment', *Journal of the Statistical and Social Inquiry Society of Ireland* 17: 438–460.

McCormick, B.J. (1992) *Hayek and the Keynesian Avalanche*, Hemel Hempstead: Harvester Wheatsheaf.

Meenan, J. (1974) 'George O'Brien 1892–1973', *Studies* 63: 17–28.

Meenan, J. (1980) *George O'Brien: a Biographical Memoir*, Dublin: Gill and Macmillan.

Mirowski, P. (2002) *Machine Dreams: Economics Becomes a Cyborg Science*, Cambridge: Cambridge University Press.

Mirowski, P. (2006) 'Twelve theses concerning the history of postwar neoclassical price theory', in *Agreement on Demand: Consumer Theory in the Twentieth Century*, Annual Supplement, *History of Political Economy* 38: 343–381.

Morgan, M.S. and Rutherford, M. (1998) 'American economics: the character of the transformation', in *From Interwar Pluralism to Postwar Neoclassicism*, Annual Supplement, *History of Political Economy* 30: 1–26.

Murphy, A. (2006) 'George Alexander Duncan, 1902–2005', *Quarterly Journal of Austrian Economics* 9(3): 71–74.

Murphy, W. (2005) 'Cogging Berkeley?: *The Querist* and the rhetoric of Fianna Fáil's economic policy', *Irish Economic and Social History* 32: 63–82.

O'Brien, G. (1920) *An Essay on Medieval Economic Teaching*, London: Longman.

O'Brien, G. (1925) 'Dr. Samuel Johnson as an economist', *Studies* 14: 80–101.

O'Brien, G. (1929) *Agricultural Economics*, London: Longmans.

O'Brien, G. (1933a) 'Review of *The Theory of Unemployment*', *Studies* 22: 518–519.

O'Brien, G (1933b) 'Review of *The Economics of Imperfect Competition*', *Studies* 22: 519–521.

O'Brien, G. (1933–34) 'Monetary policy and the depression', *Journal of the Statistical and Social Inquiry Society of Ireland* 17: 1–15.

O'Brien, G. (1934) 'Review article', *Studies* 23: 520–523.

O'Brien, G. (1940) 'New Zealand and Ireland: a parallel study', *Studies* 29: 623–628.

O'Brien, G. (1940–41) 'Some recent developments in economic theory', *Journal of the Statistical and Social Inquiry Society of Ireland* 16: 1–30.

O'Brien, G. (1942–43) 'Economic relativity', *Journal of the Statistical and Social Inquiry Society of Ireland* 17: 1–41.

O'Brien, G. (1944) 'Stability of employment: its possibility as a post-war aim', *Studies* 33: 305–315.

O'Brien, G. (1946a) 'John Maynard Keynes', *Studies* 35: 188–198.

O'Brien, G. (1946b) 'The impact of the war on the Irish economy', *Studies* 35: 25–39.

O'Brien, G. (1948a) *The Phantom of Plenty*, Dublin: Clonmore and Reynolds.

O'Brien, G. (1948b) 'Review of *Ordeal by Planning*, *Studies* 37: 249–252.

O'Brien, G. (1962) 'The economic progress of Ireland 1912–1962', *Studies* 41: 9–26.

Ó Gráda, C. (1997) *A Rocky Road: the Irish Economy since the 1920s*, Manchester: Manchester University Press.

Ó Grada, C. and O'Rourke, K. (1996) 'Irish economic growth, 1945–88', in N. Crafts and G. Toniolo (eds) *Economic Growth in Europe Since 1945*, Cambridge: Cambridge University Press.

O'Hagan, J.W. (ed.) (1995) *The Economy of Ireland: Policy and Performance of a Small European Country*, Dublin: Gill & MacMillan.

Ó Nualláin, L. with other discussants (1958–59) 'Symposium on *Economic Development*', *Journal of the Statistical and Social Inquiry Society of Ireland* 20(2): 112–148.

Peacock, A. (1949) 'Review of *The Phantom of Plenty*', *Economica* 16(62): 174–175.

Quinn, R. (2005) *Straight Left: A Journey in Politics*, Dublin: Hodder Headline.

Schumpeter, J.A. (1942) *Capitalism, Socialism and Democracy*, London: Unwin University Books.

Skidelsky, R. (2006) 'Hayek versus Keynes: the road to reconciliation', in E. Feser (ed.) *The Cambridge Companion to Hayek*, Cambridge: Cambridge University Press.

Spencer, J. (1997) 'R.C. Geary: his life and work', in Conliffe, D. (ed.) *Roy Geary, 1896–1983: Irish Statistician*, Dublin: Oak Tree Press.

Stationery Office (1938) *Commission of Inquiry Into Banking, Currency and Credit 1938 Reports*, Dublin: Stationery Office.

Tintner, G. (1948–49) 'Scope and methods of econometrics illustrated by applications to American agriculture', *Journal of the Statistical and Social Inquiry Society of Ireland* 18: 161–177.

Venn, J.A. (1929) 'Review of *Agricultural Economics*', *Economic Journal* 39(155): 420–422.

Weintraub, E.R. (1999) 'How should we write the history of twentieth-century economics?', *Oxford Review of Economic Policy* 15(4): 139–152.

Whitaker, T.K. (1955–56) 'Capital formation, saving and economic progress', *Journal of the Statistical and Social Inquiry Society of Ireland* 19: 184–210.

Whitaker, T.K. (1986) 'Economic Development, 1958–1985', in K.A. Kennedy (ed.) *Ireland in Transition: Economic and Social Change Since 1960*, Dublin: Mercier Press.

15 Learning lessons from Ireland's economic development

Frank Barry

Introduction

The 'conditional convergence' proposition of modern growth theory holds that, *other things being equal*, poorer countries can be expected to grow more rapidly than rich ones. In the mid-1980s however, Irish income per head remained at around two-thirds of the UK level, as had been the case as far back as 1913, so that little convergence had been achieved. A crucial question, then, concerns the precise meaning of the phrase 'other things being equal'. The extensive empirical literature on the issue draws attention to a number of factors, ranging from institutional capacity, trade orientation and the educational attainment levels of the population to labour-market structures and micro and macroeconomic policies. These issues are the focus of attention of the present paper, which seeks to understand the factors that facilitated the gradual improvement in Irish economic policymaking and the adoption of growth-enhancing policies.

Independence in 1922, though followed rapidly by a descent into civil war, brought with it the expectation of more rapid economic progress, though Charles Stuart Parnell, the great political leader of the late nineteenth century, had tried to temper these expectations, allegedly warning a roadside supporter that 'Ireland will be free, but you will still break stones'. Irish governments from the 1930s to the late 1950s adopted protectionist policies, though it can be seen in hindsight that the goal of achieving economic as well as political independence from Britain was much more successfully achieved under the later outward-oriented strategy.

The present paper focuses on Ireland's post-war development experience. It seeks to understand the process by which lessons were learnt from economic policy errors and institutions were developed to help rectify them and to insulate against the possibility of their arising again. Much of the paper is concerned then with systemic learning, whether in the political arena, at the level of the organisation or in the institutional sphere in which organisations interact. Given competing interests and varying leadership talents, however, it is not surprising that this process has rarely worked perfectly. It is hoped however that the paper might unearth insights of relevance to other states and regions attempting to replicate Ireland's rapid growth of the last two decades, which has seen it finally bridge the gap in income per head that had long separated it from the UK and the rest of Western Europe.

A brief overview of Irish post-war economic history

Ireland remained protectionist for about a decade after most of Western Europe had moved towards freer trade. The post-war boom of the 1950s saw Western Europe achieve growth rates of almost 6 per cent per annum while protectionist Ireland stagnated with a growth rate of less than 2 per cent, an employment growth rate of less than 1 per cent, and recurrent balance of payments crises precipitated by the need to import the more sophisticated capital and consumer goods that the country could not produce for itself. Over the course of the 1950s, more than 400,000 Irish people emigrated out of a population of less than three million.

Like the other traditionally poorer Western European countries of Greece, Spain and Portugal – the group collectively known as the EU 'cohesion countries' – Ireland moved to liberalise trade only over the course of the 1960s, culminating in the coming into force of a free trade agreement with the UK – Ireland's main trading partner – in 1966, followed by EU membership in 1973. The shifting balance of forces that delayed liberalisation and that ultimately saw it adopted will be analysed below.

Though the economy performed much more strongly in the 1960s, trade liberalisation was not by itself sufficient to unleash the forces that generate convergence. As Figure 15.1 shows, there would be little convergence on Western EU income per capita until the 1990s.[1]

Ó Gráda and O'Rourke (1996) provide a comprehensive analysis of the factors inhibiting convergence over this period, which Barry (2003) supplements by comparing Ireland's growth record to that of the other cohesion countries. Microeconomic policymaking remained deficient throughout the period (if not

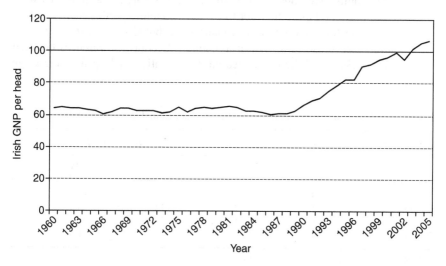

Figure 15.1 Irish GNP per head (PPS); EU15 = 100 (source: Eurostat AMECO database; Central Bank of Ireland Quarterly Bulletins for Irish GNP relative to GDP).

beyond); educational throughput remained far below Western European levels until the issue began to be addressed in the 1960s and 1970s (though it would take many more years for these reforms to impact on the educational attainment levels of the labour force); a malfunctioning labour market hindered convergence prospects for many years, and growth was severely impacted by the macroeconomic policy errors of the late 1970s and beyond.

Table 15.1 provides data that assist in tracking how Irish educational attainment levels caught up on those of the OECD over the last half-century. It is clear that Ireland was a long way behind the OECD average in the 1960s and it is only among the youngest age cohort shown that the country has now pulled clear of the OECD.

Prima facie evidence of labour-market malfunctioning over the decades is presented in Figure 15.2, which charts the gap between the Irish unemployment rate and the EU15 average.

Notwithstanding high unemployment, low productivity growth (by both EU15 and cohesion country standards) and continued emigration, Irish real wage growth and days lost to industrial relations disputes in the 1960s were both higher than in either of these other country groupings. Unsurprisingly, this was reflected in a relatively low investment-to-GDP ratio.

The Irish industrial relations system of the time was similar to that of pre-Thatcher Britain. As described by Hardiman (1994):

> Groups in the strongest bargaining position assumed a role of wage leadership, establishing the norm for the pay round which later entrants sought to emulate ... No single bargaining group believed it had to pay any attention to the impact of its activities on the overall state of economic performance. Yet the cumulative consequences of everyone's bargaining practices were proving more and more harmful to overall economic performance ... Divisions within the trade union movement contributed to the extent of wage inflation and the scale of industrial conflict. Sectional differences between skilled workers and the rest increased the potential for leap-frogging wage claims.

Table 15.1 Percentage of population classified by educational attainment, 2004

Age group	At least upper secondary		At least tertiary B	
	Ireland	OECD	Ireland	OECD
55–64	39	53	16	18
45–54	54	64	22	23
35–44	68	71	29	27
25–34	79	77	40	31

Source: OECD (2006).

Note
'At least Tertiary B' refers to occupational specialisations and university or professional equivalents.

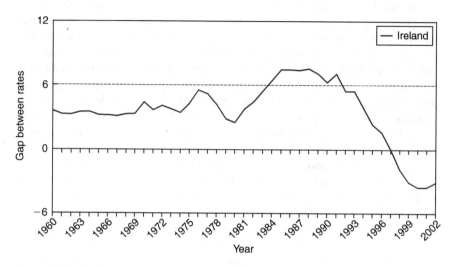

Figure 15.2 Gap between Irish and EU15 unemployment rates.

This conforms closely to the industrial relations structures that Calmfors and Driffill (1988) associate with the poorest macroeconomic outcomes.

The macroeconomic errors of the 1970s and 1980s further reduced the potential for real convergence. The cohesion countries found it particularly difficult to rein in macroeconomic policy in the wake of the oil shocks of the 1970s (as evidenced by substantial inflation differentials and fiscal deficits relative to the rest of Western Europe), while a surge in wage demands – though associated with the return to democracy in Greece, Spain and Portugal – also occurred in Ireland around this time.[2]

The first oil shock saw Ireland break the budgetary 'Golden Rule' against running a deficit on the government current account. Once broken, it proved difficult to re-establish. Even after the oil-induced recession had passed, fiscal policy remained expansionary, though it was by now strongly pro-cyclical, giving rise to the rapid real wage growth mentioned above.[3] With the jump in world interest rates in the early 1980s and a slowdown in the UK economy (the primary destination for Irish emigrants), Irish unemployment grew, debt-service and social welfare payments soared, and the debt ratio spiralled out of control. Government attempts at stabilisation through tax increases were thwarted as the tax burden fuelled wage demands, with knock-on effects on unemployment.

By the mid-1980s Ireland was in severe crisis. The unemployment rate stood at 17 per cent of the labour force and government debt rose to 120 per cent of GDP. No one at the time could have foreseen that a fortuitous combination of policy-induced changes and beneficial external shocks would create the conditions, within the space of a mere few years, for the economic dynamism of the 1990s and beyond.

Several developments that had been taking place in the background, such as the growing FDI-intensity of the economy and the accumulation of educated labour, proved important for the strength of the subsequent boom. The FDI orientation of the economy explains why the Single European Market had particularly beneficial effects for Ireland. MacSharry and White (2000) describe how several larger EU countries, in the pre-SEM era, 'had suggested to potential investors that publicly funded purchases of their products might be blacklisted if the new investment was located in Ireland' (rather than in the countries from which the threats emanated). Such non-tariff barriers could not, of course, have been used to equal effect by smaller economies such as Ireland. The outlawing of restrictive public procurement practices under the Single Market initiative therefore enhanced Ireland's well-established attractiveness as a destination for foreign direct investment. The increasing share of high-tech sectors in European manufacturing over the 1990s also helped, as did the high profits of the period, as both increase the attractiveness of a low corporation-tax environment.[4] MNCs, furthermore, would have found Ireland a much less attractive location in the 1990s were it not for the availability of skilled labour, whether already present in Ireland or 'latent' as in the case of emigrants prepared to return from abroad.[5]

Besides the Single Market, the other factors triggering the boom included the restoration of fiscal stability – associated with an enhancement of competitiveness – and a doubling in real terms in the scale of EU regional aid inflows from the late 1980s. How the fiscal consolidation was engineered, and the benefits of EU aid inflows maximised, are dealt with in detail below, as we turn now to discuss the processes by which certain political and economic problems were resolved at particular points in time, allowing newly emerging opportunities to be grasped.

Overcoming problems and availing of opportunities

The interlocking system of parliamentary, judiciary, press and civil-society scrutiny of government that characterises democratic electoral systems is clearly not sufficient to ensure that growth-enhancing economic policies are always adopted expeditiously. *Growth-inhibiting* policies can result, for example, from interest-group pressures, from outdated ideologies or as the outcome of a prisoner's dilemma imposed by the electoral system.[6] The task for democratic political systems is to develop institutions that help overcome these dilemmas and that prevent political parties from being locked into outdated ideologies or being unduly susceptible to adverse interest-group pressures. An efficient public-sector bureaucracy is necessary, furthermore, not just for the effective implementation of policy but also as a source of innovative policy proposals.

These are the themes of the present section of the paper, which considers the evolution of policy along seven broad dimensions which have surfaced as important in the brief outline of post-war economic history presented above. These are, in turn, the abandonment of protectionism, the development of the education system, correcting the malfunctioning of the labour market, overcoming fiscal instability, attracting foreign direct investment, maximising the benefits of EU regional aid and promoting microeconomic reform.

Abandoning protectionism

Marshall Aid was one of the driving forces behind post-war trade liberalisation in Europe, with recipient countries required to sign up to a code of liberalisation under the auspices of the OEEC (forerunner of the OECD). Only low-level pressures appear to have been exerted on Ireland, however, in that the Irish programme agreed under the Marshall Plan accepted protectionist measures to 'enable industries to gain a sound foothold in countries underdeveloped industrially' (Ó Gráda 1997: 49).

The ideological resistance to outward orientation resided mainly in the negative attitude of the dominant Fianna Fáil party to foreign ownership.[7] The drive to attract foreign capital was initiated by the non-Fianna Fáil coalition governments of the periods 1948–51 and 1954–57. The first coalition government established the Industrial Development Authority within the Department of Industry and Commerce in 1949 to initiate proposals for the creation of industries and to attract foreign industrialists. The second coalition granted the Authority the power to offer industrial grants in furtherance of this mandate. These had hitherto been employed only as a means of diverting new industrial activity to the less developed western regions of the country. It also took the crucial and imaginative step in 1956 of introducing Export Profits Tax Relief, the forerunner of Ireland's long-standing low corporation-tax regime. This triggered the entry of foreign corporations and helped reorient indigenous industry towards export markets.[8]

The Fianna Fáil party opposed many of these measures while in opposition but fully embraced them upon returning to power, as the policy shift implemented by the second coalition government began to bear fruit. Manufacturing employment grew from 1957 onwards, with the increase accounted for by new foreign firms adopting Ireland as an export platform into Europe. Manufactured exports expanded by 20 per cent in 1957 and by 100 per cent between 1956 and 1960, by which time the new export-oriented foreign firms established in the 1950s employed up to 3,000 people.

Many analysts date the shift in thinking on outward orientation to the report on *Economic Development* prepared in 1958 by T.K. Whitaker, the chief civil servant in the Department of Finance, which strongly influenced the government's *First Programme for Economic Expansion* published at around the same time. Whitaker himself, however, as quoted in Fanning (1978: 511), observes that Sweetman, the Finance Minister in the second coalition government, was singularly unfortunate in that his government was overthrown before the 'ideas which he implemented could bear fruit'. To the extent to which these ideas were focused on FDI they were timely. As Kennedy *et al.* (1988) note, attracting internationally mobile export industries would not have been possible in the inter-war period and outward orientation more generally would have been difficult to sustain in the protectionist world environment of the time. Hence the policy error to be focused upon is the decade-long delay in adopting outward-oriented policies, which caused Ireland to miss out on the general post-war boom.

The improvement in the conditions of industry influenced the overall assessment of the Committee on Industrial Organisation which had been established in 1961 and which reported on the prospects for individual industrial sectors under free trade conditions over the first five years of the 1960s. 'Public opinion', according to Fitzgerald (1968: 64), 'was struck by the conclusion of almost all these investigations that there was a viable industrial base, with individual inefficient firms rather than a series of industries incapable of withstanding competition'. As to how the resistance of groups who gained from protection was overcome, Fitzgerald (1968), in analysing the response to the 1957 publication of an OECD working party on the creation of a free trade area in Europe, writes that 'so rapidly were public attitudes on the issue reversed that those who had an interest in maintaining industrial protection ... found it impossible to resist this movement of opinion, and the proposal (that Ireland would join the proposed free trade area) met with surprisingly little serious opposition'.

We can see in outline, then, the constellation of factors that eventually promoted the reversal of protectionist policies. The very poor performance of the economy over the course of the 1950s would have weakened the political power of the protected industrial base and possibly even its commitment to protectionism. The change of government allowed new policy initiatives – particularly on attracting foreign industries – to be tried. This represented genuine policy innovation which would have had no guarantee of success. Its subsequent success facilitated a change in ideology on foreign ownership and, by stimulating growth, appeared to have reduced fears over the removal of protection.

It is important to bear in mind as well, however, the exogenous shock that the formation of the Common Market and the European Free Trade Association represented and which caused other similarly protectionist economies such as Portugal and Finland to move towards freer trade, even though their economic performances had been much stronger than Ireland's over the course of the 1950s. The attractions of Common Market membership would have been obvious to the powerful agricultural sector from an early stage and the tariff reductions of the early 1960s and the signing of the Anglo-Irish Free Trade Agreement in 1965 were advertised as stepping stones on the way to ultimate accession to the European Economic Community.

'Political cover' for the shift away from protectionism was provided by the government's publication of the *Economic Development* report alongside the *First Economic Programme*. By doing so, as Fitzgerald (1968) points out, 'the government made it clear that the Programme was not, and was not claimed to be, a policy prepared by the government party, but was a national programme, prepared by the head of the civil service'. This allowed it to be seen as transcending party politics. The growing interactions between government and external organisations and expertise were a further factor, though this element will loom larger in our account of developments in the sphere of education.

The development of education

Growing outward orientation in the 1960s was reflected in an increased desire to benchmark against international standards. The Irish government of the time, recognising that the changing occupational structure associated with the growth of manufacturing would place significant demands on education and training systems, volunteered to have its entire educational system surveyed by the OECD.[9] The subsequent report, *Investment in Education*, issued in 1965, made newspaper headlines when it reported that over half of Irish children left school at or before the age of thirteen, a far higher proportion than for most of Western Europe. 'Free' second-level education and free access to special transport networks for all second-level school pupils were introduced shortly thereafter. Thirty years later the numbers at school had trebled, with 80 per cent completing the full cycle (compared to only 20 per cent in 1965), while numbers at third-level had increased even more substantially – by a factor of six.

Over the period from 1965, as the third-level system expanded, the composition of the institutions comprising the system also changed. Seventy-five per cent of full-time third-level students in the mid-1960s were enrolled in universities, about 20 per cent were in teacher training colleges and other specialist institutions, and only 5 per cent were in vocational and technological education. By the late 1990s, universities accounted for a much lower 54 per cent share, while that of the broad vocational and technological sector had risen to 37 per cent. The subject areas in which third-level graduates received their qualifications had also shifted towards a more vocational and technological orientation.

The UK's early industrialisation had ensured the evolution of a well-developed system to provide an intermediate layer of technicians. It was recognised in Ireland that the education system would need to provide this intermediate layer from scratch if human resources were to be available to sustain the industrial expansion that followed in the wake of liberalisation. The main components of the technical-education system developed in Ireland over the course of the 1970s were the Regional Technical Colleges (RTCs). These offered programmes of shorter duration than those of the universities. There was also a limited range of subjects on offer – mostly in the fields of engineering and business studies – while curricula had a practical orientation designed to be responsive to the needs of local industry and business.

The Institutes of Technology (as the RTCs were later renamed) contribute hugely to the outcome whereby Ireland now surpasses the OECD in terms of the proportion of the cohort aged 25 to 34 with tertiary education, and has one of the highest proportions in the world of science and engineering graduates among this age group (European Commission 2003).[10] These outcomes, in turn, are largely responsible for the high ranking accorded to the Irish education system in the annual surveys of global executives carried out by the Swiss-based International Institute for Management Development and published as the *World Competitiveness Yearbook*. In the 2005 edition, for example, Ireland was ranked number two out of sixty OECD and medium-income developing countries in terms of how well the educational system meets the needs of a competitive economy, and number five in terms of how well university education meets these needs. The UK, by contrast, was ranked number thirty-six and thirty-eight respectively.[11]

The development and expansion of the Regional Technical Colleges owed something to the commitment to the system of senior civil servants in the Department of Education. Indeed, White (2001: 174), in his history of the Irish tertiary-level education system, suggests that a particular named senior civil servant was the main driving force behind the promotion of non-university higher education in the period from 1966 to 1980. Significantly, new policy initiatives are known globally to emerge from within best-practice public-sector bureaucracies.

Civil servants were also instrumental in the decision to apply for EU regional aid to fund the RTC system when a special European Social Fund provision was made in 1975 to facilitate the employment and geographical and professional mobility of young people. One of the applications, from the Irish Department of Education, covered training in middle-level technician skills in the newly established RTCs. By 1986 almost 90 per cent of all new entrants to full-time courses at the RTCs – i.e. about 20 per cent of those entering third-level education in Ireland – were in receipt of European Social Fund grants.[12]

Ireland remains somewhat unusual by developed-country standards in terms of the responsiveness of the education system to government policy objectives.[13] The Manpower Consultative Committee was established in 1978 to provide a channel of communication between the Industrial Development Authority (IDA) and the education system. The state agency, concerned by the looming disparity between electronics graduate outflows and its own demand projections, convinced the government to fund a massive expansion in educational capacity in these areas. The output of engineering graduates, as a result, increased by 40 per cent between 1978 and 1983, while the output from computer science increased tenfold over the same short period. The IDA in turn was able to use the rapidity of this response – exemplified by the immediate introduction of a range of one-year conversion courses to furnish science graduates with electronics qualifications – as a further selling point to foreign investors.

It is worthwhile to point out however that expanding educational throughput in an economy such as Ireland's – whose workers have easy access to labour markets abroad – will not be sufficient to stimulate growth. Indeed, a significant proportion of the return to Ireland's investment in education over the pre-boom period accrued to other economies. It was only with the turnaround in the Irish economy that the expansion in education and the availability of well-educated emigrant pools willing to return would have had their full potential effects realised, as has happened in the case of India also.

Resolving the malfunctioning of the labour market

Citing Olson, Calmfors and Driffill (1988) note that organised interests are most harmful when they are 'strong enough to cause major disruptions but not sufficiently encompassing to bear a significant fraction of the societal costs associated with pressing their own claims'. The UK under Mrs Thatcher moved towards a US-type system of wage determination while Ireland, influenced by the exposure of Irish trade union and business leaders to the models of consensus-based partnership in many European countries, moved in a corporatist direction (O'Donnell 2000).

The year of 1987 saw the introduction of pay determination via social partnership in Ireland, with government, unions and employers coming together every three years to chart a course for future wage increases. This corporatist structure stands in sharp contrast to the way pay rates had been determined in the 1960s and 1970s. In terms of the Calmfors–Driffill analysis, the new system meant that participants in the negotiations were now sufficiently encompassing to take into account the macroeconomic consequences of the pay deals struck.

In line with this analysis, Baccaro and Simoni (2007) find that social partnership changed the wage leadership process. Pre-1987 wage increases had been driven by the rapid productivity growth of the foreign-owned modern sector, while increases under the partnership process they find to have been driven by the much slower productivity growth of the largely indigenous traditional sector (at least until full employment was reached as the 'Celtic Tiger' era progressed).

The partnership process was influenced by ongoing change within the structure of the trade union movement (as well as by declining union membership). Crafts unions, which had played a major wage leadership role in the 1960s and which were amongst the most militant unions, accounted for a steadily declining proportion of total membership, while a steady decline in the number of unions reduced the potential for conflict between unions which had been a characteristic of the unsettled industrial relations environment of earlier periods. The process of negotiating the partnership agreements, furthermore, has been argued to have promoted a shared understanding of how the economy functions and of the appropriate response to different economic shocks.

The role of partnership in ensuring industrial peace and maintaining competitiveness is contested. Days lost to industrial relations disputes fell all across Europe over the same period. Alternative analyses hold that wage pressures in Ireland were bound to moderate as pay rates converged on UK levels and that the income tax reductions implemented since the late 1980s would have further moderated wage demands.[14] Partnership was critical in its early phase at least, however, in providing a channel of communication through which wage moderation could be purchased by government through the promise of future tax reductions. It also provided a forum for the advance involvement of private-sector stakeholders in the decision-making process. Thus it is difficult to conceive of a case such as that witnessed in France in 2006 – where the government was forced to withdraw its proposed labour-market reforms in the face of widespread outrage – arising in Ireland. It must be recognised on the other hand, however, that the much higher union coverage of public sector workers, in combination with partnership, may impart a degree of sclerosis to the economy.

Overcoming fiscal instability

A number of factors serve to produce a deficit bias on the part of governments. These include a failure on the part of voters to understand the intertemporal budget constraint, asymmetries in the cost/benefit spread of spending programmes, electoral cycles, and inefficiencies caused by self-interested stakeholders such as bureaucrats or politicians who wish to secure bigger budgets and avoid budget cuts, however necessary.

Similar considerations led to the choice of tax increases over expenditure cuts as successive governments in the early to mid 1980s wrestled with the spiralling government debt problem. Patrick Honohan (1988), who was an economic adviser to government at that time, notes that 'it was immediate political pressures rather than any intellectual argument that resulted in the choice falling on tax increases rather than spending reductions. In short, it was the familiar consideration that expenditure cuts tend to hit particular identifiable interest groups, while tax increases can be spread more thinly across society.'

Even when it became obvious that tax increases were not effective in bringing the crisis under control, political wrangling prevented the implementation of expenditure reductions, since trenchant opposition criticism encouraged the defection of government coalition partners or the withdrawal of support for minority governments.[15] The newly developed social partnership process helped secure a way out of this prisoner's dilemma, as is acknowledged in the following account by Ray MacSharry, the Finance Minister who implemented the fiscal cutbacks of the 1987–89 period:

> In 1987, for the first time, a political consensus on fiscal policy was beginning to emerge to underpin the economic consensus already outlined in the NESC report *Strategy for Development 1986–1990*, which had been published the previous November. The NESC analysis of what was wrong and the prescription of what needed to be done was agreed by all the social partners – including employers, trade unions, farmers and others – without dissent. The NESC described the economic and social problems facing the country as 'extremely grave' and set debt stabilisation as a minimum objective of fiscal policy, while relying on public-spending cuts – not taxation – to achieve that adjustment. This was the most critical part of its overall strategy. The boldness of the NESC approach, the consensus of the social partners in backing it, and Fine Gael's generous promise of political support on fiscal policy all created a new opportunity to tackle, finally, the public finances.[16]

> (MacSharry and White 2000: 62)

In theory, the Maastricht criteria and the Stability and Growth Pact can offer political cover which can help keep fiscal crises at bay. This has not always been availed of however. Irish fiscal policy has remained stubbornly procyclical, as Lane (1998) has shown. The antagonistic response of then Finance

Minister Charlie McCreevy to Ecofin's (2001) criticism of this aspect of Irish fiscal policy represented a lost opportunity to employ external fiscal commitments to best advantage.

Attracting foreign direct investment

As mentioned earlier, the success of the Export Profits Tax Relief measure introduced by a short-lived alternative government in the mid 1950s helped shift Fianna Fáil, the dominant political party, away from its hostility to foreign-owned industry. The distinguishing feature of Ireland's development strategy since then has been the emphasis placed on FDI. The FDI strategy having been stumbled upon, it turned out with hindsight to accord well with Ireland's advantages: its Atlantic location and English-speaking environment, relatively low labour costs by Western European standards, cultural connections with the US, and a reasonably corruption-free business and public-administration environment. The country had been remarkably successful in attracting FDI even before the Celtic Tiger era, and is now by far the most FDI-intensive economy in Europe, as seen in Table 15.2.[17]

The long-running nature of this FDI orientation and the resulting FDI-intensity of the economy have encouraged the co-evolution of the country's institutional structure to ensure a rapid and flexible response to changes in the characteristics of global FDI flows. In the late 1980s, for example, it was noticed that factors such as global deregulation of financial services and the emergence of an electronic marketplace resulting from telecommunications developments had created an opportunity for a regional location like Ireland to become a player in the international financial services industry. Focused government policies since then have seen Ireland's International Financial Services sector become one of Europe's leading off-shore financial centres. Another example of diligent response is seen in the massive increase in the funding of science, technology and innovation policy over the 2000–06 period, in line with the global trend towards the offshoring of R&D functions by MNCs.

Table 15.2 Comparative FDI-intensity of the Irish economy

	Share of foreign affiliates in manufacturing employment	*Share of foreign affiliates in services employment*	*FDI inward stock (US$) per head of population (2004)*
Ireland	49	22	57,372
EU15	23	10	9,796
CEE	33	16	2,403

Notes
Affiliate employment shares (2002 or closest date) come from OECD (2005, tables E6 and E7). CEE refers to the country average for Hungary, Poland and the Czech Republic. FDI Inward Stock data come from the UNCTAD (2005).

The importance of FDI in the Irish economy has given the Industrial Development Agency enormous clout within the public-service bureaucracy and the agency is widely regarded internationally as exemplary of best practice in the field. An important element of governance in the agency's operations is that it is subject to frequent external reviews, which have led to substantial changes in structures and procedures in the 1960s, the 1980s and the 1990s. The IDA is facilitated in continuously adapting to changing Irish circumstances and global business trends by its 'transnational strategic network': its overseas offices and its links with investors already in Ireland. These provide information about trends in targeted sectors and about newly emerging sectors that warrant the agency's attention. The resulting feedback to headquarters not only influences the industries or subsectors targeted by the IDA but also guides efforts to inform and persuade the government about required legislative changes, necessary additions to infrastructure, and specific training programmes required.

The development agencies (Forfás, IDA-Ireland and Enterprise Ireland), furthermore, through the strong position they have attained in the policymaking hierarchy, have had an impact in areas not traditionally recognised as lying within the industrial promotion remit. They played a major role, for example, in forcing through the modernisation of the country's telecommunications infrastructure in the late 1970s and early 1980s and in the development and upgrading of the human capital necessary to facilitate the country in ascending the ladder of comparative advantage. They were also instrumental in convincing government to reduce the rate of corporation tax on services at a time when services offshoring was emerging as a global phenomenon, and pushing for the massive increase in government spending on R&D seen in the National Development Plan 2000–06 and beyond.[18]

It is interesting to note that the allegations of corruption investigated by the various tribunals and inquiries of recent times have been confined to sectors such as property, retail banking, beef and domestic telecommunications, and have not included any of the sectors dominated by export-oriented foreign MNCs. The importance of FDI to the economy may have helped ensure that the latter sectors have remained rigorously insulated from corruption.

Maximising the benefits of EU regional aid

Ireland devoted a substantially higher share of its EU regional aid inflows to human capital development than did the other cohesion economies. This was largely influenced by the successful targeting of its much lower pre-1989 aid funds to develop the non-university third-level sector, as detailed earlier. Another element entering the mix however was the highly centralised nature of the Irish decision-making process. EU agreement had been secured to have Ireland treated as a single region for EU regional aid purposes, while decisions in the other cohesion countries were much more influenced by representations made at the regional level. Sub-national governments have tended to prioritise spending on roads and other 'hard infrastructure', possibly because human capital is perceived to be highly mobile between regions. Though many criticisms have been raised about the centralised nature of Irish decision making, central control – in this case at least – appeared to facilitate the capture of externalities that might have been ignored by sub-national authorities (Oates 1999).

The fact that the EU regional aid process requires agreement between Brussels and the national authorities on spending priorities (to the extent that they are co-funded) also served to reduce the extent to which domestic political considerations and interest-group pressures could adversely affect outcomes.[19]

Another beneficial institutional outcome of the EU regional aid process is the embedding of monitoring and evaluation procedures within the national public-service bureaucracy. As FitzGerald (1998) notes:

> the need to satisfy the donor countries, through the EU Commission, that their money is well spent has resulted in the introduction of a set of evaluation procedures which has helped change the way the administration approaches public expenditure. In the past the only question, once money had been voted by parliament, was whether it had been spent in accordance with regulations. Now there is increasing interest in assessing how effective the expenditure has been.

Microeconomic reform

It is in the area of microeconomic reform that the development of Irish policy has been poorest, though the country scores well in international rankings of the ease of doing business and freedom from red tape.[20] While the openness of the manufacturing sector leaves little room for anti-competitive practices, barriers to entry remain widespread in many services sectors. Furthermore, as Fingleton (1995) points out, progress in implementing competition in services has been driven more by European law and technological developments (which allow existing regulations to be bypassed) than by an explicit policy agenda.

The commercialisation of the telecommunications sector in the late 1970s and early 1980s, in which the IDA was instrumental in wresting control from a moribund government department, has been alluded to earlier. The most advanced European digital-based network outside of France was brought into operation shortly thereafter, allowing Ireland to capture a range of newly offshoring IT-enabled services sectors in which first-class international telecommunications were a key factor. The privatisation of the system in the late 1990s had very much poorer results, given the monopoly nature of the fixed-line telecommunications infrastructure. Government ministers have since accepted that this has been a factor in the subsequent slow roll-out of broadband access across the country.

The liberalisation of air access in the mid-1980s, which was associated with the birth of Ryanair, reduced air fares between Ireland and Britain by over 50 per cent in a short period of time, bringing down sea fares in its wake and providing a major stimulus to tourism.

The recent privatisation of the former state airline, Aer Lingus, however – as in the case of the telecomms privatisation – seems also to have had unanticipated and possibly undesirable results. In any case, it is clear that the implications of these two recent bouts of privatisation were not fully thought through.

Ireland also does poorly in terms of infrastructural provision. While ranking among the top quartile of the sixty or so countries assessed by the *World Competitiveness Yearbook* (IMD 2005) in terms of various competitiveness factors, including quality of governance, human capital development, infrastructure and technological environment, the international business community ranks Ireland only forty-seventh in terms of the extent to which the 'maintenance and development of infrastructure are adequately planned and financed'. In line with this, the May 2003 report of the National Roads Authority recorded that the cost of the national roads programme had escalated by over 50 per cent since 1999 while the expected completion date had shifted to 2010 – four years behind target. The fact that these issues are being addressed only at this late stage identifies a substantial weakness in this area of Irish governance.

It is in the area of urban and regional planning, however, that Irish decision making is at its worst. Year after year, reports surface of inadequate infrastructure – such as a lack of school places – in newly developed commuter areas. It is widely accepted today that the shelving of an important 1960s report on regional planning (the Buchanan Report) in response to localist pressures has had highly adverse consequences for the country as a whole. A mere couple of years after the 2002 publication of the much-vaunted National Spatial Strategy, however, the government announced a major programme of decentralisation of government departments to locations that were dictated by political considerations and that bore no relationship to the new spatial strategy.

A related problem also rooted in the realm of political economy concerns the land-rezoning mechanism for property development. Notwithstanding the levels of corruption in urban planning decisions exposed by recent Planning Tribunals and the fact that house-price inflation over the boom period has had a detrimental impact on national competitiveness, the status quo remains that the gains from the rezoning decisions of public officials are pocketed in their entirety by private-sector developers. It is to be hoped that the systemic learning seen in Ireland in the sphere of macroeconomic policy will someday extend to the microeconomic arena as well.

Conclusions

There is by now fairly widespread agreement on the range of factors and policies necessary to promote growth and economic convergence. These range from outward orientation, strong institutional capacity and an educated workforce to labour-market flexibility, macroeconomic stability and market-oriented productivity-enhancing microeconomic policies.[21]

While economic thought and economy policy have co-evolved worldwide to yield this intellectual consensus, it has been arrived at through an extensive process of trial and error at the level of individual economies. Much of the present paper has been concerned with charting the trials and errors that have character-ised the Irish experience. That the general consensus in the developed world had swung against protectionism by the 1950s is evident from the academic advice proffered to the Irish governments of the time (Bew and Patterson 1982). The political and ideological resistance took longer to overcome however.

The global consensus in favour of foreign direct investment has taken even longer to emerge. Indeed Markusen (2006) notes that it was only over the course of the 1980s that most developing countries reversed their traditionally hostile stance and began to compete actively for greenfield FDI. The experiences of Ireland and of some of the dynamic economies of East Asia have been influential in this general reversal of sentiment.

The Irish fiscal crisis of the 1980s and its ultimate resolution provide further food for thought in the matter of co-evolving theory and policy. Patrick Honohan (1988) notes how the pendulum swung away from naïve Keynesianism in offi-cial circles in the early 1980s in the wake of the budgetary and balance-or-payments crises wrought by excessive fiscal expansion. Unfortunately the macroeconomic perspective that displaced it contained its own flaws:

> One oversimplified view enjoyed an early vogue, and was, I believe, influen-tial in determining the course of policy between 1981 and 1984. According to this view the Government's overspending was closely matched by national overspending, as reflected in the balance of international payments, which had increased in line with the Government's borrowing. Accordingly the task facing the Government was a mechanical one with limited adverse con-sequences: if the Government's overspending could be reduced – by whatever means – the impact would be on national spending, and not on production. It was held by many that the expansion of the Government's deficit had created jobs abroad rather than at home. If so, then by an argument of symmetry, the elimination of that deficit need have little effect on jobs at home.
>
> There were (several) policy implications of this position. First, expendi-ture cuts involving public sector job losses should be avoided. After all, the theory stated that the needed financial adjustment could be accomplished without much adverse effect on overall employment, so why impose unnec-essary disruption? Second, since it takes time to identify with precision the sources of waste in Government spending programmes, the immediate need for balancing the budget could just as well be achieved by short-term increases in taxation while the waste was being rooted out.

As described earlier, it was only when this policy was reversed and expenditure cuts implemented that the country was extricated from fiscal crisis. The sub-sequent growth experiences of both Ireland and Denmark in the wake of the sharp fiscal contractions of the 1980s in turn led to a new and controversial aca-demic literature, triggered by Giavazzi and Pagano (1990), on the possibility of 'expansionary fiscal contraction'.

Given the fairly widespread international consensus on long-term growth-enhancing policies, however, the question remains as to why it proves so difficult to have such policies adopted. Here our discussion has revolved around several issues. What are the sources of economy-specific policy innovations? How can growth-enhancing policies be adopted in the face of interest-group and other pressures? And how can such policies be implemented efficiently?

The advantage of occasional changes in government springs immediately to mind. The success of the policies adopted by a short-lived non-Fianna Fáil coalition government to attract export-oriented foreign businesses in the 1950s facilitated Fianna Fáil in dropping its ideological objections to foreign direct investment. Something similar can be seen in the legacy bequeathed to subsequent UK Labour governments by the administration of Mrs Thatcher. The policy learning process may take much longer in non-democratic or effectively single-party systems, as evidenced by the prolonged economic failures of the Soviet system and of China under Mao, or the long stagnation of Northern Ireland under single-party domination.

More effective policies can also emerge through external influences, as illustrated by the galvanising 1965 OECD-sponsored report on education. A more recent example of how changes in the global economic *zeitgeist* can impact on Irish policymaking is provided by the growing recognition of the importance of competition policy.

Organisational and institutional learning are also clearly of importance. Openness to external review has been critical to the IDA's development as a learning organisation, and its 'transnational strategic network' has been crucial in helping the agency keep abreast of relevant global developments. In fact the entire Irish public service scores well on indicators of *institutional capacity*, though several recent failures in the public-administration arena suggest that a Whistleblower's Charter could be of benefit if due accountability is to be enforced.[22]

In the managerial literature, 'institutional learning' is used to refer to improvements in the quality of interactions between organisations that relate to each other in a given context. The comments made earlier about how social partnership may have promoted a shared understanding of the functioning of the economy are apposite here. It is one component of the extensive consultation process undertaken – as frequently remarked upon by foreign observers – before many key decisions are made in the Irish system.

Consensus is rarely reached in the political sphere however. Hence the availability of 'political cover' can be hugely beneficial when major reform programmes are being implemented. We saw how the Fianna Fáil government of the late 1950s used a document written by the head of the civil service as political cover in moving away from protectionism. EU fiscal commitments and WTO agreements – examples of what New York Times columnist Thomas Friedman (2000) terms 'the golden straightjacket' – can also be used in this way. The availability of political cover is of value however only if elected governments actually desire to withstand detrimental interest-group or populist pressures.

Notes

1 GNP is the preferred measure of Irish income per head (and is adjusted in Figure 15.1 for purchasing power differences). GDP figures overstate Ireland's achievements as they include the massive profits recorded by foreign multinational corporations operating in Ireland. Irish GDP exceeds GNP by more than 20 per cent, a difference not reflected in the data for any other EU country.

2 It took time for policymakers everywhere to realise that the oil price increases represented supply shocks which required a different response from the demand shocks with which they were more familiar. Excessive wage increases would further worsen the supply potential of the economy.

3 A later Finance Minister, Ray MacSharry, astutely critiqued his own party colleague's policy, writing that '... all the benefits were front-loaded, and the payback never came. Tax cuts were delivered in anticipation of pay moderation rather than in response to it' (MacSharry and White 2000).

4 Manipulation of transfer prices in order to shift profits to low-tax locations is easiest in R&D and advertising-intensive sectors as these factors obfuscate the exact source of value added.

5 One of MacSharry and White's anecdotes, concerning the battle to attract Intel to Ireland, is illustrative in this regard. At the final stage of the decision-making process the company remained fearful that engineers with the requisite experience might be difficult to find. The Industrial Development Agency (IDA) commissioned interviews with over 300 appropriately experienced Irish engineers, working mainly in the US, and was able to report to Intel that over 80 per cent of them expressed a willingness to return to Ireland if offered a good career opportunity with a quality company.

6 The prisoner's dilemma, a familiar concept in game theory, refers to a situation in which a group whose members pursue rational self-interest may end up worse off than a group whose members act contrary to rational self-interest.

7 As Bew and Patterson (1982: 70) point out, for nationalist ideologues 'foreign capital was a far more explosive issue than protection. After all, protection was only a means to an end – the building up of a native Irish industry.' The psychological impact of the shift in policy on foreign ownership, when it finally occurred, is apparent from the reaction of one leading Fianna Fáil deputy, who recalls that: 'I was bewildered and shocked to find that the principle of Irish ownership of industry, which was central to the Republican policy as I had always understood it, was gone...' (quoted by Bew and Patterson 1982: 121).

8 The initial Act gave 50 per cent tax remission on profits derived from increased manufactured exports. The political acceptability of the measure was greatly enhanced by the fact that it did not undermine protected industry. Nor did it impact on the existing tax base. The relief was increased to 100 per cent by the new Fianna Fáil government two years later.

9 An important feature of the report, according to one observer, was that 'technocratic expertise was being given unprecedented attention and might now be heard alongside the party political and denominational interests which had previously dominated ministerial councils'.

10 Wickham and Boucher (2004) criticise Ireland's 'inexpensive "volume production of technical graduates", undertaken without incurring the "costs" of tackling educational disadvantage or developing a research-based innovation system'. Such a system may be appropriate however for a country at a lower stage of economic development, as Ireland has been until recently.

11 Gunnigle and McGuire (2001), in a survey of executives of ten major US MNCs, find that education and skill levels rank second in importance to the corporation-tax regime in drawing these firms to Ireland.

12 The introduction of Social Fund aid to the RTCs entailed an element of subterfuge on the part of the Irish authorities since EU regulations at the time permitted the funding of *training* only, rather than *education*. White (2001) recounts how civil servants quickly reined in a newly appointed Minister of Education who inadvertently almost revealed the subterfuge to Brussels.

13 The Irish system offers a finite number of places in most third-level courses, and though these numbers are decided within the universities they are subject to government influence given that the latter provides the bulk of funding.

14 Tax cuts are estimated to have accounted for up to one-third of the rise in real take-home pay between the late 1980s and the early 2000s.

15 Even the political party that won the election of 1987 and implemented far sharper spending cuts than proposed by the previous government had campaigned on the slogan that 'health cuts hurt the old, the poor and the handicapped'.

16 NESC – the National Economic and Social Council – can be loosely described as the social-partnership secretariat. Fine Gael is the country's second largest political party and has led all non-Fianna Fáil coalition governments.

17 Luxembourg records a higher FDI stock per head of population than Ireland but this is largely concentrated in financial services and is much less employment-intensive.

18 It is important to note that though the Irish corporation tax rate is low by EU standards, this does not translate into low corporation tax revenues as a share of GDP (European Commission 2006: Table A.2.2.G).

19 Eurostat's refusal to allow Kerry and Clare to be included in the (Objective 1) Border, Midlands and West region when the country was subdivided into two NUTS II EU regions for the 2000–06 planning period provides an example of how localist-driven policies have been thwarted by the EU in the past.

20 Thus Koedijk and Kremers (1996) find that Ireland comes out best of all EU15 countries in terms of product-market freedom from regulation, and that it also scores well in terms of a freely functioning labour market. A broadly similar picture emerges from the World Bank's 'Doing Business' indicators (www.doingbusiness.org/EconomyRankings/).

21 This takes institutional factors such as property-rights protection and the rule of law as given. The strong emphasis here on institutional capacity goes beyond the 'Washington Consensus' range of policies however, though most of the features that Stiglitz (2002) identifies as lacking within that paradigm – such as the need for land reform, adequate social security nets and appropriate sequencing of reforms – relate more to developing than to developed countries.

22 Evans and Rauch (1999) show that characteristics such as the degree to which core state agencies employ meritocratic recruitment and offer predictable rewarding long-term careers significantly enhance a country's prospects for economic growth, even when initial levels of GDP per capita and human capital are controlled for. Ó Riain (2004) has recently evaluated the Irish civil service and industrial development bodies on the fourteen-point scale established by these authors. Ireland emerges with a score of 12.5, which compares favourably to the highest scoring of the thirty-five 'developing countries' to which Evans and Rauch confine their analysis – Singapore at 13.5, Korea at 13 and Taiwan at 12.

References

Baccaro, L. and Simoni, M. (2007) 'Centralized Wage Bargaining and the "Celtic Tiger" Phenomenon', *Industrial Relations* 46(3): 426–455.

Barry, F. (2003) 'Economic Integration and Convergence Processes in the EU Cohesion Countries', *Journal of Common Market Studies* 41(5): 897–921.

Bew, P. and Patterson, H. (1982) *Seán Lemass and the Making of Modern Ireland 1945–66*, Dublin: Gill and Macmillan.

Calmfors, L. and Driffill, J. (1988) 'Bargaining Structure, Corporatism and Macroeconomic Performance', *Economic Policy* 3(6): 13–61.

Fanning, R. (1978) *The Irish Department of Finance 1922–58*, Dublin: Institute of Public Administration.

Ecofin (2001) 2329th Council Meeting, Brussels, 12 February. Online. Available at http://europa.eu/rapid/pressReleasesAction.do?reference=PRES/01/35.

European Commission (2003) *Third European Report on Science and Technology Indicators*.

European Commission (2006) *Structures of the Taxation Systems in the European Union 1995–2004*.

Evans, P. and Rauch, J. (1999) 'Bureaucracy and Growth: A Cross-national Analysis of the Effects of "Weberian" State Structures on Economic Growth', *American Sociological Review* 64(5): 748–765.

Fingleton, J. (1995) 'Competition and Efficiency in the Services Sector', in J. O'Hagan (ed.) *The Economy of Ireland: Policy and Performance of a Small European Country*, Dublin: Gill and Macmillan.

FitzGerald, G. (1968) *Planning in Ireland*, Dublin: Institute of Public Administration.

FitzGerald, J. (1998) 'An Irish Perspective on the Structural Funds', *European Planning Studies* 6(6): 677–694.

Friedman, T. (2000) *The Lexus and the Olive Tree*, New York: Farrar, Straus & Giroux.

Giavazzi, F. and Pagano, M. (1990) 'Can Severe Fiscal Contractions be Expansionary? A Tale of Two Small Economies', in O. Blanchard and S. Fischer (eds) *National Bureau of Economic Research Macroeconomics Annual*, pp. 75–110.

Gunnigle, P. and McGuire, D. (2001) 'Why Ireland? A Qualitative Review of the Factors Influencing the Location of US Multinationals in Ireland with Particular Reference to the Impact of Labour Issues', *Economic and Social Review* 32: 43–67.

Hardiman, N. (1994) 'Pay Bargaining: Confrontation and Consensus', in D. Nevin (ed.) *Trade Union Century*, Dublin: Mercier Press.

Honohan, P. (1988) 'The Role of the Adviser and the Evolution of the Public Service', in M. Hederman (ed.) *The Clash of Ideas: Essays in Honour of Patrick Lynch*, Dublin: Gill and Macmillan.

Institute for Management Development (2005) *World Competitiveness Yearbook*, Lausanne: IMD.

Kennedy, K., Giblin, T. and McHugh, D. (1988) *The Economic Development of Ireland in the Twentieth Century*, London and New York: Routledge.

Koedijk, K. and Kremers, J. (1996) 'Market Opening, Regulation and Growth in Europe', *Economic Policy* 23: 445–467.

Lane, P. (1998) 'On the Cyclicality of Irish Fiscal Policy', *Economic and Social Review* 29(1): 1–16.

MacSharry, R. and White, P. (2000). *The Making of the Celtic Tiger: the Inside Story of Ireland's Booming Economy*, Dublin: Mercier Press.

Markusen, J. (2006) 'Multinationals and Development', Paper presented to conference on *Ireland and Global Development: Strengthening Financial, Trade and Health Systems*, Trinity College Dublin, 5–6 July. Available at: www.tcd.ie/iiis/pages/events/irlglobald-evschedule.php.

Oates, W.E. (1999) 'An Essay on Fiscal Federalism', *Journal of Economic Literature* 37: 1120–1149.

O'Donnell, R. (2000) 'The New Ireland in the New Europe', in R. O'Donnell (ed.) *Europe: The Irish Experience*, Dublin: Institute of European Affairs.

OECD (2005) *Science, Technology and Industry Scoreboard*, Paris: OECD.

OECD (2006) *Education at a Glance*, Paris: OECD.

Ó Gráda, C. (1997) *A Rocky Road: The Irish Economy since the 1920s*, Manchester: Manchester University Press.

Ó Gráda, C. and O'Rourke, K. (1996) 'Irish Economic Growth, 1945–88', in N. Crafts and G. Toniolo (eds) *European Economic Growth*, Cambridge: Cambridge University Press.

Ó Riain, S. (2004) *The Politics of High-Tech Growth: Developmental Network States in the Global Economy*, Cambridge, UK: Cambridge University Press.

Stiglitz, J. (2002) *Globalisation and its Discontents*, New York: W.W. Norton and Co.

UNCTAD (2005) *World Investment Report: Transnational Corporations and the Internationalization of R&D*, New York and Geneva: UN.

White, T. (2001) *Investing in People: Higher Education in Ireland from 1960 to 2000*, Dublin: Institute of Public Administration.

Wickham, J. and Boucher, G. (2004) 'Training Cubs for the Celtic Tiger: The Volume Production of Technical Graduates in the Irish Educational System', *Journal of Education and Work* 17(4): 377–395.

World Competitiveness Yearbook (2005) Lausanne: International Institute for Management Development.

Index